Leipziger Altorientalistische Studien

Herausgegeben von
Michael P. Streck

Band 7, 3

2022
Harrassowitz Verlag · Wiesbaden

Michael P. Streck and Janine Wende

Supplement to the Akkadian Dictionaries

Vol. 3: G, K, Q

With the collaboration of Bert Kouwenberg,
Nadezda Rudik, Jonas Klöker and Frank Simons

2022

Harrassowitz Verlag · Wiesbaden

Bibliografische Information der Deutschen Nationalbibliothek
Die Deutsche Nationalbibliothek verzeichnet diese Publikation in der Deutschen Nationalbibliografie; detaillierte bibliografische Daten sind im Internet über https://dnb.de abrufbar.

Bibliographic information published by the Deutsche Nationalbibliothek
The Deutsche Nationalbibliothek lists this publication in the Deutsche Nationalbibliografie; detailed bibliographic data are available in the Internet at https://dnb.de.

For further information about our publishing program consult our website https://www.harrassowitz-verlag.de

Printed on permanent/durable paper.
Printing and binding: Memminger MedienCentrum AG
Printed in Germany

ISSN 2193-4436
ISBN 978-3-447-11027-3

Table of Contents

Introduction vii
Bibliography ix
Bibliographical Abbreviations xxxi
Other Abbreviations xliii
Supplement G 1
Supplement K 29
Supplement Q 113

Introduction

1. Volume G/K/Q of the Supplement to the Akkadian Dictionaries

For the goals and organization of SAD cf. in general the introduction of volume B/P. In the following, some additional information pertaining to volume G/K/Q will be given.

The reader is kindly referred to the website of the project (https://www.gkr.uni-leipzig.de/en/draft/altorientalisches-institut/forschung/supplement-to-the-akkadian-dictionaries) where all results published in the present volume are accessible online. In addition, the website also offers much material for the other letters of the alphabet. New material and corrections for the letters B/P, as well as D/T/Ṭ, not published in the pertinent volume, are marked in yellow on the website.

The present volume is a collaborative effort of Michael P. Streck (sometimes indicated by the abbreviation MPS at the end of the lemma) and Janine Wende (JW). All lemmata not claimed by any author remain the joint responsibility of Streck and Wende. Old Assyrian material was kindly sent to us by Bert Kouwenberg (NJCK). Minor contributions were made by Nadezda Rudik (NR) and Jonas Klöker (JK). The English text was corrected by Frank Simons who also made further additions (FJMS).

The list of reviewed publications given in volume B/P (cf. LAOS 7/1 p. xii–xiv) and D/T/Ṭ (cf. LAOS 7/2 p. vii–viii) has been further expanded to include the following:

AML (OB and OA incantations)
ARM 33 (OB letters from Mari)
Foster/George 2020 (ZA 110, OB literature)
KAL 8 and 11 (lexical texts from Assur)
KAL 10 and 12 (literary texts from Assur).

2. Statistics

The following table provides the numerical breakdown for the volume G/K/Q of SAD.

	G	K	Q	Total
Number of entries in AHw	412	1,143	335	1,890
Number of entries in CAD	480	1,170	424	2,074
Number of entries in SAD	215	574	212	1001
New words in SAD in total	52	102	42	196
New nouns	43	89	32	164
New verbs	6	3	4	13
New adjectives	1	3	3	7
New adverbs	1	7	1	9
New prepositions	1	–	1	2
New verbal stems in total	4	11	6	21
New G-stems	1	1	–	2

	G	K	Q	Total
New Gt-stems	–	1	1	2
New Gtn-stems	–	2	–	2
New D-stems	1	2	2	5
New Dt-stems	1	2	–	3
New Š-stems	–	1	1	2
New Št-stems	–	–	2	2
New N-stems	1	1	–	2
New Ntn-stems	–	1	–	1

Bibliography

Abraham K. 2004: Business and Politics under the Persian Empire. Bethesda.

Abraham K. / Sokoloff M. 2011: Aramaic Loanwords in Akkadian. A Reassessment of the Proposals, AfO 52, 22–76.

Adamthwaite M. R. 2001: *Late Hittite Emar: the chronology, synchronisms, and socio-political aspects of a Late Bronze Age fortress town* (= ANES Suppl. 8). Louvain.

Ahmed K. M. 2012: The Beginnings of Ancient Kurdistan (c. 2500–1500 BC). A Historical and Cultural Synthesis (PhD Diss.) Leiden.

Albayrak İ. 1998: Koloni Çağında Yerli Bir Bayan "Madawada". 3. UHKB, 1–14.

Albayrak İ. 2001: Kültepe Metinlerinde mā'ū "Su" Kelimesi. AMMY 2000, 300–311.

Albayrak İ. 2002: Kültepe'den Değişik Bir Masraf Listesi. ArAn. 5, 1–10.

Albayrak İ. 2005: Fünf Urkunden aus dem Archiv von Peruwa, Sohn von Šuppibra. JEOL 39, 95–105.

Al-Rawi F. N. H. / Dalley S. 2000: Old Babylonian Texts from Private Houses at Abu Habbah, Ancient Sippir (= Edubba 7). London.

Alster B. / Oshima T. 2007: Sargonic dinner at Kaneš: The Old Assyrian Sargon legend, Iraq 69, 1–20.

Anbar M. 1991: Les tribus amurrites de Mari (= OBO 108).

Arkhipov I. 2012: Le vocabulaire de la métallurgie et la nomenclature des objets en métal dans les textes de Mari (= ARM 32). Paris.

Arkhipov I. 2012a: Les véhicules terrestres dans les textes de Mari. II. Le harnachement et l'équipement de chars en cuir et en tissu: Babel und Bibel 6, 5–14.

Arnaud D. 1991: Textes Syriens de l'Âge du Bronze Récent (= AulaOr Suppl. 1).

Bagg A. 2000: Assyrische Wasserbauten (= BagF 24). Mainz.

Baker H. D. 2010a: Babylonian shops, NABU 2010/88.

Balkan K. 1967: Contributions to the Understanding of the Idiom of the Old Assyrian Merchants of Kanish. Or. 36, 393–415.

Balkan K. 1974: Cancellation of Debts in Cappadocian Tablets from Kültepe, in Fs. Güterbock (PIHANS 33), 29–41.

Barjamovic G. / Larsen M. T. 2008: An Old Assyrian Incantation against the Evil Eye, AoF 35, 144–55.

Bayram S. 2000: *ina nadītim ša naruā'im*. ArAn. 4, 29–48.

Bayram S. 2001: The *nadītum* of the stele. in: Fs. Veenhof, 1–8.

Bayram S. 2016: Kültepe Metinlerinde *ĒZIBTU(M)*. ArAn. 10/1, 15–28.

Bayram S. / Çeçen S. 1995: 6 neue Urkunden über Heirat und Scheidung aus Kaniš. ArAn. 1, 1–12.

Bayram S. / Kuzuoğlu R. 2015: Takı Takma Âdetinin Eski Asur Toplumundaki İzleri, in Fs. Günbattı, 29–37.

Beaulieu P.-A. 2003: The Pantheon of Uruk during the Neo-Babylonian Period (= CunMon. 23). Leiden / Boston.

Beckman G. 2002: The Pantheon of Emar, in P. Taracha (ed.), Silva Anatolica (= Fs. Popko), 39–54.

Bennett E. A. 2021: The Meaning of Sacred Names and Babylonian Scholarship (= dubsar 25). Münster.

Bilgiç E. 1964: Three Tablets from the City Mound of Kültepe, Anatolia 8, 145–163.

Black J. A. 1991: Sumerian Grammar in Babylonian Theory. Second, revised Edition (StPohl S.M. 12). Rome.

Black J. A. / Al-Rawi F. N. H. 1987: A Contribution to the Study of Akkadian Bird Names, ZA 77, 117–126.

Bloch Y. 2013: *qubbatu*, *qubbutu* "mourning, wailing", NABU 2013/28.

Böck B. 2007: Das Handbuch Muššu'u „Einreibung". Eine Serie sumerischer und akkadischer Beschwörungen aus dem 1. Jt. vor Chr. (= BPOA 3). Madrid.

Bongenaar A. C. V. M. 1997: The Neo-Babylonian Ebabbar Temple at Sippar: its Administration and ist Prosopography (= PIHANS 80). Leiden.

Borger R. 1973: Die Weihe eines Enlil-Priesters, BiOr 30, 163–176.

Borger R. 1975: Review of CAD K, BiOr 32, 70–72.

Borger R. 1985: Review of CAD N and Q, BiOr 42, 348–353.

Borger R. 2010a: Review of CAD T, Ṭ, BiOr 67, 344–348.

Borger R. 2010b: Mesopotamisches Zeichenlexikon (= AOAT 305). Münster.

Bottéro J. 1965: Review of AHw Lieferung 4-5, Or. 34, 376–379.

Bottéro J. 1995: Textes culinaires mésopotamiens. Winona Lake.

Butz K. 1984: On Salt Again ... Lexikalische Randbemerkungen, JESHO 27, 272–316.

Cavigneaux A. 1981: Le temple de Nabû ša Harê: Rapport préliminaire sur les textes cunéiformes, Sumer 37, 118–126.

Cavigneaux A. 1982: Remarques sur les commentaires à Labat TDP 1, JCS 34, 231–241.

Çayır M. 2006: Anadolu Tüccar Nini'ye ait Tabletler. ArAn. 9/1, 1–26.

Çayır M. 2016: Kültepe'den Bir Mektup ve Liste, in: Fs. Ünal, 97–104.

Çeçen S. 1995: *mūtānū* in den Kültepe-Texten. ArAn. 1, 43–56.

Çeçen S. 1997: Kaniš Kārum'unun Diğer Kārum ve Wabartumlar'a "kù.an" (*amūtum*) İle İlgili Önemli Talimatları. Belleten LXI/231, 219–232.

Çeçen S. 1998a: Yerli Kralların Mabedleri Ziyareti ve Çıkan Neticeler. 3. UHKB, 119–24.

Çeçen S. 2002: Kültepe Belgelerine Göre Anadolu Şehir Devletlerinde Ayaklanma. ArAn. 5, 65–68.

Çeçen S. / Erol H. 2018: Kültepe'den Değişik bir Ticari mal listesi (Kt n/k 1697). ArAn. 12/2, 53–75.

Çeçen S. / Gökçek L. G. 2016: Asurlu Bayan Akadia'nın Ağabeyi Uṣur–ša–Ištar'a Göndermiş Olduğu Üç Mektup. Cappadocia Journal of History and Social Sciences 7, 247–264.

Çeçen S. / Gökçek L. G. 2017: Uṣur-ša-Ištar Ailesinden ^{f}Šimat-Su'en'e Ait Dört Mektup, Cappadocia Journal of History and Social Sciences 9, 463–82.

Çeçen S. / Hecker K. 1995: *ina mātīka eblum*. Zu einem neuen Text zum Wegerecht in der Kültepe–Zeit, in Fs. von Soden, 31–41.

Chambon G. 2008: L'écriture des mesures de longueur à Emar, in: L. d'Alfonso/Y. Cohen/D. Sürenhagen (eds.): The City of Emar among the Late Bronze Age Empires. History, Landscape, and Society (= AOAT 349), Münster. 141–151.

Chambon G. 2011: Normes et pratiques: L'homme, la mesure et l'écriture en Mésopotamie. I. Les mesures de capacité et de poids en Syrie Ancienne, d'Ébla à Émar (= BBVO 21). Gladbeck.

Charpin D. 1989-90: Compte rendu du CAD volume Q (1982), AfO 36/37, 92–106.

Charpin D. 1990a: Review of van de Mieroop 1987, RA 84, 89–90.

Charpin D. 1992: Les malheurs d'un scribe, in: DeJong Ellis (ed.), Nippur at the Centennial (= CRRAI 35 / OPSNKF 14), 7–27.

Charpin D. 1994: *Kallâm* "rapidement", NABU 1994/62.

Charpin D. 2016: Chroniques bibliographiques 18. Les débuts des relations diplomatiques au Proche-Orient ancien, RA 110, 127–186.

Charpin D. / Durand J.-M. 2004: Prétendants au trône dans le Proche-Orient amorrite, in: Fs. Larsen, 99–115.

Cherry Z. 2017: Aramaic Loanwords in Neo-Assyrian, 900–600 B.C. Uppsala.

Choukassizian Eypper S. 2019: *kasû*(^{Ú}GAZI^{SAR}) Revisited, JMS 33, 35–49.

Civil M. 1984a: Notes on the Instructions of Šuruppak, JNES 43, 281–298.

Civil M. 1990: Ninmešarra 89 and qinû 'jealousy, anger', NABU 1990/59.

Cohen E. 2006: Syntactic Marginalia. JAOS 126/4, 551–65.

Cohen Y. 2010: The "Second Glosses" in the Lexical Lists from Emar: West Semitic or Akkadian?, in: RAI 53/1, 813–839.

Cohen Y. 2018: An Old Babylonian List of Sheep Body Parts (BM 29663), Fs. Geller 131–148.

Cole S. W. 1996: The Early Neo-Babylonian Governor's Archive from Nippur (= OIP 114). Chicago.

Da Riva R. 2002: Der Ebabbar-Tempel von Sippar in frühneubabylonischer Zeit (640–580 v. Chr.) (= AOAT 291). Münster.

Da Riva R. 2012: The twin inscriptions of Nebuchadnezzar at Brisa, Wadi Esh-Sharbin, Lebanon: a historical and philological study (= AfO Bh. 32).

de Ridder J. J. 2018: A Descriptive Grammar of Middle Assyrian (= LAOS 8). Wiesbaden.

de Ridder J. J. 2020: Middle Assyrian Letters from Kār-Tukultī-Ninurta, SAAB 26, 23–57.

de Ridder J. J. / Zomer E. 2019: Botanical *qaqullu*(*m*)/*qāqullā*: A Halophyte Plant in Semitic Languages, WZKM 109, 287–298.

De Zorzi N. 2014: La serie teratomantica *Šumma izbu*. Testo, tradizione, orizzonti culturali. I-II (= HANE/M 15). Padova.

Degraeve A. 1996: Mesopotamia and ist Northern Neighbours: Part I, Akkadica 99–100, 15–35.

Deller K. 1983: Gab es einen König von Arrapḫe namens Muš-teja?, Assur 3/4, 18–27.

Deller K. 1985: *kurru* "Mehlbrei", Or. 54, 327–330.

Deller K. 1987: Review of VS 21 = MARV 2, AfO 34, 58–66.

Deller K. 1991: Neuassyrisch *qanû*, *qinītu* und *tidintu*, in: Fs Garelli, 345–355.

Deller K. 1992b: *gurrudu* "kahlköpfig" und *qerdu* "abgeschabte Wolle", NABU 1992/79.

Deller K. / Finkel I. J. 1984: A Neo-Assyrian inventory tablet of unknown provenance, ZA 74, 76–91.

Deller K. / Mayer W. R. / Oelsner J. 1989: Akkadische Lexikographie: CAD Q, Or. 58, 255–282.

Dercksen J. G. 1996: The Old Assyrian Copper Trade in Anatolia (= PIHANS 75). Leiden.

Dercksen J. G. 2001: "When we met in Ḫattuš": Trade according to Old Assyrian texts from Alishar and Boğazköy, in: Fs. Veenhof, 39–66.

Dercksen J. G. 2003: A New OA Text from Kültepe about Mules, NABU 2003/45.

Dercksen J. G. 2004a: Old Assyrian Institutions. MOS Studies 4 (= PIHANS 98). Leiden.

Dercksen J. G. 2005b: Adad is King! The Sargon Text from Kültepe (with an appendix on MARV 4, 138 and 140), JEOL 39, 107–129.

Dercksen J. G. 2007: On Anatolian Loanwords in Akkadian Texts from Kültepe, ZA 97, 26–46.

Dercksen J. G. 2011: Weeks, Months and Years in Old Assyrian Chronology. BiOr 68, 233–243.

Dercksen J. G. 2015a: Six Texts with New and Rare Toponyms from the House of Ali–ahum (Kt c/k)m in Fs. Günbattı, 49–58.

Dercksen J. G. 2015b: The Goddess Who was Robbed of her Jewellery. Ishtar and her Priest in an Assyrian Colony. Anatolica 41, 37–60.

Dietrich M. 1990: Die akkadischen Texte der Archive aus Emar, UF 22, 25–48.

Dietrich M. / Loretz O. 1964: Die soziale Struktur von Alalaḫ und Ugarit: I. Die Berufsbezeichnungen mit der hurritischen Endung -ḫuli, WO 3, 188–205.

Donbaz V. 2001: *Maḫar patrim ša Aššur* – A New Interpretation, in: Fs. Veenhof, 83–101.

Donbaz V. 2008: Three Court Proceedings Concerning Walaliašu'e an Anatolian woman, in: Fs. Darga, 209–222.

Donbaz V. / Stolper M. 1993: Gleanings from Murašû Texts in the Collections of the Istanbul Archaeological Museums, NABU 1993/102.

Donbaz V. / Veenhof K. R. 1985: New Evidence for Some Old Assyrian Terms, Anatolica 12, 131–55.

Dornauer A. 2018: Proso, Sorghum, Tiger Nut. Some Minor Crops in the Cuneiform Sources (= BBVO 27). Berlin.

Durand J.-M. 1987d: *Kaššilu*, NABU 1987/42.

Durand J.-M. 1988: Archives Epistolaires de Mari I/1 (= ARM 26/1). Paris.

Durand J.-M. 1989a: *Compte Rendu*: Daniel *Arnaud*, Recherches au Pays d'Aštata, *Emar VI,* RA 83, 163–191.

Durand J.-M. 1990b: Compte Rendu: Daniel Arnaud, Recherches au Pays d'Aštata, Emar VI, RA 84, 49–85.

Durand J.-M. 1992: Unité et Diversités au Proche-Orient à L'Époque Amorrite, CRRAI 38, 97–128.

Durand J.-M. 1995: La religión en Siria durante la época de los reinos amorreos según la documentación de Mari, in: G. del Olmo Lete, Mitología y Religión del Oriente Antiguo. II/1 Semitas Occidentales (Ebla, Mari) 125–233. Sabadell.

Durand J.-M. 1997: Documents épistolaires du palais de Mari I (= LAPO 16). Paris.

Durand J.-M. 1998: Documents épistolaires du palais de Mari II (= LAPO 17). Paris.

Durand J.-M. 2000: Documents épistolaires du palais de Mari III (= LAPO 18). Paris.

Durand J.-M. 2005: Le culte des pierres et les monuments commémoratifs en Syrie Amorrite (= FM 8). Paris.

Durand J.-M. 2009: La nomenclature des habits et des textiles dans les textes de Mari (= ARM 30). Paris.

Durand J.-M. / Guichard M. 1997: Les rituels de Mari, in: Gs. Barrelet (= FM 3), 19–78.

Durand J.-M. / Joannès F. 1990: *kubuddâ'u* à Mari et à Emar, NABU 1990/70.

Edzard D. O. 1974: Review of CAD K, ZA 64, 123–126.

Edzard D. O. 1978: Zu den altbabylonischen Präpositionen *itti* und *qadum*", in: Fs. Matouš I, 69–89.

Edzard D. O. 1983: Review of CAD Q, ZA 73, 132–136.

Edzard D. O. 1987: Zur Ritualtafel der sog. „Love Lyrics", in Fs. Reiner, 57–69.

Fales F. M. 1987: Aramaic Letters and Neo-Assyrian Letters: Philological and Methodological Notes, JAOS 107, 451–469.

Fales F. M. 2000: Neo-Assyrian *karāmu*: A Unitary Interpretation, in: Gs. Cagni, 261–281.

Farber W. 1973: Review of van Driel, The Cult of Aššur, BiOr 70, 433–436.

Farber W. 2014: Lamaštu: An Edition of the Canonical Series of Lamaštu Incantations and Rituals and Related Texts from the Second and First Millennia B. C. (= MesCiv. 17). Winona Lake.

Feliu L. 2003: The God Dagan in Bronze Age Syria (= CHANE 19). Leiden.

Fincke J. 2000: Augenleiden nach keilschriftlichen Quellen. Untersuchungen zur altorientalischen Medizin. Würzburg.

Fincke J. 2011: Spezialisierung und Differenzierung im Bereich der altorientalischen Medizin, in: Selz (ed.), The Empirical Dimension of Ancient Near Eastern Studies – Die empirische Dimension altorientalischer Forschungen (= WOO 6), 159–210.

Finet A. 1956: L'Accadien des lettres de Mari. Bruxelles.

Finkel I. L. 1999: The Lament of Nabû-šuma-ukîn, in: Renger (ed.), Babylon: Focus mesopotamischer Geschichte, Wiege früher Gelehrsamkeit, Mythos in der Moderne (= CDOG 2), 323–342.

Finkel I. 2014: The Ark before Noah. London.

Fleming D. E. 1992: The installation of Baal's high priestess at Emar: A window on ancient Syrian religion (= HSS 42). Atlanta.

Fleming D. E. 1993: The *kilûtum* Rites of Mari, NABU 1993/3.

Fleming D. E. 2000: Time at Emar: The Cultic Calendar and the Rituals from the Diviner's Archive (= MC 11). Winona Lake.

Fleming D. E. 2000a: Mari's Large Public Tent and the Priestly Tent Sanctuary, VT 50, 484–498.

Frahm E. 1997: Einleitung in die Sanherib-Inschriften (= AfO Bh. 26). Wien.

Frahm E. 2002: Assur 2001: Die Schriftfunde, MDOG 134, 47–86.

Frahm E. 2009: Warum die Brüder Böses planten. Überlegungen zu einer alten Crux in Asarhaddons 'Ninive A'-Inschrift, in: Gs. Sima, 27–49.

Frahm E. 2011: Babylonian and Assyrian Text Commentaries. Origins of Interpretation (GMTR 5). Münster.

Franke S. / Wilhelm G. 1985: Eine mittelassyrische fiktive Urkunde zur Wahrung des Anspruchs auf ein Findelkind, Jahrbuch des Museums für Kunst und Gewerbe Hamburg 4, 19–26.

Frankena R. 1978: Kommentar zu den Altbabylonischen Briefen aus Lagaba und anderen Orten (= SLB 4). Leiden.

Freydank H. 1976: Untersuchungen zur sozialen Struktur in mittelassyrischer Zeit, AoF 4, 111–130.

Freydank H. 1980: Zur Lage der deportierten Hurriter in Assyrien, AoF 7, 89–117.

Freydank H. 1997: Noch einmal zum Vorgang *pišerti karū'e*, AOAT 247, 129–143.

Gallery M. L. 1980: Service Obligations of the *kezertu*-Women: Or. 49, 333–338.

Gaspa S. 2009: "Wiping the Pot Clean": On Cooking Pots and Polishing Operations in Neo-Assyrian Sources, in: Fs Parpola, 83–98.

Gaspa S. 2009–2010: Organizing the Festive Cycles at the Aššur Temple: Royal Dispositions for the Provision and Processing of Foodstuffs in First Millennium BC Assyria, SAAB 91–144.

Gaspa S. 2018: Textiles in the Neo-Assyrian Empire. A Study of Terminology (= SANER 19). Boston / Berlin.

Gelb I. J. 1984: *šîbût kušurrā'im*, "Witnesses of the Indemnity", JNES 43, 263–276.

Geller M. / Wiggerman F. A. M. 2008: Duplicating Akkadian Magic in: R. J. van der Spek (ed.), Studies in Ancient Near Eastern World View and Society. Presented to Marten Stol on the Occasion of his 65th Birthday (Bethesda) 149–160.

George A. R. 1991: Babylonian Texts from the Folios of Sidney Smith. Part Two: Prognostic and Diagnostic Omens, Tablet I, RA 85, 137–167.

George A. R. 2003: The Babylonian Gilgamesh-Epic. Oxford.

George A. R. 2013: Babylonian Divinatory Texts Chiefly in the Schøyen Collection (= CUSAS 18). Bethesda.

Gesenius W. 1987–2010: Hebräisches und Aramäisches Handwörterbuch über das Alte Testament.

Gökçek L. G. 2017: Kültepe'den Kaçakçılıkla İlgili Yeni Bir Belge. ArAn. 11/2, 39–44.

Greenfield J. C. / Shaffer Aaron 1983: *qlqlt'*, *tubkinnu*, Refuse Tips and Treasure Trove, AnSt 33, 123–129.

Groneberg B. R. M. 1993: Les meilleurs vœux d'Alfred, NABU 1993/44.

Guichard M. 2005: La vaisselle de luxe des rois de Mari. Matériaux pour le Dictionnaire de Babylonien de Paris, tome II (= ARM 31). Paris.

Guichard M. 2015: Une prière bilingue inédite de Mari l'art d'amadouer son dieu et seigneur de la littérature à la pratique, in: Durand/Marti/Römer (eds.), Colères et repentirs divins (= OBO 278), 343–376.

Günbattı C. 1995: More Examples of Correspondences Between kārum's. ArAn. 1, 107–15.

Günbattı C. 1997: Kültepe'den Akadlı Sargon'a âit bir tablet, ArAn 3, 131–55.

Günbattı C. 2004: Two Treaty texts found at Kültepe, in: Fs. Larsen, 249–68.

Günbattı C. 2014: The Letter Sent to Hurmeli King of Harsamna and the Kings of Kaniš. Türk Tarih Kurumu Yayınları, V. Dizi – Sayı 3. Ankara.

Günbattı C. 2016: *Ina šapat Humātim kalā'um* "Humātum Kenarında Alıkoymak", in: Fs. Ünal, 275–280.

Haas V. 1993: Hurritologische Miszellen, AoF 20, 261–268.

Hasselbach 2005: Sargonic Akkadian. A Historical and Comparative Study of the Syllabic Texts. Wiesbaden.

Haul M. 2009: Stele und Legende (= Göttinger Beiträge zum Alten Orient 4).

Hecker K. 1997: Über den Euphrat… Ortsbezogene Restriktionen in aA Kaufurkunden, in: Gs Bilgiç (= Archivum Anatolicum 3), 157–172.

Hecker K. 2001: Akkadische Texte, TUAT Ergänzungslieferung, 11–60.

Hecker K. 2003: *kunuk kārim ṣeḫer rabi*, in: Fs. Kienast, 183–96.

Hecker K. 2004a: *kaspum mādum ša ṭuppē mādūtim*, in: Fs. Pettinato, 63–69.

Hecker K. 2004b: Beim Tode unseres Vaters…. Der leidige Streit ums Erbe, in: Fs. Larsen, 281–297.

Heide M. 2010: The Domestication of the Camel, UF 42, 331–384.

Heimpel W. 1996c: Euristic Dog behaviour, NABU 1996/45.

Heimpel W. 1996d: Cases of ga_{14} and dì, NABU 1996/44.

Heimpel W. 1997d: My-Father-is-my-Rock, NABU 1997/2.

Heimpel W. 2003: Letters to the King of Mari (= MesCiv. 12). Winona Lake.

Heimpel W. 2009: Workers and Construction Work at Garšana (= CUSAS 5). Bethesda.

Heltzer M. 1989: Akkadian katinnu and Hebre kīdōn, “Sword”, JCS 41, 65–68.

Hrůša I. 2010: Die akkadische Synonymenliste *malku* = *šarru* (= AOAT 50).

Huehnergard J. 1987: Ugaritic Vocabulary in Syllabic Transcription (= HSS 32). Winona Lake.

Jacquet A. 2011: Documents relatifs aux dépenses pour le culte (= FM 12). Paris.

Jakob S. 2003: Mittelassyrische Verwaltung und Sozialstruktur (= CunMon. 29). Groningen.

Jakob S. 2009: Die mittelassyrischen Texte aus Tell Chuēra in Nordost-Syrien. Wiesbaden.

Jiménez E. 2017: The Babylonian Disputation Poems (= CHANE 87). Leiden.

Joannès F. 1982: Textes économiques de la Babylonie récente (= ERC Cah. 5).

Joannès F. 1984: Contrats de mariage d’époque récente, RA 78, 71–81.

Joannès F. 1989a: Le bijou *karalla*, NABU 1989/1.

Joannès F. 1995: Lépreux fantômes?, NABU 1995/20.

Jursa M. 1997a: Aromatika, NABU 1997/34.

Jursa M. 1997/1998: Review of OIP 114, AfO 44/45, 419–424.

Jursa M. 1999: Das Archiv des Bēl-rēmanni (= PIHANS 86). Leiden.

Jursa M. 2006: Agricultural Management, Tax Farming and Banking: Aspects of Entrepreneurial Activity in Babylonia in the Late Achaemenid and Hellenistic Periods, in: Briant, P. / Joannès, F. (eds.), La transition entre l’empire achéménide et les royaumes hellénistiques (vers 350–300 av. J.-C.) (= Persika 9), 137–222.

Jursa M. 2009: Die Kralle des Meers und andere Aromata, in: Gs. Sima, 147–180.

Jursa M. 2010: Aspects of the Economic History of Babylonia in the First Millennium BC. Economic Geography, Economic Mentalities, Agriculture, the Use of Money, and the Problem of Economic Growth (= AOAT 377). Münster.

Kendall T. 1981: *gurpisu ša awēli*: The Helmets of the Warriors at Nuzi, in : SCCNH 1, 201–231.

Kienast B. / Sommerfeld W. 1994: Glossar zu den altakkadischen Königsinschriften (= FAOS 8). Stuttgart.

Kilmer A. D. 1991: An Oration on Babylon, AoF 18, 9–22.

Kilmer A. D. 1995: Musik A. I. In Mesopotamien, RlA 8, 463–482.

Kilmer A. D. / Tinney S. 1996: Old Babylonian Music Instruction Texts, JCS 48, 49–56.

Kinnier Wilson J. V. 1972: The Nimrud wine lists: a study of men and administration at the Assyrian capital in the eighth century B.C. (= CTN 1). Hertford-London.

Kinnier Wilson J. 2005: On the Cryptogams in the lexical and related texts, JMC 6, 1–21.

Kleber K. 2008: Tempel und Palast. Die Beziehungen zwischen dem König und dem Eanna-Tempel im spätbabylonischen Uruk. (= AOAT 358). Münster.

Kleber K. 2011: Review of Zawadzki 2006, OLZ 106, 86–90.

Klein J. / Sefati Y. 2019: From the Workshop of the Mesopotamian Scribe. Literary and Scholarly Texts from the Old Babylonian Period. University Park.

Kogan L. 2011: On Some Orthographic Oppositions in the Old Babylonian Copies of the Sargonic Royal Inscriptions (I), BiOr 68, 33–56.

Kogan L. / Krebernik M. 2021: A History of the Akkadian Lexikon, in: P. Vita (ed.) History of the Akkadian Language (= HdO 152), 366–476.

Kogan L. / Militarev A. 2002: Akkadian Terms for Genitalia: New Etymologies, New Textual Interpetations, in: CCRAI 47, 311–319.

Kouwenberg N. J. C. 2010: The Akkadian Verb and Its Semitic Background (= LANE 2). Winona Lake.

Kouwenberg N. J. C. 2012: Spatial Deixis in Akkadian. Demonstrative Pronouns, Presentative Particles and Locational Adverbs, ZA 102, 17–75.

Kouwenberg N. J. C. 2015: Sargon's *tūdittum*, or how to make fools of your enemies, in: Fs. Günbattı, 165–70.

Kouwenberg N. J. C. 2018–2019: The Old Assyrian Incantation Tablet Kt 91/k 502, JEOL 47, 57–72.

Kraus F. R. 1973: Vom mesopotamischen Menschen der altbabylonischen Zeit und seiner Welt.

Kraus F. R. 1984b: Königliche Verfügungen in altbabylonischer Zeit (= SD 11). Leiden.

Krebernik M. 1984: Die Beschwörungen aus Fara und Ebla. Untersuchungen zur ältesten keilschriftlichen Beschwörungsliteratur (= TSO 2). Hildesheim/Zürich/New York.

Kryszat G. 2004: Zur Chronologie der Kaufmannsarchive aus der Schicht 2 des Kārum Kaneš (= OAAS 2; PIHANS 99). Leiden.

Kupper J.-R. 1996: Les differents moments de la journee d'apres les textes de Mari, in Fs. Limet, 79–85.

Kupper J.-R. 2006: Une unité d'élite à Ebla, NABU 2006/27.

Kuzuoğlu R. 2016: Eski Asur Kaynaklarında Tanrıça İšhara ve Akrep Sembolü. ArAn. 10/1, 29–54.

Lacambre D. 2008: 10. Le bureau de la bière, in: Ö. Tunca / A. el-M. Baghdo (eds), Chagar Bazar (Syrie) III. Les trouvailles épigraphiques et sigillographiques du chantier I (2000–2002), 179–210.

Lackenbacher S. 1982b: Un texte vieux-babylonien sur la finition des textiles, Syria 59, 129–149.

Lambert W. G. 1967: Review of AHw. Lieferung 5–6, JSS 12, 100–105.

Lambert W. G. 1975: The Problem of the Love Lyrics, in: Goedicke (ed.), Unity and Diversity. Essays in the History, Literature, and Religion of the Ancient Near East, 98–135.

Lambert W. G. 1989: A Babylonian Prayer to Anuna, in: Fs. A. W. Sjöberg, 321–336.

Lambert W. G. 1990: A New Babylonian Descent to the Netherworld, in: Fs. Moran (= HSS 37), 289–300.

Lambert W. G. 1991: Metal-working and its Patron Deities in the Early Levant, Levant 23, 183–186.

Landsberger B. 1934: Die Fauna des Alten Mesopotamien nach der 14. Tafel der Serie HAR-RA-hubullu, unter Mitwirkung von I. Krumbiegel. Leipzig.

Langlois A.-I. 2017: Les archives de la princesse Iltani découvertes à Tell al-Rimah (XVIIIe siècle av.J.-C.) et l'histoire du royaume de Karana/Qaṭṭara, Tome 2 (= Mém. N.A.B.U. 18 = Archibab 2). Paris.

Larsen M. T. 1976: The Old Assyrian City-State and its Colonies (= Mesopotamia 4). Copenhagen.

Leichty E. 2000: *qabūtu*, *šāḫu* and *mê qāti*, in: Fs Oelsner (= AOAT 252), 243–244.

Limet H. 1976: Textes administratifs de l'époque des Šakkanakku (= ARM 19). Paris.

Linssen M. J. H. 2004: The Cults of Uruk and Babylon. The Temple Ritual Texts as Evidence for Hellenistic Cult Practices (= CunMon. 25). Groningen.

Lion B. 2004: Les familles royales et les artisans déportés à Mari en ZL 12, in: CRAI 46 = Amurru 3, 217–224.

Lion B. / Michel C. 1997: Criquets at autres insectes à Mari, MARI 8, 707–724.

Lion B. / Michel C. 2000: Poissons crustacés en Haute-Mésopotamie au début IIe millénaire av. J.-C., TOPOI Sup. 2, 71–116.

Llop J. 2011: The Food of the Gods. MARV 3, 16. A Middle Assyrian Offerings List to the Great Gods of the City of Aššur, SAAB 18, 1–46.

Loktionov A. 2014: *Kušû*: Crocodile after all?, NABU 2014/103.

MacGinnis J. 1995: Letter Orders from Sippar and the Administration of the Ebabbara in the Late-Babylonian Period. Bonami.

Matouš L. 1974: Beiträge zur akkadischen Lexikographie (Review of CAD K and AHw Lieferung 9-10), ArOr 42, 167–172.

Maul S. M. 1988: 'Herzberuhigungsklagen'. Die sumerisch-akkadischen Eršaḫunga-Gebete. Wiesbaden.

Maul S. M. 2009: Die Lesung der Rubra DÙ.DÙ.BI und KÌD.KÌD.BI, Or. 78, 69–80.

Mayer W. R. 2003: Waffen und Stricke in einer altbabylonischen Urkunde, Or. 72, 368–389.

Mayer W. R. 2007: Das akkadische Präsens zum Ausdruck der Nachzeitigkeit in der Vergangenheit, Or. 76, 117–144.

Mayer W. R. 2009: Akkadische Lexikographie: CAD T und Ṭ, Or. 78, 423–438.

Mayer W. R. 2016: Zum akkadischen Wörterbuch A–L, Or. 85, 181–235.

McEwan G. J. P. 1981a: Priest and Temple in Hellenistic Babylonia (= FAOS 4). Stuttgart.

McEwan G. J. P. 1984: A Greek Legal Instrument in Hellenistic Uruk, AoF 11, 237–241.

McEwan G. J. P. 1986: Sons of the Hunchback, RA 80, 188.

Menzel-Wortmann B. 1986: Der ^{LÚ}GAL *danibata*, Mesopotamia 21, 213–227.

Michalowski P. 1989: The Lamentation over the Destruction of Sumer and Ur (= MesCiv. 1). Winona Lake.

Michel C. 2001b: Correspondance des marchands de Kaniš au début du IIe millénaire avant J.-C. (= LAPO 19). Paris.

Michel C. 2004b: Deux incantations paléo-assyriennes. Une nouvelle incantation pour accompagner la naissance, in: Fs. Larsen, 395–420.

Michel C. 2006: Bigamie chez les Assyriens au début du IIe millénaire avant J.–C. Revue historique de droit français et étranger 84/2, 155–76.

Michel C. 2008a: Les assyriens et les esprits de leurs morts, in. Gs. Garelli, 181–97.

Michel C. 2016: Le pain à Aššur et à Kaneš, in: Fs. Milano, 221–35.

Michel C. / Nosch M.-L. 2010: Textile Terminologies in the Ancient Near East and Mediterranean From the Third to the First Millennia BC (= Ancient Textiles 8). Oxford.

Michel C. / Veenhof K. R. 2010: The Textiles Traded by the Assyrians in Anatolia (19th–18th centuries BC), in: Michel/Nosch 2010, 210–271.

Militarev A. / Kogan L. 2000: Semitic Etymological Dictionary, Vol. 1: Anatomy of Man and Animals (= AOAT 278/1). Münster.

Militarev A. / Kogan L. 2005: Semitic Etymological Dictionary, Vol. 2: Animal Names (= AOAT 278/2). Münster.

Moran W. L. 1992: The Amarna Letters. Baltimore/London.

Negri Scafa P. 1982: A proposito del termina *kašku* nei testi di Nuzi, OrAnt. 21, 123–142.

Niedorf 2008: Die mittelbabylonischen Rechtsurkunden aus Alalaḫ (Schicht IV) (= AOAT 352). Münster.

Numoto H. 2009: Excavations at Tell Taban, Hassake, Syria: Preliminary report on the 2007 season of excavations, and the study of cuneiform texts. Tokyo.

Oshima T. 2011: Babylonian Prayers to Marduk (= ORA 7). Tübingen.

Oshima T. 2014: Babylonian Poems of Pious Sufferers (= ORA 14). Tübingen.

Parpola S. 1983a: Letters from Assyrian Scholars to the Kings Esarhaddon and Assurbanipal. Part II: Commentary and Appendices (= AOAT 5/2). Kevelaer / Neukirchen-Vluyn.

Paulus S. 2014: Die babylonischen Kudurru-Inschriften von der kassitischen bis zur frühneubabylonischen Zeit: Untersuchung unter besonderer Berücksichtigung gesellschafts- und rechtshistorischer Fragestellungen (= AOAT 51). Münster.

Pasquali J. 2005: Il Lessico dell'Artigianato nei Testi di Ebla (= QS 23). Firenze.

Pasquali J. 2014: Eblaïte *ga-zi-a-tum* = néo-babylonien $^{\check{s}im}$*ka-ṣi-'a-a-tu*$_4$, NABU 2014/75.

Pentiuc E. J. 2001: West Semitic Vocabulary in the Akkadian Texts from Emar (= HSS 49). Winona Lake.

Podany A. H. 2002: The Land of Hana. Kings, Chronology, and Scribal Tradition. Bethesda.

Postgate J. N. 1974: The *bit akiti* in Assyrian Nabu Temples, Sumer 30, 51–74.

Postgate J. N. 1976: Fifty Neo-Assyrian Legal Documents. Warminster.

Postgate J. N. 1980: Review of Freydank, Mittelassyrische Rechtsurkunden und Verwaltungstexte (VS NF. 3), BiOr 37, 67–70.

Postgate J. N. 1987: Some Vegetables in the Assyrian Sources, BSA 3, 93–100.

Postgate J. N. 1994a: Rings, torcs and bracelets, in: Fs. Hrouda, 235–245.

Postgate J. N. 2000a: The Assyrian Army in Zamua, Iraq 62, 89–108.

Postgate J. N. 2003: Documents in Government under the Middle Assyrian Kingdom, in: M. Brosius (ed.), Ancient Archives and Archival Traditions, 124–138.

Postgate J. N. 2007: The Land of Assur and the Yoke of Assur. Studies on Assyria 1971–2005. Oxford.

Postgate J. N. 2008: The Organization of the Middle Assyrian Army: Some Fresh Evidence, in: P. Abrahami / L. Battini (eds.), Les armées du Proche-Orient ancien (IIIe–Ier mill. av. J.-C.) (= BAR International Series 1855), Oxford, 83–92.

Postgate J. N. 2013: Bronze Age Bureaucracy. Writing and the Practice of Government in Assyria. Cambridge.

Postgate J. N. et al. 2019: Documents from the Nabu Temple and from Private Houses on the Citadel (= CTN 6).

Potts D. T. / Parpola A. / Parpola S. / Tidmarsh J. 1996: *Guḫlu* und *Guggulu*, WZKM 86, 291–305.

Powell M. A. 1987–1990: Masse und Gewichte, RlA 7, 457–517.

Quillien L. 2019: Dissemination and price of cotton in Mesopotamia during the 1st millennium BC, Revue d'ethnoécologie 15.

Radner K. 1997: Die neuassyrischen Privatrechtsurkunden als Quelle für Mensch und Umwelt (= SAAS 6). Helsinki.

Reiter K. 1989: *kikkullu/kilkillu*, "Raum zur Aufbewahrung des Eidleistungssymbols (šu.nir = *šurinnum*) des Šamaš, NABU 1989/107.

Reiter K. 1991: *kilkillu*, archäologisch, NABU 1991/84.

Renaut L. 2007: A Short Note on JA Scurlock's Recent Identification of the *kamantu*-Plant with *Lawsonia inermis L.*, JMC 10, 47–48.

Richter T. 1992: Weitere Anmerkungen zu CAD Q, NABU 1992/24.

Richter T. 2005: Kleine Beiträge zum hurritischen Wörterbuch, AoF 32, 23–44.

Richter T. 2012: Bibliographisches Glossar des Hurritischen. Wiesbaden.

Riemschneider K. K. 1977: *kappu-rapšu* and *pattarpalḫi-*, JCS 27, 233–234.

Roth M. T. 1989–90: The Material Composition of the Neo-Babylonian Dowry, AfO 36/37, 1–55.

Sallaberger W. 1995: Eine reiche Bestattung im neusumerischen Ur, JCS 47, 15–17.

Sallaberger W. 1996: Der babylonische Töpfer und seine Gefäße nach Urkunden altsumerischer bis altbabylonischer Zeit sowie lexikalischen und literarischen Zeugnissen (= MHEM 3). Ghent.

Sallaberger W. 2000: Das Erscheinen Marduks als Vorzeichen: Kultstatue und Neujahrsfest in der Omenserie Šumma ālu, ZA 90, 227–262.

Sallaberger W. 2011: Sumerian Language Use at Garšana. On Orthography, Grammar, and Akkado-Sumerian Bilingualism, in: D. I. Owen (ed.), Garšana Studies (= CUSAS 6, Bethesda) 335–372.

Salonen A. 1969: Die Fussbekleidung der alten Mesopotamier nach sumerisch-akkadischen Quellen. Eine lexikalische und kulturgeschichtliche Untersuchung (= Annales Academiae Scientiarum Fennicae. Ser. B, Tom. 157). Helsinki.

Salonen A. 1973: Vogel und Vogelfang im Alten Mesopotamien. Helsinki.

Salvini M. 1998: I testi cuneiformi delle campagne 1989 e 1993 a Tell Barri / Kahat, in: P. E. Pecorella (ed.) Tell Barri / Kahat 2 (= Documenta Asiana V), 187–198.

Salvini M. 2014: Neuassyrische Schrift und Sprache in den urartäischen Königsinschriften (9.–7. Jahrhundert v. Chr.), in: E. Cancik-Kirschbaum / J. Klinger / G. G. W. Müller,

Diversity and Standardization: Perspectives on ancient Near Eastern cultural history, München: Akadmie Verlag, 113–143.

Sanmartín J. 2019: A Glossary of Old Syrian. Volume 1: ʔ – ḳ (= LANE 8/1). Winona Lake.

Sassmannshausen L. 2001: Beiträge zur Verwaltung und Gesellschaft Babyloniens in der Kassitenzeit (= BagF 21). Mainz am Rhein.

Sasson J. M. 1994: Divine divide: re FM 2 : 71 : 5, NABU 1994/42.

Sasson J. M. 2007: Scruples. Extradition in the Mari Archives, in: Fs. Hunger (= WZKM 97), 453–473.

Schaudig H. 2001: Die Inschriften Nabonids von Babylon und Kyros' des Großen samt den in ihrem Umfeld entstandenen Tendenzschriften. Textausgabe und Grammatik (= AOAT 256). Münster.

Schaudig H. 2013: Explaining Disaster: Tradition and Transformation of the "Catastrophe of Ibbi-Sîn" in Babylonian Literature. In preparation for: AOAT 370.

Schwemer D. 1995: Das alttestamentliche Doppelritual *'lwt wšlmym* im Horizont der hurritischen Opfertermini *ambašši* und *keldi*, in: SCCNH 7, 81–116.

Schwemer D. 2005–6: Lehnbeziehungen zwischen dem Hethitischen und dem Akkadischen. AfO 51, 220–234.

Schwemer D. 2007: Abwehrzauber und Behexung. Studien zum Schadenzauberglauben im alten Mesopotamien.

Scurlock J. A. 1993: Once more *ku-bu-ru*, NABU 1993/21.

Scurlock J. A. 1997: Cur's *kurru* encore, NABU 1997/91.

Scurlock J. A. 2007: A Proposal for Identification of a Missing Plant: *kamantu* / ^{Ú}ÁB.DUḪ = *Lawsonia inermis L.*, WZKM 97, 491–520.

Scurlock J. A. / Andersen B. R. 2005: Diagnoses in Assyrian and Babylonian Medicine. Urbana.

Selz G. 1993: *kaparru*(*m*), ein sumerischen Lehnwort im Akkadischen? Untersuchungen zu sumerischen Nominalformen des Typus /gabil/ und ihren akkadischen Entsprechungen, RA 87, 29–45.

Sever H. 1995: Yeni Belgelerin Işığında Koloni Çağında (M.Ö. 1970–1750) Yerli Halk İle Asurlu Tüccarlar Arasındaki İlişkiler. Belleten 59/224, 1–16.

Shaffer A. / Wassermann N. / Seidl U. 2003: Iddi(n)-Sîn, King of Simurrum: A New Rock-Relief Inscription and a Reverential Seal, ZA 93, 1–52.

Shehata D. 2001: Annotierte Bibliographie zum altbabylonischen Atramhasis-mythos *Inūma ilu awīlum* (= GAAL 3). Göttingen.

Sigrist M. 1993: Seven Emar Tablets, in: A. F. Rainey (ed.), Kinattūtu ša dārâti. Raphael Kutscher Memorial Volume, 165–187.

Sjöberg Å. W. 1975: Der Examenstext A, ZA 64: 137–176.

Sjöberg Å. W. 1996: UET 7 no. 93. A Lexical Text or a Commentary?, ZA 86, 220–237.

Sjöberg Å. W. 1996a: UET 7, 73: An Exercise Tablet Enumerating Professions, Fs. Limet 117–139.

Sjöberg Å. W. 1998: Studies in the Emar Sa Vocabulary, ZA 88, 240–283.

Sjöberg Å. W. 2003: Notes on Selected Entries from the Ebla Vocabulary $eš_2$-bar-kin_5 (IV), in: Fs. Wilcke, 251–266.

Sokoloff M. 2009: A Syriac Lexicon. Winona Lake.

Sollberger E. 1987: A Bead for Sennacherib, Fs. Reiner (= AOS 67), 379–380.

Sommerfeld W. 1985: Der Kurigalzu Text MAH 15922, AfO 32, 1–32.

Sommerfeld W. 1990: Review of AbB 10, ZA 80, 141–143.

Sommerfeld W. 1990a: Review of CAD Q, OLZ 85, 29–34.

Sommerfeld W. 2013: Review of Hasselbach 2005, WZKM 102, 193–284.

Sommerfeld W. 2021: Old Akkadian, in: J.-P. Vita (ed.) History of the Akkadian Language. Volume 1: Linguistic Background and Early Periods (HdO 152/1), 513–663.

Stol M. 1979: On Trees, Mountains, and Millstones in the Ancient Near East. Leiden.

Stol M. 1980–1983: Leder(industrie), RlA 6, 527–543.

Stol M. 1983: Review of CT 55–57, ZA 73, 296–300.

Stol M. 1983–1984: Cress and its Mustard, JEOL 28, 24–32.

Stol M. 1985: Beans, peas, lentils & vetches, BSA 127–139.

Stol M. 1987a: The Cucurbitaceae in the Cuneiform Texts, BSA 3, 81–92.

Stol M. 1987b: Garlic, Onion, Leek, BSA 3, 57–80.

Stol M. 1989: Leprosy. New Light from Greek and Bablonian Sources, JEOL 30, 22–31.

Stol M. 1991: Old Babylonian Personal Names, SEL 8, 191–212.

Stol M. 1993b: *Epilepsy* in Babylonia (= CunMon. 2). Leiden.

Stol M. 1993c: Milk, Butter, and Cheese, BSA 7, 99–113.

Stol M. 1994: Beer in Neo-Babylonian Times, in: Milano 1994, 155–183.

Stol M. 1995b: Old Babylonian Cattle, BSA 8, 173–213.

Stol M. 1998: Einige kurze Wortstudien, in: Fs. Borger (= CunMon. 10), 343–352.

Stol M. 2004a: Review of VS 29, BiOr 61, 133–134.

Stol M. 2006: The Digestion of Food according to Babylonian Sources, in: Battini/Villard (eds.), Médecine et médecins au Proche-Orient ancien (= BAR IS 1528), 103–119.

Stol M. 2007b: Reis, RlA 11, 300–301.

Stol M. 2009: Schwefel, RlA 12, 317–319.

Stol M. 2011–2013: Strauß, RlA 13, 211–212.

Stol M. 2011–2013b: Teer. A. Philologisch, RlA 13, 498–500.

Stol M. 2014: Trüffel, RlA 14/1, 149–150.

Stol M. / Vleming S. P. 1998: The Care of the Elderly in the Ancient Near East (= Studies in the History and Culture of the Ancient Near East 14). Leiden.

Stolper M. W. 1977: Three Iranian Loanwords in Late Babylonian Texts, in: BiMes 7, 251–266.

Stolper M. W. 1985: Entrepreneurs and Empire: the Murašû Archive, the Murašû Firm, and Persian rule in Babylonia (= PIHANS 54). Istanbul.

Streck M. P. 1995a: Zahl und Zeit. Grammatik der Numerialia und des Verbalsystems im Spätbabylonischen (= CunMon. 5). Groningen.

Streck M. P. 1999: Review of OIP 114, ZA 89, 286–295.

Streck M. P. 2000a: Das amurritische Onomastikon der altbabylonischen Zeit (= AOAT 273/1). Münster.

Streck M. P. 2003a: Die akkadischen Verbalstämme mit *ta*-Infix (= AOAT 303). Münster.

Streck M. P. 2004: Dattelpalme und Tamariske in Mesopotamien nach dem akkadischen Streitgespräch, ZA 94, 250–29.

Streck M. P. 2009–2011b: Schlitten. A. Philologisch. RlA 12, 228–230.

Streck M. P. 2010: Notes on the Old Babylonian Hymns of Agušaya, JAOS 130, 561–571.

Streck M. P. 2017: The Terminology for Times of the Day in Akkadian, in: Y. Heffron / A. Stone / M. Worthington (eds.), At the Dawn of History. Ancient Near Eastern Studies in Honour of J. N. Postgate. Winona Lake, 583–609.

Streck M. P. 2021: Akkadian Lexicography: New Discoveries, in: R. Hasselbach-Andee/N. Pat-El (eds.), Bēl Lišāni. Current Research in Akkadian Linguistics (Winona Lake), 219–228.

Streck M. P. / Wasserman N. 2008: The Old Babylonian Hymns to Papulegara, Or. NS 77, 335–358.

Streck M. P. / Wasserman N. 2012: More Light on Nanāya, ZA 102, 183–201.

Streck M. P. / Wasserman N. 2018: The Man is Like a Woman, the Maiden is a Young Man: A new edition of Ištar-Louvre, Or. NS 87, 1–38, pl. II–III.

Steinkeller P. 1984: The Eblaite Preposition *qidimay* "Before", OrAnt 23, 33–37.

Steinkeller P. 1991: The Container *kabkūru*, NABU 1991/4.

Steinkeller P. 1995: Sheep and goat terminology in Ur III sources from Drehem, BSA 8, 49–70.

Sturm T. 1995: Qannuttum – eine Dame in Assur zur aA Zeit, NABU 1995/37.

Such-Gutiérrez M. 2018: Die Sprachsituation in Adab während der altakkadischen Periode, in: S. Fink / M. Lang / M. Schretter (eds.), Mehrsprachigkeit. Vom Alten Orient bis zum Esperanto (= dubsar 2), 131–150.

Thavapalan S. 2020: The Meaning of Color in Ancient Mesopotamia (= CHANE 104). Leiden.

van de Mieroop M. 1987: Crafts in the Early Isin Period (= OLA 24). Leuven.

van Driel G. 1969: The Cult of Aššur. (Studia Semitica Neerlandica 13).

van Driel G. 1992: Wood, Reeds and Rushes. A note on Neo-Babylonian practical texts, BSA 6, 171–176.

van Driel G. 1995: Cattle in the Neo-Babylonian period, *BSA 8*, 215–240.

van Driel G. 2002: Elusive Silver. In Search of a Role for a Market in an Agrarian Environment (= PIHANS 95). Leiden.

van Koppen F. 2001: Sweeping the court and locking the gate: The palace of Sippir-ṣērim, in Fs. Veenhof, 211–224.

van Soldt W. H. 1978: Review of UET 7, JAOS 98, 491–501.

Veenhof K. R. 1970: Review of N. B. Jankovskaja, Klinopisnye Teksty iz Kjultepe v Sobranijach SSSR (Cuneiform Texts from Kültepe in Collections in the USSR), BiOr 27, 367–369.

Veenhof K. R. 1972: *Aspects* of Old Assyrian Trade and its Terminology. Leiden.

Veenhof K. R. 1976: The Dissolution of an Old Babylonian Marriage According to CT 45, 86, RA 70, 153–164.

Veenhof K. R. 1995–96: The Old Assyrian *ḫamuštum* Period: A Seven–day Week. JEOL 34/36, 5–26.

Veenhof K. R. 1997: Two Marriage Documents from Kültepe. ArAn 3, 357–381.

Veenhof K. R. 1998: Old Assyrian and Ancient Anatolian Evidence for the Care of the Elderly, in: Stol/Vleming 1998, 119–160.

Veenhof K. R. 2001: The Old Assyrian Period, in: Westbrook R. / Jasnow R. (eds.), Security for Debt in Ancient Near Eastern Law (= CHANE 9), 93–159.

Veenhof K. R. 2003: The Old Assyrian List of Year Eponyms from Karum Kanish and its Chronological Implications. Publications of the Turkish Historical Society, VI/64. Ankara.

Veenhof K. R. 2005: Letters in the Louvre. Transliterated and Translated (= AbB 14). Leiden.

Veenhof K. R. 2008: Communication in the Old Assyrian Trading Society, Gs. Garelli (= PIHANS 112), 199–246.

Veenhof K. R. 2008a: The Old Assyrian Period, in: id. / J. Eidem (eds), Mesopotamia. The Old Assyrien Period. Annäherungen 5 (OBO 160/5), 13–264.

Veenhof K. R. 2010: Kültepe Tabletleri V. The Archive of Kuliya, son of Ali-abum (Kt. 92/k 188-263). Türk Tarih Kurumu Yayınları VI/33c. Ankara.

Veenhof K. R. 2012: Last Wills and Inheritance of Old Assyrian Traders with Four Records from the Archive of Elamma, in: Fs. Skaist, 169–202.

Veenhof K. R. 2014: Silver in Old Assyrian Trade. Its Shapes, Qualities and Purification, in: Gs. Vargyas, 393–422.

Veenhof K. R. 2017b: The Old Assyrian contract H.K. 1005–5534, NABU 2017/8.

Veenhof K. R. 2018a: On Old Assyrian Marriage and Marriage Law, ZABR 24, 7–56.

Veldhuis N. 2004: Religion, Literature, and Scholarship. The Sumerian Composition "Nanše and the Birds" (= CunMon. 22). Groningen.

von Soden W. 1975: Review of CAD K, OLZ 70, 485–492.

von Soden W. 1977: Aramäische Wörter in neuassyrischen und neu- und spätbabylonischen Texten. Ein Vorbericht. III, Or. 46, 183–197.

von Soden W. 1980a: Review of Alster (ed.), Death in Mesopotamia (CRRAI 26), ZA 70, 274–275.

von Soden W. 1981a: Review of Greengus, Old Babylonian Tablets from Ishchali and Vicinity, ZA 71, 149–151.

von Soden W. 1985: Review of CAD Q, JSS 30, 274–278.

von Soden W. 1986: Review of AbB 10, BiOr 43, 732–736.

von Soden W. 1989: Zu dem altbabylonischen Hymnus an Anmartu und Ašratum mit Verheissungen an Rīm-Sîn, NABU 1989/105.

von Soden W. 1991: Review of SAA 3, WO 22, 189–195.

Waerzeggers C. 2006a: Neo-Babylonian Laundry, RA 100, 83–96.

Walker Ch. / Dick M. 2001: The Induction of the Cult Image in Ancient Mesopotamia. The Mesopotamian Mis Pi Ritual (= SAALT 1). Winona Lake.

Wasserman N. 2011: Adzes, not Skirts in CUSAS 10, No. 7, NABU 2011/53.

Wasserman N. 2012: Most Probably. Epistemic Modality in Old Babylonian (= LANE 39). Winona Lake.

Wasserman N. 2013: Treating Garments in the Old Babylonian Period: "At the Cleaners" in a Comparative View, Iraq 75, 255–277.

Watanabe K. 1987: Die *adê*-Vereidigung anlässlich der Thronfolgeregelung Asarhaddons (= BagM Beih. 3). Berlin.

Watson W. G. E: 2011: Akk. *kumānu* in a wider perspective, NABU 2011/82.

Watson W. G. E. 2014: Akk. *katappu* and *katinnu* revisited, NABU 2014/24.

Wehr H. 1985: Arabisches Wörterbuch für die Schriftsprache der Gegenwart. 5. ed. Wiesbaden.

Weidner E. 1959–1960: Review of CAD D, E, G, Ḫ, AfO 19, 155–156.

Westbrook R. 1996: zíz.da/*kiššātum*, WZKM 86, 449–459.

Westenholz A. 1987: Old Sumerian and Old Akkadian Texts in Philadelphia. Part Two: The 'Akkadian' Texts, the Enlilemaba Texts, and the Onion Archive (= CNIPublications 3). Copenhagen.

Westenholz A. 1999: The Old Akkadian Period: History and Culture, in W. Sallaberger / A. Westenholz, Mesopotamien: Akkade-Zeit und Ur III-Zeit (= OBO 160/5), 17–117.

Westenholz J. G. 1993: One more *ku-bu-ru*, NABU 1993/21.

Westenholz J. G. 1997: Legends of the Kings of Akkade (= MesCiv. 7). Winona Lake.

Westenholz J. G. 2000: Cuneiform inscriptions in the collection of the Bible Lands Museum Jerusalem: the Emar tablets. Vol. 1. (= CunMon. 13). Groningen.

Wilcke C. 1991: Die Lesung von ÁŠ-da = *kiššātum*, NABU 1991/16.

Wilcke C. 1998: Care for the Elderly in Mesopotamia in the Third Millennium B.C., in: Stol/Vleming 1998, 23–57.

Wilhelm G. 1985: Das Archiv des Šilwa-Teššup, 3: Rationenlisten II. Wiesbaden.

Wilhelm G. 1988: Zu den Wollmaßen in Nuzi, ZA 78, 276–283.

Yoffee N. 1998: The Economics of Ritual at Late Old Babylonian Kish, JESHO 41, 312–343.

Zaccagnini C. 1994: Joint Responsibility in Barley Loans in the Neo-Assyrian Period, SAAB 8, 28–42.

Zadok R. 1982: Lexical, Onomastic and Geographical Notes, RA 76, 174–178.

Zadok R. 1997: On Aromatics and Reeds, NABU 1997/2, 51f., 55.

Zadok R. 2020: Arameo-Akkadica II, NABU 2020/128.

Zadok R. 2020a: Four Loanwords in Neo-/Late-Babylonian, NABU 2020/129.

Zawadzki S. 2006: Garments of the Gods, Vol. 1: Studies on the Textile Industry and the Pantheon of Sippar According to the Texts from the Ebabbar Archive (= OBO 218). Fribourg/Göttingen.

Zawadzki S. 2010: Garments in Non-Cultic Context, in: Michel/Nosch 2010, 409–429.

Zawadzki S. 2013: Garments of the Gods, Vol. 2: Texts (= OBO 260). Fribourg – Göttingen.

Zeeb F. 2001: Die Palastwirtschaft in Altsyrien nach den spätaltbabylonischen Getreidelieferlisten aus Alalaḫ (Schicht VII) (= AOAT 282). Münster.

Bibliographical Abbreviations

AbB	Altbabylonische Briefe in Umschrift und Übersetzung.
ABL	R. F. Harper, Assyrian and Babylonian letters belonging to the Kouyounjik collection of the British Museum.
Adš	G. Wilhelm / D. L. Stein, Das Archiv des Šilwa-Teššup, 1–9.
AfO (Beih.)	Archiv für Orientforschung (Beihefte).
AHw.	W. von Soden, Akkadisches Handwörterbuch.
Akkadica	Akkadica. Revue semestrielle de la Fondation Assyriologique Georges Dossin.
AKT	Ankara Kültepe Tabletleri (Ankaraner Kültepe-Tafeln).
ALL	N. Wasserman, Akkadian Love Literature of the Third and Second Millennium BCE (= Leipziger Altorientalische Studien 4).
AlT	D. J. Wiseman, The Alalakh Tablets.
AMD	(Studies in) Ancient Magic and Divination.
AML	N. Wasserman/E. Zomer 2021: Akkadian Magic Literature. Old Babylonian and Old Assyrian Incantations: Corpus – Context – Praxis (= LAOS 12).
AMMY	Anadolu Medeniyetleri Müzesi Yıllığı, Ankara.
AMT	R. C. Thompson, Assyrian medical texts from the originals in the British Museum (London 1923).
Amurru	Amurru (Paris 1996ff.).
ANES	Ancient Near Eastern Studies. An annual (publ.) by the School of Fine Arts, Classical Studies and Archaeology University of Melbourne.
AnSt.	Anatolian Studies. Journal of the British Institute of Archaeo-logy at Ankara.
AO	Tablets in the collections of the Musée du Louvre.
AOAT	Alter Orient und Altes Testament.
AoF	Altorientalische Forschungen.
AOS	American Oriental Series.
API	E. Herzfeld, Altpersische Inschriften.

ArAn	Archivum Anatolicum.
ARM	Archives Royales de Mari.
ArOr.	Archív Orientální.
AS	Assyriological Studies (Chicago).
ASJ	Acta Sumerologica.
Ass.	Field number of tablets excavated at Assur.
ATHE	B. Kienast, Die altassyrischen Texte des Orientalischen Seminars der Universität Heidelberg und der Sammlung Erlenmeyer-Basel.
Atra-ḫasīs	W. G. Lambert / A. R. Millard, Atra-ḫasīs. The Babylonian story of the flood.
AUCT	Andrews University Cuneiform Texts.
AulaOr.	Aula Orientalis. Revista de estudios del Próximo Oriente Antiguo.
AUWE	Ausgrabungen in Uruk-Warka. Endberichte, DAI Baghdad (Mainz 1987–).
AWTL	F. Ismail, Altbabylonische Wirtschaftsurkunden aus Tall Leilān Syrien (PhD thesis Tübingen 1991).
BagF	Baghdader Forschungen.
BagM	Baghdader Mitteilungen.
BAM	F. Köcher et al., Die babylonisch-assyrische Medizin in Texten und Untersuchungen.
Banca d'Italia	1: F. Pomponio/G. Visicato/A. Westenholz, Le tavolette cuneiformi di Adab delle collezioni della Banca d'Italia. 2: F. Pomponio/M. Stol/A. Westenholz, Le tavolette cuneiformi di varia provenienza delle collezioni della Banca d'Italia (Rome 2006).
BATSH	Berichte der Ausgrabung Tall Šēḫ Ḥamad / Dūr-Katlimmu.
BE	The Babylonian Expedition of the University of Pennsylvania.
Bēl rēmanni	M. Jursa, Das Archiv des Bēl-rēmanni (= PIHANS 86).
Belleten	Belleten. Türk Tarih Kurumu, Ankara.
BiMes.	Bibliotheca Mesopotamica.
BIN	Babylonian Inscriptions in the Collection of James B. Nies, Yale University

BiOr.	Bibliotheca Orientalis.
BL	S. Langdon, Babylonian liturgies: Sumerian texts from the early period and from the library of Ashurbanipal, for the most part transliterated and translated, with introduction and index (Paris 1913).
BM	Tablets in the collections of the British Museum.
BMS	L. W. King, Babylonian magic and sorcery.
Bo.	Field number of tablets excavated at Boghazköy.
BSA	Bulletin on Sumerian Agriculture.
BVW	E. Ebeling, Bruchstücke einer mittelassyrischen Vorschriftensammlung für die Akklimatisierung und Trainierung von Wagenpferden (Deutsche Akademie der Wissenschaften zu Berlin Institut für Orientforschung: Veröffentlichung 7, 1951).
BWL	W. G. Lambert, Babylonian wisdom literature.
CAD	The Assyrian Dictionary of the University of Chicago.
CBS	Tablets in the collections of the University Museum of the University of Pennsylvania, Philadelphia).
CCT	Cuneiform Texts from Cappadocian Tablets in the British Museum.
CDA	J. A. Black / A. George / N. Postgate, A concise dictionary of Akkadian.
CH	Codex Hammurapi.
CHANE	Culture and History of the Ancient Near East.
Chuera	S. Jakob, Die mittelassyrischen Texte aus Tell Chuēra in Nordost-Syrien.
CNIP	Carsten Niebuhr Institute Publications.
CRRAI	Compte rendu, Rencontre Assyriologique Internationale.
CT	Cuneiform Texts from Babylonian Tablets in the British Museum.
CTMMA	Cuneiform Texts in the Metropolitan Museum of Art.
CTN	Cuneiform Texts from Nimrud.
CunMon.	Cuneiform Monographs.
CUSAS	Cornell University Studies in Assyriology and Sumerology.

DCCLT	N. Veldhuis (ed.), Digital Corpus of Cuneiform Lexical Texts. http://oracc.museum.upenn.edu/dcclt/.
DUL	G. del Olmo Lete/J. Sanmartín (transl. by W. G. E. Watson), A dictionary of the Ugaritic language in the alphabetical tradition, 1–2 (= HdO 1/67 1–2, 2004 [2nd rev. ed.]).
EA	J. A. Knudtzon, Die El-Amarna-Tafeln. Cf. W. L. Moran, The Amarna letters.
Edubba 7	F. N. H. Al-Rawi / S. Dalley, Old Babylonian Texts from Private Houses at Abu Habbah, Ancient Sippir.
Tell ed-Dēr	D. O. Edzard, Altbabylonische Rechts- und Wirtschaftsurkunden aus TeIl ed-Der (= ABAW NF72, 1970).
Ee	Enūma elîš (W. G. Lambert, Babylonian Creation Myths [2013]; T. R. Kämmerer / K. A. Metzler, Das babylonische Weltschöpfungsepos Enūma elîš [= AOAT 375, 2012]).
Emar	D. Arnaud, Recherches au Pays d'Aštata. Emar 6/1–4. Textes sumériens et accadiens.
Ešḫ	S. M. Mau, 'Herzberuhigungsklagen'. Die sumerisch-akkadischen Eršaḫunga-Gebete. (1988)
FAOS (Beih.)	Freiburger Altorientalische Studien (Beihefte).
FLP	Tablets in the collections of the Free Library of Philadelphia.
FM	Florilegium Marianum (= Mémoires de NABU).
FNALD	J. N. Postgate, Fifty Neo-Assyrian legal documents (Warminster 1976).
Fs. Charpin	G. Chambon / M. Guichard / A.-I. Langlois (eds.), De l'argile au numérique. Mélanges assyriologiques en l'honneur de Dominique Charpin (Leuven/Paris/Bristol 2019).
Fs. Darga	T. Tarhan / A. Tibet / E. Konyar (eds.), Muhibbe Darga Armağanı (Istanbul 2008).
Fs. De Meyer	H. Gasche / M. Tanret / C. Janssen / A. Degraeve (eds.), Cinquante-deux réflexions sur le Proche-Orient ancien: offertes en hommage à Léon De Meyer (= MHEO 2, 1994).
Fs. Donbaz	Ş. Dönmez (ed.), DUB.SAR É.DUB.BA.A Studies Presented in Honour of Veysel Donbaz (Istanbul 2010).

Fs. Geller	S. V. Panayotov / L. Vacín (eds.), Mesopotamian Medicine and Magic. Studies in Honor of Markham J. Geller (Leiden/Boston 2018).
Fs. Günbattı	İ. Albayrak / H. Erol / M. Çayır (eds.), Studies in Honour of Cahit Günbattı (Ankara 2015).
Fs. Güterbock	K. Bittel / Ph. H. J. Houwink ten Cate / E. Reiner (eds.), Anatolian Studies Presented to Hans Gustav Güterbock on the Occasion of his 65th Birthday (Istanbul 1974).
Fs. Klein	Y. Sefati et al. (ed.), "An experienced scribe who neglects nothing": Ancient Near Eastern studies in honor of Jacob Klein (Bethesda 2005).
Fs. Kraus	G. van Driel / Th. J. H. Krispijn / M. Stol / K. R. Veenhof (eds.), Zikir šumim: Assyriological studies presented to F. R. Kraus on the occasion of his seventieth birthday (= Studia Francisci Scholten memoriae dicata 5, Leiden 1982).
Fs. Lambert	A. R. George / I. L. Finkel (eds.), Wisdom, gods and literature: Studies in Assyriology in Honour of W. G. Lambert (Winona Lake 2000).
Fs. Larsen	J. G. Dercksen (ed.), Assyria and beyond: studies presented to Mogens Trolle Larsen (= PIHANS 100).
Fs. Matouš	B. Hruška / G. Komoróczy (eds.), Festschrift Lubor Matouš, 1–2 (Assyriologia 5/1–2 = Az Eötvös Loránd tudományegyetem Ókori történeti tanszékeinek kiadványai 24–25, Budapest 1978).
Fs. Milano	P. Corò / E. Devecchi / N. de Zorzi / M. Maiocchi (eds.), Libiamo ne' lieti calici. Ancient Near Eastern Studies Presented to Lucio Milano on the Occasion of his 65th Birth-day by Pupils, Colleagues and Friends (= AOAT 436).
Fs. N. Özgüç	M. J. Mellink / E. Porada / T. Özgüç (eds.), Aspects of Art and Iconography. Anatolia and its Neighbors. Nimet Özgüç'e armağan. Studies in Honor of Nimet Özgüç (Ankara 1993).
Fs. T. Özgüç	K. Emre et al. (eds.), Anatolia and the Ancient Near East. Studies in Honor of Tahsin Özgüç (Ankara 1989).
Fs. Pettinato	H. Waetzoldt (ed.), Von Sumer nach Ebla und zurück. Festschrift Giovanni Pettinato zum 27. September 1999 gewidmet von Freunden, Kollegen und Schülern (= HSAO 9).
Fs. Reiner	F. Rochberg-Halton (ed.), Language, Literature and History. Philological and Historical Studies Presented to Erica Reiner (= AOS 67, 1987).

Fs. Sjöberg	H. Behrens / D. Loding / M. T. Roth (eds.), DUMU-E2-DUB-BA-A. Studies in honor of Åke W. Sjöberg (= OccPubl. S. N. Kramer Fund 11, 1989).
Fs. Skaist	K. Abraham / J. Fleishman (eds.), Looking at the Ancient Near East and the Bible through the Same Eyes. Minha LeAhron: A Tribute to Aaron Skaist (Bethesda, Maryland 2012).
Fs. Ünal	S. Erkut / Ö. Sir Gavaz (eds.) ANTAḪŠUMSAR "ÇIĞDEM" Studies in Honour of Ahmet Ünal (Istanbul 2016).
Fs. Veenhof	J. G. Dercksen et al. (eds.), Veenhof Anniversary Volume. Studies presented to Klaas R. Veenhof on the occasion of his sixty-fifth birthday (= PIHANS 52, 2001).
Fs. von Soden	M. Dietrich and O. Loretz (eds.), Vom Alten Orient zum Alten Testament, Festschrift für Wolfram Freiherrn von Soden zum 85. Geburtstag am 19. Juni 1993 (= AOAT 240).
Fs. Walker	C. Wunsch (ed.), Mining the archives. Festschrift for Christopher Walker on the occasion of his 60th birthday 4 October 2002, (= BabA 1, 2002).
Fs. Wilcke	W. Sallaberger / K. Volk / A. Zgoll (eds.), Literatur, Politik und Recht in Mesopotamien. Festschrift für Claus Wilcke (= Orientalia Biblica et Christiana 14, 2003).
GAG	W. von Soden, Grundriß der akkadischen Grammatik.
GAO	N. J. C. Kouwenberg, A Grammar of Old Assyrian.
Gilg.	A. R. George, The Babylonian Gilgamesh-Epic (Oxford 2003), and recent publications.
Gs. Garelli	C. Michel (ed.), Old Assyrian Studies in Memory of Paul Garelli (= PIHANS 112).
Gs. Vargyas	Z. Csabai (ed.), Studies in Economic and Social History of the Ancient Near East in Memory of Péter Vargyas (= Ancient Near Eastern and Mediterranean Studies 2, 2014).
HANEM 2	G. Beckman, Texts from the Vicinity of Emar in the Collection of Jonathan Rosen (History of the Ancient Near East 2).
Hermitage	Tablets in the collections of the Hermitage St. Petersburg.
Ḫg	Lexical series ḪAR-gud, published MSL 5–11.
Ḫḫ	Lexical series ḪAR-ra = ḫubullu, published MSL 5–11.
HSAO	Heidelberger Studien zum Alten Orient.

HSS	Harvard Semitic Series.
ICK	Inscriptions cunéiformes du Kultépé.
IM	Tablets in the collections of the Iraq-Museum.
IPLA	R. de Boer, The Ikūn-pîša Letter Archive from Tell ed-Dēr (= PIHANS 131, 2021).
Iraq	Iraq. Journal of the British Archaeological Institute.
Ištar Bagdad	M. P. Streck, Die Klage „Ištar Bagdad", in: Fs. Wilcke, 304–309.
Ištar Louvre	M. P. Streck / N. Wasserman, The Man is Like a Woman, the Maiden is a Young Man. A new edition of Ištar-Louvre.
ITT	Inventaire des tablettes de Tello.
Izi	Lexical series izi = išātu, published MSL 13, 154ff.
JAOS	Journal of the American Oriental Society.
JCS	Journal of Cuneiform Studies.
JEOL	Jaarbericht van het Vooraziatisch-Egyptisch Genootschap "Ex Oriente Lux".
JRAS	Journal of the Royal Asiatic Society.
JSS	Journal of Semitic Studies.
KAJ	E. Ebeling, Keilschrifttexte aus Assur juristischen Inhalts (= WVDOG 50).
KAL	Keilschrifttexte aus Assur literarischen Inhalts.
KIM	Kültepe International Meetings (Turnhout 2015–).
KKS	L. Matouš / M. Matoušov-Rajmová, Kappadokische Keilschrifttafeln mit Siegeln aus den Sammlungen der Karlsuniversität in Prag.
KTT	M. Krebernik, Keilschrifttexte aus Tuttul.
KUB	Keilschrifturkunden aus Boghazköi 1–60 (Berlin 1921–1990).
Lamaštu	W. Farber, Lamaštu. An Edition of the Canonical Series of Lamaštu Incantations and Rituals and Related Texts from the Second and First Millennia B.C.
LANE	Languages of the Ancient Near East (Winona Lake 2008ff.).
LAPO	Littératures Anciennes du Proche-Orient (Paris 1967ff.).

LKA	E. Ebeling, Literarische Keilschrifttexte aus Assur.
M.	Field number of tablets excavated at Mari.
Malku	Lexical series malku = šarru, published AOAT 50.
MAM	A. Parrot et al., Mission Archéologique de Mari (Paris/Beyrouth 1956–2003).
MARI	MARI. Annales de recherches interdisciplinaires.
MARV	H. Freydank et al., Mittelassyrische Rechtsurkunden und Verwaltungstexte.
MBLET	O. R. Gurney, The Middle Babylonian legal and economic texts from Ur.
MDP	Mémoires de la Délégation en Perse.
MEE	Materiali Epigrafici di Ebla (Neapel 1979–).
MesCiv.	Mesopotamian Civilizations (Winona Lake 1989ff.).
MHEM / MHEO	Mesopotamian History and Environment. Memoirs / Occasional Publications.
MRWH	H. P. H. Petschow, Mittelbabylonische Rechts- und Wirtschafts-urkunden der Hilprecht-Sammlung Jena (= AbhLeipzig 64/4, 1974).
MSL	Materialien zum sumerischen Lexikon / Materials for the Sumerian lexicon.
NABU	Nouvelles Assyriologiques Brèves et Utilitaires (Paris / Rouen 1987ff.).
NBC	Tablets in the collections of the Nies Babylonian Collection (Yale University, New Haven).
ND	Field number of tablets excavated at Nimrud (Kalḫu).
Nidaba and Enki	SEAL no. 7507.
NPN	I. J. Gelb/P. M. Purves/A. A. MacRae, Nuzi Personal Names (= OIP 57, 1943).
OA Sarg.	Alster/Oshima 2007.
OAA	Old Assyrian Archives (Leiden 2002ff.; in PIHANS).
OBO	Orbis Biblicus et Orientalis.

OBTR	S. Dalley / C. B. F. Walker / J. D. Hawkins, Old Babylonian Tablets from Tell al Rimah.
OECT	Oxford Editions of Cuneiform Texts.
OIP	Oriental Institute Publications (Chicago 1924ff.).
OLA	Orientalia Lovaniensia Analecta.
Or.	Orientalia.
ORA	Orientalische Religionen in der Antike (Tübingen 2009ff.).
Parfümrezepte	E. Ebeling, Parfümrezepte und kultische Texte aus Assur.
PBS	The Museum Publications of the Babylonian Section, University of Pennsylvania.
Persika	Persika (Paris 2001ff.).
PIHANS	Publications de l'Institut Historique-Archéologique Néerlandais de Stamboul.
POAT	W. C. Gwaltney, The Pennsylvania Old Assyrian texts (= HUCA Suppl. 3).
Prag	K. Hecker / G. Kryszat / L. Matouš, Kappadokische Keilschrifttafeln aus den Sammlungen der Karlsuniversität Prag. 1998.
PRU	C. F.-A. Schaeffer (ed.), Le Palais Royal d'Ugarit.
QS 3	T. Richter / S. Lange, Das Archiv des Idadda (Qaṭna Studien 3).
QuadSem.	Quaderni di Semitistica.
RA	Revue d'Assyriologie et d'Archéologie Orientale.
RATL	J. Eidem, The Royal Archives from Tell Leilan (= PIHANS 117, 2011).
RE	G. Beckman, Texts from the vicinity of Emar in the collection of Jonathan Rosen (= HANEM 2, 1996).
REL	Revised Eponym List (Barjamovic, Hertel and Larsen 2012).
RIMA/E	The Royal Inscriptions of Mesopotamia. Assyrian Periods / Early Periods.
RINAP	The Royal Inscriptions of the Neo-Assyrian Period.
RlA	Reallexikon der Assyriologie und Vorderasiatischen Archäologie.
ROMCT	Royal Ontario Museum Cuneiform Texts.

RSM	S. Dalley, A Catalogue of the Akkadian Cuneiform Tablets in the Collections of the Royal Scottish Museum Edinburgh. Art and Archaeology 2 (Edinburgh 1979).
RSO	Ras Shamra – Ougarit
SAA	State Archives of Assyria.
SAAB	State Archives of Assyria. Bulletin.
SAAO	State Archives of Assyria Online.
SAAS	State Archives of Assyria Suppl.
SAD	M. P. Streck (ed.), Supplement to the Akkadian Dictionaries.
Sadberk	V. Donbaz, Cuneiform Texts in the Sadberk Hanım Museum (Istanbul 1999).
SANER	Studies in Ancient Near Eastern Records.
SCCNH	Studies on the Civilization and Culture of Nuzi and the Hurrians.
SCTRAH	M. Molina/M. E. Milone/E. Markina, Sargonic Cuneiform Tablets in the Real Academia de la Historia. The Carl Lippmann Collection (Real Academia de la Historia I.1.6., Madrid 2014)
SD	Studia et Documenta ad Iura Orientis Antiqui Pertinentia.
SEAL	M. P. Streck / N. Wasserman, Sources of Early Akkadian Literature. http://www.seal.uni-leipzig.de.
SEb	Studi Eblaiti.
Shemshara 1	J. Eidem / J. Læssøe, The Shemshara Archives. Vol. 1: The Letters (Copenhagen 2001).
Shemshara 2	J. Eidem, The Shemshara Archives. 2: The Administrative Texts (Copenhagen 1992).
SpTU	Spätbabylonische Texte aus Uruk.
StAT	Studien zu den Assur-Texten.
StBoT	Studien zu den Boğazköy-Texten.
StPohl SM	Studia Pohl. Dissertationes scientificae de rebus Orientis antiqui, Series Maior.
STT	O. R. Gurney / J. J. Finkelstein / P. Hulin, The Sultantepe tablets.
Subartu	Subartu, edited by the European Centre for Upper Mesopotamian Studies (Turnhout 1995ff.).

Sumer	Sumer. A Journal of Archaeology and History in Arab World.
Šūpê-amēli	Line numbering after Y. Cohen, Wisdom from the Late Bronze Age (Atlanta 2013) 84–101.
TBER	J.-M. Durand, Textes babyloniens d'époque récente.
TCL	Textes Cunéiformes. Musée du Louvre.
TCS	A. L. Oppenheim et al. (eds.), Texts from cuneiform sources.
TDP	R. Labat, Traité akkadien de diagnostics et pronostics médicaux.
TIM	Texts in the Iraq Museum.
TLT	C. A. Vincente, The 1987 Tell Leilan tablets dated by the Limmu Habil-kinu, 1–2.
TMH	Texte und Materialien der Frau Professor Hilprecht Collection of Babylonian Antiquities im Eigentum der Universität Jena.
Torino 1	A. Archi/F. Pomponio, Testi cuneiformi neo-sumerici da Drehem: N. 0001–0412 [= Catalogo del Museo Egizio di Torino. Serie seconda, Collezioni 7, Milano 1990].
TPAK	C. Michel / P. Garelli, Tablettes paléo-assyriennes de Kültepe.
UCP	University of California Publications (Berkeley 1907–).
UET	Ur Excavations. Texts.
UF	Ugarit-Forschungen. Internationales Jahrbuch für die Altertumskunde Syrien-Palästinas.
UHKB	Uluslarası Hititoloji Kongresi Bilderileri (Acts of the International Congress of Hittitology).
VAT	Tablets in the collections of the Vorderasiatische Abteilung (Staatliche Museen zu Berlin).
VS	Vorderasiatische Schriftdenkmäler.
WO	Welt des Orients.
WVDOG	Wissenschaftliche Veröffentlichungen der Deutschen Orient-Gesellschaft.
WZKM	Wiener Zeitschrift für die Kunde des Morgenlandes.
YBC	Tablets in the Babylonian Collection, Yale University.
YOS	Yale Oriental Series.
ZA	Zeitschrift für Assyriologie.

ZABR	Zeitschrift für Altorientalische und Biblische Rechtsgeschichte

Other Abbreviations

acc.	accusative
add.	additional
adj.	adjective
Amor.	Amorite
Arab.	Arabic
Aram.	Aramaic
Assyr.	Assyrian
astron.	astronomical
Bab.	Babylonian
Bogh.	Boghazkoy
cf.	confer
coll.	collation, collated
comm.	commentary
corr.	correction
court.	courtesy (of)
det.	determinative
dict.	dictionary
diff.	different(ly)
disc. (sect.)	discussion section
DN	divine name
dupl.	duplicate
ed.	edition / edited
Eg.	Egyptian
etym.	etymology
f.	following
fem.	feminine
ff.	following pages
Gilg.	Gilgameš
Gk.	Greek
GN	geographical name
gramm.	grammatical
Hebr.	Hebrew
Hell.	Hellenistic
Hitt.	Hittite
Hurr.	Hurrian
i.e.	id est
ib.	ibidem
incant.	incantation
inf. constr.	infinitive construction
inscr.	inscription
interpret.	interpretation
intrans.	intransitive
LB	Late-Babylonian
l.e.	left edge
lex.	lexical
lex. sect.	lexical section
lit.	literature / literary / literally
logogr.	logogram / logographical(ly)
loc.	locative
lw.	loanword
MA	Middle-Assyrian
masc.	masculine
MB	Middle-Babylonian
med.	Medical
MN	month name
mng.	meaning
n.	unknown number of items
n.	note
NA	Neo-Assyrian
NB	Neo-Babylonian

NN	nomen nominandum	r.	reverse
no.	number	ref.	reference
NWSem.	Northwest-Semitic	s.v.	sub verbo / sub voce
OA	Old-Assyrian	s.	see
OAkk	Old-Akkadian	Sab.	Sabean
OB	Old-Babylonian	SB	Standard Babylonian
Old Pers.	Old-Persian	sg.	singular
Off. Aram.	Official Aramaic	sim.	similar(ly)
p.	page	stat. cstr.	status constructus
pl.	plural / plate	Sum.	Sumerian
PN(N)	personal name(s)	trans.	transitive
PNf	personal name feminine	Ugar.	Ugaritic
pret.	preterite	unkn.	unknown
prev.	previous(ly)	unpubl.	unpublished
prob.	probably	var.	variant
quot.	quoted (in)	WSem.	West-Semitic

G

gabadibbu, *gabadippu* "parapet, crenellation"

ištū uššēšu adī ga-ba-dip-pe-šú BBVOT 2, 24 no. 1: 9 "from its foundations to its crenellations", s. Maul ib. 32.

gabagallu "an object made from leather or fabric; part of a wagon"; Sum. lw.

1. Early OB GABA.GÁL BIN 9, 75, 463 (of leather, van de Mieroop 1987, 136 with Charpin 1990a, 90).

2. OB *gaba-gal-lu* ARM 7, 243: 4; túg*gaba-gál-lu* ARM 22, 324 ii 11. S. Durand 2009, 34 with add. Mari refs.

3. SB DIŠ giš*gaba-gál-la* : *pitnu ereqqi ša* 1-*en parû ū lū* 1-*en* ANŠE.x [...] RA 85, 152: 49a "(if he sees a *g.*): the box of a cart, which a single mule or a single donkey (?) [...]; *gaba-gál-la* : *pitnu* ib. c "*g.* = a box". Sim. RA 73, 167: 19 (comm. to TDP I, 42').

4. Arkhipov 2012a, 7f. The SB comm. and lex. attestations suggest the floor or body of a small cart (George 1991, 162). In OB, the word describes an object made from leather or fabric that could have served multiple purposes (Durand 2009, 34). Cf. Ur III *gaba-gál kù-sig*17 UET 3, 335: 2, perhaps a pectoral or breastplate, s. Sallaberger 1995, 17.

gabalaḫḫu s. *gabaraḫḫu*

gabānu s. *gapānu*

g/kabaraḫḫu, + *gabalaḫḫu* "mourning, distress"; Sum. lw.

1. In Sum. lit. as an Akk. lw., indicated by the nominative ending: *ga-ba-ra-ḫum* MC 1: 65, cf. *ga-ba-ra-ḫu-um*/*ḫum* Inninšagura 22 (Michalowski 1989, 78).

2. OB lit. *pasāqum*!? *ga-ba-ra-a*[*ḫ-ka*] AML 100: 1 "[your] distress is choking(!?)".

3. SB [*g*]*a-ba-ra-ḫu ana ummānīya imaqqut* KAL 5, 93: 7 "distress will befall my troops".

4. SB *gaba-la-aḫ-ḫu* (will befall my troops) KAL 5, 19: 7, 8.

5. The transl. "rebellion" suggested in CAD G 1f. is not warranted by the texts.

gabarû "copy"; + OB

OB (oil) *ša ana* PN *ina ga-ba-re-e-em tamû* AbB 14, 74: 25 "that had been assigned to PN under oath according to a duplicate (tablet)" (s. Veenhof ib. p. 67 n. e.).

gabāšu s. *kapāšu* I and II

+ **gabbu III**, *gappu* "pedestal; back(?)"; OB

1. OB "pedestal": **a)** *inūma* DN *ina gáb-bi-ša uzzīzū* FM 3, 238 no. 73: 9 "when they installed DN on her pedestal".
b) *ina gáb-bi-ša ušzīzū*! ib. 248 no. 95: 31.
c) [*inan*]*na ga-ap-pa-am* [*g*]*apšam ša ṣalmim* [*an*]*a talbīš napād mešetti* [*up*]*atteḫ* ARM 13, 11: 23 "now I have drilled through the *large* pedestal of a statue (in order to make) cladding of the fastener of the *mešettu*-lance" (Durand 1997, 281f., cf. M.13259).
d) Durand 2005, 144f. Cf. Hebr. *gab* I HAL I 163, Ugar. *gb* I and II DUL I 291. However, some of the Ugar. refs. per-

haps belong to *gubbu* "cistern" (= Hebr. *gēb* I HAL I 163).

+ **gabdi/u** "next to, adjoining"; NA; Aram. lw.?

1. (an estate) *gab-di* PNf *gab-di* PN *gab-di eqli ša* PN2 *gab-di eqli ša* PN3 SAA 6, 22: 4–7 "adjoining PNf, adjoining PN, adjoining the field of PN2, adjoining the field of PN3".

2. (a house) *gab-du bīt* PN *gab-du bīt* PN2 *gab-du ḫarrān šarre mušēṣī'u gab-du ḫi*[*rīṣi š*]*a āli* StaT 2, 207: 7–11 "adjoining the house of PN, adjoining the house of PN2, adjoining the king's road leading out, adjoining the m[oat o]f the city".

3. Further refs. and disc. in Cherry 2017, 103–106. Lw. from Aram. *gb*(ʾ) "side" + pronoun *dī/ū*?

+ **gabḫallu** "mng. unkn."; SB

Lex. *gab-ḫa-lum* = *ḫa*-BAD AOAT 50, 348: 204A (malku). Hrůša (following H. Waetzoldt) ib. p. 220 suggests var. of *gabagallu* "part of a wagon".

+ **gabīʾan(n)u** "(a substance similar to) alum"; early OB

1. 20 GÍN *ga-bi-an-nu* ARM 19, 330: 1 "20 shekels of alum".

2. 12 [GÍN] *ga-bi-a-nu* ARM 19, 315: 2 "12 [shekels of] alum (for a textile)".

3. Cf. *gabû* I.

gabību "land of inferior quality"

Zadok 2020, 266 suggests derivation from Aram. *gbb* "to bend over", "presumably referring to a peculiar topographical elevation ("bent, curved, convex, hunchbacked")".

g/kabīdu "liver"

1. OB *ka-bi-da-am* YOS 11, 26 i 62 (among ingredients). Reading after Stol 2006, 112 (pace Bottéro 1995, 76: *qà-qá-da-am*).

2 LB *naṣrapi ša* ⌜*ga*⌝-*bi-d*[*u*] Jursa 1999, 81 BM 4+: 5 "a *n.* piece of meat of the liver". S. Jursa ib. p. 67; Stol 2006, 112.

+ **gabīnu?** "hillock; hunchback"; Ugar.; LB; NWSem. lw

1. MB [A.ŠÀ]$^{\text{ḫi.a}}$: *ga-bi-ni* [*qadū d*]*imti-šu* PRU 3, 119f.: 12 "[field]s: 'hillock' with its tower" (for etym. s. Huehnergard 1987, 115).

2. LB "hunchback" *mārū ša ga-bi-in*^{EGIR} TCL 13, 228: 4 "sons of the hunchback" = Aram. *gᵊbīn* (McEwan 1986, 188).

gābištu s. *kāpišu*

gablu s. *qablu* III

gabru, pl. *gabrātu* "strong one, man(?)"; MB, SB; NWSem. lw.

1. Lex. *ga-ab-rum* = ⌜*gaš*⌝[*rum*] AOAT 50, 435: 140f. (malku) "man = strong". Hrůša ib. p. 159 and 284 suggests a lw. from NWSem. (s. Aram. *gabrā* etc.); if correct, the verb *gapāru* (AHw. 281) is in fact *gabāru* and denominated (s. already CAD G s.v. *gubburu*).

2. *šarram gab-ra-tu-šu izzibāšu* Emar 6/4, 668: 5 "his troops will abandon the king".

gabʾu "mountain peak"; + OB, + MB; NWSem. lw.

1. OB [*in*]*a ga-ab-i-im ša* GN *akkalīma* ARM 26/2, 215 no. 388: 12 "I was held back [o]n the hill of GN".

2. OB *aššum na-re-e-am ša ga-ba-i* [x] *napālim* ARM 26/2, 294 no. 414: 25 "concerning the stela to be broken (out of?) the mountain peak" (s. Streck 2000a, 88).

3. MB Emar *ana bēl ga-ab-a* Emar 6/3, 373: 104 "to the Lord of the hill" (s. Pentiuc 2001, 49).

4. NA *[ū]mu u mūšu ina pani gab-ʾi ša nēši šarru uṣal[la]* SAA 10, 294: 39 "day and night I pray to the king in front of the lion's hill(?)". S. Cherry 2017, 101f. with disc., possibly to be derived from Aram. *gb* "pit, well, cistern" (cf. *gubbu*).

gabû I, *gabbû* "alum"; + MB

1. OB *ga-bi-im* pass. in ARM 23, 158ff. nos. 139–170 for dyeing and tanning (s. Degraeve 1996, 25–28).

2. MB (5 talents) *ga-bi-i* Emar 6/3, 87: 7.

3. LB CT 57, 255: 16, 29; CT 55, 353: 2; 862: 3; 259: 6–7, 865: 5.

4. For dyeing and tanning in LB s. Zawadzki 2006, 44. Cf. *gabīʾan(n)u*.

+ **gabû II** "to gather(?)"; OB; Amor. lw.

D *ištū ḫalaṣ* GN *nawâm ug-da-ab-bi-im* Amurru 3, 143f.: 12 "I gathered (the inhabitants of) the steppe from the district of GN" (s. Streck 2000a, 88). Cf. *gibêtu*.

gadāru s. *kadāru* II

gaddāʾu "cane or wood cutter"; + NA, LB; Aram. lw.

1. NA: **a)** ^{lú}*gad-da-a-a* SAA 12, 83 r. 9.
b) 6 *ebilāte ša tam-me ...* ^{lú}*ga-da-a-[a] iddunū* SAA 12, 69 r. 20 "the wood cutters will give 6 bundles of poles(?)" (*tammu* = *timmu*?).
c) ^{lú}GAL-*gad-da-a-a* SAA 12, 86 r. 31 "chief wood cutter".
d) NA PN ^{lú}*gad-a-[a]* StAT 2, 141: 13.

2. LB: **a)** ^{lú}*ga-ad-da-a-a* CT 55, 426: 3; YOS 19, 142: 2; ^{lú}*gad-da-a-a* VS 20, 49: 20.
b) The refs. in AHw. s.v. *gaddāja* and CAD s.v. *gadāʾa* belong here.

3. Cherry 2017, 108–110. Although GAD may well stand for *gaṭ* (pace Cherry), *ga* does not favor the root QṬʿ (for which s. AHw. and CAD *qāṭû* and *qettāʾu*). JK/JW/MPS

gaddāya s. *gaddāʾu*

+ **gaddu I** "fortune (name of a deity)"; MB Emar; NWSem. lw.

bīt ga-ad-dá Emar 6/3, 369: 36 "temple of Fortune", *bīt* ^{d}*ga[-ad-dá]* ib. 34; *ga*$_{14}$-*ad[-da]* Emar 6/3, 461: 5, 4; *gad-dá* Emar 6/3, 373: 165. S. Pentiuc 2001, 50. The deity corresponds to Papsukkal, s. Beckman 2002, 43; Dietrich 1990, 36.

+ **gaddu II** "tattered(?)"; LB

šittā gammidātu 1-*et eššetu* 1-*et ga-di-it-tum* Zawadzki 2010, 415 BM 76136: 4 "2 *gammidu*-garments, one new, one tattered(?)". < *gadādu* "to cut off" (AHw. 273).

gadmāḫu, *gad(a)maḫḫu*, + *gadmuḫḫu* "a fine linen garment"

Lex. [^{túg}*maḫ* = *ga*]*d-mu-*⌜*ḫu*⌝ KAL 8, 112: 7 (murgud).

gadmuḫu s. *gadmāḫu*

+ **gadru** "a precious stone, a jewel"; NB

2 ^{na_4}*ga-ad-ru* KÙ.GI OIP 122, 120 ii 10 "2 *g.* (with) gold (mounting)".

gadû "male kid"; NWSem. lw.

1. NA (may they [slaughter] you) *kī ḫurāpi ga-de-e* SAA 2, 6: 636C "like a spring lamb, a kid"; s. already AHw. 1555.

2. Abraham/Sokoloff 2011, 30 consider *g.* a cognate rather than a lw., but since the word is common in Aram. and only attested in NA and LB, the latter seems more likely (Cherry 2016, 104f.; Kogan /Krebernik 2021, 439).

gāgamu s. *gayyānu*

gāgu "(neck) ring, torc"

NA 2 *ga-gi* KÙ.BABBAR FNALD 14: 11. S. Postgate 1994a, 244.

+ **gaḫḫibu** "cough"; OB

kīma ga-aḫ-ḫi-bu-ma ana [*ašrišu*] *lā iturru* RATL L.T. 3 v 12 "like a cough does not return to its place (of origin)", cf. the parallel L.T. 2 iv 9" (Ziegler apud Charpin 2016, 175). Diff. Eidem in RATL p. 394. Cf. *guḫḫubu* "to cough".

g/kaʾiššu "traveling merchant"

1. Logogr. RAŠ:GA for GA.EŠ$_{8}$ in Pre-Sargonic Mari (FAOS 7, MP 10: 7, 33: 3).

2. OB *ka-i-šu lēmū maḫāram* CUSAS 36, 168: 8 "the merchants were unwilling to accept (the dates); *ka-i-šu suluppī limḫurūšu* ib. 17 "the merchants may accept the dates from him".

gajāte s. *kâ/ātu*

galābu "to shave"

+ **G** OA (expenses made when) *a-ḫa-<at>-ni qaqqassa ana* DN *ta-ag-lu-ub* Albayrak 2002, 3 kt 88/k 71: 61 "our sister had her head shaved for Ištar". The unusual G-stem in this specific context is likely a detransitive derivation from the D-stem.

D 1. OB as punishment: *qaqqassu ana gu-lu-bi-im iddinū* Haradum 2, 23: 7 "they (= the judges) gave his head to be shaved".

2. […] *liṭrudma ūlūma li-ga*$_{14}$*-li-ib-šu-nu-ti* […] *liškunšunūtima ana kaspim liddinšunūti* ARM 26/2, 260 no. 404: 73 "[whether] he sends […] or shaves them, place them [in shackles] and sell them for silver" (after Heimpel 1996d).

3. Said of a field (s. AHw. 297 g. 3a): *eṣṣid ú-ga-lab* CTN 6, 108: 4 "he will harvest and 'shave' it".

+ **Dt** OB *abuttašu ug-da-la-ab* ARM 26/1, 282 no. 115 r. 5 "his slave hair-style will be shorn off" (Streck 2003a, 111).

Š 1. OA lit. *ša* GN *qabalti qaqqadātī-šunu ú-ša-ag-li-ib* OA Sarg. 61 "I had the middle of the heads of (the men of) GN shaved".

2. OB s. AHw. 1557.

NJCK (G, Š), JW (D, Dt), MPS (D, Š)

galālu I "building stone, gravel"; Aram. lw.

On the etym. s. Kogan/Krebernik 2021, 440. Cf. Aram. GLL (DNWSI 24), Mand. *glala*.

galālu II "to roll"

NA *a-⸢ga-lal⸣* SAA 9, 2 iii 4' "I will roll" (in broken context).

+ **galammû** "trickery, deception"; Sum. lw.

1. SB *ga-la-ma-a-šú eli pātiqu zārûʾa* ORA 7, 322: 66 "his trickery lasts upon the creator, my begetter".

2. SB *ibnû ga-la-*[*ma-a*] ORA 7, 322: 65 "they created trick[ery]"; cf. [*bā*]*nû ga-la-ma-a* ib. 75 "he who [crea]tes trickery".

3. SB *šimē ga-la-ma-a ša erimmīya* ORA 7, 322: 72 "hear the trickery of my enemies!".

4. SB *š[u?-bil] šāru meḫû ga-la-ma-a-šú zaqīqū lipaṭṭirū riksīšu* ORA 7, 322: 73 "[make(?)] the tempest, the storm, [carry away(?)] his trickery, may the winds loosen his fetters".

5. Cf. also SB *galam-me-e* ORA 7, 322: 64 and *ga-la-ma-a* ib. 67, both refs. in broken and unclear context.

6. Streck 2021, 225f.

galātu, NA *galādu* "to tremble, to be afraid"

G 1. NA /*gt*/ preserved: GN *ig-ta-al-du* SAA 5, 202 r. 8 "GN became afraid".
2. NA a-class: *kī* GN *ig-la!-du-u-ni* SAA 5, 202 r. 12 "when GN became afraid".

Gtn OB lit. *gi-ta-lu-tu šakikku* CUSAS 10, 115: 41 "it is given to you to be always frightened".

D 1. OB lit. *šittašu ú-ga-al-li-is-sú* CUSAS 10, 5: 2, 31 "his sleep frightened him".
2. OB lit. *mannum idkēʾanni mannum ú-ga-li-ta-ni ṣeḫrum idkēka ṣeḫrum ú-ga-li-it-ka* ZA 61, 62: 7f. "who has awakened me? Who has frightened me? The child has awakened you, the baby has frightened you".

Štn OB lit. *[u]l-ta-nag-la-at? namrirrū-ša malû p[uluḫta]* Lamaštu FsB 15 (Farber 2014, 267) "she spreads fear, her aura is filled with t[error]".

galāšu "to darken, obscure"; SB

SB *Sîn ina tāmartišu ana imitti ga-liš* // (blank) // *ina imittišu a-dir* Borger, Fs. Böhl, LB 1321: 23 (var. *ana šumēli* l. 24) "(if) the moon is obscured in its appearance on the right side". Cf. 81-2-4, 281: 14f. (cit. Borger ib. 42) and VAT 9901 (quot. Weidner 1959–1960, 156a).

galdanibātu "an official"; NA

1. PN ^{lú}*gal-da-ni-ba-te* CTN 1 p. 103 ii 51; SAA 5, 143 r. 8; 7, 5 ii 50; 13, 61 r. 1; 141: 14 and pass.

2. S. CTN 1, 103 n. 11; Extensively Menzel-Wortmann 1986. Cf. Hurr. *kaldeniwa/e(š)* (a quality of cereal, Richter 2012, 182). S. already AHw. 1555, CAD D 87, CAD G 20 s.v. *galteniwa.* The editors of SAA(o) parse the word as *rab danibāt(ē)*.

galgallu s. *qalqālu*

galītu "deportation"

NA *ga-li-te* SAA 5, 203 s. 1 in broken context. S. *galû*.

gallābu "barber"; + OA

1. Lex. *é šu-i* = *bīt gal-la-be* CUSAS 12 p. 40: 47 (Ugumu) "barber's shop".

2. OA **a)** *ṣuḫāram* PN *ga-lá-ba-am ana* 1/2 MA.NA *kaspim* (…) *taddinam* UF 7, 316 no. 2: 5, 13 "you sold the servant PN, the barber, to me for 1/2 mina of silver".
b) *ṣuḫāram ga-lá-ba-am* AKT 8, 213: 4.
c) *šinā ṣuḫārē ga-lá-be* <<IM>> *emqūtim šāmāne* kt k/k 47: 7 "buy two young competent barbers for me", quoted by Hecker 2003, 184 n. 3.

3. MB Ugar. ^{lú}*ga$_5$-la-b[u]* PRU 6, 136: 10 (list of professions). S. Huehnergard 1987, 116.

4. OB *bīt g.*: *bīt ga-la-bi pitēma tīnātim u ša-qí-di šūṣêma* Fs. Veenhof, 130 T.135: 8 "open the house of the barbers and bring out figs and almonds!".

MPS (1), NJCK (2), JW (2–4)

gallābūtu "the function of barber"

OA (he will give the servant) *ana ga-lá-bu-tim* KTK 19: 24.

gallu "rolling"

SB [*ti'ām*]*at gal-la-at* Jiménez 2017, 170 Ic 30, s. *ḫamṭussu*.

gallû "a type of demon"

1. OB lit. *u gal-lu-šu/ku-nu* [En]nugi Atr. I 10, 127 "and their/your (= the gods) *g*. was DN". Note that Ennugi is elsewhere titled *gugallu* "canal inspector" (s. Shehata 2001, 27). Mistake?

2. OB lit. *ūmum lemnum ga-lu-um šipir* DN UET 6/2, 395: 12 "an evil spirit, a *g*., messenger of DN"; *ga-al-la-šu* ib. 16; *ana g*[*a-li-im*] ib. 17; DNf *ga-la-i-iš-šu tasaqqaršum* ib. r. 14 "DNf addresses his *g*." (ed. Lambert 1990, 291–3).

3. SB *ušāḫizki kalba ṣalma gal-la-ki/ka* Lamaštu I 14 (Farber 2014, 71, 146–7) "I have made you seize a black dog as your *g*."

4. Mayer 2016, 209.

***galmar** (CAD G 20) s. *kalmarḫu*

galtabbu, *galtappu* "a (fat-tailed) sheep"; Ur III

1. 1 *u*8 *gal-tab-bu-um niga* Torino 1, 291: 1 "1 *g*.-ewe for fattening", cf. 305: 6.

2. n *sila*4 *gal-tab-bu-um niga* FAOS 16, 1052 iii 7 "n *g*.-lambs for fattening", s. iii 20, iv 6 3, iv 14 (in groups with *udu kun-gíd* and *gukkal* "fat-tailed sheep"); cf. 1067: 3; 1086: 3.

3. AHw. 286 s.v. *gerṣeppu* considers this word a variant of *kaltappu* "footstool", which is only attested in NA. *g*. clearly denotes a sheep in Ur III, suggesting that the two words are not connected (Steinkeller 1995, 51).

galteniwa s. *galdanibātu*

galtû "fearful, fearsome"

SB *bēlu šibbu gal-tu* KAL 9, 30 obv. r. col. 9 (// *umun mir-ša*4 *ḫu-luḫ-ḫa*) "lord, fearsome snake".

galû II "to be deported, to go into exile"; Aram. lw.

G NA *ina libbi ūme ša ig-lu-u-ni* SAA 1, 194: 18 "the day they went into exile".

Š 1. NA PN *u rabûtīšu ana* GN *ul-te-eg-lu* TCS 5, 1 ii 28 "he led PN and his officers away to GN".

2. NA *lu-šag-li-a-šú* SAA 15, 169: 10 "I will deport him".

3. NA ⌜*ú?-še-eg-la*-⌝*áš-šú* SAA 10, 112 r. 5 (context unclear).

4. NB GN *u* GN2 ... *u bēl piqitti* ... *ul-ta-ga-liš* SAA 13, 181: 16 "he took GN and GN2 and the official into exile". Pace Cole/Machinist ib. 150 not from *galātu*.

Disc.: < Aram. *gly*, s. Cherry 2016, 105–108 and Kogan/Krebernik 2021, 441 pace Abraham/Sokoloff 2011, 30.

gamālu "to be obliging"

G Stative: OB lit. *ga-am-lu-ni-ik-ka* OECT 11, 1: 4 "they please you".

+ **D** NB *tagmīlti ša* P[N] *u* PN2 *mārūšu ša dīnu itti aḫāmiš ú-gam-me-lu* Fs. Klein 624 (BM 26523, 87281): 4 "agreement, which P[N] and PN2, his son, have mutually reached".

gamāmu "to cut"; + OB

1. OB lit. *ga-am-ma-ši-im abbunata*[*m*] UET 6/3, 889 ii 7 "they have cut for her the umbilical cor[d …]", cf. Streck/Wasserman 2012, 200.

2. For a lex. ref. (now MSL 14, 345: 78) s. AHw. 276 and CAD Q 76 s. v. *qamāmu* "to dress hair", which is probably to be distinguished from *g*.

gamārtu "totality, completion; a grammatical term"; + OA

1. OA n URUDU *rubā'um* GN *ana ga-ma-ar-tim ēpulka* AKT 5, 71: 6 "the ruler of GN promised to pay you n (minas of) copper for a final settlement", s. Veenhof 2010, 186.

2. OA *anāku u šūt ina ga-mar*x(BAR)-*tí ḫarrānim nimmeḫer(ma)* AKT 6B, 451: 5 "he and I met at the completion of the journey".

3. OB "the current state of affairs, circumstances(?)", s. *gašīšu*. S. also *gamertu*. NJCK (1–2), JW (3)

gamāru "to complete"

G 1. Lex. *til* = *ga*14-*ma-rum* Emar 6/4, 537: 604 (Sa), cf. [*t*]*il* = *ga-ma-rum* Ugaritica 5, 137: 22 (Sjöberg 1998, 273).
2. OB PN? [*i*]*k-sú*!-*ma qadūm mārim u mārti* [*i*]*g-mu-ur-ma* FM 2, 260 no. 126: 9 "he bound PN(?) and finished (him) off together with (his) son and daughter".
3. *panum ga-mi-ir* JCS 58, 78: 46 "the surface (of the original tablet) is complete" (copyist's notation).

D 1. OB *bēlī ana* PN *li-ga-am-me-er-ma* FM 7, 105 no. 28: 36 (s. also 32) "may my lord fully report(?) to PN". J.-M. Durand, ib. p. 109f. suggests an abbreviation for *libba gummuru ana* "to come to an understanding with".
2. Cf. *gammuru*?

N SB *nag-mir išdiḫu* ZA 61 p. 50: 36 "fulfil the profit(?)", mng. of N unclear.

+ **gamāzu?** "to jib, balk, move restively (of horses)"; NA; Aram. lw.

D NA (horses) *ga-mu-zu*! SAA 5, 64 r. 4 "are restive(?)", s. SAD B/P 46 s. v. *burbānu*. Cf. Syr. *gmḏ*, s. Cherry 2016, 110f.; AHw. 1556 s.v. *ga-mu-zu*.

gamertu "totality"

1. OA "full share (in a common fund)" (s. Dercksen 2004a, 203–6):
a) PN *ana ga-me-er-tim izzāz* BIN 4, 37: 20 "PN will stand for a full share" (sim. ib. 14; CTMMA 1, 92 no. 71: 39).
b) *ana nikkassē ana gám-ra-tim-ma nuštazzizka* KTS 1, 11: 19 (= OAA 1, 100) "at the settlement of accounts we have made you stand for full shares" (Dercksen 2004a, 209: "for the entire settlement").
c) *ana ga-me-er-tim lā kašdāku* AKT 5, 5: 20 "I am not able (to participate) for a full share" (sim. ib. 38 and BIN 4, 37: 9; also AKT 5, 5: 24 with *gi*5-*me-er-tem* in the same expression).

2. As a grammatical term for Sumerian verbal forms with *ba-*/*-ma-* (var. of *gamārtu*): NA [*nì*]-*til-la-a* // *ga-mer-ta* ZA 64, 142: 16 (exam text A), cf. MSL 4, 151 (*gamārtu*); Sjöberg 1975, 157f.; Black 1991, 95–98.

3. S. also *gamārtu* and *gimertu*. NJCK (1), JW (2)

gamgammu "a bird"

S. Salonen 1973, 166f. (a sea bird?); for possible Sem. cognates s. Militarev/Kogan 2005, 115f.

gāmilu "merciful, sparing"

NA *ina patrišu lā ga-me-li* SAA 2, 6: 455 "with his merciless sword".

gamirtu s. *gamertu*

gamlu, + *gammalu*; pl. *gamlātu* "crook"; + OA

1. OA *adī eblim u sikkatim ga-*⌜*am-li*⌝-*im u mimma šumšu* Fs. Larsen, 257 ii 17 "(you shall pay the full amount for any losses that occur) including a rope and bent-stick(?) and anything (else)". The known instances of *g.* do not show any parallels of this use, so perhaps OA *g/k/qamlu* is a different word.

2. OB *ṣalam* ^{d}MAR.TU *ga-am-la-am našī* FM 8, 132 no. 38: 20 "the image of Amurru bears a curved staff".

3. Fem. sg.: OB lit. *ga-am-la-am elletam* OECT 11, 1: 7 "holy crook" (of Amurru). Cf. ib. 8, 9, 11 and pass.

4. Fem. pl.: OB IGI Šamaš Ninsianna *u ga-am-la-ti-šu-nu* Fs. Kupper, 35 no. 1: 5 "before DN, DNf, and their crooks".

5. SB as magical tool: GÀM *siparri* SpTU 1, 56: 3 "sickle of bronze"; also of gold (l. 2), tin (l. 4), tamarisk wood (l. 5), boxwood (l. 6), *musukkanu*-wood (l. 7); cf. SpTU 1, 57.

6. Var. *gammalu*: SB *šīḫa lānšu gam-ma-la-ma ikappap* Fs. Kraus, 194 ii 12 "he bent his lofty stature like a crook (resting his head beside his feet)".

7. For add. Mari refs. s. Arkhipov 2012, 106. Refs. cit. in AHw. s.v. *gamlu* 1 c read *pilšu* (s. AHw. s.v.). S. also *gizû* below. NJCK (1), JW (1, 4–7), MPS (2–3)

gammalu I, *gammalû* "very merciful"

SB [*g*]*a-am-ma-*⸢*la*⸣*-at qāt* ⸢…⸣ KAL 9, 6 i 15 "very merciful is the hand …" (prayer to Gula).

gammalu II "camel"

1. NA *immerē* $^{anše!}$*gam*!-⸢*mal*!⸣^{meš} ⸢*lā*⸣ *iḫabbutū nišē iḫabbutū* SAA 1, 82 s. 1 "they do not plunder sheep or camels, they plunder people".

2. NB 2 ANŠE.A.A[BA^{meš}] SAA 17, 4: 4 (broken context, but in l. 5 the Arab. tribe Saba' is mentioned).

3. NB **a)** ANŠE.A.AB.BA *suluppī in-damma* OIP 114, 39: 16 "load a camel with dates".

b) *rē'i* ⸢ANŠE⸣.A.AB.BA ib. 62: 21 "camel herder".

c) ANŠE.A.AB.BA^{meš}*-šú-nu ḫabtū* ib. 32: 5 "their camels were plundered".

d) For further refs. s. ib. p. 310.

4. For the reading of ANŠE.A.AB.BA (more likely *gammalu* than *ibilu*) s. Heide 2010, 351.

S. also *ibilu* 2.

gammidatu s. *gammidu*

gammidu "a garment"; Aram. lw.

1. NA 81 ^{túg}*ga-me-da-te* StAT 1, 39: 3; StAT 3, 1: 14.

2. NA 1 *šupālītu ḫalluptu ša* ^{túg}*ga-me-de-te* StAT 1, 39: 10 "1 reinforced undergarment for a *g.*-garment".

3. LB ^{túg}*gam-mi-da-*⸢*tum*⸣ Zawadzki 2010, 415, BM 76136: 3, s. *gadittu*.

4. LB 10-*ta* ⸢^{túg}⸣*gam-mid-da-a-ta ša tabarri ebbeti ṣuppāta* dubsar 3, 43: 31 "10 *g.* garments of red, clean and combed wool".

5. Probably a loan from Aram. *gmd* "to press, mangle" (Cherry 2016, 108–110). JW (1, 3, 5), JK (2), MPS (4)

gammiš s. *ṣumlalû*

+ **gammuru** "completion, complete(?)"; MB Emar

1. *tuppu ša gammuri* "tablet of completion(?)": [*anūmm*]*a tuppu ša ga-mu-ri* [*in*]*a pisanni ša* PN *šakin* AulaOr. 5, 5: 32 "now the tablet of completion(?) is placed in the basket of PN"; *ša gám-mu-ri* Emar 6/3, 90: 16.

2. *tuppu g.* "completed tablet (?)": *tuppu ga-mu-ru* AulaOr. 5, 9: 18; *ga-mu-rum*

AulaOr. 1, 55: 23; [*g*]*a*$_{14}$*-mu-ru* Emar 6/3, 194: 9; *gam-mu-ru* ib. 207: 34.

3. Pentiuc 2001, 51; Durand 1990b, 50. All known instances describe a tablet and perhaps refer to a completed transaction.

gamru "complete"

Unique spelling: OB PN *qadūm awīlī ga-aw*(PI)*-ri-šu-n*[*u*] ARM 27, 63: 12 "PN together with all the men".

gana "come on"

Note the plene spelling in MB lit. *ga-a-na* ALL no. 11: 15.

ganāṣu "to sniff, to wrinkle one's nose, to sneer"

D *kīma ḫarriri ú-gan-na-ṣa* Lamaštu FsB 10 (Farber 2014, 267) "like a vole(?) she wrinkles (her nose)".

gandu s. *kamdu*

ganīnu s. *ganūnu*

gannu, *gannatu* "garden"; + OB; NWsem. lw.?

1. OB PN *ša ga-an-nim ana ṣēr bēliya aṭṭardam šassuqī ana* GN *lir*[*tedd*]*ī'am* ARM 13, 38: 28 (= LAPO 17, 831) "I have sent PN of the garden to my lord so he may continuously bring *šassuqu*-trees to GN".

2. OB [*tēbibtu*]*m edištum* [*in*]*a ga-an-nim ša bāb nēšim* M.6337 (cit. Durand 1998, 648 n. j) "new [censu]s in the garden of the lion's gate".

3. According to Kogan/Krebernik 2021, 440, Aram. lw. in LB (pace Abraham/Sokoloff 2011, 30). Cf. Syr. *gantā*, Off. Arm. *gn*. If correct, the OB attestations suggest an Amor. lw.

ganūnu, *ganīnu*, + *kunūnu* "storeroom"

1. OA lit. *e-BA-ki malā ga-ni-nim* JEOL 47, 59: 3 "your capacity(?) is equal to a storeroom", s. Kouwenberg 2018/19, 62, incant. concerning a *diqārum*-vessel.

2. OA (the *kārum* passed a verdict that) [é]*ga-nu-nu ša* PN *mamman merā Aššur ulā iša''amšu* AKT 7A, 296: 2 "no Assyrian will buy PN's storeroom (from him?)".

3. SB *ana eṭli ša kunnunū ku-nu-nu-šu išpi*[*kūšu šap*]*kū* Gilg. MB Ur 56; s. Gilg. SB VII 159 "to a man whose storerooms are well off, whose sto[cks are hea]ped up".

4. SB *ga*$_{14}$*-ni-ni-ni-šu malī Nisaba* Šūpê-amēli 136 "his storeroom is full of grain" (s. already AHw. 1556).

5. S. also *kunnunu*. For OA s. also *kanūnu*. NJCK (1–2), MPS (3–4)

ganzir, *ganṣir* "(frontgate of the) netherworld; part of a temple where damaged statues are kept"; Sum. word

Mayer 2016, 209–10:

1. SB *mēlīt šamāmī simmilat ga-an-zìr/ṣir* Iraq 47, 4 ii 15 "(Imgur-Enlil, great wall of Babylon,) stairway to heaven, stairs to the underworld".

2. [*m*]arkas *ermi Anu u ga-an-zìr/ṣir* Iraq 48, 133 B 5 "(tablet of destiny), which connects Anu's canopy with the underworld".

3. [*š*]*a ina ga-an-zìr/ṣir nadû* [...] [*ša*] *ina karašê nadû* BM 68031: 9 "who is thrown into the underworld, who is headed for disaster".

4. *ušaṣbissunūtu ga-an-zìr/ṣir* MesCiv 16, 328: 12b "(DN) have them (= the 'dead gods') take their place in G.", referring to a room in Eturkalamma (s. Lambert ib. 49f.).

gapaḫšu "proud, overbearing"

The hapax *ga-pa-aḫ-šu* (now TMH 12, 4: 7) has been interpreted as a by-form of *gapšu* "proud, overbearing" by Kilmer 1991, 18 and E. Zomer in TMH 12. The form remains, however, unexplained.

+ **gapānu** "to harness(?)"; OB; Amor. lw.?

D 1. [*ger*]*rašunu*? *ú-ga-ap-pí-nu-ma it*[*t*]*allakū* FM 9, 71: 26 "they harnessed(?) their [cara]van(?) and moved on".

2. *gu-up-pí-in-ma alik* A.559 (cit. FM 9 p. 285) "harness and go!".

3. Cf. Ugar. *gpn* "harness" DUL I 304 (however, the Hebr. cognate mentioned there is wrong: rather "vine"). The translation assumes a denominated D-stem. Diff. Ziegler ib.: "se préparer au voyage, s'équiper, se ravitailler".

gapāru "to be superior, to overpower"

D OB (the letter) *ša aššum paḫār ḫanî ina gu-up-pu-ri-ma* ARM 26/1, 158 no. 27: 4 "concerning the gathering of Hanaeans by force". The transl. follows Durand 2000, 1233b, cf. id. 1988, 159f. Heimpel 2003, 191 considers the word a place name without determinative.

Dt For VS 10, 214 iii 1 (AHw. 281) s. *kapāru* Dt.

gapāšu "to rise up, swell"

SB *ag-da-pu-uš allak urḫu* Gilg. SB II 262 "having grown bold, I will walk the path".

gappu "pedestal" s. *gabbu*

gappu "wing" s. *kappu* I

gapru s. *gabru*

garābu "a (skin-)disease"

The conventional identification with leprosy (cf. Syr. *garbā*) is inaccurate, as *g*. affects sheep and cattle as well. It describes skin conditions like those caused by leprosy, but also other conditions (Scurlock/Andersen 2005, 232). S. also Stol 1989, 29f. (a fungal infection?). S. also *garību* and *garabānu*.

garabānu, *garbānu* "afflicted with *garābu*-disease"

1. NA ^{lú}*ga-ra-ba-nu* SAA 17, 110 r. 9 (broken context).

2. SB *ga-ra-ba-nu* SpTU 5, 255: 4 in broken context.

3. Del. refs. from UET 4 (AHw. 282), read LÚ *šá ba-nu-ú-tu* (Joannès 1995).

4. Cf. *garību*.

+ **garāḫu** "to copulate"; SB

1. *garāḫu* = *na*-[*a-ku*] cit. AHw. 282 s.v. *garāś*/*šu*

2. SB *ag-ra-aḫ-ki* DN *ag-ra-aḫ-ki* DN *kīma immeri* KBo. 36, 27: 15f. "I am copulating with you, oh DN, I am copulating with you, DN, like with a sheep". The *a*-class of the verb is further proof that *garāḫu* is not a variant of *garāś*/*šu* since the latter has *u* in the pret.

garāru s. *qarāru*

garāṣu s. *karāṣu*

garāšu I "to come, to approach"

G 1. OAkk KN *ig-ru-sa-am* MesCiv 7, 226: 7 "KN approached".
2. OAkk *idiššu ig-ru-ús* RIME 2, 108 v 35 "he went to his side", also ib. 221 i 9; 224 iv 3; 226 x 2 (Mayer 2016, 210).
3. OAkk [*a*]*dī lā tág-ru-*⌜*sa*⌝*-am* FAOS 19, Ad 12: 14 "before you come here".

4. OAkk *ga-ra-si-im iškun* RIME 2, 42: 34 and passim in Rīmuš inscriptions "he assigned (them) to be deported(?)" (after Westenholz 1999, 41 n130 and cf. Hebr./Ugar. *grš* "to drive away, expel", which would then suggest that the mng. "to come" is a result of the ventive. The difficult passage may alternatively belong to *karāšu* I or II).
5. OB "to consort"(?): (brother made brother declare a sacred oath and they sat down to drink) *ištū ig-ru-šu u kāsam ištû* ARM 26/2, 263 no. 404: 63 "after they consorted(?) and drank from the goblet (brother brought a gift to brother)", cf. Heimpel 2003, 345 n. 204.

+ **N** Mayer 2016, 210:
1. "to set off": SB *ig-dar-šu-ú-ni illakū-ni bābiš* Iraq 58, 160: 59 "they set off and went towards the gate", cf. *ig-gar-šu-nim-ma illa*[*kūni*] Ee III 129.
2. "to be made love to":
a) SB *aššāt amēlī i-gar-ru-šá-ma arkī zikarī idullā* CunMon. 11, 48 VAT 10218 iii 15 "men's wives will commit adultery and run after men", var. *ig-gar-ri-šá-ma* p. 72 BM 40111: 17; p. 180 K.229 r. 23.
b) SB *nišū ig-gir-ra-šá* CunMon. 11, 106 K.3632: 25 "people will have intercourse".

Cf. CAD G 51 s.v. *gārišu* "mating".

garāšu II s. *qarāšu* 3.

gardu "worker"; LB

Stolper 1985, 56–59.

+ **garību** "afflicted with *garābu*-disease"; OB

(Cedar oil) *ana lī'ātim ga-ri-ba-tim* JMC 10, 42, M.12765 "for the cows with *garābu*-disease".

garinnu s. *agarinnu*

garīṣtu, *girīṣtu* "a bread"; Aram. lw.

S. Cherry 2016, 111–114 (cf. Syr. *gərīṣ-tā, gārṣā* "a round flat loaf of bread"); diff. Abraham/Sokoloff 2010, 30f.

+ **gārišu** "a type of messenger"; OA

1. *ištē* PN *ulā ištē ga-ri-ší-im ša ibattu-quni šēbil* Prag 744 r. 3 "send [...] with PN or with a *g.* who travels separately".

2. *ṣuḫāram ištēn ga-ri-ša-am ašappa-rakkum* Prag 598: 22 "I will send you a single servant as *g.*"

3. Veenhof 2008, 216. Probably < *garāšu.* NJCK/JW

garmartu s. *kalmartu*

+ **GarZu** "a textile or a qualification of a textile"; OA

TÚG *Ga-ar-Za-am kabram* PN *naš'ak-kum* Prag 487: 4 "PN has brought you a thick *g.*-textile". Cf. *karāṣu*? NJCK/JW

gaṣṣatu "firewood"

1. NA LÚ *ša* [giš]*gaṣ-ṣa-te-šú* CTN 6, 3: 32 "firewood supplier".

2. LB 60-*šu dibbīya ša ṣarbatu* ME [giš]*ga-aṣ-ṣa-a-ta* ... PAP 70 *dibbīya* 1 ME *ga-aṣ-ṣa-a-ta* dubsar 3, 146: 18, 24 "60 boards of poplar, 100 logs (or bundles?) of firewood ... together 70 planks, 100 logs (or bundles?) of firewood".

gaṣṣu I "cruel, murderous"

OB lit. *bēlet ga-ṣú-ti-im šadū'ī u ḫuršā-nī* AfO 50, 13 iii 12, 14 "lady of the cruel hills [and] mountains". Already quot. AHw. 282 *g.* 1.

gašāru "to be(come) strong"

OB lit. *ga-še-er nišikšu* AML 64: 4 "strong is his (= the dog's) bite".

gašīsu, + *gišīšu* "stake, pole"

1. OB *ina gamartim dannatim annītim ša ina māti ga-ši-šu zaqpū* CUSAS 36, 123: 7 "under these hard circumstances(?), when stakes are raised throughout the land".

2. OB *ina* ${}^{\text{giš}}$*gi-ši-ši-im iškunšu* RATL 117: 8 "he impaled him", cf. ${}^{\text{giš}}$*ga-[ši-ši-im]* ib. 186: 20.

3. OB [*ina*] *gi-ši-ši-im* [*lišš*]*akinma* ARM 13, 108 r. 14 "he shall be impaled".

4. SB in agricultural use: *gi-ši-ša ay imḫaṣ šumēlû alapka* Šūpê-amēli 51 "your left-hand ox should not hit the stake".

gaššu "an official" (OA) s. *Kaššu*; "part of the temple of Aššur" s. *qaššu.*

gattu I "stature, build"; + OA

1. OA *ša*! GU4 *ša ga-tám e-li-ú-ni* (...) *šēri'am* kt j/k 623: 15 "have (one) of the oxen that are tall in stature brought here!", s. Dercksen 2003. Perhaps also GU4 *ša ga*(! sign BI)-*tám rabī'u* KTS 1, 3a: 5 "an ox that is large in stature".

2. SB [*ina* ..]. *pašalli gat-ta-ki ušarraḫ* KAL 9, 4: 9 "he makes your form splendid with *pašallu*-gold". NJCK (1), JW (2)

gaṭṭā'a s. *gaddā'u*

****ga'û** (AHw. 1556)

The passage reads *i*-BI-*ú*, now AbB 11, 85 (Streck 2000a, 89).

gā'u, *gâ'u* s. *gayyu*

gayyānu, *gāgamu* "shed"; + OB, SB

1. OB lit. *ina ga-ga-am suluppī* PBS 1/1, 2: 80 "in the date shed". S. Lambert 1989, 327: 94 with comm. ib. p. 335.

2. S. Hrůša 2010, 219 ad I 267.

+ **gayyišam** "clan by clan"; OB; Amor. lw.

têrētim ana mārī ālim ga-ji-ša-am ušēpišma ARM 26/1, 15 n. 42 A.3993: 38' "I had omens taken for the inhabitants of the city, clan by clan" (Anbar 1991, 78; Streck 2000a, 89; < *gayyu*).

gayyu "clan"; Amor. lw.

1. OB 4 *awīlū ga-ji* PN ARM 24, 235: 5 "4 men of the tribe of PN"; cf. l. 8, 15.

2. Spellings indicate *gayyu* rather than *gā'/wu* s. Streck 2000a, 89, 321 Anm. 6. Cf. Hebr *gôy*, Sabaic GWY. S. also *gayyišam.*

3. In AbB 4, 69: 41 (cit. AHw. 1556) read *a-na-ga-ḫi-im*, s. Streck 2000a, 89.

+ **gazālu** "to steal, carry off"; NA; Aram. lw.

11 *sarrūti* 70 UDU${}^{\text{meš}}$ *ig-da-az*?-*lu* CTN 2, 119 r. 19 "11 criminals carried off 70 sheep". S. Cherry 2016, 114f. (< Aram./Syr. *gzl* "to rob").

+ **gazāru** "to cut"; NA; Aram. lw.

nipšu ša m[*uḫḫi* ...] [*i*]-*ge-zi-ir*! *ina išāti ika*[*rra*]*r* Parfümrezepte 21+ r. 15 "(the priest) cuts off a tuft from the sk[ull of ...] and places it in the fire". S. Cherry 2016, 115f. (< Aram. *gzr* "to cut").

gazāzu "to shear"

1. SB *ga-za-az ša šārat enzi* SpTU 1, 51: 3 "shearing of a goat's hair", s. *gizzatu.*

2. Object "wool": NB *šīpāti ig-*⌈*zu*⌉*-zu* OIP 114, 46: 12; *šīpāti* ... *ag-zu-zu* ib. 24 "he/I sheared the wool".

3. NB *ni-ig-zu-zu* ib. 47 "let us do the shearing".

gazzu, *kazzu*, + fem. *gaziztu* "shorn; ram"; + OA

1. OA as a designation of fabric:
a) 2 TÚG *ga-zi-iz-ti-in* Prag 428: 33 "2 shorn textiles". Note that the partial duplicate JCS 41, 40: 28 has *kusītēn*.
b) 1 *išram ga-zi-iz-tám damiqtam* kt c/k 710: 15 "a shorn sash of good quality" (cit. Dercksen apud Michel/Veenhof 2010, 233).
c) 5 TÚG *ga-zu-tù-um* kt c/k 488: 8 (courtesy J. G. Dercksen).
d) A type of low-pile fabric, presumably made by cutting the nap of the pile to achieve a uniform surface. This process has also been called "shearing" in European textile manufacturing since the middle ages. The Bab. equivalent is *gizzu*. S. also *gizzatu*.

2. OB "ram":
a) lit. *ka-az-za-*⌜*am*⌝ *imme*[*r*]*tam* CUSAS 10, 1: 11a "ram (and) ewe".
b) *ka-az-zu-um etellum ālišu* ib. 35 "the ram, prince of his city".
c) [*k*]*a-az-zum* ib. 2.
d) Cf. CAD G 115 *gizzu* A "adult male goat", AHw. 496 *kizzu* I "(junger) Ziegenbock". Derivation of *g*/*kazāzu* is likely. NJCK (1), JW (1), MPS (2)

gebû s. *gabû* II

gegunnû s. *gigun*(*n*)*û*

gelduḫlu s. *keltuḫlu*

+ **gennu** "a musicological term"; OB; Sum. lw.?

zennum u ge-en-nu-um JCS 48, 52 r. i 4 and *pass*. The term always co-occurs with *zennu* and both are repeated multiple times in the music instruction texts. Kilmer/Tinney (ib.) propose a tentative translation "tune and test" and derive the word from Sum. *ge-en* (s. OB Proto-Lu 622–627 and cf. Kilmer 1995, 477 § 5.2).

genû "to thrust, butt"

S. *qanû* D 2.

gerdu "wool or fur that has been removed from a hide"

1. NA ^{siki}*ge-er-du* Nimrud 43 (cit. Deller 1992b), cf. Aram./Hebr. *grd* "to scrape off" and s. *gurrudu*.

2. S. AHw. 915a; CAD Q 227f. s.v. *qerdu*.

gergīlu "a bird"

OB *ge-er-gi-lum*^{mušen} Edubba'a 7, 100: 55 (in list of birds).

gergiššu "(fruit of the) strawberry tree; a red skin condition"

OB *šipat ge-er-gi-iš-ši-im* KTT 379: 12 "incantation against *g*.".

germadû s. *gir*(*i*)*madû*

gerru I, *kerru* "way, journey, military campaign"

1. Early OB *ana* PN *ge-ra-am ittabal* RIME 4 p. 708: 10 "(GN) waged war against PN".

2. OB *aššum ge-ri ereqqī* AbB 7, 3: 17 "concerning the caravan of wagons".

3. OB *ge-ru-um rūqma* AbB 7, 44: 7 "the journey is long".

4. OB *awīlī ša ke-er-ri-i*[*m š*]*a eqlim* ARM 28, 171: 18 "the men on campaign in the countryside".

5. OB *ṣuḫārūya ina ke-er-ri-i*[*m*] *lišbū* ARM 28, 39 r. 5 "let my servants remain on course".

6. OB *inūma ke-er-ra-šu uṣammidu* CUSAS 15, 187: 6 "when he readied his caravan".

7. SB *ger-ru Tiʾāmat akbusa* SAA 3, 19: 3 "I trod the sea route".

8. NA *ge-ri ramānika* SAA 1, 181: 17 "on your own authority (lit. by way of yourself)", s. CAD R 125 *ramanu* f7'.

gerseqqû "a palace or temple attendant"

MB new logogr.: *šutāpū ša mārī* KI.IR.SI.GA CT 51, 41: 4 "the associates of the attendants" (Sassmannshausen 2001, 28 n. 418).

gerṣeppu, *kilzappu*, *kaltappu*, *kištappu*, + *girtappu* "a footstool, also as part of a threshing sledge"

1. OAkk *kištappu*: 1 ^{giš}*kiš-tap-um* CUSAS 27, 236 r. 3.

2. OB *girtappu*: 8 KUŠ UDU.GAL *iš gìr-tab-ba-tìm* ARM 19, 104: 2 "8 skins of big sheep for footstools".

3. Pace AHw. 286, Ur III *galtabbu* "a fat-tailed sheep" is to be differentiated from NA *kaltappu* (s. *galtabbu*).

4. The (gold) ornament *kaltappu* is considered a separate word by AHw. 427a.

5. Streck 2009–2011b, 229 for the threshing sledge.

gerû "to be hostile to, attack; to exert pressure"

G 1. OA *tamkārī* (…) *ag-ri-ma* CCT 6, 35a r. 11 "I aggressively approached merchants (with offers)".
2. OA *ippanītim ig-ri-ú*!*-ni-ma umma šunūma ūmē ṣibīšum* Prag 714: 12 "before, they put pressure on me saying: 'extend (fem.) his term!'".
3. OA *annākam malā u šinēšu ag-ri-šu-ma kaspam laqāʾam lā imūʾa* RSM 10: 21 "here I pressed him several times but he refuses to accept the silver".
4. OA *ḫusārī mamman ig-ri-a-ni-ma* TC 3, 49: 37 "someone has put pressure on me for my lapis lazuli"; for add. refs. s. Veenhof 2015a, 247–249.
5. LB PN: *Ig-ra-a* ROMCT 2, 52: 1 (cf. CAD G 63 s.v. *gerû* 4a', Oelsner in Deller/Mayer/Oelsner 1989, 281).

Gtn OA *ig-da-na-ri-ú-ni umma šunūma šumma ašīʾum ayyākamma ibaššī šupurma* [PN] *u* PN$_2$ *iltanaqqēʾū* BIN 4, 45: 10 "they keep pressing me saying: 'if anywhere *ašīʾum*-iron is available, send a written order that [PN] and PN$_2$ keep trying to get it".

N "to quarrel": OA *annākam ištē* PN *a-ge$_5$-ri(-ma)* BIN 4, 79: 9 "here I have quarrelled with PN"; for further refs. s. Veenhof 2015a, 247–249.

JW (G), NJCK (G, Gtn, N)

gērû, *gārû* "foe, adversary, rebel"

1. MB Emar *ge-ri-šu* Emar 6/4, 778: 77 "his foe" (?) in broken context (Steinkeller apud Pentiuc 2001, 53).

2. SB *ge-ru-šu ul ibbašši ša ina adêšu ibb⌜alkitu?⌝* SAA 3, 22 r. 12 "no foe will emerge who rebels against his treaty".

+ **gêsu III** "mng. unkn."; LB

gabû ana ge-e-su ša DN CT 57, 255: 16 "alum for the *g.* of DN". Based on context possibly a garment.

geššu s. *gilšu*

gešû "to belch"

OB lex. KAxBAL? = *ge-šu-ú* Klein/Sefati 2019, 90 ii 19. S. also *gišûtu*.

FJMS/JW

gêšu II "to spend the night" (AHw. 287)

Streck 2017, 598: malku = šarru III 46 reads *bâtu* = *utūlu* (Hrůša 2010, 362).

gibbu s. *kibbu* II

+ **gibêtu?** "recruits?"; OB; Amor. lw.

1. *ṣābum kalûšu gi-bé-tum* ARM 26/1, 158 no. 27: 10 "the whole troop is (made up of) *g*."; *gi-bé-e-tum* ARM 26/2, 145 n. 39.

2. *warkat ṣābim anāku parsāku ša ina ṣābim gi-⸢bé-tim⸣ bēlī illakma* FM 2 p. 206: 44 (= ARM 33, 154) "I myself inspected the troops, so that my lord might go with the help of a troop of *g*."

3. Possibly to be derived from the rare verb *ga/ebû* (Durand 1988, 94, s. *gabû* II). Streck 2000a, 89f.

gibillû "tinder"; + NB

1. Lex. *ki* = GIBIL = *gi₅-bil-lu* Emar 6/4, 537: 311 (Sa), Sjöberg 1998, 261.

2. *nagāru* [..]. *gi-bil-li-ka idīka lū* TUKU SAA 17, 27 r. 15 "let the carpenter … take your tinder as your pay".

+ **gibʾu** "red truffle(?)"; OB

1. *gi-ib-i*, *gi-ib-ú* ARM 27, 54: 12–16, s. *kamʾatu*.

2. Cf. Heimpel 1997c; id. 2003, 429: "toadstools", "specifically perhaps *agaricus xanthoderma*"; Stol 2014, 149: cf. arab. *ğebaʿ* "red truffles".

+ **gību** "a locust?"

OB lex. … (broken and unclear) = [*g*]*i-bu* UET 7, 93 r. 3, between *lamṣatu* "dust fly" and *kurṣiptu* "butterfly". Cf. Hebr. *gēbīm, gōbāy*; Aram. *gōb*; Arab. *ğābīʾ* "locust(s)" (Sjöberg 1996, 229; Militarev/Kogan 2005, 112f.).

gidlu, *gidlû*, + *gidalu*? "plaited string, rope; a door curtain"

1. LB ⸢*gid-di-il*⸣ *ina šūmi ešrû ša* DN CT 22, 8 (= AOAT 414/1, 3): 5 "a plait of garlic, tithe of DN".

2. LB $^{gada!}$*gi-id-lu-ú* CT 55, 439: 10; $^{gada!}$*gi-*<*id*>*-lu-ú ša* DN CT 55, 858: 7.

3. LB *gi-id-lu šakk*[*ūtu*] *ša* SUM.HUŠ.SAR CBS 88: 1–2, 8–9 (cit. Stol 1987b, 74) "strung bundles of (red?) onions".

4. LB (wool) *ana nīri ša* $^{gada!}$*gi-da-lu-ú u šiddānu* CT 4, 27 Bu 88-5-12, 336: 14 "for ropes for door curtains and covers", cf. *gi-da-lu* YOS 6, 146: 11; $^{gada!}$*gi-da-lu-ú* GCCI 2, 360: 25 (both cited in CAD K, 148 s.v. *kandalu*).

5. LB $^{⸢kuš⸣}$*šiddānu ana gi-di-il-ʾ ša* PN CT 56, 10: 2 "covers for the door curtains of PN" (s. Beaulieu 2003, 381f. with add. refs.).

6. For the variant *gidalu* s. Stol 1983, 299 and Oelsner in Deller/Mayer/Oelsner 1989, 278.

7. The LB refs. read *bulû* in CAD B 313 and AHw. 138 belong here (Beaulieu 2003, 381f.).

8. For etym. s. Cherry 2016, 116f.: "the West-Semitic evidence points probably to an early West-Semitic loan in Babylonian, which lingered in LB, as well as a later borrowing into NA particularly from Aramaic in the sense 'braid, plait'."

9. Cf. ^{túg}*gadalû* (CAD G 8).

gīdu "sinew, gristle; bowstring"

1. OB *šerʾānū ana gi-di ša tilpānī* ARM 23, 187 no. 207: 2 "tendons for the strings of composite bows".

2. OB 2 *tilpānū ša gi-di-im* ARM 23, 202 no. 228: 16 "2 composite bows with bowstrings", cf. *tilpānū ša lā gi-di* no. 454: 1 "composite bows without bowstrings".

3. SB *gi-de našbūti* AulaOr. (Suppl.) 23, 14: 5 "putrid(?) sinews".

4. Uncert.: LB 5 MA.NA *kidinnê ana* PN *ana gi-i-di nadin* Zawadzki 2013, 572: 3 "5 minas of *k.* for PN for *g.*" Cf. *kītu* "mat" (?).

5. Instead of *sagû* C (CAD S 27), read SA *lummargû*/*lamragû* "string of *l.* instrument". MPS/JW (1–4), FJMS (5)

gigallu s. *kigallu*

gigamlu, *gugamlu*, *kigamlu* "paddock"

1. OA *ina ki-ga-a*[*m-lim*] *anāku u att*[*a*] *ninnamerma* KTS 2, 16: 3 "we, me and you, met in the paddock".

2. SB (a sheep) *ša gu-*⸢*ga*⸣*-*[*am-li* (?)] KAL 9, 55: 9.

gigun(n)û, *kikun*(*n*)*û* "temple tower"

1. OB lit. *ullūtam ki-ku-na* AfO 50, 16 r. i 11 "(Mama, whose) temple tower is high".

2. OB lit. *ki-ku-un-na-a-ak lušalbiš warqam* MesCiv. 7, 13: 29 "let me clothe your temple tower in green!"

3. OB lit. *kīma epēr gi-gu-un-ne-em*! JCS 66, 41 i 2 "in order to provide (regular offerings) for the temple tower".

gigurru, + *gikurru* "a container"

1. OB 5 *gi-ku-*⸢*rum*⸣ *ša ṣubātī* OBTR 170: 1 "5 *g.*-containers with textiles". S. Langlois 2017, Vol. 2, 171.

2. OB 1 *gi-ku-rum* OBTR 205: 6.

giḫa/innu "a basket"

(3 oxen and 12 sheep) *ša ina* 2 *gi-ḫi-ni* 15 *pānī kankū* ARM 23, 199 no. 224: 3 "which are sealed up in 2 *g.*-baskets and 15 *pānu*-baskets".

gikurru s. *gigurru*

gildu "animal hide, skin"; Aram. lw.

On etym. s. Kogan/Krebernik 2021, 440; Abraham/Sokoloff 2011, 31; Militarev/Kogan 2000, no. 78.

gillatu "crime, sin"

OB *ḫiṭītum u gi-la-tum ul ibbaššī* ARM 26/1, 174 no. 39: 25 "there will arise neither sin nor crime", cf. ib. 16.

+ **gillu II** "roll of leather"; NA; Aram. lw.

1. LB ^{kuš}*gi-il-lu* CT 56, 18: 1; cf. 12: 1.

2. < NWSem. *gll* "to roll", cf. *magallatu* "parchment scroll". Diff. van Driel 1995, 241, who considers the word a var. of *gildu* "animal hide".

****gillu C** (CAD G 73a)

George 2003, 688, l. 170 reads ^{giš}*má-gi-il-la* "an ocean-going boat". S. also p. 872 ll. 169-170. S. already CAD M/1 44. FJMS

gilšu, *geššu* "hip, flank"; in Emar also "kidney"

SB *qaqqada* ^{uzu}*ge*$_5$*-eš-ša* 1/2 *errī alpi šarri māti ilaqqī* Emar 6/3, 388: 62 "the king of the land receives the head, the kidney and one half of the intestines of an ox", sim. ^{uzu}*ge-eš-šu* Emar 6/3, 447: 3. Other texts mentioning the king's portion have ^{uzu}ELLÁG ("kidney"), once ^{uzu}ELLÁG-*šu* (Emar 6/3, 406: 2). This would suggest that *geššu* has taken on the mng. "kidney" in these text (Fleming 1992, 153; Pentiuc 2001, 52f.).

gimartu s. *gimirtu*

gimillu s. also *gum*(*u*)*lu* and *gumālu*

+ **gimirrāyu** "Cimmerian"; LB

^{lú}*gi-mir-ra-a-a* BE 10, 69: 6 "Cimmerians", cf. TMH 2/3, 189.

gimirtu, *gimertu*, + *gimartu* "totality; OA full share"

1. OA said of (part of) a temple:
a) RN (...) *ana* DN *bēlīšu* (…) *bīti gi-me-er-ti i-Za-re ana* DN *īpuš* RIMA 1, 28: 13 "for DN, his lord, PN built a temple (and?/in the form of?) a complete *iZārum* for DN" (sim. ib. 22: 7 and 25: 13; cf. also ib. 20: 11 with *gi*$_5$*-me-*<*er*>*-tí* and 27: 10 with ⌜*ga*⌝*-me-er-ti*). Replaced by *siḫertu* "circumference, totality" in PN *ana* DN *bēlīšu* (…) *sí-ḫe-er-ti i-Za-re ša bēt* DN (…) *īpuš* RIMA 1, 26: 12.
b) OA PN (…) *bīt* DN *gi-me-er-tù-šu īpuš* RIMA 1, 38: 11 "PN built a temple for DN (in) its totality(?)".

2. OA "full share" (cf. *gamertu*):
a) *ana nikkassē a-gi*$_5$*-me-er-tim u mišlē lā kašdāku* AKT 5, 5: 24 "for the accounting I am not able (to participate) for a full share or (even) a half share" (cf. ib. 20 and 38 with *ana gamertim*).
b) *ana šazzuzātīka* [*g*]*i-me-er-tám šuprāšunūti ana* 30 MA.NA KÙ.BABBAR *lū ana* 40 MA.NA KÙ.BABBAR *awīlam a-na gi-me-er-tim-ma lissuḫūšu* KBo. 28, 158: 4, 7 "send/order (pl.) a *g.* to your representatives that they … the man for 30 or 40 minas of silver for precisely this *g.*" (in fragmentary context, unclear).

3. OB Mari "main force":
a) *ina gi-ma-ar-ti-šu* ARM 27, 148: 15 "through his entire (force)".
b) *qadūm gi-me-ra-ti-ia* ARM 10, 178: 14 "together with my entire (force)".
NJCK (1–2), MPS/JW (3)

+ **gimku** "a ritual?"; OB

OB lit. *ūm gi-im-ki-im qersū iššakkanū* FM 3, 68 no. 4 ii 7 "on the day of the g. the tent frames will be installed" (// *ūm biblim* ib. 1 "on the day of the new moon").

gimru "totality, costs, expenses"

1. OA *g. gamārum* "to reach a settlement" (cf. *awātam gamārum* "to settle a case"): *ana* PN *niṭḫēma gi*$_5$*-im-ra-am nigmur*(*ma*) VS 26, 72: 6 "we approached PN and reached a settlement".

2. On N/LB g. "transport costs" s. van Driel 2002, 171f. NJCK

ginindanakku s. *nindanakku*

+ **ginisû** "a leather object"; NA

8 ^{kuš}*gi-ni-se-*⌜*e*?⌝ SAA 7, 120 ii 9 (between a shoe and a dish).

ginnu "a mark on or form of silver"

S. Jursa 2010, 480–485.

ginû "regular offering"

In MB s. Sassmannshausen 2001, 166f.

gipû "baskets for (baked?) dates"

1. LB 20 *gi-pu-u* AOAT 414/1, 81: 11 "20 baskets of baked dates".

2. LB *tuḫallāta g*[*i-p*]*e-e u lurindu* AOAT 414/1, 95: 11 "palm-leaf baskets, baskets of baked dates and pomegranates".

****gipû II** (CAD G 86 *g.* B, AHw. 291) s. *kibbu*.

girītu "an aquatic animal", probably "moray eel"

1. Lex. **a)** $^{\text{gi-ri-tum}}$*a-dar-ḫáb*$^{\text{ku}_6}$ OB Ḫḫ IV 333 (among fish).
b) *mi-si-*IŠ$^{\text{ku}_6}$ = *gi-ri-tum*, *uḫ naĝ-e*$^{\text{ku}_6}$ = MIN *taʾî*, *a-ta-gur*$_4$$^{\text{ku}_6}$ = MIN UET 6/2, 406 r. 17–19 (Ḫḫ XV-XVIII) "*m.*-fish = moray eel, turtle-like animal that drinks

= foraging moray eel, *azaggur*-fish = foraging moray eel"

c) *mu-ur-ra*$^{\ulcorner\mathrm{ku}_6\urcorner}$ = *gi-ri-*⸢*tum*⸣, *uḫ?-gu*$_7{}^{\ulcorner\mathrm{ku}_6\urcorner}$ = MIN, ⸢*a-da?-gur*$_5{}^{\mathrm{ku}_6}$⸣ = MIN AOAT 275, 607, BM 73313 r. 10–12 (Ḫḫ).

2. OB lit. *mašak gi-ri-ti*[*m*] *tarakkass*[*u*] CUSAS 32, 25: 21 "you bandage him with the skin of a moray eel".

3. SB [*…šu ša g*]*i-ri-tú* Fs. Walker, 220: 9 "[its … is that of a] moray eel" (= BM 55551, description of the body of a god).

girmadû, *girimadû* "pole for the slipway"

1. 60 *nāḫam ana* ⸢*gi-ri*⸣*-ma-de-e* Finkel 2014: 57 "60 (kor of) lard for the poles of the slipway".

2. On the ref. Gilg. XI 78 s. now George 2003, 883 on l. 79. MPS (1), FJMS (2)

****girmaduššu**

The ref. Ḫḫ IV 393 belongs to *girmadû* (s. MSL 9, 172).

girratu s. *kirratu*

\+ **girribu** "a bird"; MB Emar

Lex. *tu-maḫ* (*mušen*) = *tù-ma-ḫu* : *gir-ri-bu* Emar 6/4, 555: 72 "big dove : *crow*(?)". The word may be connected to *ā/ēribu* "crow" with reflex of the original initial ġ (Y. Cohen 2010, 818).

girûtu "hostility"

NA *gír-ru-tú memēni laššu* SAA 5, 113: 18 "there is no hostility at all".

gisallu "reed fence or screen (on the roof)"

OB *gi-sa-al-lu ša mūtim ina muḫḫiya ḫariṣ* AbB 1, 52: 19 "the reed fence (holding back) death is broken above me" (metaphorical).

****gisanda/udû** "reed effigy"

1. The Sum. reading is to be corrected according to a gloss: *gi-saĝ-du-*DI^{sa}*-a* = ŠU Ḫḫ IX 294 (MSL 9, 183).

2. The Akk. explanation is to be corrected to *qa-*[*an an-d*]*u-na-nu* "reed substitute" (MSL 9, 186 L6 1).

gisandussû s. *gisanda/udû*

giskimmu "sign, omen"

SB DNf *muzakkirat gis-ki-me nišī šadî u māti*[*tān*] BM 75974 r. 5 (Mayer 2016, 211) "DNf, who proclaims the signs for the people of the mountains and all the lands"; cf. *gis-ki-*[*im-mu*] BM 65617 ii 11'.

giṣṣu, + *kiṣṣu* "thorn(bush)"

OB lit. [*u*]*llul kīma ki-ṣí-i-im* VS 17, 4: 1 "tufted like a thornbush".

gišḫummu "a bench (of a boat or wagon)"

Lex. *giš-ḫu-um/ḫum-mu* = *kippatu* AOAT 50, 347: 191 (malku) "bench" = "circumference", i.e. a bench going around an edge? Often said of wagons and boats. MPS/FJMS

\+ **gišḫuppu** "a tool"; Sum. lw.

Lex. [^{giš}]*ḫub* = *giš-ḫup-p*[*u*] KAL 8, 26: 6; *giš-ḫu-up-pu* AOAT 275, 633 r. 12.

gišḫūru "plan, magic circle"

1. SB [*ina* GI]Š.ḪUR*-ia izzazzū ilu u šarru* Jiménez 2017, 170 Ic 27 "god and king stand [in] my (poplar's) magic circle".

2. The writing GIŠ.ḪUR*-r-* is half logographic and does not point to a form ***gišḫurru*, which is not attested.

gišimmaru "date palm"

1. OB lit. *gi*4*-ši-ma-ar-šu ul ikkis* CUSAS 10, 15: 13 "he did not cut down its date-palm".

2. SB ^giš^GIŠIMMAR *šūki ili* Šūpê-amēli 50 "the date-palm is the door-pole of god".

3. LB *ḫepê* ⌜giš⌝GIŠIMMAR[^meš^] AOAT 414/1, 189: 12 "cutting down of date palms".

gišnû "bed"

Lex. *giš-nu-ú* = MIN (*ēru*) AOAT 50, 454: 261 (malku).

gišnugallu, *ašnugallu* "alabaster"

NB [GABA.R]I *tuppi ša* ^na4^GIŠ.NU11.GAL *ša* PN BM 54060: 2 "copy of the alabaster tablet of PN", s. Jursa 2009, 150.

gišparru "trap, snare"

1. OB lit. *ge*6*-eš-pa*!*-ar pūtim qarnī īšū* AML 86: 3 "the snare of the forehead has horns" (referring to a scorpion).

2. SB *ušandû ana giš-par-ri-šú iṭam eblu* Jiménez 2017, 250: 21 "the bird-catcher plaits the rope for his trap".

gišrinnu, + *kišrinnu* "balance"

OB lit. *našīma zikru ki-iš-*⌜*ri*⌝*-nam-ma qātiššu* Or. 87, 19 ii 5 "the man carries a balance in his hand".

gišru "bridge"

1. NA *gi-iš-r*[*u*] *ša* [*el*]*eppēte* SAA 10, 364: 8 "bridge of ships".

2. NA *ētebir ina muḫḫi giš-ri issakna* ... PN *ultu muḫḫi giš-ri ussaḫḫira* ... *ultu muḫḫi giš-ri* ... *ittalak* ... *adū libbi giš-ri* [...] SAA 19, 82: 5–16 "he has crossed (the river) and set camp at the bridge ... He turned PN back from the bridge ... From the bridge he went to ... as far as the bridge ...".

****gištalgiddû** s. *talgiddû* (Borger 2010a, 345).

gištallu?, *gištalû* "a joist"

1. OB **a)** ḪAR ŠU (...) *gi-iš*7*-ta-lu* ARM 22, 290 ii 12, cf. *gi-iš-ta-lu-ú* M.6495 ii 16 and Arkhipov 2012, 97 for add. refs. and disc.
b) ^giš^GU.ZA *gi-iš-ta-li-tim* ARM 31, 494 no. 196: 5 "a chair with braces(?)", either a fem. pl. of the form *gištalû* (*gištalêtim*, Guichard 2005, 204) or a fem. adj. (Arkhipov 2012, 494).

2. NB *gušūrī giš-tal-li* ^giš^SAG.KUL BABBAR *šīpī u ṣupru* OIP 114, 89: 15 "beams, joists, a white(?) bolt, rafters and a 'claw'" (for roofing houses).

3. Perhaps to be read ^giš^*tallu*.

+ **gištašalu?** "part of a vessel"; OB [...] *gi-iš-ta-ša-lu* ARM 31, 351 no. 14 r. 20. S. Guichard 2005, 130 (mistake for *gištallu*?).

gištû "a joist"

OB *iḫzi ša* ^giš^*gi-iš-ti-im arkim* ARM 25, 540: 3 "setting for long joists" (reading with Guichard 2005, 204).

gištuppu s. *nišduppu*

gišûtu, + *gisûtu* "burp, belch"

1. OB lex. KAxBAL? = *gi-šu-tum* Klein/Sefati 2019, 90 ii 20. S. also *gešû*.

2. SB *kīma gi*5*-i-su-ti nap-šá-ti* AulaOr. (Suppl.) 23, 21: 40 "like a burp of the throat". FJMS/JW (1), MPS (2)

gitmālu, *gitamlu* "equal; noble, perfect"

1. Lex. [*g*]*i*/*gít-tam-lu* = *gít-ma-lu₄*/*lu* AOAT 50, 305: 67 (malku). S. Hrůša ib. p. 200.

2. OB lit. *gi-it-ma-la-ku* AML 126: 3 "I am perfect".

3. SB *gít-ma-lu ina ilānī* SpTU 5, 247 r. iv 8 "perfect among the gods".

4. SB *aplu gít-*[*ma-l*]*u* AOAT 275, 459 r. 1, cf. 483 r. 1 "perfect heir".

gizillû, + *gizallû*? "torch, brand"

1. Lex. MIN(= ^{gi}).*izi-lá* = *gi-zi-lu-u* = *šab-bu-ṭu* Emar 6/4, 546: 9, s. *šabbiṭu* "staff".

2. SB *šar kibrāt gi-zal-lu-ú* (// *gi-izi-lá*) *mut*[*tanbiṭ*]*u Gula ittaṣâ* SpTU 5, 227: 8 "the king of the world, the sh[in]ing torch, Gula, went forth". In LB orthography, *zal* may stand for /*zil*/.

3. SB Spelling *gi-zi-la*/*lá* (syllabic or late var. of the logogr.?): NÍG.NA GI.ZI.LÁ KÙ *uš-bi-ka-nu-uš* JMC 36, 25: 10 "has moved the holy censer (and) torch past you", cf. GI.Z[I.LA] AMD 8/2, 8.15: 38, and GI.ZI.LA Fs. Hallo, 153 text C: 1, 4 (BM 29383).

MPS (1–2), FJMS/JW (3)

gizinakku "offering for the moon god Sîn"

OB (fat) *inūma gi-zi-na-ki* ARM 21, 105: 3 "at the occasion of the offering for Sîn".

+ **gizû?** "a sort of cane"; OB; Sum. lw.

OB lit. *malkū wāšib kussī'āt g*[*i*?]*-zi-im dadnī* ⌜*ibēlū*⌝ *ina gamlika* OECT 11, 1: 9 "the kings sitting on thrones of *gizi*-cane(?) ruled the inhabited world with your crook". Von Soden 1989 and 1989/90, 118 suggests *s*[*í*]*-sí-im* from *sissimu* "granary" (hapax, s. CAD S 325) and translates "Thronen der Schatzkammern(?) der Wohnstätten". For the tentative interpretation as thrones of *gizi*-cane cf. *gu-za-lá gi-zi* "*gizi*-chair-carrier" (Wilcke 1998, 50: 25).

gizzatu "shearing, wool yield; metal shaving; a textile; hairloss"

1. (2 shekels of gold) *issu libbi gi-za-a-ti ana kirkī ša tamlīt ša urki ša-ku*?*-ri*? CTN 2, 145: 2 "out of the shavings, for rolls for the inlay of the back of the *šukurru-emblem*(?)", s. Postgate ib.

2. The mng. "gold shaving" also applies to ABL 1458 (now SAA 1, 52) cit. AHw. 295 and ADD 676 (both sg. *gi-zu-tú*).

3. SB "hair loss":

a) *gi-iz-za-tum* SpTU 1, 43: 18 (in list of diseases).

b) *gi-iz-za-tú* : *ana muḫḫī gazāz ša šārat enzi* SpTU 1, 51: 3 "hair loss : related to shearing of a goat's hair" (medical comm.).

c) Refs. in AHw. 489 *k*/*gišṣatu* "Haarausfall, Abblättern der Haut" and CAD K 443 *kiṣṣatu* "a skin disease" probably belong here. S. also *gizzutu*

gizzu "shearing; shearling; shorn (of fabric)"

1. OB a low-pile textile (cf. OA *gazzu*): 2 TÚG *gi-zu* BAR.KAR.R[A] ARM 22, 119: 1 (coll. ARM 30 p. 195) "2 shorn garments of *barkarrû*-quality". The word corresponds to ^{túg}GUZ.ZA in parallel texts. S. Durand 2009, 34f. for add. refs. and disc.

2. NA "shearling?": 1 GUD 25 *gi-zi* (…) 1 ANŠE 20 *gi-zi* CTN 2, 222 A 1–2 "1 ox, 25 *g.* (…), 1 donkey, 20 *g.*" S. Postgate ib. p. 216 (a type of goat?).

3. LB (van Driel 1995, 228):

a) (wool) *gi-zi* CT 55, 761: 1.

b) *serpī parzilli ana gi-iz-zi* CT 55, 252: 2 "(13 new) iron knives for shearing".
c) *bīt gi-iz-zi* CT 57, 162: 4 "shearing shed".

4. NA (n silver) *ša* UDU^{meš} *kaspi* SIKI *gi-zi* SAA 11, 100: 3 "of sheep, price of the wool from shearing".

5. Pl. *gizzānū*:
a) NA [*adi*] *remēšunu adi gi-za-ni-šú-nu* BATSH 6/2, 20 r. 4 "(sheep) together with their young and their shearlings" (diff. Radner ib.: "fleeces").
b) NA (300 sheep) *ana lid*(*d*)*ā*[*nīšunu*] *ana gi-za-ni-šú-nu* SAAS 5, 51: 5 "to bear young and to be shorn"; sim. BATSH 6/2, 110: 8–9.

JW (1–3, 5), MPS (4), JK (5)

gubāru s. *gupāru*

+ **gubbatu** "reed pipes?"; LB; Aram. Lw.

[x] GUN *gu-ub-ba-tum* NBC 6140: 1 (Fs. Klein, 652). Cf. Syr. *gwbtʿ* (hapax).

gubbu "cistern"

1. NA ⸢*bītu*?⸣ *gu-ub-bu* ŠE.NU[MUN^{meš}] SAA 5, 15: 12 "house(?), cistern, arab[le land]".

2. NA *mê šūt gu-ub-bu* SAA 12, 3: 4f. "water of the cistern".

3. S. Cherry 2016, 117–119. Cf. *gabbu*, *gabʾu*.

gubbuḫu, *qubbuḫu* "bald"

SB […] *gub-bu-ḫu immar* KAL 1, 5 iii 17 "[when…] a bald (man) is seen".

gubbunu s. *gapānu*

gubburu s. *gapāru*

+ **gubību** "a golden object or ornament"; NA

tudittu KÙ.GI *g*[*u*?]-*bi-bi* KÙ.GI *kasūsu ina muḫḫi* SAA 7, 81: 3 "a golden dress-pin (with?) a golden *g.* and a falcon on it".

gublāyu "from Byblos"

OB 1 TÚG *gu-ub-la-ji/u* ARM 30, 353 M.5260 "1 Byblos-style garment". S. Durand 2009, 100 with add. refs.

gubnatu "cheese"

Aram. lw., s. Kogan/Krebernik 2021, 440 (cf. Syr. *gəbettā*, Off. Aram. *gbnh* (DNWSI 210)).

+ **gudappu** "a commodity"; OB

1 MA.NA *gu-da-ap-pu* CT 45, 99: 5 (von Soden 1980a, 274).

****gudilû** (CAD G 119b)

Read ḪA.A = *gu-di-id*?-⸢*du*?⸣-*um* MSL 14, 131.

+ **gudil(l)û** "single(?)"; SB

Lex. *ūmu gu-di-lu-ú* // [*g*]*u-dil-ú* // *gu-dil-lu-ú* = *ištēn ūmu* AOAT 50, 370: 164 (malku) "a single day" = "one day". Hrůša ib. p. 87: < Sum. *ugu-dili*.

MPS/FJMS

gudūdu I "patrol, band, battle troop"

1. SB 20 ^{lú}*gu-du-du ša Aramu* BagM 21, 345 iii 14 "a patrol of 20 of the Arameans".

2. NB ^{lú}*gu-du-da-nu ša rab-šāqê* SAA 19, 4: 12 "the battle troops of the chief cupbearer".

3. NB ^{lú}*gu-du-du ša Bīt-Yakīn ... iḫtabtū* OIP 114, 18: 4 "the patrol of the Bīt-Jakīn stole (people and donkeys)".

\+ **gudūdu? II** "part of a bed, a textile?"; LB

LB 1-*et* ^giš^NÁ *ia-a-nu-mi-ʾ-tum adī ṣip-rīti* 1-*en gu-du-di-šú* AOAT 222, 38: 13 (CT 49, 165) "1 bed of *y.*-type together with dyed linens, 1 (of) its(?) *g.*".

gudugudû, *guduguttû* s. *guduttû*

guduttû, + *gudugudû*, + *guduguttû* "offering table"

1. Lex. *gu-du-*⸢*gu-ut*⸣*-tu-ú* // *gu-du-ut-tu-u* // ⸢*gu*⸣*-du-gu-du-u* = *paššūru* AOAT 50, 347: 186 (malku) "offering table = table". Delete the var. *dugudû* in CAD G 120 *guduttû*.

2. SB [*g*]*u*?*-du-ut isinni* [*š*]*a* ⸢*tarā*⸣[*ṣi*] KAL 9, 1: 4 "offering table for the festival, for preparation(?)", s. the comm. ib. p. 18.

\+ **gugalippu** "mng. unkn"; SB

[*g*]*u-ga-lip*!*-pi*!*-šu-n*[*u*] KAL 12, 37 A 12, *gu-ga-lip*!-[*pi-šu-nu*] ib. B 9 (among foodstuffs in ritual instruction).

gugguru "a long, bottle-like container"

OB ^dug^*gu-gu-rum* TMH 10, 192: 1, 7.

gugūtu "a designation of sheep"; Ur III

1. SILA$_4$ *gu-gu-tum* MVN 3, 344: 32; AUCT 2, 375: 10; ASJ 15, 136: 2.

2. Likely a type of meal or ritual designation (Steinkeller 1995, 56).

guḫaṣṣu s. *guḫaššu*

guḫaššu, *guḫaṣṣu*, *guḫalṣu* "braided wire, torc"; + NA

1. OB *šarḫullu* GAL KÙ.GI ⸢ŠÀ.BA⸣ 1 *gu-ḫa-šu* ARM 32, 244 M.12668 ii 18 "a large golden *š.*-ornament with *g.* in its center", Arkhipov 2012, 75 with add. refs; Guichard 2005, 135; S. also *kirādu*.

2. NA (the tip of a thornbush) *kī gu-ḫa-ṣu epiš* SAA 10, 382: 10 "is made like a wire".

guḫlu "bdellium(?)"

1. LB *še rebītu gu-uḫ-li* AOAT 414/1, 80: 16 "bdellium(?) for 1/4 shekel" (next to *murru*).

2. After Potts et al. 1996, 291–305, *g.* is not "antimony" but rather bdellium (gum of *Commiphora mukul*), and Sanskrit *guggulu* is borrowed from Akk. Note that bdellium is also identified with *buduḫlu* (s. Jursa 2009, 158 n. 51; s. *buduḫlu*).

guḫšû "a reed altar"; + MA

2 ^gi^*gu-uḫ-še*$_{20}$*-e* Chuera 11: 16.

\+ **gulātu** "a garment"; SB

[^túg^*g*]*u-la-a-t*[*u*] SpTU 4, 128: 23; 1-*en* ^túg^*gu-la-a-a-tu*[*m*] ib. 92.

gulēnu, *gulānu* "cloak, mantle"; Aram. lw.

1. NB 200 ^túg^*gu-la-a-ni* SAA 17, 69 r. 21 "200 *g.* garments". S. also Zawadzki 2010, 419.

2. Cherry 2016, 120f. for add. NA refs. Cf. Aram. *glym* "cloak, mantle".

gulgull(at)u "skull"

NA *gul-gu-lat-ku-nu umarraqa* SAA 16, 88: 13 "I will crush your skulls".

gulgultu s. *qulqultu*

gulībātu "hair-trimmings"; + OB

Lex. *umbin*-TAR-*ĝu*$_{10}$ = *gu-li-ba-*⸢*tu-ú*⸣*-a* CUSAS 12 p. 154 ii 19 (Ugumu) "my hair trimmings".

gullatu "a bowl, ewer; an ornament (Qaṭna); a column base (NA, NB)"; + MB Emar

1. OB (a vessel) s. Guichard 2015, 189–193 for add. refs.

2. MB Emar "ewer":

a) 4 *gu-la-tù* ZABAR CunMon. 13, 27: 2 (cult inventory).

b) 3 *gu-ul-la-a-ta* ZABAR Emar 6/3, 186: 9, cf. ib.: 15; 187: 9; 283: 14.

3. In many cases *g.* may in fact be the pl. of *gullu* (s. below).

gullu, pl. *gullātu* "a bowl; link (of a chain)"

1. OB lex. GAL = *gu-lu*!*-um* Klein/Sefati 2019, 93 iv 23.

2. NA 1 *šeršerrutu gul-lat* KALAG!^{meš} ditto 1 ditto ditto *qàl*^{meš} ditto SAA 7, 72: 17f. "1 chain with big links of ditto (gold), ditto (1 chain with) small ditto (links) of ditto (gold)".

3. (gold) *ana* 1 ^{kuš}BÀN.DA *gul-lat* x! SAA 7, 64 r. ii 7 "for 1 leather chain with ... links".

4. S. Guichard 2015, 189–193. Cf. *gullatu*. MPS/JW/FJMS

gullubu s. *galābu*

gullubūtu "barber service"; + LB

LB *pappasu ša* ^{lú}*gul-lu-bu-tu* dubsar 3, 47 (= YOS 3, 80): 10 "prebendary payment for the barber service", cf. CAD G 129 and AHw. 297 s. v. *gullubu*.

gullultu "sin"

OB *u aššum ṭēmim annîm ittī* PN *gu-ul-lu-ul-tum ittabšī* FM 8, 69 no. 15: 26 "and because of that matter a sin occurred on the part of PN".

gullulu I "to commit a sin, crime; to cause harm"

1. OB *ana nawêm ana gu-lu-li-im p*[*anūš*]*u*[*nu ša*]*knū* AbB 8, 38: 13 "(500 soldiers) are planning to attack the meadow". Alternatively *qullulu* "to diminish".

2. OB [*wa*]*rkīssina ana gu-lu-li-ši-na ašâlki* CUSAS 36, 55: 13 "I am asking you about what will happen to them (= the mollies) (lit. what will be their future), in case they get harmed"; *mimma ú-ga-la-al-ma* ib. 19 "he will cause harm in some way".

+ **gullulu II** "to blind"

1. MA *gal-lu-le* KAV 1 viii 56 (inf., Deller in id./Mayer/Oelsner 1989, 264).

2. NA PN: ^{I}*Ga-lu-lu* ADD 218 r. 4 (cit. CAD G 131b).

3. In Ass. instead of Bab. *napālu* (Watanabe 1987, 206b).

4. CAD Q s.v. *qullulu*; CAD G s.v. *gullulu* adj.

gul(u)būtu "a legume"

S. Postgate 1987, 94f.: Perhaps *Lathyrus sativus* (cf. Aram. *gilbōna*, Arab. *jilbān*).

gumāḫu "choice bull"

The rare word *qumaḫḫu* (CAD Q 304) is perhaps a phonetic variant (Sommerfeld 1990, 32).

+ **gumakil(l)u** "a wooden object"

NA *bēlī udda ummeʾānū* [*i*]*ssu panīya ittūṣīʾū lā ana batqi* [*lā*] *ana* ^{giš}*gu-ma-ki-li epāši ... lurammīšunu* SAA 1, 179 r. 20 "my lord knows that the artisans have run away from me. May he not set them free for repairing or making *g.*s".

+ **gumālu** "mercy, clemency, salvation"; SB

lušalmidma nišī qitruba gu-ma-al-šin Iraq 60, 193: 39 (Ludlul 1) "let me teach the people how close their salvation is", with var. *gi-[mil-*] (Oshima 2014, 384).

gumāru "charcoal, ember"

< Aram. *gwmrh*, cf. Syr. *gūmrā* (s. Cherry 2016, 121–123).

gumatu s. *gummātu*

+ **gum(u)lu** "mercy, clemency"; OB In Mari PNN only (Stol 1991, 195):

1. *Gu-mu-ul*-DN FM 9, 13: 11 (and *pass.*).

2. *Ì-lí-gu-um-li-ia* ARM 13, 1 viii 45; *Ì-lí-gu-um-la-ia* ARM 21, 403 viii 6.

3. DN-*gu-um-li* ARM 13, 1 iv 39

4. *Gu-mu-lum* ARM 22, 14 ii 17; 38: 3.

gummātu "summer"; LB

Del. the var. *ḫummātu* (AHw. 298), s. *ḫummātu*. The word is only attested in BE 9, 29 and 30. Abraham/Sokoloff 2011, 32, doubt the derivation from Aram. *ḥmm*, "to be hot", as proposed by von Soden.

****gum(m)urtum** (kt 88/k 487: 9, s. Kuzuoğlu 2016, 36–37) s. *kumurtum*.

gummuru s. *gammuru*

gunakku "a garment"; LB

1. 1-*en* [túg]*gu-nak-ku* BM 76968/72: 13 (Roth 1989/1990, 30).

2. 2 [túg]*gu-nak-ku* Zawadzki 2010, 415 BM 76136: 2 and comm. ib. 418.

3. S. Abraham/Sokoloff 2011, 32.

gungītu, + *guggittu* "a box"

Lex. *šakkabakku* = *gu-(un-)gi-it-t[um]* AOAT 50, 388: 140 (malku).

guninnu s. *kuninnu*

gunnuṣu "nose-wrinkling"

OB lit. *dabbi šabašītum dalp⌜um epšatum gú-nu-ṣum⌝* Fs. Stol, 151 = CT 42, 32: 16 "the gossipy person, the enraged woman, the restless man, the sorceress, the nose-wrinkling man" (forerunner of SAG.GIG/*muššuʾu*).

Cf. *ganāṣu*.

gunû, *gunnu* "a storage space for tablets"

1. OB (PNN) *ṣuḫārū ša gu-ni* ARM 23, 219 no. 240: 19 "servants of the *g.*"

2. SB (he wrote this tablet and placed it in the temple of DN, the house of his great lordship) *ana* GÚ *ana kan[akki] ša Esagil* CTMMA 2, 65 r. 8 "in the *g.*, in the *kanakku* of Esagil", s. Gesche ib. 260.

3. SB [(dug)]*gu-un-nu* pass. in *Nabu ša harê*, s. Cavigneaux 1981, 123f.

gunurû s. *kunurû*

gupāru I "neck, necklace": + NB

GÚ.BAR *ḫurāṣi* SAA 17, 58: 4 "a golden necklace".

+ **gupāru II** "a type of military camp"; OB

1. (I have seen the general) *ittī aḫḫātīya ana gu-pa-ri-im ūṣêm* ARM 10, 29: 5 "together with my sisters I went to the camp."

2. (light fires surrounding GN) *u šumma ālum* GN *gu-pa-ra-am ul leyī* A.2821, 8 // A.3857+: 8 (cit. ARM 26/1, 159f.) "and if the city of GN is not capable of (maintaining?) a camp (…)".

3. *gu-pa-ra-am niʾam* [*ṣā*]*bum ša* GN ⌜*īmur*⌝ Shemshara 1, 56: 31 "the troops of GN saw our camp".

4. Durand, ARM 26/1, 159f. Cf. *gupru*?

gupnu "tree"

1. NA ^giš^*gup-ni maḫiṣ* SAA 19, 87 r. 4; 156: 10 "the tree(s) are cut".

2. NA (stones will be put) *ina muḫḫi* ^giš^*gup-ni ma-ḫi-ṣi* SAA 19, 156: 10 "on the cut tree(s)".

gupru, *kupru* "shepherd's hut"

1. OB (lit.) *kupru*: *tibût*/*miqitti ku-up-ri-im* RA 63 p. 155: 18, 20 "rising/falling of the camp"; sim. *ku-up-ri* RA 65, 67–84 AO 7539: 76; *ku-up-ra-am* YOS 10, 18: 46, 48; *ku-up-ri* RA 101, 66: 78 (Gilg.), s. George 2013, 139, diff. CAD K 484 s.v. *kubru*.

2. Does lex. *gu-up-rum* = *būlu* AOAT 50, 397: 23 (malku) "hut = cattle" belong here? Hrůša ib. p. 251 suggests a var. of *kubru* "thickest part" (said of sheep).

guqqû, pl. *guqqānû* "an offering"; + MB

1. MB (flour) *gu-qá-nu-ú* BE 14, 148: 24. S. Sassmannshausen 2001, 155 and 167.

2. S. McEwan 1981a, 166f.; Joannès 1982, 214; MacGinnis 1995, 156ff.; Bongenaar 1997, 145f.; Da Riva 2002, 268ff.; Linssen 2004, 163f.

****gurābu I/B** "leper" (AHw. 299; CAD G 136)

Read *gu-lu-bu* in OB Lu Ser. A. 409 (MSL 12, 243).

gurābū "sack, wrapping"

On etym. s. Abraham/Sokoloff 2011, 32 with lit. (not Aram., possibly of Iranian origin).

+ **guramīru** "mng. unkn."; MB Emar

Lex. ḪAR = *gu-ra-mi-rum* Emar 6/4, 537: 58 (Sjöberg 1998, 245).

guraštu s. *kuraštu*

gurbizu s. *q/gurpisu*

+ **gurdimu** "an axe"; MB Emar

1. Lex. *a-ga* = *aga*$_x$(ÍL) = *a-gu* = *gur-di-*[*mu*] Emar 6/4, 545: 345.

2. Cf. Ebla ^giš^*àga* = *gur-du-mu-um* MEE 4, 2 xiii 44; 13 xiv 2''; 65+ xii 27'.

S. Pentiuc 2001, 54; Y. Cohen 2010, 818.

+ **gurgubû** "a foodstuff?"; OB

gu-úr-gu-bu-ú BBVOT 3, 28: 12, 15 (among flour and grain in a list of cult provisions).

****gurištu** s. *kurištu* "vulva"

The ref. CT 19, 45 + (list of diseases) belongs to *kuraštu*. The only remaining ref. (Nabnitu i) has *ku-*.

+ **gurnatu?** "a wooden object"; OB

^giš^*gur-na-*[*tum a*/*in*]*a*? *mātim nadnat* [(…)] ARM 26/1, 417 no. 194: 11 "a *g*. is given [fo]r/[i]n the land". The interpretation as pyre, var. of *gurunnu*, by Durand ib. p. 418f. and 2005, 105, is doubtful, as already stated by Heimpel 2003, 249.

gurnu, *gunnu* II "of average quality"; + OA?; + NA

1. OA lit. *nuḫitimmī gu*$_5$*-ur-na-am urrir*(*ma*) OA Sarg. 37 "my cook let *g*.(-

meat?) burn". In view of the occurrence of *kursinnu* "lower leg, shank" in l. 27, it is possible that here, too, we should read *ku-ur-<sí>-na-am*.

2. OB of wool: 18 GÚ SÍG *gur-nu* ARM 30, 447 M.6700: 4, cf. 10, 16, 22. Cf. Durand 2009, 1f. with a diff. interpretation.

3. OB of barley: [*ina*] *libbū gu-un-nim šanîm* […] *nuzakkīma* AbB 7, 84: 11 "we have dehusked […] from among the second average quality".

4. ⌜KAŠ?⌝ *gur-nu* SAA 12, 48: 14 "beer of medium quality".

MPS (1), NJCK (1), JW (2–4)

gurpissu s. *q*/*gurpis*(*s*)*u*

+ **gurru II?** "mng. unkn."

NA [*ana*] *mīni* [*p*]*an gur-ra-te tallak* StAT 1, 57: 16 = StAT 2, 248 r. 4 "why are you going to …" (coll. in StAT 2).

JK

gurrubu "a color designation?"

LB 1 MA.NA SÍG.ZA.GÌN.KUR.RA *gu-ru-ub-tum ana nēbeḫu ša* DN Zawadzki 2013, 479: 2 "1 mina of blue-purple wool of *g*.-quality for the *n*.-belt of DN".

gurrudu "bald"

CAD Q s.v. *qurrudu* (adj.) and *qarādu* B; AHw. *qurrudu* and *qarādu* I; s. also *gerdu*.

gursippu s. *q*/*gurpis*(*s*)*u*

g/quršu I "a (ritual) meal"

1. NA *kappī ḫurāṣi ša ina gur-še ušēlûni* CTN 6, 58: 2 "golden *kappu*-bowls which they dedicated during the *g*.".

2. NA *gur-šu ša* DN *šākin māti ušakkal* Ass. Tempel II, T 44 r. 18 "the governor will serve the *g*.-meal of DN"; cf. ib. T 54 8 and RA 69, 183: 36.

3. NA *qur-šu mar'ēk*[*a*] SAA 10, 185 r. 24 "meal of your sons".

4. NA (on the 4th day) *gur-šu ša* DN SAA 13, 78: 10 "the *g*. of DN (takes place)".

5. *bīt g*/*q*/*ḫurši* means "abattoir, kitchen" (Deller in id./Mayer/Oelsner 1989, 265–6, < *q*/*garāšu*).

6. On the mng. s. Postgate 1974, 70 ("feast, meal", < *qarāšu* "to trim meat"). Diff. Parpola 1983a, 119 n. 251 ("wedding night, marriage", < *garāšu* "to copulate"); Deller in id./Mayer/Oelsner 1989, 265 ("Hochzeitsmahl", cf. Arab. *ʿurs*). The mng. "Hauskapelle" proposed in AHw. 299 is not supported by the known refs.

****gurummad/ḫu** (AHw. 299) s. *gurummaru* (already AHw. 1557).

gurummaru "a tree"

OB *tuppam šanêm aššum* ^giš^*gu-ru-um-ma*!*-ri-im ana ṣēr šarrim uštābilam* ARM 13, 48: 6 "I have sent a second letter to the king regarding the *g*.", cf. ARM 13, 45: 5, 11.

gūru "foliage (of reed plants)"

Fincke 2011, 197f.

gurunnu I "heap" s. *q*/*gurunnu*

+ **gurunnu II** "fruit-shaped decoration"; OB; lw. from Sum. *gurun* "fruit".

(150 grains of gold for) 18 *gu-ru-ni ša ḫubūsim* ARM 32, 371 A.4670: 2 "18 *g*.-ornaments on a *ḫ*.-weapon". The same implement is described as decorated with *inbu*, "fruit", elsewhere, s. Arkhipov 2012, 45, 109.

gusānu "a leather bag"

1. 1 ^{kuš}*gu-sa-nu ša ṣubātī* OBTR 170: 2 "1 leather bag with textiles"; 4 ^{kuš}*gu-sa-nu* OBTR 205: 4.

2. Durand 2009, 175 for add. Mari refs. S. also *kursānu.*

+ **guššu** "a textile"; OB

1. ^{gú}*gu-úš-šu* ARM 30, 185 M.12030: 4 (among other textiles).

2. ^{túg}*gu-úš-šu-um* ARM 24, 190: 1; ^{túg}*gu-úš-šum* SAG ARM 25, 120: 1; (5 minas of wool for) ^{túg}*gu-šum* ARM 24, 177: 2; ^{túg}*gu-uš-šu* ARM 21, 257: 21.

3. Durand 2009, 36. The term has been misread as *gunušu* in older Mari publications. Cf. AHw./CAD s.v. *gušû.*

gušû s. *guššu*

gušurrāʾu s. *kušurrāʾu*

gušūru "tree-trunk, log"

1. OB lit. *ḫur[bāš]u ṣillu [iṣṣ]ī qīštim gu-šu-r[i!-šu-nu] azzīmma lā ḫerû lišān pāšim* FM 14 ii 42 "(there is) fearsomeness (in) the shade of the forest trees, as long as the blade of the axe has not felled their logs".

2. OB 170 ^{giš}ÙR[$^{ḫi.a}$] *ša* 10 *am-ma*^{àm} FM 2, 69 no. 35: 14 "170 tree-trunks, which are each 10 cubits (long)"; cf. ib. 5, 9.

3. OB *[i]na mātim [el]ītim nukurtumma [i]štū mātim elītim* ^{giš}ÙR$^{ḫi.a}$ *leqêm ul eleʾʾī* ^{giš}ÙR$^{ḫi.a}$ *ina qīšātim ša* GN *ibaššû* 100 ^{giš}ÙR$^{ḫi.a}$ *ša* 1 1/2 NINDA 4 KÙŠ^{àm} *u elīšma adī* 2 NINDA^{àm} FM 2, 162 no. 87: 4–8 "there is hostility in the upper land, therefore I cannot fetch tree-trunks from the upper land. There are tree-trunks in the forests of GN, which are 1 1/2 NINDA 4 cubits (ca. 11 m) (long) or even more up to 12 m (long)".

4. On N/LB s. van Driel 1992, 173 (use in building work).

gutappû "part of a donkey harness"

1. Lex. *[kuš-gú-tab-ba]-anše = gú-tap-pu-u* MSL 9, 199 (130 B2 2').

2. OB 15 *gú!-tap-pu* ARM 7, 161: 11 (coll. MARI 2 p. 82); 4 *gu-tap-pu* ARM 25, 210 iii 22; S. ARM 30, 182 for add. refs.

+ **guw(w)a/ālu** "circuit?"; Ugar.; lw. from Ugar. *gwl*?

(royal fields) *ša eqlī gu-wa-*⌜*li*⌝ PRU 3, 151f.: 12 "in 'circuit fields'". Cf. Arab. *ǧawl(at)* "circuit, round" and the Hebr. GN *gôlān*, s. Huehnergard 1987, 116.

guzallu "scoundrel"

SB Designation for a disease: GÚ.ZAL *š[umšu]* SpTU 4, 152: 60 "scoundrel is [its] n[ame]" (cf. *šaḫšaḫḫu šumšu* ib. 58 "slanderer is its name").

guzalû "chair bearer"

1. OB *ina panī* GU.ZA.LÁ *qaqqadī attanabbal* AbB 14, 123: 29 "I have to constantly excuse myself in front of the chair bearer"; cf. AbB 206: 12.

2. Veenhof 2014, 207; Westenholz/Westenholz 2006, 123–127 with add. refs. and disc.

guzguzu "a garment"

NB 3 ^{túg}*gu-uz-gu-za*^{meš} *ša tabarri* dubsar 7, 39: 25 "3 *g.* (made) of dyed wool".

guzullu s. *kuzullu*

K

Kaʾāšu "to wrap up"; OA

1. *ina maškim ki-i-ša-šu-ma danninãma kunkāšuma* AKT 3, 84: 17 "wrap it (= the tablet) up firmly in a fleece and seal it" (also ib. 82: 24; 83: 22; 88: 43; 89: 35; 100: 18).

2. *tuppam ša talaqqûni ki-i-šu-ma ina kunukkēni ana* PN *lu*[*put*] TC 2, 26 r. 17 "wrap up the tablet that you will obtain, (seal it) with our seals and write on it '(addressed) to PN'".

3. 1 *tuppam kà-i-iš-ma* PN (...) *ēzibam* CTMMA 1, 116 no. 84a: 47 "one tablet in a wrapping (lit. it has been wrapped up and) PN has left with me" (sim. AKT 3, 104: 12).

4. The forms point to a II/ʾ verb *g/k/qaʾāšum* of the *i/i* class (GOA § 18.6). By lack of any plausible cognate, the nature of the initial velar remains unknown. NJCK

kabābu I "shield"

OB lit. *ša ka-ba-bi* UET 7, 73 i 34 (Westenholz 1997, 148ff.) "the one (in charge) of the shields" (followed by *ša qašti* "bowman"). Cf. Sjöberg 1996a, 118.

kabābu II "to burn"

1. OB *puḫād bārîm ša maḫar il*[*im*] *ik-bu-bu* ARM 26/1, 280 no. 113: 6 "the lamb of the diviner which they burnt in front of the god".

2. LB *libbaka ik-ta-ba-ab-ka* dubsar 3, 29: 8 "your heart burnt you".

+ **kabal-** "to plunder"; Hurr. word in MB Qaṭna

GN *eqlīšu* : *ga-pa-lu-uš-a* QS 3, 4: 20 "who plundered his fields?", s. 22, 24; : *qa-pa-lu-uš-u u lāma* GN_2 GN_3 : *qa-pa-lu-uš-a* ib. 29–31 "you plundered GN before GN_2 plundered GN_3".

kaballu "a garment for legs and/or feet"

OB 4 *tāpal ka-ba-li* ARM 23, 444: 3 "4 pair of *k.*". S. Durand 2009, 49 for add. Mari refs. S. also Salonen 1969, 64.

kabaraḫḫu s. *gabaraḫḫu*

kabāru "to be(come) thick"

1. Said of trees: OB *ka-ab-ru* FM 2, 168 no. 89: 6, 7, 9.

2. Said of *ṣērū* "ribs" and *imdū* "stanchions" in Finkel 2014: 14, 16, s. *pānu*.

kabāsu "to step, tread, trample"

G 1. OA "to tread upon s.o." i.e. "to harm (financially), to treat unfairly, to neglect s.o.'s interests":
a) *ammala taleʾʾeʾu gumurši lā ta-kà-bi-sí* BIN 6, 42: 10 "settle it (i.e. my case) as well as you can; do not treat me unfairly!"; s. AKT 3, 62: 30; ATHE 65: 31; AKT 8, 1: 23?.
b) (may DNN be my witnesses that ...) *mimma* KÙ.BABBAR 1 GÍN *lā ak-bu-sú-kà* AKT 3, 62: 10 "I have not deprived you of a single shekel of silver"; s. BIN 4, 51: 14 (= OAA 1, 64).
c) KÙ.BABBAR 1 GÍN *ina šiʾim* (…) *ramākka ku-ub-sà-am* CCT 2, 26a: 18 "settle for a shekel of silver less from the proceeds"; sim. ICK 1, 192: 23; KTS

1, 22a: 16; kt h/k 347: 15, s. Balkan 1967, 395.

2. OA "to remit, to waive" (interest): *ša* 2 ITU.KAM *ṣibtam ak-bu-sà-kum* TC 3, 40: 24 "I have waived for you 2 months' interest"; also kt c/k 680: 11 (Balkan 1967, 401); sim. AKT 11A, 113: 20; BIN 4, 145: 16; CCT 6, 46a: 11; TC 3, 40: 34.

3. OA "to deduct": 18 GÍN *ammassu-ḫuttim ni-ik-bu-ús* AKT 8, 41: 13 "we deducted 18 shekels for impurities"; s. also AKT 6C, 636: 6, 671: 34; BIN 4, 51: 45 (= OAA 1, 64); kt c/k 1087: 21f. (s. Balkan 1967, 407).

4. OA "to annul": *māmītum šīt kà-áb-sá-at* Balkan 1967, 410 kt c/k 1548: 8 "that oath has been annulled".

5. OA "to end, to resolve": *nuštam-geršunuma rugummā'ēšunu ni-ik-bu-us(-ma)* Balkan 1967, 409 kt g/k 100: 14 "we made them come to an agreement and we resolved their complaints"; *awātam ku-bu-ús* CCT 3, 25: 19 "wind up the affair!"; sim. OIP 27, 62: 22.

6. OA "to disregard, to overlook": *mimma kasapni lā ta-k*[*à*]*-ba-sà* RA 59, 151 no. 23: 14 "do not overlook any silver of ours!"; s. also AKT 6C, 530: 11.

7. OA "to give up, to relinquish": PN *u* PN_2 *ana* PN_3 *u* PN_4 *qāssunu ik-bu-sú(-ma)* AKT 8, 175: 12 "PN and PN_2 have given up their share (of silver) in favor of PN_3 and PN_4".

8. OA without direct object:

a) *ana ayyītim balū'a ta-ak-bu-ús* AKT 8, 1: 12 "why have you proceeded without me?"; sim. ib. 16.

b) PN *ulā ušašqal ulā a-kà-ba-sú-um* Fs. Veenhof p. 139: 16 "I will not make PN pay nor will I take action against him(?)".

9. OB lit. *ka-bi-iš-ti eqel niš*[*ī*] UET 6/2, 404: 6 (ZA 102, 196) "(DNf,) who paces out the field of mankind" (Mayer 2016, 222).

10. OB *ša kīma ka-ba-si-im* [*al*]*pū u immerū i-ka-ab-ba-su* ARM 27, 29: 18f. "[ox]en and sheep were trampling any (locusts) that could be trampled".

11. OB *ša kīma ka-ba-si-im ik-bu-sa* ARM 27, 28: 23f. "they trampled any (locusts) that could be trampled".

12. Del. HSS 13, 119 (CAD K 7 ad 2 e), s. ***kaniniwe*.

13. S. also Š, below.

+ **Gt 1.** OB *kīma immerāt mātikama puḫur li-ik-ta-ab-sa* RATL 117, 10: 19 "they (= sheep) shall run around together just like the sheep of your land" (Mayer 2016, 222).

2. MB Emar [...] *ūmi ki-it-bu-u*[*s*] Emar 6/3, 445: 3.

3. Reflexive: SB *ak-ta-ba-as-ku-nu-ši* SpTU 2, 24: 8 "I humbled myself before you", s. *karā'u*.

D OA "to deduct, to waive, to balance": *mimma abūša šalṭam ḫabbulu kà-bu-ús(-ma)* kt 91/k 158: 18 "whatever her father owes in cash has been waived", s. Veenhof 1997, 374; s. also BIN 4, 187: 5; kt c/k 101: 15 (Balkan 1967, 403).

Dt OA *ši'im ṣubātī'a ší-li-ip-kà-im ina barēkunu lā tù-uk-tá-ba-sà* KTH 19: 32 "do not remit to each other (part of) the price of my *šilipkā'um*-textile".

Š 1. OA *tuppam ša ūmē adī mišl*[*išu*] *ša* PN *ūmē nu-ša-ak-bi-i*[*s*] TC 1, 20: 13 "as to the tablet with the term regarding the half share of PN, we have had the term reduced(?)".

2. OB *ša kīma k*[*ab*]*āsim ú-ša-ak-bi-ìs* ARM 27, 27: 20 "I made them trample any (locusts) that could be trampled".

N 1. OA *gumurma malā lā a-kà-bu-sú kaspam* (...) *šuqul* CCT 3, 30: 33 "settle (the case) and pay the silver, so that I will not be harmed".

2. OA (silver) *attāma na-ak-bi4-sú-ma alkam* KTS 1, 4b: 20 "give up(?) (some 10 or 20 shekels of silver) for him and come here!" (uncert. *nakbissumma* may also come from *kabātu*).
3. OB *ana eqlim ina erēšim lā ik-ka-bi-su* AbB 12, 137: "they shall not step on the field during cultivation!" (ingressive N is otherwise attested in NB, s. CAD K 11 ad 8).
4. NB (the Borsippeans) *ik-kab-ba-su-ú* SAA 10, 118 r. 9 "will be subdued".

NJCK (G, D, Dt, Š, N), MPS (G, Gt, Š, N), JW (G, Gt, N)

kabātu, *kabādu* "to be(come) heavy"

G 1. OA "to be(come) heavy", of tablets: *mīššum tuppum ik-bi4-it-ku-nu-tí-ma lā tušēbilānim* BIN 4, 26: 49 "why has a tablet become too heavy for you to send me one?"
2. OA "to be(come) serious" (of conditions):
a) PN *mariṣ kà-bi4-it* AKT 9A, 41: 6 "PN is seriously ill" (s. OB *maruṣ kabit* Sumer 14, 68 no. 43: 16); sim. ib. 27.
b) *dullum ina ālim ik-tí-bi4-it* Prag 467: 5 "distress has caused aggravation in the city".
3. With *panū*, "to be(come) worried, anxious":
a) OA *ištū* 3 *šanātim ū* 4 *šanātim aššumi mera* PN *panū'a kà-áb-tù(-ma)* AKT 9A, 152: 6 "for 3 years or 4 years I have been worrying about PN's son".
b) OA (may good news from you reach me in the City) *panū'a ana ṣērika lā i-kà-bi4-tù* KBo. 9, 9 r. 7 "so that I need not be worried about you'; s. also VS 26, 71: 7; kt n/k 1377: 22 (Gökçek 2017, 41); AKT 3, 67: 19.
4. OA uncertain: (I will no longer keep sending you textiles) *ša i-kà-bu-tù* CCT 3, 23b: 5 "that are heavy" (*ikabbitūni* expected).
5. OB *ik-bi-us-sú-um-ma dullašu* RB 59 = Fs. Reiner 190: 5 "his toil became too heavy for him".
6. Var. *kabādu*: OB *biltum ik-ta-ab-da-an-né-ši-[im]* ARM 27, 37: 47 "the load has become too heavy for us".
7. SB *ša nešmûšu ik-bi-tu* (var. [*i*]*k-bit*) *tu*[*ša*]*ptâ uznu tazquššuma ša ramānuš i*[*k-bi*]*-tú* (var. *ik-bit*) *elīšu* AfO 19, 64 iii 1-2 // BM 61649+ iii 8–9 // BM 87226: 12–13 "you allowed the ears of him who has become hard of hearing to open, you raised up him who has become a burden to himself" (Mayer 2016, 222).

D 1. OB *ammīnim panīki tu-ka-ab-bi-tim* OBTR 141: 19 "why did you make your face heavy towards me?", i.e. "become stubborn" (Mayer 2016, 222).
2. *ṣābam li-ka-bi-du-nim-ma* ARM 27, 179 no. 102: 22 "they shall heavily equip workers for me (for harvesting)", cf. *ṣābum kibittum* (MARI 5, 666). For the var. *kabādu* s. also ARM 26/1, 243 M.11371: 12 and *kabtu*.
3. OB *kalakkam elīšina u-ka-ab-bi-it* ARM 14, 18 r. 9 "I made the dug-out material heavy on them (the dams)".

+ **Dt** OA "to act honourably, in accordance with one's honour": *ṣuḫārtum irtibī ku-ta-bi4-it-ma alkamma ana sūn* DN *šukušši* BIN 4, 9: 21 "the girl has grown up: act in accordance with your honor, (i.e.) come here and place her on DN's lap" (not Dtn, because intrans.).

MPS (G, D), JW (G, D), NJCK (G, Dt)

+ **kab/pa'u,** + *kipa'u* "canebrake"; MB Emar

1. [SA]G.KI 2.KÁM.MA *ki-pa-ú* Emar 6/3, 147: 13 "the second front side: the reed marsh".

2. Pentiuc 2001, 104.

kabbartu "part of the foot or leg; hock"

MB Emar uzu*ka-bar-tum ana ēnti* DN Emar 6/3, 369: 57 "the hock to the *ēntu*-priestess of DN". S. Emar 6/3, 370: 36; 446: 33. S. Pentiuc 2001, 93.

+ **kabbāru** "a type of copper ingot"; OA

šulūšā'um ana kà-ba-ri-im Anatolica 12, 131 Ka 435: 6 "(they offer (to pay) a rate of) three (units of wool) for (one) *k*.". S. Donbaz and Veenhof 1985, 131–34; Dercksen 1996, 58f. for translation and disc. Cf. OB *g/kubāru*, also a type of ingot. NJCK/JW

+ **kabbā'u** "seamster"; OB

ka-ba-ú inaddûninnima ittallakū AbB 10, 41 r. 35 "(send the garments to PNN). The seamsters will abandon me and walk away" (reading after von Soden 1986, 473).

kabbilu s. *qabbilu*

kabbu "burning"

Lex. *anqullum* = MIN (*šāru*) *kab-bu* AOAT 50, 373: 191A (malku) "heat" = "burning wind"; s. *an-qú-ul* = *šāru ka-ab-bu* RA 17, 185: 17 (Hrůša 2010, 236).

kabilli s. *qawili*

kābilu s. *qabbilu*

+ **kabilukku** "a dish or fruit"; NA

1 BÁN *ka*!-*bi-lu-ki* SAA 11, 28: 8 "1 seah of *k*." (between wine and fig cakes).

+ **kab/pkurru** "metal part of a wheel"; OB

1. OB (bronze and tin) *ana sappī kakkī ka-aB-ku-ur-ri ša* 2 *magarrī* GAL ARM 25, 693: 15 (= ARM 32 p. 272) "for *s*., pegs, and *k*. for 2 large wheels", sim. ARM 22, 203+ ii 40 (= ARM 32 p. 277f.)

2. Separated from OAkk *kab/pkūru* on semantic grounds, cf. Arkhipov 2012, 156.

kab/pkūru, + *kabkullu*? "a container"

Lex. kuš*káb-ku*[*l*] = ŠU-*lum* (= *kabkul*(*l*)*um*) MSL 7 p. 133 with M. Civil *apud* Steinkeller 1991. Perhaps Presarg. and Sarg. (giš)NAG.KUD/KU/KUL, read *káb-kud*(*r*)/*ku*/*kul* (Steinkeller ib. with refs.). S. also *kab/pkurru*.

kablu "leg of a piece of furniture"; + OA

1. OA *kà-ab-lu* (of a table) AKT 3, 66: 35.

2. OB of table: *ka-ab-la-tu-šu* FM 8, 46 no. 6: 11, s. *kamiššaru*.

3. Cf. Ebla *ga-bí-lum* MEE 2, 23: 2 (decorative element on a vessel, s. Pasquali 2005, 128).

+ **KaBrānu** "mng. unkn."; OA

1. (if PN comes back to PNf, he has to pay five minas of silver) *u šu'āti ina GA-ÁB-ra-nim idukkūšu* Veenhof 2018a, 39 kt 89/k 345: 14 "and/or they will kill him in..." (also ib. 19, in a marriage contract, corresponding to *ina i-DÍ-nim* in the same phrase in other texts). S. Veenhof ib.: "Several Anatolian contracts stipulate alongside (or as substitute for?) a monetary fine the death penalty for breaking a promise of non-vindication."

2. Prob. also *i-GA-ÁB-ra-n*[*im*!] OIP 27, 19A: 16 in the same clause. NJCK

kabru "thick"

1. OA also of textiles: Prag 487: 5, s. *garzu*.

2. LB 4 *ka-ba-ri* (followed by dates and wood) AOAT 414/1, 69: 4 "4 fattened (sheep?)".

S. also *kapru*.

kabrūtu "thickness(?)"

Lex. [...]-⌜*a*⌝ = *kab-ru-tum* MSL 11, 87: 292. Read perhaps *kaprūtu* "a (salpeter-based) cleaning product", < *kapāru* II "to wipe clean" (Butz 1984, 306f.). The word appears between *kasû*-mustard and salt.

kabsu "young (male) sheep"; + OB

1. OB ^{udu}*ka-ab-si qallūtim* AbB 9, 162: 12 "small young sheep".

2. NA *ana mīnimma*! PN *ēpuš muk amēlu kab-su raddīʾu šū* SAA 16, 5: 6 "why did PN do it? I say: The man is a sheep, a follower".

3. Cherry 2017, 291f.: not an Aram. lw. in Akk.

kabtu, + *kabdu* "heavy"

1. OA *ana barīte šarrē kà-áb-tù-tim niʾāti mīnam ṭaḫḫuʾātunu* 01/k 217: 48 "what business do you (merchants) have among us, mighty kings?" (s. Günbattı 2014, 90).

2. Var. *kabdu*: OB *ka-ab-di-im* ARM 33, 346 n. 154: 59, s. *qaqqadu*.

3. Lex. KAB = *kab-tum* Emar 6/4, 537: 735 (Sa), Sjöberg 1998, 277.

NJCK (1), JW (2–3)

kabû I "dung"; + OA

1. OA *nēmalam šuʾāti* DN *u* DN2 *a-kà-bi-im lidīšū* CCT 6, 14: 51 "may DN and DN2 trample that profit into dung!" (Veenhof 2008a, 83 n. 348).

2. OB *šurīpa*[*m*] *lipaḫḫirū ina iṣṣim ka-bi-i u šittam* ⌜*damq*⌝*iš limsû* ARM 1, 21 r. 14 "they shall gather ice. Using wood they shall clean (it) of dung and faeces" (Mayer 2016, 223).

3. OB *aššum ka-bi-i u* [*s*]*umuktim ša arḫātim* OBTR 327: 4 "concerning cow dung and waste" (Mayer 2016, 223).

4. NB *ka-bé-e-šú-nu iḫaššalū inappûma ana libbi aḫāmiš usammaḫūma iṭennūma ippû ikkalū* ABL 1000: 9 (AOAT 242, 292) "they crush (wild donkeys') dung, sieve it, mix it together, grind it, bake it, and eat it" (said of foreign tribes, s. Mayer 2016, 223 + n. 10).

5. SB [...] ⌜*kī*⌝ *labūku ka-bé-e kī lā risni ša ašlākī* JSS 4, 10 (LKA 92): 10 "(the smell of cattle) [...] like (something) steeped in dung, like it has not been soaked by the fuller". Diff. Lambert ib. and 1975, 123: "like something not mended by the tailor", connecting it with *mukabbû*. S. Mayer 2016, 224.

NJCK (1), JW (2–5)

kabû II "pod"

In UET 5, 590: 10 (s. CAD K 29) read *ka-b/pu-ú ma-li*! *qú-lu-p*[*u*] "pods, as many as are peeled" (von Soden 1975, 460).

****kabû B** (CAD K 29)

ARM 1, 21 r. 14) belongs to *kabû* I (von Soden 1975, 460).

****kābû** "mng. unkn." (CAD K 29)

In Aa II/7 iv 10' (AO 3930, in CAD erroneously II/8) read *ka-a* : *ṣa-a-pu* (MSL 14, 298). The ref. iii 41' given in CAD is a mistake. FJMS

kabūtu "dung"

1. OB lit. *ka-bu-ut alpim* CUSAS 10, 12: 17 "ox dung".

2. OB *šumma aḫi Purattim gulgullātim lā umallī u ka-bu-ut sisî* ⌜*mala*⌝ *qanê lā ušzīz* AbB 13, 60: 12 "I will (surely) fill the Euphrates with skulls and I will (surely) let the horse dung rise up as high as the reeds" (Edzard 1974, 125; Mayer 2016, 223).

3. SB *liḫtī ka-bu-ut-ka* (var. *ka-bu-ut-ta-ka*) *liqmā* dG[IBIL] LKA 153 r. 18 // BMS 61: 19 (= KAL 10, 116: 77) "the god of fire shall gather up your faeces and burn them" (Mayer 2016, 223).

4. NA *ka-bu-ut alpī emārī immerē sisê ina mātišu ay ibšī* SAA 2, 2 iv 7 "may there be no more dung of oxen, asses, sheep, and horses in his land" (Mayer 2016, 223).

5. S. also *kabû*.

****kabûtu** (CAD K 29: "a part of the body of the horse") s. *kabūtu*

+ **kad-** "to speak"; Hurr. word in MB Qaṭna

kīmê : *ur-ḫu ka-ta-ša-nu-ni-ia* QS 3, 5: 45 "that he is speaking the truth", s. the comm. ib. p. 73.; cf. *ur-ḫu ka-du-uk-ku* ib. l. 57.

kadabbedû "oral paralysis, aphasia"

Schwemer 2007, 14: Correct the reading KA.DIB.BI.DA.A (Maqlû I 90 in CAD K 31a) to KA.DAB.BÉ.DA.

ka-da-bi-bu s. *dābibu*

kadādu "to rub"

D SB *ú?-ka-di-id* SpTU 2, 32 r. 4 in broken context.

kadammu "a building; dungeon(?)" + LB

1. NA 14 *ka-da-am-me* SAA 19, 156: 4 in broken context. S. *katammu*.

2. LB *ka-dam-mu* SpTU 4, 121 ii 16 in broken context.

kadānu I s. *kuddunu*

+ **kadānu II** "a plant"

SB (the *pappānu* plant bearing wool: its name is) ú*ka-da-nu* SpTU 3, 106 r. 2.

kadāru II, + *kedēru*, + *gadāru* "to be wild, goring; (of hair, clothing) to be disheveled; to bend downwards"

1. OB lit. **a)** *sinnišātu pērēte ga-ad-ra-ma* Or. 87 19 ii 4 "the women are untidy regarding (their) hair".
b) *sinništum kī zikri lubuštaša ga-ad-ra-at-ma* ib. ii 11 "the woman, like a man, her dress is untidy".

2. SB **a)** *šumma* KI.MIN *ana maḫrišu/ arkišu ke-di-ir* SpTU 2, 35: 4f. "if ditto (i.e., when Marduk sits down in Esangil) he is declined forward/ backwards".
b) *šumma* KI.MIN *ina aṣîšu ana imittišu/šumēlišu/maḫrišu/ana arkišu ke-di-ir* ib. 29–32 "if, when *ditto* (i.e. Marduk) goes out, he is declined to his right/to his left/forward/backwards".
c) Sallaberger 2000, 235: *k.* is frequently said of aurochsen, whose attack stance is characterized by the lowering of the head – AHw.'s "sich aufbäumen" is therefore inaccurate, as it denotes the opposite movement. When said of images and objects, *k.* should therefore be understood as "to bend forward or downward".

kadaššu "celebration"

OB lit. *ištanaḫḫiṭā ka-da-aš-ša-am* YOS 11, 92: 11 "(the girls) keep twirling in celebration".

kadāšu (AHw. 419, CAD K 31) s. *kadaššu*

+ **kadītu** "an implement"; LB

1 *ka-di-tum* CT 55, 216: 5.

kadrāyītu "aggressive"

S. CAD K 32 **kadriu* "an epithet of Ištar", BAM 3, 237 i 19'. Rather than to derive from *kadrû* "bribe" (Edzard 1974, 125), the word belongs to *kadāru*.

****kadriu** (CAD K 32) s. *kadrāyītu*

kad/trû, + *ked/trû* "greeting gift"

1. OB lit. *bāb⸢iš ina⸣ ke-ed-⸢ri⸣-im lušīl* CunMon. 8, 110: 5 "I will rejoice at the gate with a gift of greeting".

2. OB lit. *luddinma ke-ed-ri-a-am* UET 6/2, 395 r. 16 "I shall give a gift".

kādu I "watch, outpost"; + OB

ina nawêm ḫibram u ka-di ul nīšū Durand 1992, 118: 37 "we have neither a (nomadic) group nor outposts in the steppe". Earlier disc. with further lit.: Streck 2000, 101.

\+ **KāDu II**, *KaDDu*? "a small object"; OA

2 *Ga-De*$_8$*-en*$_6$ kt c/k 399: 9 (s. Dercksen 2015a, 51); 4 *GA-ḪI* kt c/k 441: 39 (ib. 54). A small object mentioned in lists of expenses among other poorly known items such as *dulbātum*, *saḫertum* and *ZiBārātum*. NJCK

kā/adû? "a profession(?)"

OB lex. *lú* ḪI-*ak* = *ka-⸢du⸣-ú* MSL 12, 205: 27.Cf. *lú* UD-*a* (= *ḫád*?)-*ak* = *ka-du-ú* MSL 12, 160: 72, already cited in CAD K 35. Cf. *lú* ḪI-*a-ak* = *mu-zi-bu* MSL 12, 205: 29 (AHw. 1576).

kâdu I "to be distressed(?)"

D 1. OB **a)** Lex. *te-te-ḫé* = *mu-ki-du* (after *mu-re-šu-um* "slanderer") ZA 94, 230 ii 7 "molester". **b)** *lillum mu-ki-id bēli emūqi* ib. 231 v 7 "the fool is a molester of the mighty one".

2. OB *aganna* 1 *awīlum ina libbišunu ša ú-ka-du-šu ulūma e-bé-el-⸢lu*!?⸣/<*lu*>-⸢*šu*⸣ ⸢*awīlum šū liqbī* ARM 27, 116: 18 "now then, a single man amongst them whom I am molesting or oppressing, let that man speak".

3. S. CAD K 35 *kâdu* B.

kâdu II "to take into custody"; + NB

G NB *mannu kī* ⸢*i*⸣*-kud-da-*⸢*áš-šum*⸣*-ma tašapparamma* OIP 114, 2: 18 "you shall send somebody who will take him into custody".

****Gt** s. Streck 2003a, 77.

kagallu, *kigallu* "a kind of waste land"

Lex. *ki-ga*[*l*]*-lu*/*la* = MIN (*erṣetu ša mērešti*) AOAT 50, 330: 22 (malku) "waste land = agricultural land".

kaḫšu "a chair"; EA; NWSem. lw.(?)

In EA 120: 18 read 1 [G]U.ZA *ka-aḫ-šu* (cf. CAD K 36 s.v., s. Borger 1975, 71a; Moran 1992, 199 n. 8). Ugar. *kḥṯ* is perhaps borrowed from Hurr. *ke/išḫe/i*, the etym. of which is disputed (s. Richter 2012, 216f. for bibliogr.).

\+ **kāʾilu** "a musician(?)"; OB

1. DUMU^{meš} NAR$^{⸢\text{meš}⸣}$ [...] *a*[*št*]*alû u* ^{lú}*ka-i-lu* DN FM 9, 246 no. 63 r. 3 "the musicians [...] the *aštalû*-musicians and the *k.* of DN".

2. *ka*!*-i-li* ARM 1, 13: 31 and *ka-i*!-[*li*?] ib. 34, both in broken context.

3. The suggestion that *k.* is a variant of *kalû* "lamentation priest" (Durand 1997, 27; id./Guichard 1997, 63; Ziegler 2007, 65) is difficult on morphological grounds.

kaʾiššu s. *g/kaʾiššu*

kajj- s. *kayy-*

kakardinnu, *karkadinnu* "victualler; confectioner"; + OA

1. OA PN *kà-kà-ar-dí-nu-um* Prag 496: 17.

2. *taqrībatam ša kà-kà-ar-dí-nim* "the *taqrībatu*-ritual(?) of/for the victualler" kt 87/k 178: 7 (unpubl., court. K. Hecker).

3. MA PN ^{lú}*ka-kar-*⸢*di*⸣*-nu* MARV 3, 49: 8, as recipient of honey.

4. NA 12 ^{lú}*kar-*⸢*ka*⸣*-di-ni* SAA 5, 215: 17 (in list of craftsmen, followed by bakers and cooks).

5. NA ^{lú}*kar-ka-din* SAA 12, 83 r. 3 (between brewer and cupbearer).

6. Jakob 2003, 395–398 with add. MA refs.; Richter 2012, 180 (possibly Sem. *kkr* + Hurr. *-tennu*).

JW (1, 4, 6), NJCK (2), MPS (3, 5)

kakdâ, *qaqdâ* "constantly"; + OB

OB lit. *Ga-aG-da-am* Lambert 1989, 325: 27 (broken context), s. the comm. ib. 333: "Its etymology is unknown since first-millennium writings begin variously *ga-*, *ka-* and *qa-*. A form *qaqda* derived from *qaqqadu* is unlikely in view of the writing here when compared with *ka-aq-qá-ra* in 24 above."

kakikku s. *kakkikku*

kakkikku "an official"; OB

Syll. spelling: ^{lú}*ka-ak-ki-ki-i*[*m*] NABU 1992/122 A.3357: 10.

kakkabānu, *kabkabānu* "starlike; a bird"

1. OA PN *kà-áb-kà-ba-nu-um* AKT 8, 70: 24 "PN the starlike" (*līmu* REL 74, s. Veenhof 2003, 25).

2. NA [1]00 *kak-kab-nat issi*! *kirrute*! SAA 7, 148 iii 12 "[1]00 *k.* birds from the *kirratu* vessel".

3. NA 5 *kak-kab-nat naptune*! SAA 7, 149 ii 7 "5 *k.* birds for the meal".

4. NA 5 *kak-ka-*⸢*ba*!*-nat*?⸣^{mušen} *ša* PN *masenne* SAA 7, 172: 4 (= ADD 1020 in CAD K 44 *k.* a) "5 *k.* birds of PN, the treasurer".

5. NA 2 *kak-kab-nat*^{mušen} SAA 7, 160: 3 (= ADD 1087 in CAD K 44 *k.* a).

NJCK (1), MPS (2–5)

kakkabtu "star (symbol)"; + OB

1. OB lit. [x *ka*]*-ak-ka-ab-ti-ša talappatamma* [*ša*l]*ā*⸢*šīšu*⸣ *kī'am taqabbī* [*kakk*]*ab kakka*[*b*] *šinnī marṣat* AML 47: 34 "you touch the [...] of her star symbol and you say three times: 'Star, star, my tooth is sick'".

2. NA *kak-kab-tú ša ḫurāṣi* SAA 9, 11: 7 (s. also 11) "golden star".

kakkabu, + *qakkabu*? "star"

1. OA 17 *kà-ku-bu-ú ša kaspim* kt c/k 18: 45 "17 stars of silver" (in a list of precious objects, s. Dercksen 2015b, 39).

2. OA as an epithet of Ištar, s. also AKT 6C, 526: 15; 11A, 163: 4.

3. OB lit. *aṣbat pī ka-ka-bi* AML 84: 1 "I seized the mouth of the stars" (referring to the constellation scorpio in an incantation against scorpions?).

4. OB lit. [*ka-ak-k*]*a-ab ka-ak-ka-a*[*b*] AML 47: 36, s. *kakkabtu*.

5. OB *qa-ka-ba-at kaspim u ḫurāṣim* A.2576: 5 "stars of silver and gold" (Charpin 1989–90, 94). S. Arkhipov 2012, 46f. for add. refs.

NJCK (1–2), MPS (4), JW (5)

kakkallu s. *qalqālu*

kakkartu "round loaf of bread; a metal ingot", + OA

1. OA 5 *kà-kà-ra-tum* 57 MA.NA *šuqultum* AKT 2, 59: 9 "5 *k.* weighing 57 minas"; s. ib. 1; Prag 482 r. 5; CCT 6, 19b: 27. S. Dercksen 1996, 59.

2. OB *ka-ka-a[r-tum]* ARM 21, 258: 33 "(2 talents and 29 1/2 minas of copper) in ingots".

3. MB Emar ${}^{\text{ninda}}$*ka-ak-kar-tum* Emar 6/4, 560: 90.

4. S. also *kakkaru.* NJCK (1), JW (1–3)

kakkaru, + *kaqqaru* ,+ *kikkiru*?, "talent; a bread"

1. OB URUDU *ša* 1 ⌜GÚ *ka*⌝-*ka-ri* (or 1 ${}^{\text{gú}}$*ka-*) FM 8, 164 no. 47 r. 5 "copper (in the weight) of a disk of 1 talent". S. Durand ib. p. 166.

2. Early OB Mari *kikkiru* (Limet 1976, 165 n. 11):
a) 5 BÁN ŠE *ki-kir* ARM 19, 378: 2 "50 liters of barley (for) *k.*".
b) 1 A.GÀR 3 GUR 8 SÌLA Š[E] *ki-kir* ARM 19, 379: 2 "1568 liters of barley (for) *k.*".
c) *ki-kir* [...] ARM 19, 380: 3 (in broken context).

3. MB Emar "talent": *ka-qa-rum* GUŠKIN *ša* PN Emar 6/3, 59: 1 "(1) talent of gold from PN".

4. MB Emar "a bread": *zarḫa ana* ${}^{\text{ninda.meš}}$*ka-ak-ka-ri* Emar 6/3, 387: 5 "*z.*-flour for *k.*"; s. also Emar 6/3, 393: 25, 434: 8; 436: 12. ${}^{\text{ninda}}$*ka-ka-ru* TUR Emar 6/3, 460: 21 "small *k.*"

5. Likely NWSem. lw. (Huehnergard 1987, 136). S. Pentiuc 2001, 91. Cf. Hurr. *gaḫari*-and *kakkari* (Richter 2012, 179f.). S. also *kakkartu*.

kakkassu s. *kakkussu*

****kakilu** (CAD K 44) "a bird" s. *kurmadillu*

kakkišu "weasel?"

NA pl. [*ka-ki*]*š-a-ti* (in broken context) SAA 9, 4: 3.

kakku "stick; weapon, mace"

1. OB lex.:
a) ${}^{\text{giš}}$*tukul-sík-ĝu*$_{10}$ = *ka-ak-ki pērtiya* CUSAS 12 p. 154 ii 3 (Ugumu) "bun(?) of my hair".
b) ${}^{\text{giš}}$*tukul zú-ĝu*$_{10}$ = *ka-ak-*⌜*ki*⌝ *šinniya* ib. 155 v 11 "my canine tooth".

2. OA lit. *kakka nadānu*: *ana* 70 *ālānī kà-kà-am a-dí-in* OA Sarg. 9 "I waged war with 70 cities".

3. OA *mīššu ša kīma awīlim raggim kà-ku-šu ilqē'uma a*–GN *ittalku* LB 1206: 7 (unpubl., court. K. R. Veenhof) "why has he taken his weapon like an evil man and gone to GN?"; sim. TC 3, 25: 18.

4. "mace" in lists of (precious) objects: OA 5 *kà-ku-ú* AKT 6B, 468: 9 "5 maces" (inventory of a chapel, s. Barjamovic/Larsen 2008, 153f.); s. also kt c/k 18: 46 (Dercksen 2015b, 39).

5. OA *ana kà-ki-im qadēšuma ušteneṣ-ṣûni'āti(-ma)* Çeçen 2002, 67 kt 92/k 526: 13 "they are trying to make us go out with him (the ruler) for fighting".

6. *rabī k.* "overseer of the weapons": OA PN *rabī kà-ki-im* AKT 10, 54A: 4; BIN 4, 163: 4; TC 3, 158: 9.

7. NA PN *bēl k.*: EN-TUKUL-KUR-*u-a* BATSH 6/2, 53 r. 5; 54 r. 7; 60 r. 8"; 145 r. 14"; EN-TUKUL-*ša*!-*du-ú-*(*a*) 55 r. 17 "the lord of the weapon is my mountain".

8. *ša k.*: OA PN *ša* ${}^{\text{giš}}$GAG-*ki* kt 92/k 193: 37 (= KEL A) // *ša kà-ki*! kt 91/k 555: 26 (= KEL B) // *ša* GAG-*im* kt n/k 517+1571: 41 (= KEL D), s. Veenhof

2003, 10 and 26 "the one (in charge?) of the weapon(s)"; s. also AKT 11A, 153: 5.

9. For OB refs. s. Arkhipov 2012, 110–112.

S. also *kaksappu.*

MPS (1–2), NJCK (2–6, 8), JK (7)

kakkû "lentil(s)"; + OA; + MA

1. OA lit. *kakkā'um*: *addīšim kà-kà-a-am lā abārašši* kt 90/k 178: 29 "I threw lentil(s) at her but I did not catch her" (incant., s. Michel 2004b, 398). Pace Michel *kakkā'am* rather than *kakkam* "weapon", cf. the sequel: "I threw beer bread, thyme and salt at her".

2. MA ^{šim}*ka-ak-⸢ku⸣* StAT 5, 47: 6.

NJCK (1), JW (2)

kakkullu, *qaqqullu*, + *kukkallu*(?), + *kukkullu* "mash-tub, a wooden container"

1. OB *šaman rēštim daqqāt qa-qú-ul-lim* AbB 2, 87: 28 "first-rate oil, small amounts left over from the *q*.-vessel"; cf. Bottéro 1965, 378 (*kak*!-*ku-ul-lim*).

2. OB Alal. var. *kukkallu*?: 1 *kāsum* KÙ.BABBAR *ku-uk-ka-al-li* AlT 366: 4 "1 silver cup (of) *k*.-type".

3. *kukkullu*: **a)** MA in personnel lists "quiver(?)" or "container of sling-stones(?)" and its carrier: PN *ku-ku-lu* BATSH 18, 58: 8, 18, 20; 74 r. 13, 15f., 22; 75: 20f.; PN *ku-kúl-lu* BATSH 18, 74 r. 35; 76: 6 and pass.; Chuera 71: 11; PN *ša ku-kúl-⸢li⸣* Chuera 70: 11, 23, 55; VS 2 1, 6 pass. (s. Freydank 1980, 103f. and n. 19); ⸢*ša*⸣ ^{giš}⸢*ku-ku-li*⸣ KAM 7, 8: 6. For add. refs. s. BATSH 18, 246 n. 883. S. Postgate 2008, 87; Jakob 2009, 101.

b) NA 2 ^{giš}*ku-kul*?-*u ḫaḫḫī* SAA 11, 85: 4 "two *k*.-containers with plums".

4. NA uncert.: *qu-qu-la-tum* SAA 7, 180: 4 (in broken context).

5. Pace AHw., there is no need to separate *kakkullu* I "Maischbottich" and *kakkullu* II "Früchte-, Abfallkorb", s. Sallaberger 1996, 85–87. S. also *kakkultu.*

kakkultu "mash-tub"; OB, MB, SB

OB *k.* (*īni*) "iris": … = *kak-kúl-la-tum* UET 7, 93: 42, followed by *šapiltu* and *tē'u īni*, both designating parts of the eye.

kakkusakku s. *kakkušakku*

kakkussu, *kakkūsu*, *kakkassu* "a domesticated plant"; + OA; + OB

1. OA lit. uncert.: *adī Ga-Ku-Za-am u pitiltam a-na-⸢dí-ú-ki⸣-ni lā tappaššerī* kt 91/k 502: 12 "until I put a ... and a string on you, you shall not come loose(?)" (incantation, s. Kouwenberg, 2018–19). The addressee is a *diqāru*, a pot or vessel, hence this *Ga-Ku-Za-am* may be a different word referring to a kind of lid or stopper.

2. OB (n) *ka-ka*!-*sà-tum ša ana* GN *buṭumtašin*[*a*] *ibbabla* Stol 1979, 22 A.5861: 4 "(n) *k*., the green seed of which was brought to GN".

NJCK (1), JW (2)

kakkušakku "a medicinal plant; a stone"

SB [$^{\text{na}_4}$]*kak-ku-šak-ku* KAL 9, 37 iv 30 (among stones used to make a magic charm).

kakmû "from Kakmu"

1. OB *ṣubātum Zuḫû ka-ak-mu* SAG AWTL 94: 1, 3 "*Zuḫû*-garment in the *Kakmu*-style of best quality".

2. OB [*i*]*na qabê manni ka-ak-mi-a-am ana bīt napṭarišu tanaddī* ... *ka-ak-me-a-am ana bītišu tanaddī* ... *ka-ak-me-a-*

am ša bītišu šūṣī CUSAS 15, 1: 6 – r. 4 "by whose order are you throwing the Kakmean into his (= my lords) guest house? (I have shown you my lord's sealed tablet, and yet) you throw the Kakmean into his house! … Evict the Kakmean from his house!".

+ **kaksappu** "(part of) a weapon"; OB

1. 1 *ka-ak-sà-pu* ARM 25, 33 (= ARM 32, 325 M.10710): 1 (made of silver); ARM 21, 430: 1.

2. Derived from a genitive construction: *ka-ak*(-)*sà-pí* ARM 31, 72: 16 and ^{giš}TUKUL *sà-ap-*[*pí*] ARM 32, 478 M.12597 r. 8 (s. *sappu* "a lance"),

3. S. Arkhipov 2012, 112f. Perhaps "spearhead".

kalakku I, + *kulukku* "excavation, silo, storeroom, box"

1. Cold storage for ice:

a) OB *ka-la-ka-tim-m*[*a*] FM 2, 140 no. 76: 18, s. *kaṣāru* G.

b) ⸢*ina ka-la-ka*⸣-[*tim*] *ša mê umallû*! 3 A.GÀR *šurīpam upaḫḫi*[*r*] ib. 12 "in the (cold) stor[es] that I had filled with water I collected 3 *ugār* (ca. 3600 l) of ice".

2. Astronomically: SB *ina pan ka-lak-ku ša Pabil* SpTU 4, 171: 8 "in front of the quiver(?) of P. (Sagittarius)"; 3 KÙŠ *elât ka-lak-ku* ib. 12 "3 cubits above the quiver(?)"; *elât ka-lak-ku ša Pabil* ib. 14 "above the quiver(?) of P."

3. NB *ṣidītu ana ku-lu-ku-šú attadu* OIP 114, 78: 15 "I poured travel provisions in his box".

kalakku II "raft, kelek"; + NB

NB [*lū*] *quppu lū ka-lak-ki* SAA 18, 106: 7 "[either] a guffa or a kelek".

kalāma "all, everything"

Delete ref. BBSt. No. 35: 6 in CAD K 65 (Borger 1975, 71a).

kalammu "part of a chariot(?)"; MA

1. 20 NÍG.LAL *ša* NA$_{4}^{\text{meš}}$ *ša ka-lam-me* StAT 5, 3: 20, 21 "20 bindings of stone of the *k*.", s. ib. p. 18.

2. 2 NA$_{4}$^{meš} ⸢*ša*⸣ *ka-lam-me* […] StAT 5, 6: 5 "2 stones of the *k*."

kalappu, *kalabbu*, + *kalbatu* "pickaxe"

1. OA add. refs.: Prag 625: 7; AKT 5, 17: 10; kt 88/k 310: 17 (Bayram 2016, 19); kt 88/k 972: 17 (Donbaz 2008, 219).

2. MB Emar 1 *ka-*⸢*al*⸣*-ba-tum* URUDU RE 69: 11 "1 copper pickaxe", between "1 cart" and "1 copper axe". The mng. is suggested by the context. The word is otherwise masc. in sg. with a fem. pl. Beckman (ib.) translates "copper bitch".

3. NA *ḫursān lallik* $^{\text{an.bar}}$*ka-la*!*-pu lantuḫ*! SAA 21, 15: 11 "I will go to the ordeal and lift the pickaxe".

NJCK (1), JW (2), MPS (3)

kalbānātu "(part of) a siege engine, grapnel(?)"

1. Lex. *k*[*a*]*l-ba-na-tum* = *nabalkattu* AOAT 50, 361: 34 (malku) "grapnel (?) = scaling ladder". S. Hrůša ib. p. 228.

2. OB *simmiltam u k*[*a-a*]*l-ba-na-tam* FM 1 p. 82: 42 "ladder and grapple(?)".

3. MA *kal-ba-na-ta aṣûta šeḫīta ekimta* KAL 12, 32: 5 "grapple(?), departure, *šeḫīta*, taken away" (fragment of a war ritual?, s. Schaudig ib. p. 69).

kalbāniš, + *kalbānī* "like a dog"

⸢*ka-al-ba*⸣-[*n*]*i-i*[*š*] AML 119: 87; *ka-al-ba-ni* AML 116: 3.

kalbatu "bitch"

1. OA in *rabī kalbātim* "overseer of the bitches" (as hunting dogs?): *maḫar* PN *rabī kà-al-ba-tim* AKT 3, 41: 18 "before PN, the overseer of the bitches"; s. also Chantre 2: 22'; kt c/k 1641: 17 (Albayrak 2005, 98); kt g/t 36: 8, 10, 12 (Bilgiç 1964, 148). S. Veenhof 2008a, 221.

2. OB lit. *ka-al-ba-tam uššar* CUSAS 10, 10: 43 "I will let the bitch go" (said of a woman).

3. MB Emar, uncert. (*Flurname?*): *eqel mērešu ina nārān ina ka-al-ba-ti* AulaOr (Suppl.) 55: 1 "farmland in between the rivers, in/among *k.*" Arnaud 1991, 11 interprets the word as *qalbātu* "well" (cf. Arab. *qalībun*).

NJCK (1), MPS (2), JW (3)

kalbu "dog"

1. OA as an epithet or a nickname: *kunuk* PN *kà-al-bi₄-im* AKT 6B, 492: 5 "seal of PN, the 'dog'"; referring to the same person also in kt m/k 148: 18 (Hecker 2004a, 65), kt c/k 515: 8 and 678: 2 (court. J. G. Dercksen).

2. OB *kalab Šamaš* (CAD K 62, AHw. 425 *kalbu* 8d): *ur-me* = *k*[*a-l*]*a-ab* ^{d}UTU UET 7, 93: 37. S. Sjöberg 1996, 228.

3. SB *ka-lab-*^{d}KIN.SIG Fs. Lambert, 169 no. 15: 22, perhaps an insect.

4. NB *anāku kal-bi pāliḫi* SAA 18, 71 r. 13 "I am a fearsome dog".

NJCK (1), MPS (2, 4), JW (3)

kalgukkû, + *kalkukku* "a mineral, a lead-based yellow colorant" red ochre"; + OB

1. OB *aššum ka-al-gu-uk-ki-im gabîm u liqtim* ARM 18, 15: 5 "concerning the *k.-mineral*, *gabû*-alum and *liqtu*-alum."

2. OB 4 MA.NA *ka-al-gu-uk-ki-im* ARM 22, 259: 4 "4 minas of *k.*-mineral".

3. OB 1 MA.NA *ka-al-gu-ku ana šipir narkabtim rēštîm* ARM 23, 188 no. 208: 1 "1 mina of *k.*-mineral for work on a first-quality chariot"; cf. 209: 1, 210: 1, 211: 1.

4. OB *aššum annu*[*ḫa*]*ri aššum gabî aššum ka-al-*[*gu*]*-uk-ki* Fs. Birot, 98 no. 1: 7 "concerning *annuḫaru*-alum, concerning *gabû*-alum, concerning *k.*-mineral" (memorandum).

5. OB *ka-al-ku-uk-ki-im* Fs. De Meyer, 270: 6, 8 (s. *kalû* IV).

6. On the mng. "a lead-based yellow colorant" s. Thavapalan 2020, 342–346.

JW (1–5), FJMS (6)

kalītu "kidney"

1. OB lex. *ellag gùn-ba-ra-ĝu₁₀* = *ka-li-it birkīya* CUSAS 12, 157 ix 10 (Ugumu) "my testicles = kidneys of my knees/lap".

2. OB lex. *ellag gùn-šà-ga-ĝu₁₀* = *ka-li-it libbiya* ib. 11 "my kidney".

+ **kallâm** "quickly, promptly"; OB

1. PN *ka-al-la-a-am ana ṣērika išpuran-nêti* Fs. von Soden, 52 A.2435: 13 "PN sent us promptly to you".

2. (*tuppam*) PN *ka-al-*[*lam*] *ana ṣēriya ušābilaš*[*šu*] ARM 3, 68: 19 "PN had (the tablet) promptly sent to me".

3. *ka-al-la-a-am ana ṣēr bēliya awīlē šunūti šurrī* ARM 14, 105: 19 "bring these men to my lord, quickly". S. also ARM 18, 8: 18 and ARM 33, 101: 33.

4. Charpin 1994: Most Mari refs. cit. s.v. AHw./CAD s.v. *kallû* are adverbial. Apparently < *kalla-am* with adverbial acc. ending (but s. final *-i* in NA *kalliʾu*).

kallamāre, + *kannamāre* (MA), + *kalla-nāri* (NA) "early in the morning"

1. MA **a)** *ka-na-ma-ri arḫiš lublūni* Chuera 1: 6 "they must quickly bring (them) in the early morning".
b) *ūma ka-an-na-ma-ri lillik* Chuera 5: 6 "he shall go the same day, in the early morning".
c) *ka-na-ma-ri šamma [ikkulū]* BVW A 8, Ab: 7 "[they will eat] grass at dawn" cf. D 5; M+N r. 5. cf. H 2.

2. NA *ka-[l]a-na-ri-šú* SAA 15, 6: 7; *kal-la-ma-a-re* SAA 13, 88 r. 6, 100: r. 9; *ka-la-ma-re* SAA 5, 243 r. 14.

3. Etym. likely < *kal-* + *namāri*, lit. "entire (time of) shining", cf. *kal ūme*, *kal mūše* (Streck 2017, 598–9; de Ridder 2018 §491).

kallanāri s. *kallamāre*

kallāp/bu "foot soldier, auxiliary troops"

1. NA pl. fem.: 80 ^{lú}*kal-ba-*⸢*te*⸣ SAA 5, 215: 20.

2. *rab k.*: NA ^{lú}GAL KAL!-*bi* Orient 29, 120 no. 8: 3 (seal legend); ^{lú}GAL-*kal-lap* BATSH 6/2, 127 r. 3; 127 r. 9.

3. NA pl. (PNN) *kal-la-pa-nu* BATSH 6/2, 121 r. 6.

4. Borrowed into Aram. as *klbʾ* (Fales 1987, 469). On mng. (infantry rather than a type of courier or dispatch rider) s. Postgate 2000a, 104.

MPS (1), JW (2, disc.), JK (2, 3)

kallatu "bride, daughter in law"

1. OB ^{f}*ka-al-*⸢*la-tam ana māriya*⸣ *ušērib* FM 2, 76 no. 40: 6 "I made a bride enter (the house of) my son"; cf. ib. 8.

2. OB 7 *aššātum ka-la-tum* FM 4, 215 no. 36: 2 "7 wives (of the king)". Cf. Ziegler ib. p. 45f.

3. OB *ka-la-at-ni ēzib* CUSAS 36, 207: 9 "I divorced our daughter in law".

4. OB É.GI4.A *bītim* OBTIV 5: 1, 6: 1, 7: 1 "bride of the house". S. Kraus 1973, 53f.

5. OB *kallat Šamaš* "dragonfly, lit. bride of the Sungod" (AHw. 426 *kallātu* 3a; CAD K 79 as a separate lemma): *ní-dúb-dúb-bu/za-an-za-na-?* = *ka-la-at* ^{d}UTU UET 7, 93 r. 9f. S. Sjöberg 1996, 229f.

kallu "bowl"

SB ^{dug}*kal-lu ša ina šarūri šamši* SAA 3, 35: 9 "a bowl in the rays of the sun".

kallû, *kalliʾu* "express messenger, courier"; + MA

1. MA PN ^{lú}*kal-li-*⸢*ú*⸣ Chuera 58: 4.

2. With *ina/ana* "posthaste", MA:
a) *a-na kal-le-e* BATSH 4/1, 5 r. 10; 9: 34; 19 r. 4.
b) *i+na kal-le-*⸢*e*⸣ ib. 13: 14.
c) *ana ka-li-ia* StAT 5, 54: 13.

3. S. also *kallâm*.

kallūtu "status of bride, marriage"

OB lit. *sissinni ka-al-lu-tim* Or. 87, 17 i 44 "date spadix of marriage".

kalmak/qru "an adze or axe"

OB (bronze for) 1 *ka-al-ma-aK-ri* ARM 32, 223 M.7190: 4. S. Arkhipov 2012, 113.

kalmarḫu "a tree"

1. In SMN 708 r. 8 (cit. CAD K 86a) read after coll. *gal-ma-ar-ḫ[é]* (SCCNH 8, 364).

2. CAD suggested the mng. "tamarind", which is, however, more likely to be identified with *kasû* (Choukassizian Eypper 2019).

JW (1), FJMS (2)

kalmartu, + *garmartu* "a month name, a festival".

NA *nadbaku ša gar-mar-te* SAA 12, 69: 35 "expenditure for the *g.*"

kalmatu "parasite, louse"

1. OB *qēmam ... ka-al-ma-tum iltapat* ARM 14, 74: 7 "the parasites have infested the flour".

2. OB PN: *Ka-al-ma-ta-nu* JCS 23, 127: 4 (von Soden 1975, 460).

3. Lion/Michel 1997, 720–722.

+ **kaltu**, *ke/iltu*? "rival, opponent, pretender to the throne"; OB

1. *ša* PN *ward*[*ī*] [*ana k*]*a-de-e-im ana ka-al-ti-*{TI-}*ia* [*tatt*]*anaššē'am u anāku mār* PN$_2$ [*waradka*] *ša inanna maḫrīya* ⸢*waš*⸣*bu* [*ana k*]*a-al-te-ka ul attanašši*[*ku*]*m*] Fs. Larsen 99–115 (A.1215): 44, 48 "(what? Is it acceptable) that you should ceaselessly promote my servant PN against me as my *kadû* (and) my rival, while I should not keep promoting against you as your rival the son of PN$_2$, your servant, who now stays with me?" (transl. Sasson 2007, 455 n. 9, cf. Charpin/Durand 2004, who take *kadû* to mean "protect" or the like, cf. *kīdūtu.*).

2. *ana ka-al-ti-ia šiprī i*[*št*]*anappa*[*r*] *u da'atī ul iš*[*â*]*l* ARM 26/2, 71 no. 312: 23 "he keeps sending messengers to my rival but does not care about me".

3. PN *maḫar bēliy*[*a ikš*]*udanni* [*umm*]*ami* [lú]*ki-il-ti ittī* P[N$_2$ *wa*]*šib* [*an*]*āku maḫar bēliya kī'am āpulšu u*[*mmami wu*]*ddī bēli awīlī šunūti innaddinakkum u* [*bēl*]*ī ana* PN *kī'am iqbī umma*[*mi*] [...]x *aḫḫīka luterrakkum assurr*[*ri bēlī*? *ki-i*]*l-ti šunūti ana* [...] ARM 28, 53: 8, 13 "PN [cam]e to me before my lord, saying: 'My rival [st]ays with PN$_2$'. I thus answered him before my lord: '[Cer]tainly my lord will give those men to you'. And my [lo]rd thus said to PN: '[...] I will return your brothers to you'. Hopefully [my lord(?)] will [...] those ⸢rivals⸣".

4. [*a*]*mmīnim ki-il-ti ina* GN *wašib* ARM 28, 115: 36 "why is my rival staying in GN?"

5. *sarrar*[*u ... š*]*a ittī ki-il-ti-*[*ia*] *ana qaqqadiya leqîm* ⸢*illi*⸣*kūnim* RATL 112: 6 "the bandits (…) who came with my rival to take my head".

6. S. perhaps [DUMU *ka-a*]*l-ti-im* ARM 26/2, 189 no. 377: 30.

7. Charpin/Durand 2004; Sasson 2007, 455ff.; Lion 2004, 219f; Durand 2004b, 183 n. 388. S. also *kaltūtu*.

+ **kaltūtu** "rivalry"; OB

[P]N *ana ka-al-tu-ut* [P]N$_2$ *našû* ARM 28, 44: 28 "they are positioning PN as a rival (against) PN$_2$". S. *kaltu*.

kalû II "all, everything" S. *kalummû*.

kalû IV "yellow ochre"

1. OB lit. *ka-lu-um* // *ka-lu-ú panūšu* AML 51: 8; 50: 20; 60: 3 "his face is yellow-ochre paste", s. *qitmu*.

2. OB *aššum ka-li-im u kalkukkim* Fs. De Meyer, 270 (M.11050). 5 "concerning the yellow ochre and *kalkukku*-mineral".

3. Stol 1998, 347f. (yellow ochre, not orpiment). S. Thavapalan 2020, 346ff. for extensive disc..

kalû V "to hold, detain"

G *aššum nēbaḫim ka-*⸢*le-ni*⸣ CUSAS 36, 63: 6 "we are detained because of the *nēbaḫu*-payment" (*kalêni* instead of *kalênu* < *kalī-ānu*).

Gt(n) *ta-ak-/tak-te-el-lu-a-ma* AOAT 275, 226 r. ii (Streck 2003a, 68).

kālû "dam; a designation of fields"

For LB (designation of fields) s. Da Riva 2002, 88f.

+ **KalūBu,** *KalluBu*(?) "a valuable object"; OA

(thieves have entered the temple of Aššur) *mēšurum kà-lu-bu-ú zamruʾā-tum u katāpū tablū* Bab. 6, 187 no. 7: 13 "the *mēšuru*-symbol, *K.*, *zamrūtu* and *katāpu*-vessels have been taken away".

NJCK

+ **kalummû** "all, everything"; OB

[*kasp*]*um u ka-lu-um-mu-ia* ARM 26/2, 533 no. 541: 16 "silver and everything that belongs to me". Lafont (ib.), following a suggestion by Durand, proposes a new word *kalummû* "everything", and compares Nuzi *kalûmānu*. Heimpel 2003, 408 considers the form erroneous, noting the otherwise unexplained reduplicated *m*. Perhaps frozen *kalûmma* + *ū* (pl. nom.) + poss. suff.; cf. *mimmû* < *mimma* + *ū*.

+ **kalûmma** "in every respect"; OB

1. OB lit. *ka-lum-ma iššuš* FM 14 iii 10 "he was suffering in every respect".

2. *kalûm* (loc.) + *ma*, s. also *kalummû*.

kalūmtu "female lamb"

1. OB lit. ⌜*luwaʾʾir*⌝ *rēʾî* ... *arḫāti u ka-*⌜*lu-ma*⌝*-ti-im lilqûnimmi šitta ša arḫā-ti*[*m*] *u ka-lu-ma-ti* AML 120: 13, 16 "let me instruct the herders of cows and she-lambs so that they grab for me the sleep of cows and she-lambs".

2. OB lit. *aḫzā ka-lu-ma-tum maḫrīšu* AML 125: 10 "she-lambs are seized in front of him".

kalūmu "(male) lamb"

1. OB lit. *aḫzū immerū ka-lu-mu* AML 125: 9 "sheep and lambs are seized".

2. OB PN *qadū* [*k*]*a-lu-me-ka* ARM 33, 91 no. 27: 38 "PN together with your lambs".

3. MA *lalāʾū* 16? *ka-lu-mi-ia* BATSH 4/1, 12: 28 "the kids and my 16? (male) lambs".

4. LB 3 *ka-lu-mu par-rat* AOAT 414/1, 184 r. 6 "3 male (and) female lambs".

5. S. also *ḫadīru*.

MPS (1, 4), JW (2), JK (3)

kalzu "a military unit"; NA

1. [*ina*] *pan* PN *rab kiṣir šanê aptiqissu lā immaggur mā ina kal-zi-a-ma alas-su*[*m*] SAA 1, 236: 5 "I appointed him [to] the service of PN, the second cohort commander. He did not agree, saying: 'I will serve as a runner in my own unit'".

2. PN *ša ka*[*l-zi*]*-šú ša ka*[*l-zi* ⌜*nišīšu*⌝ SAA 1, 171: 9f. "PN of his *k.* unit and of the *k.* unit of his people".

3. *ša* ⌜*kal*⌝*-*[*z*]*i ittalkūni* ib. 28 "the (members) of the *k.* unit came".

4. *ana* PN *ana ša kal-zi šarru bēlī lišʾala* ib. 32 "let the king, my lord, ask PN and the (members) of the *k.* unit".

5. SAA 1 p. 216: "community".

kamādu "to beat (fabric)"; + OB

1. OB n MA.NA *šutûm* [*k*]*āmidū li-i*[*k*]*-mu-du-nim-ma* BagM 23, 186: 7 "n minas of woven textiles – the *kāmidu*-craftsmen shall beat".

2. OB *ka-ma-du-um* Lackenbacher 1982b i 29', ii 16, ii 32, and pass. A step during textile fabrication taking two days, after cleaning (*zukkû*) and needle repairs(?) (*eṣēru*), and before carding (*mašāru*).

3. NB [*i-ká*]*m-ma-du-šú-nu-ti* SAA 17, 11 r. 2 "they will beat(?) them"; *ṣubātī lik-mu-du-ú-ma* ib. r. 6.

4. The mng. "to beat (in order to soften)" (AHw.) rather than "to weave" (CAD) is supported by cognates (Arab. *kamada* "to soften (a fabric)"; Syr. *kmd* "to become flaccid") and ITT 5, 9996 (already cit. CAD K 121 s.v. *kamdu*). For possible cognates in Ebla and Ugar. s. Sanmartín 2019, 307f. The procedure in question may be a kind of felting (Lackenbacher 1982b, 141f.; Wasserman 2013, 264). S. also *kamdu*, *kimdu*, *kāmidu*.

kamālu "to become angry"

G With acc.: OB lit. [*k*]*a-mi-il-ka libbī*! ZA 110, 45 iii 64 "my heart is angry with you".

Gt SB *māt* GN *kit-mu-lat* SpTU 2, 35: 27f. "the land of GN is irascible".

kamamtu "a herb or spice"; OAkk, Ur III

1. Ur III *kà-ma-am-tum* CUSAS 3, 442: 15; 557: 6. For further refs. s. CUSAS 4, 92.

2. A spice which ceased to be used after the Ur III period (Heimpel 2009, 98 n. 64). To be distinguished from *kamantu*, s. the disc. in CAD K 109 s.v.

kamāmu "to nod, to shake the head(?); an expression of displeasure"

G OB lit. *ta-ak-ma-am* KALAM ⸢x⸣ [...] JRAS Cent. Supp. iii 7 "you nodded, the land [...]" (Lambert 1967, 103; Streck/Wasserman 2008, 347). This form shows that the verb is, pace AHw. 430, not *a*/*u*- but *a*/*a*-class.

+ **D** SB *mu-kám-mi-mu-ú-a* ORA 7, 320: 44 "those who shake the head at me".

Disc.: Mayer 2007, 132 n. 8: An expression of displeasure, perhaps "to growl, to grumble".

kamantu "a (pharmaceutical) plant"

1. SB *zēr ka-man-tú tasâk* SpTU 1, 60 r. 7 "you crush seed of the *k*. plant".

2. Del. the ref. BE 9, 99 (cit. CAD K 110), read *ka-*⸢*ra*⸣*-šú* (coll. Leichty/Zadok apud Donbaz/Stolper 1993).

3. For add. refs. s. Scurlock 2007. Her suggestion to identify *k*. with henna is not supported by the evidence (Renaut 2007).

kamānu "a cake"

1. NA 2 ^{ninda}*ka-ma-na-a-ti* SAA 12, 68 r. 11 "2 *k*.-cakes".

2. SB *ka-man teppuš libbū ka-man turatta libbi immeri* SpTU 5, 235 r. 1 "you make a cake. Into the cake, you put the heart of a sheep".

kamar(r)u, *kabar*(*r*)*u*, + *kanar*(*r*)*u* "(garden) wall"

1. OB *matī dūram luqqur matī ka-ma-ra-am lušpuk* ARM 33, 124: 13 "sometimes I need to tear down the wall, sometimes I need to pile up the rampart(?)"; 705 ÌR<^{meš}> *ana ka-ma-ri-im agmur* ib. 7 "I used up 705 slaves for (constructing) the rampart".

2. MB *ina ka*$_4$*-ma-a*[*r*(-)...] SCCNH 4, 348: 5.

3. MB *ka-na-ri* HSS 14, 5: 1.

4. Wilhelm 1985, 53; Richter 2012, 182 s.v. *kab*/*m*/*war*(*r*)*u*(*m*). AHw. *kamar-*(*r*)*u*, CAD *kamāru* A.

kamāru I, *kamarru* "snare, trap"; + OB

1. OB lit. *iṣṣūr māt lā māgirī i-ka-mar-ri išḫuḫ* RA 86, 81: 8 "the bird of the land of the disobedient wasted away in the trap".

2. in *k. šakānu*:

a) OAkk *in <a>ppārim kà-ma-ra-ma iškun* FAOS 7, 291 Fragm. C 7 ii 4 "in the marshes he set traps".

b) Early OB *kà-ma-ar-šu-n[u] išku[n]* ZA 93, 9 v 7 "he snared them", pl. *kà-ma-ri-šu iškun* ib. 8 iii 2.

c) We follow AHw. in assuming that this is a metaphor for inflicting defeat. Diff. CAD K, who assume a noun *kamāru* B "defeat". It has further been connected with *kamāru* IV "to pile up" (which is also said of bodies and ruin), s. Mayer 2016, 224.

kamāru II "defeat" s. *kamāru* I

kamāru III "a (dried?) fish"; + OA

1. OA 49 *kà-ma-ru* Prag 740: 11 and kt 92/k 241: 7 (unpubl., cit. Dercksen 2001, 44 n. 23). S. Lion/Michel 2000, 78–80. S. also *kamāru* V.

2. OB ^{ku_6}*ka-ma-ri* ... *[ā]kulma [mā]diš ina pīya ṭābū [u] inanna ana kayyān[im] ina* ^{ku_6}*ka-ma-ri* ... *ātanakkal* ARM 28, 88: 6, 10 "I have eaten the *k.* fish and they were very good in my mouth,[and] now I want to eat of the *k.* fish all the time".

3. OB ⸢3?⸣ *ka-ma-ru*^{ku_6} *ana napt[an] šarrim u [ṣā]bī* ARM 21, 90: 1 "3(?) *k.* fish for the meal of the king and the soldiers".

4. OB in Tell Leilan s. TLT p. 353f.

5. For etym. s. the disc. in Kogan/Militarev 2005, 171f. S. also *kawarḫu*.

NJCK (1), JW (2–5)

kamāru IV "to pile up, accumulate"

Gt OB lit. *lā rabī'at ki-it-mu-ra-⸢at⸣ šupassu* CUSAS 10, 1: 39 "is his dwelling not big (and) heaped up high?" S. also *kamar(r)u*.

+ **kamāru V**, *g/qamāru*? "a piece of clothing or equipment"; OA

1. *ḫurši'ānum ša kà-ma-re-e* AKT 5, 58: 7 "a box with *k.*" (alongside a saddle-cloth, ropes, pack-saddles, a sack and a box with *dulbātum*).

2. (PN is bringing you) *šakūkam u kà-ma-re* kt n/k 268: 13 "a belt and *k.*" (s. Çeçen/Gökçek 2017, 467).

3. 10 *kà-ma-re* KBo. 9, 9 r. 11 (at the end of a list of clothing and unidentified items).

4. Refs. listed under *kamāru* III might belong here as well, although the context is less clear. S. Veenhof 2010, 170.

NJCK/JW

+ **kamāsiš** "kneeling"; OB

OB lit. PN *ka-ma-s[í-i]š maḫar* DN *illakā dī[m]āšu* CUSAS 10, 2 iv 8 "PN, as he was kneeling, his tears constantly flowed before DN".

kamāsu I, *kamāṣu*, *kanāšu* "to gather"

G 1. OB *anāku ana* GN *ka-am-sa-ku* RATL 143: 19 "I (and my troops) gathered in GN".

2. LB *ki-in-ṣa-a-ma* dubsar 3, 135: 16 "gather!", cf. *kusītu*.

3. NB (silver) *ik-te-mis* OIP 114, 41: 11 "he collected".

D NA *eṣādu ka-ni-ši* StAT 2, 163 r. 11 "collect (masc.!) the harvest".

MPS (G), JW (G), JK (D)

kamāsu II "to kneel, to squat"

G 1. OA *lā tadaggalā kīma ammākam kī'am ina išātim kà-am-sà-ku-ni* AKT 9A, 73: 7 "do you not see that there (? sic!) I am simply sitting in the fire?" (i.e.

"things are too hot for me"? The writer is clearly in financial trouble).

2. OB lit. [*k*]*a-mi-is* ZA 110, 39 i 16, s. *šēdu*. NJCK (1), MPS (2)

kam'atu, + *kam'u* "white truffle"; + MB Ugar., + LB

1. OB *awīlī ana kam-a-tim leqêm aṭrud-ma umma anākuma pīqat ka-am-ú itât āl*[*im*] *ibaššû* ... *illikūma gib'ī tamšīl ka-am-i ublūnimma awīlī šunū*[*ti*] *utēr um-ma anākuma ištū gib'ū ibbašû ka-am-i ātammarā illikūma ka-am-i ītammarū anūmma ka-am-i ša ublūnim* [*a*]*na ṣēr bēliya ušābilam* [*ka-a*]*m-i šināti* ... ARM 27, 54: 6–21 "I dispatched men to collect white truffles, saying: 'Perhaps there are white truffles around the city.' ... They went and brought red truffles resembling white truffles, and I turned back those men saying: 'Since there were red truffles, look everywhere for white truffles!' They went and looked everywhere for white truffles. Now I have sent to my lord the white truffles that they brought. Those [white truf]fles ...".

2. MB Ugar. [*k*]*a-ma-'a-*⌜*tu*⌝ PRU 6, 159: 3 (reading after Huehnergard 1987, 137).

3. LB *ka-ma-a-tú* PIHANS 79, 18: 5 (s. NABU 1997/88).

4. On truffles s. Stol 2014, 149f.; for Ebla refs. s. Pasquali 2005, 129f.

kamdu, *kandu*, + *gandu* "a designation of textile"; + LB

LB (1/3 shekel silver) *ana* 1 *ga-an-du* Zawadzki 2013, 550 r. 5 "for 1 *g*."

S. *kamādu*.

+ **kamēšu** " a sort of bread(?)"; NA

1 *ka*!*-me-šú* SAA 7, 174: 11 in list of various breads.

kāmidu "a textile craftsman" s. *kamādu*

kamîš "like a captive"; + NA

[*l*]*išēšibšu ka-mì-iš* SAA 2, 4: 21 "may she have him sit like a captive".

kamiššaru, *kamiššuru* "pear tree"

1. OB *dippāt*[*ūšu*] *lū elammakkum u kablātūšu lū* ^{giš}*ka-mi-šu-ru-*[*um*] FM 8, 46 no. 6: 12 "its (the table's) top shall be *e*.-wood and its legs shall be pear wood".

2. OB 1 *kussûm* ^{giš}ŠENNUR.[BAB]-BAR.RA RIMA 1 p. 56: 11 "1 throne made from pear wood.

kamkammatu "a kind of ring"

1. Ur III 1 ^{urudu}*kà-am-kà-ma-tum* ArOr 87, 36 no. 3 = RA 113, 41 "1 copper *k*.". Otherwise *kam-kam-ma-tum* in Ur III (cf. CAD K 124 a).

2. For add. OB refs. s. Arkhipov 2012, 80.

+ **kamliš** "furiously"; OB

aš-ri-UŠ ⌜*ša libbiki*⌝ [*k*]*a-am-li-iš šuttu-qu kûmma Ištar* Or. 87, 16 i 30 "wherever you desire, to split (the house) furiously – is yours, Ištar".

kamlu s. *gamlu* 1

+ **Kamlu** "a bread"; MB Emar

^{ninda}KA*-am-la i-zu-ú-zu* Emar 6/3, 388: 66 "they will share (pres.!) the *k*.-bread". Huehnergard *apud* Pentiuc 2001, 146 suggests a connection to Syr. *qmal* "to become moldy", *qumlā* "blue mold on bread; barley cakes baked in the embers and allowed to grow sour".

kammakku s. *kammaku*

kammaku "cloth cover for chariots"; OB

1. *kakkabū* [*š*]*a kam-ma-ki-im ša nar-kabtim ša ḫamuḫḫim* ARM 32, 484 M.15076: 3 "(silver for) stars for the cover of the *ḫamuḫḫu*-chariot", cf. ARM 7, 115.

2. 2 gada*kam-ma-ku* ARM 21, 294: 2; cf. ARM 18, 45.

3. 1 *kam-ma*!*-ku duḫšî* ARM 21, 255: 3 "1 cover of blue-green (wool, linen, or leather)".

4. A cover usually made from wool or linen (Durand 2009, 50, 158 and Arkhipov 2012a, 9).

kammamtu s. *kamamtu*

kammu I "tablet, literary composition"

NA 3 *kam-ma-ni* SAA 7, 49 i 4 in inventory of tablets and writing boards.

kammu II "a fungus; a substance used in leather production" (CAD *kammu* A)

kammu III, pl. *kammātu* "rivet, dowel"

1. NA 37 *ka-ma-te*! KÙ.GI *ša qaqqad sisî* CTN 2, 151: 1 "37 platelets of gold for a horse's head".

2. NA (1 quiver) 2 *kam-ma-tu* SAAB 13, 8 no. 4: 2 "two rivets". The suggestion by Postgate/Collon ib. p. 8 to understand this as a "dome-headed" nail or tack in view of *kammu* II "a fungus" is unconvincing, as *k.*-fungus refers to mold- or lichen-like growths rather than dome-shaped mushrooms.

3. CAD *kammu* C, AHw. *kammu* I.

+ **kammu IV** "a wooden object used in sieges"; OB

(20 pine trees) *ana ka-am-mi* ARM 26/1, 211 no. 71-bis: 8 "for *k.*", mentioned after ladders (*simmilātum*). Durand ib. proposes a shorter type of ladder.

kamru II s. *kumru*

kamsu I "gathered"

1. A designation of cloth or garments: OA *kam-sú-tum* AKT 6A, 144: 9; *šīm kam-sí-im* AKT 7A, 176: 2 "the price of *k.*-cloth"; 1 TÚG *kam-sú-um* AKT 9A, 120: 7 "1 *k.*-garment".

2. An indicator of high quality, perhaps "finished; gathered in (of edges?)", s. Michel/Veenhof 2010, 253f.

NJCK/JW/MPS

kams/ṣu II "kneeling"

NB *kam-ṣe-e-ti* SAA 17, 201 r. 8 in broken context.

kamʾu s. *kamʾatu*

kamû II "captive"; + OAkk

OAkk logogr. LÚxKÁR/ÉŠ: n GURUŠ.GURUŠ *ušamqit* n LÚxKÁR *ik*[*m*]*ī* FAOS 7, RIM C 1: 54 and *pass.* "he fell n men, he took n captives" (s. Kienast/Sommerfeld 1994, 225).

kamû III "to capture"

D 1. SB [*mu-*]*kam-mu-ú-a* ORA 7, 320: 37 "those who capture me".
2. SB [*ku*]*-um-mu ina kamûtimma* ORA 7, 322: 70 "he is [bou]nd in captivity".

kamūnu I "cumin"

1. OA *kà-mu-ni* Prag 740: 11; 429: 26 (// OIP 27, 55: 31); AKT 4, 37: 19; *kà-mu-nu* AKT 5, 57: 9; *kà-mu-ni* ib. 58A: 8; kt 88/k 418: 2 (s. Bayram 2016, 38).

2. OB (10 litres of) *ka-mu-nu* FM 2, 25 no. 4: 10 (list of vegetables and spices).

NJCK (1), MPS (2)

kamūnu II, + *kamunû*(?) "(a) fungus"

1. SB *ina lumun ka-mu-ni-e l*[*ā ṭābi ša…*] JNES 33, 347 r. 7 "because of the evil of ill-[portending] *k*.-fungus", s. Caplice ib. p. 349; cf. *ka-mu-nu-u* BAM 329 (Kinnier Wilson 2005, 8).

2. SB NAM.BÚR *lumun ka-mu-né-e* SpTU 1, 6: 18 "namburbi ritual against the evil of a fungus".

3. "Gall" on tamarisks: SB *ka-mun bīni* JMC 5, 9: 68 (Ugu) "*k*. of the tamarisk" (as a medical ingredient, s. Worthington ib. p. 25). The mng. "gall" is supported by explanations with *gabû* "alum" in comm. and lex. texts. Both tamarisk galls and alum are historically used in tanning. Like a fungus, galls grow from the bark.

4. S. Streck 2004, 285f.; Kinnier Wilson 2005, 8–11.

kamûtu "captivity"

SB [*ku*]*mmu ina ka-mu-tim-ma adi ušteššera ramānu ukannu du*[*mqu*(?)] ORA 7, 322: 70 "he is [bou]nd in captivity, until he provides justice for himself and establishes what is g[ood(?)]".

kanaktu, *kanatku*, + *kanatḫu* "an incense-bearing tree"; + Ur III; + OA

1. Ur III n ḪAR ^{giš}*kà-na-at-ḫu-um* CUSAS 3, 1375: 35ff. "n *k*.-tree seedling(s)" (for a garden). Cf. *kà-na-at-ku* HSS 14, 198: 1 (Nuzi, CAD K 135b *k*. 2, 1') and *ka-na-a-at-ki* EA 22 iii 32. S. also Sallaberger, CUSAS 6, 358.

2. OA (1 litre) *zar'am ša kà-na-ak-tim* KTS 2, 14: 16 "of seed of the *k*.-tree".

3. OB lit. pl. *ka-na-ka-ti*, s. *munû* I.

4. After Moran 1992, 59, n. 35 and 83, n. 41, the logogr. in EA 25 iv 51, quoted in CAD B 64 s.v. *bullukku* as ŠIM.BAL, is in fact ŠIM.GIG (= *kanaktu*).

5. Jursa 2009, 161 (perhaps opopanax); Richter 2012, 183f. (Hurr. *kanagi*).

NR (1, 4), MPS (3), JW (5), NJCK (2)

kanāku "to seal"

G 1. Said of body parts: OB lit. *ak-nu-uk appam u ḫasīsam ak-nu-uk šipī'ātim ša muḫḫišu ša* DN *ú*!(I)-*ra-am-mu-šu* AML 114: 13 "I sealed the nose and the ear. I sealed the sutures of his skull, that DN had loosened".

2. OB *ina kunukkiya u kunuk mārī kārim bītam ni-ik-nu-uk* FM 2, 285 no. 130: 20 "we sealed the house with my seal and the seal of the sons of the merchants' area".

3. OB *aššum ... bāb* UR.MAḪ *ka-na-*⌜*ki*⌝*-i*[*m*] ARM 33, 125: 7 "concerning the sealing of the Lion's gate" (the text is concerned with bricks, suggesting that *k*. here refers to building activity).

D *bīssu ú-ka-ni-ik* FM 2, 285 no. 130: 8 "I sealed his house".

kanānu "to roll up, coil"

SB [*šumma*] *kīma ṣērim ik-nun* KAL 5, 70 r. 41 "[if] (the oil) has coiled up like a snake". Cf. *qanānu*.

kanāqu s. *ḫanāqu*

kanaqurtu s. *q*/*kanaqurtu*

kanasarru, *kanazerru*, *kašanšarru*, + *katanšarru* "wooden part of a wheel"

OB 3 *ka-ta-an-ša-ra-tum u* 2 *lišānū epinnim* AbB 11, 82: 9 "3 *k*. and 2 plough shares", cf. ib. 12 and 14. The text clearly distinguishes TA and ŠA.

kanāšu I "to bow down, to submit"

D 1. Lex. DU = *ku-un-nu-šu* Emar 6/4, 537: 347 (Sa) "to force into submission".

2. Early OB [*an*]*a šēpī*[*šu*] ⸢*ú*⸣-*kà-ni-í*[*s*]-*sú*-[*n*]*u-ti* RIME 4 p. 713 ii 19 "he made them fall at his feet".

3. OB (food for soldiers) *inūma ku-nu-ši-im* KTT 139//140: 10 "at the time of submission".

4. SB (the wife will say to her man) *ku-nu-uš* Šūpê-amēli 66 "submit!"

kanatḫu s. *kanaktu*

kanatku s. *kanaktu*

KA-an-DA-BI-tum s. *qanû* I

kandaku "hold of a boat"; foreign word

Abraham/Sokoloff 2011, 36: Cf. Syr. *kndwq*ʾ, "large storage jar for grain", perhaps of Persian origin (s. Sokoloff 2009, 683).

kandalu s. *qandalu*

kandarasānu, NA *kandirše, kundiraše* "a linen dress"; + NA

1. Lex. ^{túg}*kun-dar-a-ši* AfO 18, 331: 288 (practical vocabulary of Assur).

2. NA 1 *kun-dir-a-še* SAA 7, 121 i 6 (in list of cloths).

3. NA ^{túg}*kan-dir-še* SAA 7, 174: 5 (in list of cloths).

4. 4 ^{túg}*kun-dar-a-šá-ni* StAT 2, 164: 10.

5. S. CAD K 148 *kandarasanu* (LB), AHw. 436 *kandaru*, AHw. 1569 *kun-da/irašu*. S. Gaspa 2018, 283–284. *k.* sometimes co-occurs with the *sasuppu*-garment and appears to be used in ritual context.

kandirše s. *kandarasānu*

kandu, + *kindu* "a container"; NB, LB; Aram. lw.

1. 30 *ki-in-du ša kupsu* AfO 38/39, 81 no. 2: 12 "30 *k.* of (sesame) pressings", s. MacGinnis ib. 82.

2. NB 1 *kan-du* (of bronze, for measuring oil) dubsar 7, 39: 5.

3. Abraham/Sokoloff 2011, 36f.; Cherry 2017, 158f. (Aram. lw.).

kandu s. *kamdu*

kanīktu "sealed silver medal"

1. OB 10 GÍN 1 ḪAR KÙ.BABBAR 1 GÍN *ka-ni-*<*ik*>*-tum* FM 1, 140 A.486+: 63 "1 ring of 10 shekel silver, a medal of 1 shekel"; s. ib. 64–69.

2. OB 1 ḪAR *ša* 4 GÍN KÙ.BABBAR *ù* 1 GÍN KÙ.BABBAR *ka-ni-ik-tam idinšum* ARM 18, 19: 10 "give him 1 ring of 4 shekel silver and 1 shekel silver in the form of a sealed medal!"

3. OB 2 GÍN *ka-an-ka-tum nībum* [n GÍN K]I.LÁ.BI ARM 32 p. 381 M.6206: 5 "medals of 2 shekel nominal value, their [weig]ht is [n shekel]".

4. Arkhipov 2012, 17 with further refs.

+ **kāniktu** "female seal bearer"; OB

OB lit. [*ina b*]*īt makkūrim* [*ka*]*-ni-ik-ta-šu* (// *kišib-lá*) *atti* Nidaba and Enki 53 "in the storeroom, you (fem.) are its seal bearer".

kāniku s. also *kanniku*

****kaniniwe** (AHw. 437, CAD K 152)

In HSS 13, 119 read 2 BÁN! *ni-ir*!*-we a-na* <I>*Ga-a-pa-a-zi*, cf. HSS 14, 200 (Deller 1983; cf. Richter 2012, 184). S. *nirwe*.

kankannu, *g*/*kangannu* "potstand"; +MB

MB *kan-ga-an-nu* [...] BagF 21, 202: 2, 4.

kannamāre s. *kallamāre*

ka/inna/iškarakku, *ka*(*n*)*giškarakku* "a table"

1. OB 1 ^{giš}KA.GIŠ.KARA$_4$ *tuppašu elammakum* ARM 22, 306: 7 "one *k*., its top (made from) *elammaku*-wood"; cf. 316 ii 8.

2. OB *aššum* ^{giš}*ka-ni-iš-ka-ra-ki-im ša meluḫḫim* KÙ.GI GAR.RA ARM 23, 100 no. 103: 8 "(memorandum) concerning 1 wooden *k.* from Meluḫḫa, gold plated". Cf. ^{giš}BANŠUR$_x$ *ka-an-giš-ka-ra-ki* ARM 23, 190 no. 213: 13.

3. OB (1 mina of glue for making) ^{giš}*ki-in-na-aš-ka-ra-ki* ARM 21, 303: 7 and s. p. 362 n. 29 for spelling variants.

kanniku, *kāniku* "sealer, person in charge of sealing"; + OA

13 GÍN URUDU *ana* PN *kà-ni-ki-im* OIP 27, 58: 28 "13 shekels of copper for PN, the sealer". NJCK

+ **kannišu** "wooden table(?)"; OB

1. 3 DUG GEŠTIN *ana* ^{giš}*ka-ni-ši-im* FM 11, 151: 8 "3 jars of wine for the *k.* (when the messengers sat in front of the king in the date palm court)".

2. 8 DUG GEŠTIN ŠÀ.BA 2 DUG GEŠTIN *ša sīmi* ZI.GA *ana* ^{giš}*ka-an-ni-ši-im* ib. 25: 17 "8 jars of wine, among them 2 jars of red(?) wine, expenditure for the *k.*".

3. ZI.GA *ana* ^{giš}*ka-an-ni-ši-im* FM 11, 26: 12.

4. G. Chambon, FM 11 p. 29f. S. also *kannu* I.

kannu I "wooden rack for storing containers, potstand"

1. OB lit. *šaknāt ina ka-an-nim* AML 27: 7 "you (the fermentation vat) are placed on the potstand".

2. OB 1 DUG GEŠTIN *ana ka-an-nim* FM 11, 1: 2 "1 jar of wine for the rack" Cf. ib. 5: 2; 12: 4; 152: 8; 161: 2 etc.

3. With det. ^{giš}: ^{giš}*ka-an-nim* ib. 21: 9, 11, 32; 27 r. 11; 30: 4; 31: 6; 33: 8; 35: 2; 57: 2; 79: 2 etc.

4. *k. ša šarrim* "of the king": ib. 25: 29; 59: 2; 153: 2.

5. *k. ša bāb ēkallim* "of the palace gate": ib. 84: 2.

6. In ARM 9, 33: 5; 187: 4 read, instead of É *k.* (CAD K 156 *k.* A in *bīt k.*), ^{giš}*k.*, s. G. Chambon, FM 11 p. 27.

7. G. Chambon, FM 11 p. 26–29; Guichard 2005, 24–26 with add. refs. S. also *kannišu*.

kannu II "band, rope"

OB *ka-an-nu aš-la-a tāmu*[*r*] *ša* [*eleppim*] Finkel 2014, p. 359: 10 "ropes each (1) *ašlu* long – (when) you have found (them) for [the ship]".

****kannūtu** (AHw. 438), *kannûtu* (CAD K 157) s. *qunnunu*.

kanšu I "submissive"

Fem. *kanšatu* "a kind of musician", referring to her "kneeling" position: 21 *ka-an-š*[*a*]*-tum* FM 4, 21 no. 37: 2 (in list of musicians); 49 ^{f}*ka-a*[*n-š*]*a-tum* ib. 6. S. ib. 215 no. 36: 9–12. Cf. N. Ziegler, ib. p. 70.

kanšu II "work-team, array"; Aram. lw.

LB *suluppē ana imērē ša ka-an-šú* ... SUM-*na* Jursa 1999, 147 BM 42347: 14 "the dates were given for the donkeys of the work-team". S. Jursa ib. p. 100: not "donkey caravan", but "work-team, array".

kantuḫḫu, *ḫanduḫḫu* "attachment to a chariot; part of a lock"

1. OB 5 *qullum ša taskarinnim* 5 *ka-an-tu-ḫu-šu-nu* Fs. Veenhof, 219 BM 80394: 3 "5 rings of boxwood, their 5 *k.*".

2. OB (silver) *ana iḫzi ša* 4 *ka-an-tu-ḫi ša nūbal* MÁ.GAN^{an}.NA ARM 25, 351 (= ARM 32, 406 M.11273): 3 "for setting 4 *k.*s of a palanquin of Magan; cf. ARM 25, 287 (= ARM 32, 407 M.10463): 11.

3. *ana ka-an-tu-uḫ-ḫi ša nūba*[*lim*] ARM 32, 211 M.11620: 3 "for the *k.* of the chariot".

4. AHw. and CAD s.v. *ḫandūḫu* and CAD G 152a; AHw. 1559a. In BE 14, 123a: 10f. read *kam-du-ḫi* and *kam-duḫ-ḫi* with van Koppen 2001, 220 pace AHw. s.v. *ḫandūḫu* and CAD s.v. *mašīru*. Emendation to *ḫi*!-*du*/*duḫ-ḫi* is unneccesary. Rather, the word *ḫidduḫḫu*, pl. *hinduḫḫētu*, attested in the same text l. 8 and in Nuzi, is a separate lemma.

kânu "to be(come) permament, firm, true"

G OA also "to be established, confirmed, proven":

1. (if PN owes silver in the country) *ina tuppišu u šēbēšu i-ku-an*(*-ma*) AKT 6A, 294: 15 "it has to be confirmed by means of his tablet and (or?) his witnesses", sim. kt a/k 394: 17 (s. Veenhof 1995, 1725 n. 22) and kt n/k 1925: 17 (s. Veenhof 2019, 450f.)

2. PN_1 u PN_2 *uktannūma šumma ṣubātū iṣṣēr* PN_2 *ik-tù-nu* 2/3 MA.NA KÙ.BABBAR PN_2 (...) *ana* PN_3 *išaqqal* AKT 8, 101: 10 "PN_1 and PN_2 will confront one another to establish who of them is liable, and if the textiles prove to be owed by PN_2, PN_2 will pay 2/3 mina of silver to PN_3"; sim. AKT 6C, 639: 7and 7A, 23: 15.

D OA **1**. "to secure (the acquisition of copper or silver), to get hold of", s. Dercksen 1996, 53–57; CAD K 170b s.v. *kânu* A 4c-3'; AKT 2, 39: 8; 11A, 33: 38.

2. "to confirm or prove sb.'s (Acc) statement, claim, or liability" (s. Veenhof 2017a, 145f.): *šumma* PN_1 *ana* PN_2 PN_3 *lā uk-ta-in kaspam u ṣibātēšu* PN_1 *ana* PN_2 *išaqqal* AKT 8, 99B: 22 "if PN_1 cannot prove PN_3('s liability) to PN_2, PN_1 will pay the silver and its interest to PN_2"; n GÍN KÙ.BABBAR *šumma* PN_1 PN_2 *lā uk-ta-i-nam kaspam u ṣibassu* PN_1 *išaqqalam* CCT 1, 40c: 4 "if PN_1 does not confirm (or prove) that PN_2 owes n shekels of silver to me, PN_1 (himself) will pay me the silver and its interest"; s. also AKT 1, 62: env. 8 // tablet 5 ; AKT 6A, 235: 34.

3. "to bring proof against sb. (accusative)": *awīlam ina Ālem innaruāʾem u nadītem ú-kà-an* kt 92/k 543: 39 "in the City I will bring proof against the man by means of the stele and the *nadītum*"; also ib. 30 *ú-kà-a-kà*, s. Bayram 2001, 3f.

4. "to present sb. as witness": *atta tallakamma ana merʾē* PN *ú-kà-an-kà* (...) *tibʾamma atalkam lāma ūmū imluʾūni ište merʾē awīlem ku-ta-i-in* Prag 537: 25 and 31 "you must come here so that I can present you (as witness) against the sons of PN (...). Come here and before the term is over present yourself (as witness) to the sons of the man"; also TCL 1, 241: 11 and 14.

Dt 1. OA "to bring proof against each other, to confront each other to establish who is liable":
a) PN_1 *u* PN_2 *uk-ta-nu-ú-ma šumma ṣubātū iṣṣēr* PN_2 *iktūnū* 2/3 MA.NA KÙ.BABBAR PN_2 (…) *ana* PN_3 *išaqqal* AKT 8, 101: 10 "PN_1 and PN_2 will establish who of them is liable and if the textiles prove to be owed by PN_2, PN_2 will pay 2/3 mina of silver to PN_3".
b) *ammākam atta u* PN *ku-ta-i-na-ma alē* KB *iburrû* KB *lilliqī* CCT 6, 45c: 16 "there, you and PN must establish who is liable, and let the silver be obtained where the silver appears (i.e. by the person who is proved to be entitled)"; sim. AKT 7A, 23: 15; 126: 23; 8, 100: 10; 11A, 156: 11.
2. OA reflexive of D s. Prag 537: 31 quot. above, *kânu* D 4.

3. OB [*ina p*]*anī* ⸢*niqê*⸣*m uk-ti-in-nu* FM 3, 71 no. 5: 8 "they place themselves (pres.!) before the offering" (Streck 2003a, 112).

Št 1. [*awī*]*lum šū lū* [*b*]*aliṭ adī maḫar bēliya ittī* PN *uš-ta-ka-a*[*n*]*-nu* ARM 28, 105: 25 "this gentleman shall remain alive until they interrogate him before my lord together with PN" (s. Streck 2003a, 122).
2. *maḫar* PN ⸢*li*⸣*-iš-ta-ki-n*[*u-šu*] FM 3, 169 no. 15: 8 "they shall have him permanently placed before PN".

Disc.: S. Mayer 2016, 224 on the mng. of the Dtt ("to interrogate") and add. Št refs.

NJCK (G, D 1–4, Dt 1–2), MPS/JW (Dt 3, Št)

kanūnu s. *kinūnu*

kanzūzu "chin"

SB ME.ZÉ-⸢*šú*⸣ *n*[*u-u*]*š-šú* : *kan-zu-u*[*s-su* …] SpTU 1, 31: 8 "his ME.ZÉ is shaky : his chin is [shaky]" (comm. on Sa-gig 5, s. Wee 2019, Vol 2, 170ff.); *su-qat-su* : *kan-zu-us-su* ib. 26 "his *suqtu* : his chin". Cf. *uzu su-uq-t*[*ú*] = [*k*]*an-zu-zu* (Ḫg B IV, 2 = MSL 9, 34).

kapādu, + *kapātu* "to plan, take care of"

G 1. Lex. *ka-pa-tú ša* MIN (= *uznī*) MSL 3, 52: 17 (s. AHw. 443 *kapātu* G; CAD K 183 *kapātu*) "to plan, of the ears".
2. *i*-class: NB *ki-pi-id-ma* OIP 114, 35: 28, s. *qullu*; Jursa 1997/1998, 422; Streck 1999, 292.

Gtn OB *ištū alliku aḫ-ta-ap-pu-ud-ma* AbB 10, 193: 5 "since I left, I have been managing (the sesame field in GN)".

D 1. Early OB *ana kuru*[*mmātīšu*] *māru šip*[*riya*] *lū ku-pu-u*[*d*] AS 35: 16 "shall my messenger take care of his (own) rations?".
2. OB *zibbatam kīma ṣibûtim ku-pi-da* AbB 5, 172: 20 "take care (pl.) of the tail-end (of the canal) as desired".
3. OB *šumma bēlī ašariš ku-up-pu-ud* ARM 33, 56 r. 6 "if my lord has a plan for there".

S. also *kapātu.*

kapālu, *qapālu* "to coil, roll up"

G OB (rations for workers) *ša qinnazā-tim ik-pi-lu* CUSAS 15, 74: 4 "who plaited(?) whips".

Gt Streck 2003a, 29:
1. OB *šumma* 2 *ṣerrū* … *ik-ta-ap-pí-lu* Fs. de Meyer, 306: 9 "if 2 snakes coil around each other".
2. SB *ittī bēl emūqi lā ták-ta-píl* Ugar. 5, 278 ii 10 "do not wrestle with a strong man!" (cit. AHw. 924 s.v. *qitbulu*, but s. already CAD Q 292).

D *maštūtam ša ina qātī*[*ka*] *ibaššû li-qá-ap-pí-*[*lu*] AbB 6, 189: 18 "they shall roll up the weave that is available to you".

Dt OB lit. *mu-uk-ta-ap-pi-l*[*i*] TIM 9, 41: 28 "who gathered (against)".

Disc.: S. also *muktaplu* and *kaplatu*.

kapāpu, + *kabābu* "to bend, to curve"

SB *qātātušu u šēpāšu ana kišādišu ik-tab-ba* (var. *ik-tap-*[*p*]*a*) Diagnostic Handbook XXVI: 13 (Stol 1993b, 60) "(if his fit overcomes him and) his hands and feet curve towards his neck", cf. *ik-tab-ba* SpTU 2, 44 r. 17.

kaparru I "herd boy"; Sum. lw.

1. OB PN KA.BAR AbB 13, 41: 3.

2. OB lit. *kamsū rē'û maḫ*[*aršu*] *ka-pa-ar-ru uddamm*[*aṣū*] RA 101, 66 ii 82 "the shepherds were bowed down before [him], the herd boys humble[d] themselves, saying:".

3. SB *ka-par* Jiménez 2017, 248: 5, cf. *rabābu* Š.

4. Selz 1993 (loan from Sum. *gáb-ra*).

kaparru II "spadix(?); a metal implement"

1. OB 4 *ka-pa-ar-ra-tim* ZABAR *ša* 2 MA.NA.ÀM FM 8, 64 no. 14: 11 "4 bronze *k.* of 2 minas each" (mentioned between axes and shovels).

2. AHw. *k.* II = CAD *k.* B and C. Derivation from *ḫepēru*, as Durand ib. p. 12 suggests, is doubtful.

kapāru I "to strip, wipe (off), to smear"

G 1. OB (oil) *ana ka-pa-ar eleppim eššetim*/*maturrim eššim* FM 3, 229 no. 60: 14; ib. 245 no. 95: 12 "for 'smearing' (i.e. finishing the wood of?) a new ship/a new *m.*-ship".

2. OB (oil) *ana pašāš dalātim u ka-pa-ar bīt gallābim* ib. 234 no. 61: 3 "for anointing the doors and smearing the barber's house".

3. OB (oil) *ana ka-pa-ar eleppim u bīt gallābim* ib. 253 no. 113: 2 "for smearing a ship and the barber's house".

4. OB (oil) *ana ka-pa-ar* 2 *el*[*eppētim*] ib. 258 no. 125: 7 "for smearing 2 sh[ips]".

+ **Dt 1.** OB lit. *eṭlū uk-ta-ap-pa-ru ša kī arkātim* VS 10, 214 iii 1 "young men are cut off as if for spear poles", cf. disc. Streck 2010, 562.

2. OB *awāssu li-ik-tap-pe-er* AbB 1, 67 r. 13 "his matter shall be cleared up" (von Soden 1975, 460).

Disc.: S. also *kāpiru* and *kariktu*; *kezertu* 1.

kapāṣu I "a seashell (?) and its imitations in stone or metal"

1. OB *qašta u* ^na4^*ka-pa-ṣi*^sic^*-a* ^túg^BAR.SI.IG AbB 12, 94: 28 "(buy for me) a bow, a (?) *k.*, and a head-scarf".

2. AHw "ein roter Stein" (s.v. *kapaṣu*) must be rejected based on lex. and contextual evidence for *k.* made from various materials. Cf. the disc. CAD K 181.

kapāṣu II "to bend back, to distort"

1. SB *šumma* ... *īn šumēlišu kap-ṣa-at* SpTU 1, 82: 18 "if his left eye is squinting(?)".

2. Del. RB 59 in AHw. 443 *k.* 2 and CAD K 181 *k.* 1a and cf. *kabāsu*.

kapāšu I, *gapāšu* "to swell, rise up; to be(come) abundant"

G Var. *kapāšu* (cf. CAD K 128b): OB lit. *i-ka-ap-pu-ša kīma tī'āmtim* AML 173: 42 "it becomes abundant like the sea".

+ **Ntn** OB lit. *ta-at-ta-ag*/*k-pi-iš mātam qabalšu* Westenholz 1997, 196: 35 "his attack overwhelmed(?) the land." (S. ib. p. 197; Mayer 2016, 210).

kapāšu II, + *gapāšu* "to perform in disguise" s. *kāpišu*.

kapātu "to gather, collect, compile"

+ **G 1.** OB of oracles: *aššum alāk ṣābim u epēš* [*kakkī*] *kayyāniš a-ka-ap-pu-ut-*⌜*ma*⌝ ARM 26/1, 372 no. 190: 4 "concerning the marching of troops and doing [battle], I continuously compile (oracles)". Durand ib. p. 44 derives the form from *kapādu* "to plan", i.e. "to draft (queries)" but cf. *têrētim ú-ka-ap-pa-tu-ma* ARM 2, 22: 29 (coll. LAPO 17, 221), where a reading *-dú-* would be atypical.

2. For *ka-pa-*UD *ša uznī* (AHw. 443 *kapātu* G; CAD K 183) s. *kapādu*.

D (all levees are damaged) 2 *ammā kalakkam elīšina ú-ka-ap-pí-it* ARM 14, 18 r. 9 "I heaped 2 cubits of spoil on each of them".

Dt NA *uk-tap-pat* SAA 10, 117: 6 (in broken context).

CAD *kupputu*.

kapaʾu s. *kupû*

+ **kapiltu** "a bead"; OB

1. 3 *kap-la-tum* ^{na_4}PAR.PAR.DILI ARM 32, 424 M.10382: 3 "3 *k.* of *pappardilû*-stone".

2. 1 *kap-la-at uqnîm* ARM 32, 456 M.5954 r. 12 "1 *k.* of lapis lazuli".

3. Arkhipov 2012, 47. Perhaps < *kapālu* "to coil, to roll up".

kāpiru "caulker, polisher"

1. NA *k. diqāri* "dishwasher (lit. 'polisher of cooking pots')":

a) [^{LÚ}]*ka-pir* UTÚL^{meš} *lū* ^{LÚ}MUŠEN.DÙ *lū* ^{LÚ}MÁ.LAḪ$_4$ *lū* ^{LÚ}AD.KID SAA 12, 83 r. 11 "a dishwasher, or a fowler, or a boatman, or a reed-worker".

b) The emendation *ka-pir* UZU!(UTÚL) in STT 385 iii 10' suggested in CAD K 184 and the subsequent assumption of a new lemma mng. "butcher(?)" is not necessary.

2. For disc. s. Gaspa 2009.

****kāpiru B** "butcher(?)" s. *kāpiru*

kāpišu, *k/gāpištu* "a performer in disguise, cross-dresser(?)"

OB 1 ^{munus}*ga-pí-i*[*š$_7$-tum*] *i-ga-ap-pí-iš* FM 3, 60 no. 3 iii 14 "1 *g.* performs"; 7 ^{munus}*ga-pí-*[*ša-tum* (*maḫar* DN?)] *i-ga-pí-ša* [...] *usaḫḫarām*[*a* (*maḫar* DN$_2$?) *i-ga-pí-ša* ib. 20-23 "7 *g.* perform (before DN?) [...then] they turn around and perform (before DN$_2$?)". S. ib. p. 51f. and FM 11 p. 60.

+ **kappāḫu** "mason"; OB, SB

1. OB *ḫišeḫti* ^{lú}*ka-ap-pa-ḫi* 4 *ḫaṣṣin siparri* ... 4 *kaparrātim* ZABAR ... 2 *marri siparri* ... FM 8, 64 no. 14: 9 "requisites of the mason, 4 bronze axes, 4 bronze *k.*, 2 bronze shovels".

2. OB *ittī ka-pa-ḫi* [*abn*]*am li-ba-aḫ-ḫu-ú* ib. 34 "let (the men) search for [ston]e together with the masons".

3. SB *en-qa kap-paḫ*? JCS 66, 82: 308 "Cricket, Screecher, Typhoon, Screamer," Wise-One, Mason" (sons of Ḫumbaba).

4. Derivation from *ḫepû*, as Durand ib. p. 10f. suggests, is doubtful.

kappaltu "groin, loin"

On etym. s. Kogan/Militarev 2002, 316.

kapparnu s. *kapparru*

+ **kapparru** "a vessel"; MB Emar

1. 1 ^{dug}*kap-pár-ra* GEŠTIN.NA Emar 6/3, 371: 9 "1 *k.* of wine"; cf. 304: 4; 370: 112.

2. Pentiuc 2001, 97 suggests derivation from WSem. *kpr* "to cover", but cf. *kapparnu* "a pitcher" (CAD K 185, Richter 2012, 186, Hurr. lw.). S. also Huehnergard 1987, 139 (Ugar. $^{⌜du⌝g?}$*ku?-ba-ra-tu*^{meš} PRU 6, 158: 13).

kappu I "wing"

1. OB [*k*]*a-pa-an imittam u šumēlam dawdâm idūkā* FM 3, 146 no. 14: 13 "the right and left flanks inflicted defeat".

2. OB ⌜*kap*⌝(KAB) *lurmim šūbilam* ARM 28, 43: 16 "send me the wing of an ostrich!"

3. *ṣubāt kap lu-ur-me* ARM 30, 369 M.12814 ii 1 "a garment made of the wing of an ostrich"; s. ib. p. 105f. for further refs. and disc.

4. OB "a bead":

a) (bands) *ša kap-pí ša pappardilîm* ARM 21, 223: 39 "of *k.* made from *pappardilû*-stone".

b) 1 *kišādu ša kap-pí uqnîm* ARM 32, 461 M.7748: 3; 465 M.8353+: 2, 3; 483 M.14335 r. 4 "1 necklace of *k.* made from lapis lazuli".

c) 1 *kišādu ka-ap-pí uqnîm* ARM 32, 191 A.3490: 2, 4; cf. ARM 31, 546 no. 287 r. 11.

d) S. Arkhipov 2012, 47. If not identical with *kappu* I, perhaps < *kapāpu* "to curve".

5. SB *dannata kap-pí*! *summata umaššir illik itūra ušāniḫ kap-pí-ša* OBO 290, 88: 11–13 "I released a dove, strong-of-wings. She went forth and came back, exausted her wings".

6. "plumes" as decoration on a helmet, s. *q*/*gurpis*(*s*)*u*.

kappu II "(palm of the) hand, handful (as a measure); a vessel" ; + NB

1. SB *kap-pi iqnê* SAA 3, 14: 12 "bowl of lapis lazuli".

2. NA 1 *tupnīnu* 153 *kap-pi kaspi ina libbi* 1 *tupnīnu* 25 *kap-pi kaspi* SAA 1, 158: 14–16 "1 box containing 153 silver bowls, 1 box (with) 25 silver bowls".

3. NA 2 ^{giš}*kap-pu*^{meš} [(x) ^{giš}]*kap-pu* URUDU ^{giš}NÁ AN.BAR [(x) *k*]*ap-pu* URUDU StAT 2, 184: 9–11 "2 drinking bowls, a copper drinking bowl, an iron bed, a copper drinking bowl".

4. NA *kap*!*-pu* PN *ana rab ēkalli* SAA 16, 50: 1 "*k.* of PN to the palace manager", unclear.

5. NB *ina kap-pí uqatt*[*û*] SAA 17, 201 r. 3 "they destroyed (the writing boards r. 1) with (their) palms".

6. LB a measure: *ina ma-ṭi-ur-nu ša* 16 *kap-pi-šú* CT 49, 123: 7 "(n barley) by the measure of 16 handfuls"; s. ib. 122: 6; 129: 2; BM 54555: 7 (Jursa, AOAT 254, 115). MPS (1–2, 4–6), JK (3), NR (6)

kappu-rapšu "'wide-wing', a bird"

Perhaps loan-translated into Hitt. as *pattar-palḫi* of the same mng. (Riemschneider 1977).

+ **kappuṣû** "contraction(?)"; SB

kàp-pu-ṣu-ú SAA 3, 32 : 25 in broken context.

+ **kapullu** "wrap, skein"; OB

šīpātim damqātim ša ka-pu-la-ši-na laqtu AbB 12, 75: 15 "(send me) good wool whose skein has been gathered up (unclear)". Cf. *kappultu*.

kapru "village"

1. OB *ka-ap-ra-tum ana lib* GN *iktamsū* ARM 28, 53 r. 8 "the villages assembled in GN".

2. NA URU.ŠE *qanni* GN SAA 21, 140: 8 "a village outside GN".

****kapru B** (CAD K 190) "a type of sacrifice"

Read *kabru* "thickened", said of preserved *maltītu*-drinks (Sassmannshausen 2001, 453).

kaptarû "coming from Crete"

1. OB of vessels: 1 *kāsum kap-ta-ri-tum* ARM 31, 188: 7": s. Guichard 2015, 209 for add. refs.

2. OB (tin) *ana kap-ta-ra-i-im* ARM 23, 526 no. 556: 28 "for the Cretan" (i.e. the ruler of Crete).

kaptukkû, *kab/pduqqû* "a jar of two seah"

1. Lex. [*dug*$^{ban\text{-}me}$]⌜$^{-en}$⌝[*ban*]*min* = ⌜*kab-du-qu-u*⌝ KAL 8, 59 i 5 (Ḫḫ X).

2. OB 1 ^{dug}BANMIN (of first quality oil) OBTR 205: 3.

kāpu "embankment; rock"

Refs. in PNN (cit. CAD K 192 s.v. *kāpu* B "mng. uncert.") belong here (already AHw. 445 and s. Heimpel 1997d).

kâpu "to oppress"; + OB

OB lit. *na-ki-ra-at* DN *a-kà-ap* VS 10, 213 i 11 "I oppress the hostile (lands) of DN".

****kâpu C** (CAD 192)

Likely a ghostword. It is preserved only by composite: K. 2021a+ (=5r 16) i 39 [… = x]-*a-bu*?! (= DCCLT p394142), Rm-2,585 (= ASKT 198) 22' *ùr* = *ka-a-rù*.

FJMS

karābu "to pray"

G 1. OA *ikribam karābu* "to promise a votive gift": *ikribam ša ana* DNf *ta-ak-ru-bu-ni appūtum lā tamaššī* TC 3, 35: 17 "please, do not forget the votive gift you promised to DNf".

2. OB *ina panīšu ṣalam bēliya ka-ri-bu* FM 8, 132 no. 38: 21 "in front of him (the god) is a praying image of my lord".

+ Gtn OB *lu-uk-ta-ar-ra-ab* AbB 1, 15: 29 "I shall pray incessantly" (pace Edzard 1974, 125 not Dtn).

D 1. OAkk *in bīt ilī libkī'ūnim u li-kà-ri-bu-nim* CUSAS 27, 77: 5 "in the house of the gods, let them weep for me and let them pray regularly for me".

2. OA *maḫar* D[N] *ana balāṭika u šalām* GN *lū nu-kà-ri-ib* Günbattı 2014, 91 01/k 217: 75 "we will pray regularly before D[N] for your life and the well-being of GN" (cf. Gtn in 55).

NJCK (G, D), JW (G, D), JW/MPS (Gtn)

****karadnannalla** (CAD K, 198)

The ref. belongs to *karadnannu* "an ornament", with Hurr. suffix *-alla* (s. Richter 2012, 189 with lit.).

karāku "to intertwine, gather"

1. With people and animals as object: NA ^{lú}GAR-*nu-ku-nu adu sīsê … ki-ir-ka-ni arḫiš* SAA 1, 22: 9 "quickly gather your prefects and horses!"

2. NA *rēḫtu ik-ti-ri-ik* SAA 21, 138: 12 "he gathered the rest (of the people)", already cited AHw. 1566.

karallu I "prick, goad; a type of jewellery"

1. LB 4 ^{urudu}*ka-ra-al-le*^{me} AOAT 414/1, 110: 12 "4 copper pricks(?)" (after vessels and other objects made of copper and bronze).

2. LB 1-*en ka-ra-al-la* KÙ.BABBAR 2 *semerē* KÙ.BABBAR Joannés 1989, 355 NBC 8410: 9 "1 silver *k.*, 2 silver rings", s. Joannès 1989a (a nose-ring?).

+ **karammaru**, *kalammaru*, *karri ammaru* "registry"; LB; Old Pers. lw.

1. *amēlūtu ša ... ina kar-ri am-ma-ru ša šarri ... ušētiq* Dar. 551: 12 "the slave woman whom he transferred in the king's registry".

2. (that house is mine) *ina ka-*⌜*al*⌝*-am-ma-ri ša šarri ... šaṭir* PIHANS 54, 106: 10 "it was written down in the king's registry".

3. (canal) *ša ina ka-ra-am-ma-ri* BE 9, 55: 4 "which is in the registry".

4. Stolper 1977, 259–266. From Old Pers. **kāra-hmara-* "counting people", cf. Elam. *karamaraš*.

karāmu "to be(come) prepared, ready"

1. NA *kī kabbulū ik-rim-u-ni nuḫtarrip ina* MN *nissapar* SAA 21, 79: 12 "since the crippled were ready, we (could) have sent (them) already in MN", already cit. AHw. 1566.

2. NA *ša kar-me-u-ni šū urkīʾu* NALK 214: 32 "whoever is at hand – he will be the guarantor".

3. NA *šarru ka-ri-im illak* SAA 15, 164 r. 11 "the king is ready to depart".

4. NA *šumma* … PN *lā kar-me ina* GN BATSH 6/2, 2: 4 "if PN is not available in GN" (stative, s. Fales 2000, 279).

5. NA *šattu tak-tar-ma* SAA 19, 57: 6 "the year has advanced".

6. On the use in NA legal documents s. Zaccagnini 1994, 37–42. On the range of mng. s. Fales 2000 (pace AHw. "verzögern", CAD "to hinder") with refs.: transitive "to prepare (sth.); to make (sth.) ready, set, available"; intransitive "to be prepared, ready, set, present, available"; stative "is prepared, at hand"; *ḫarrānu*/*ḫūlu karim* "the going is easy"; *karintu* "preparation".

MPS (1, 5), JW (2–3), JK (4)

****karāmu B** "to pile up" (CAD K) s. *karāmu*

karānu, OA *kirānu* "vine, wine"

1. OA lit. ⌜*kī*⌝ *ṣa-ru-ú ki-ra-nim l*[*imq*]*u-tam qaqqaršu* AML 9: 19 "may it (the baby) fall down to the earth like vine-snakes".

2. OA lit. *ina ṣer ki-ra-nim kī kibtim ašaršu liṣbat* AML 11: 22 "may it (the baby) take its place on top of the vine-snake like wheat".

3. OA *ina wa-ra-ad ki-ra-nim* AKT 10, 20A: 9 "at the coming down (i.e. the harvesting) of the grapes" (// 20B: 14).

4. OA *ina qá-*[*ta-áp*] *ka-ra-nim* kt 92/k 1037: 7 "at the plucking of the grapes", s. Çayır 2006, 8;

5. OA 30.TA *ki-ra-nam* PN *u ša ki-ra-né ša rabī sikkitim našʾū* kt m/k 179: 20 and 21 "PN and the wine dealer(?) of the *rabī sikkitim* are carrying 30 (jars?) of wine each" (unpubl., court. K. Hecker); *rabī kirānim* kt 93/k 946 "overseer of the wine", s. Veenhof 2008a, 221.

6. OB lit. *kīma šātû ka-ra-ni-im kīma mār sābītim limqutaššum šittum* AML 124 r. 9 "like over a wine drinker, like over a son of a tavern keeper, may sleep fall over him".

7. OB lit. *azarrū ka-ra-na-am* AML 132 = ALL no. 23: 8 "I will sow a vine".

8. a) OB GEŠTIN (*ša*) *sīmi* "wine of red color(?)": FM 11, 8: 1; 25: 16; 33: 2.

b) GEŠTIN *ša sāmim* "wine of red color(?)": ib. 36: 1, 6; 39 iii 14; 42: 11; 45: 2, 8 etc.
c) S. G. Chambon ib. p. 14–16 for the question whether *sāmu/sīmu* is rather a toponym.

9. GEŠTIN ÚS *sīmi* "second quality red(?) wine": ib. 33: 3.

10. GEŠTIN ÚS(ḫi.a) ib. 33: 4; 42: 1; 158: 15.

11. GEŠTINḫi.a *labirum* "old wine": ib. 71: 4, 6a.

12. 11 DUG GEŠTIN *ittī* DUG GEŠTIN *labirim ša ina bīt* DN [*i*]*ḫḫīqa* ib. 21: 5f. "11 jars of wine were mixed together with a jar of old wine from the temple of DN".

13. GEŠTINḫi.a *eššum* "new wine": ib. 71: 7.

14. GEŠTIN(.NA) *ṭābum* "sweet wine": ib. 25: 4; 168: 1.

15. GEŠTIN *ma-ar-*[*ri*] "bitter wine": ib. 161: 4, 15.

16. Provenance:
a) Ugarit: ib. 11, 75: 1; 76: 3; 77: 1.
b) Qatna: ib. 76: 1.
c) Saggarātum: ib. 84: 4.
d) For other places s. , s. G. Chambon, FM 11 p. 10–16.

17. LB *kī ša ka-ra-nu ša bēliya ibaššû* 1-*en udû* 2 BÁN *ṭābu ina qātīšu bēlu lušēbil* AOAT 414/1, 80: 7 "according to the availability of my lord's wine may the lord send 1 jar of 2 seah (12 l) of good (wine)".

18. LB *dišpi u* gišGEŠTIN AOAT 414/1, 73: 6 "honey and wine".

MPS (1–2, 6–18), NJCK (3–5)

karāru "to put, set, place"; + OB

1. *u qadū ana nadānišu ak-ru-ru ak-ru-ru-ma lā iddinaššu* FM 7, 6 no. 1: 14 "and as I insisted (that) he be given to me, (although) I insisted, he did not give him to me". More likely *karāru* than *q/garāru*, suggested by J.-M. Durand ib. p. 7.

2. Lex. uncl.: PAD = *KA-ra-a-rum* Emar 6/4, 537: 42 (Sa). Sjöberg 1998, 244: *ga*14*-ra-a-rum* < Syr.-Aram. *grr* "to scrape".

karapḫu, *karpaḫu* "fallow land"; Hurr. lw.

1. NA [*k*]*a-ra-ap*⌉*-ḫi ma-aḫ-ḫa-ṣa* ... [*k*]*a-ra-ap-ḫi maḫ-ṣu* SAA 19, 20: 4–6 "break the fallow land ... the fallow land has been broken".

2. S. Richter 2012, 189 for lit.

karāṣu "to pinch off"

G OB lit. *ka-ri-iṣ-ma ina apsîm* ⌜*ṭīdašu*⌝ AML 97: 5 "the clay for it is pinched off in the Apsû".

D SB *rūʾa ṭābi ú-kar-ra-ṣa napištī* Ludlul I 88 "my good friend was 'pinching off' my life", s. Oshima 2014, 216.

Cf. GarZu?

karašu, *karšu* "leek"; + Ur III

1. Ur III 1/2 *sìla kàr-šum* CUSAS 3, 511: 74; 972: 28, 97; 975: 30, 98. Sallaberger, CUSAS 6, 359: elsewhere in Ur III Sumerian *garaš*6.

2. 7 SÌLA *ka-ar-šum* FM 2, 25 no. 4: 5 "7 liters of leek" (in list of vegetables and spices).

3. SB GA.RAŠsar *ikkib Ezida* ... *u*[*qa*]*rrib u ērib bītāti u*[*l*]*tākil* SpTU 3, 58: 17 "he brought leek, the taboo of Ezida, and made the priests eat (it)".

karā/ašu I "fieldcamp"

1. OB *adī bāb ka-ra-ši-šu ukaššissu* RATL 11: 13 "I chased him until the entrance to his camp".

2. OB *ištū* ITI-4-KAM *ka-ra-šu-um ana ka-ra-ši-im ittanaddinannêti* RATL 140: 7 "for 4 months one fieldcamp has (only) taken us to (the next) fieldcamp".

S. also *garāšu.*

karā/ašu II, + *karšu* "catastrophe, annihilation"

OB *ša bēl awātišu u ša ittātišu* GN *ana ka-ar-ši-šu ikmisū* FM 9, 200 no. 47 r. 13 "GN assembled its enemy and all who stand by his side for annihilation". In spite of the var. *karšu*, Ziegler's suggestion (ib. p. 201) to derive the word from *karšu* "belly" (mng. "to devour") seems idiomatically unconvincing.

karattu "watercourse"

1. Lex. *ka-ra-at-tum* = *nāru* AOAT 50, 332: 41 (malku) "watercourse = river".

2. *in-ni tamirti lā kuppī ka-ra-at-tu petêma* RINAP 2, p. 228 no. 4: 37 "to open up the springs of meadowland without reservoirs as(?) a watercourse", (partially quot. as Lyon Sarg 6 in AHw. 448, CAD K 215). MPS (1), FJMS (2)

karātu "to cut off, break off, detach"

G 1. NB *amēlussu ak-tar-a-ta* OIP 114, 17: 8 "I detached(?) his slave".

2. *amēlussu lū ak-ta-ra-t*[*a*] ib. 29.

3. Elsewhere the verb is *i*-class.

D SB *ana kur-ru-ti ša eqbīki* Lamaštu SKS 15 (Farber 2014, 272) "to break off your heels".

karāṭu "N to be merciful"

N SB *ik-ka-riṭ-ma zamar itarri ālittu* Ludlul I 18 "(once) he shows compassion, he quickly becomes like a mother", s. Oshima 2014, 117.

karāʾu "to bow down"; < Aram. *krʿ*

SB *ana mārat ḫazannu ša* GN *ak-ta-ra-ʾ aktabaskunūši kīma mê uṭṭabbīkunūši kīma eleppi kī ēlû attašab ana mu*[*ḫḫ*]*i-kunu* SpTU 2, 24: 8 "I bowed down to the daughter of the mayor of GN. I humbled myself before you. I dove before you as in water, like a ship. When I emerged, I sat down with you". S. von Weiher, ib. p. 128; AHw. 1566.

karballatu, + *karmallatu*, + *karrarbatu* "a piece of linen headgear"

LB *kar-mál-la-tum* CT 56, 558: 4; *kar-bar*!(MAŠ)*-lat* CT 57, 320: 11; *kar-ra-ar-ba-tum* CT 56, 382: 9.

kargullû "market value"

OB *ka-ar-gu-ul-lu uštamriṣūninni* CUSAS 36, 39: 10 "the market prices have troubled me".

kāribu "person providing offerings"

Da Riva 2002, 63: Not a profession, but a general term describing a wealthy private individual who provides temple offerings alongside the king.

+ **karīku**, *kirīku* "wrap"; OB, LB; < *karāku*

1. 1 *tāpal ka-ri-ki* ARM 30, 342 M.11535: 5 "1 pair of *k.*"

2. LB (5 shekel of blue-purple wool) *ana ki-ri-ki ša ḫuṣannē ša lubuštu ša* DN Zawadzki 2013, 502: 2, 6, 10 "for a wrap with sashes for the garment of DN".

+ karintu “preparation”

S. Fales 2000, 278.

karkamisû “from Carchemish”; OB

^{lú}*kar-ka-mi-su-ú*^{ki} ARM 31, 76: 1 “man from Carchemish”, s. Guichard 2005, 170 n. 44.

karkartu “an edible plant”; + MB

1. MB 3 *kar-ka-ra-tum* MBLET 52: 4. 1, 8 “3! *k.* (besides barley, opopanax, *muššu*, and cress)”.

2. Gurney ib. p. 143 suggests to read ^{ninda}*karkarātu* and identifies the word as a variant of *kakkartu* “a round leaf of bread”. MPS/NR

karkaṣu, + *karkasu* “a kind of mash”; + OB

OB lex. *ka gaz munu*$_4$ = *ka-ar-ka-su* TIM 9, 88 r. 4.

****karmu I** (AHw. 449; CAD K 217 *k.* adj.) s. *karintu* (Fales 2000, 278).

karmu “heap; storage”

bīt karme “storeroom”: (barley) *ina bīt kar-me ša erābe ana emetta tabik* DeZ 2528: 8 (cit. CM 29,) “is heaped up on the right-hand side when entering the storeroom”. S. ib. 323–325 for disc.

karmūtu “ruination”

SB *ummānī rubê kar-mu-tu illak* KAL 5, 19: 14 “the troops of rulers will go to ruin”.

karpassu s. *qarpāsu*

karpatu “jar”

1. OB n DUG GEŠTIN($^{\text{ḫi.a}}$) *rīqātu ša ka-ar-pa-tam ana ka-ar-pa-tim ušrīqū* FM 11, 25: 12–14; 26: 6–8; 33: 11–14 “n empty jars of wine, that had been emptied jar by jar”.

2. S. Guichard 2005, 1f. for disc. and p. 210 for add. refs. (all logogr.). Cf. Powell 1987–1990, 499, 504f.

karriru “a criminal”

1. Bogh. lex. ⸢*áš*⸣*-daḫ di* = ⸢*kar-ri-ru*⸣= *za-ap-*⸢*pí-at-tal-la*⸣*-aš* MSL 17, 98ff. A i. 45 (Erimḫuš) “criminal = *k.* = who lets (things) leak/drip away”.

2. LB lex. [*lú-kar*]*-ra* = ⸢*kar*⸣*-ri-ri* (= *sa-ar-rum*) SpTU 2, 53: 56 “fugitive = *k.* = criminal” (quote of Malku I 91).

karru II, + *kurāru* “knob, handle”

1. OB *ḫūratum ana ṣarāp ku-ra-ri ša šukurrī* ARM 21, 306: 3 “madder(?) for dying the handles(?) of lances”.

2. OB (blue wool) *ša ana šipir ku-ra-ri ša šukurrī* ARM 30, 296 M.8208: 5 “for making tassels(?) for lances”.

3. To be distinguished from the *kurāru* disease.

karru III “rags, mourning clothing”

1. OB *anūmma šārātīya ša qaqqad*[*iy*]*a u ka-ra-am ša ina pagriya nuṭṭup*(sic) *ušābilakkum* ARM 10, 32: 7 “hereby I send you my hair from my head and the rags torn from my body” (coll. and disc. Durand 2009, 50).

2. SB *kī elīša kar-r*[*a* …] KAL 9, 6 ii 18 “like upon her the mourning dress […]”.

karṣu “slander”; + OA

1. OA *awīlum ana* PN *kà-ar-ṣé-a ēkul* AKT 2, 50: 31 “the man has slandered me before PN”.

2. OB lit. *ākilāt ka-ar-*<*ṣí*>*-i-a* CUSAS 10, 9: 30, s. *ḫabību*.

3. S. also *karāṣu* D. NJCK (1), MPS (2)

karšu I "stomach, interior"

1. OB lex. *šà maḫ šu-si ĝìr-ĝ*[*u*10] = *ka-ra-aš ubān* [*šēpiya*] CUSAS 12 p. 157 xi 9 (Ugumu) "the ball of my toe".

2. Rumen, first stomach of sheep and cattle (Stol 2006, 105f.).

karšu II s. *karašu*

karšu III s. *karā/ašu* II

kartappu "groom"

OB lit. *Ḫamusisi ka-ar-ta-*⸢*pa*!?⸣-*k*[*a*] (// *kir*4-⸢*dab*⸣) ASJ 19, 262: 5 "Ḫ. is your groom" (followed by *kizû* l. 6).

karû I "pile of barley"

1. OB lit. [*k*]*a-re-e tīli* [*ka-r*]*e-e māši* [*ka-re*]-*e ki-ša-da*/-[*t*]*i-šu-nu* [*ta-ka*]-*ma*!-*ri* Nidaba and Enki 55 "[you pi]le up piles (the size) of a hill, piles (the size) of a *māšu*-measure, [pile]s …".

2. MA *pišerti ka-ru-e* BATSH 9, 60: 2 pass. "release of the grain heap" (i.e. grain distribution after threshing). On this phrase s. Röllig ib. p. 20 with prev. lit.

3. NA *ka-ru-a-ni-ia l*[*aššu*?] SAA 1, 264 r. 3 "I h[ave no(?)] storage heaps"; s. [*k*]*a-ru-*⸢*a*⸣-[*ni*] ib. r. 8.

4. NA *šummu dēnu ina muḫḫi puṣê ina ka-ru-e-šú-nu* StAT 2, 263 s. 3 "(they swear there is no) lawsuit concerning the empty lot (and/in?) their granary".

5. LB *udû ḫepû ū ḫal-qa ina ka-ri-šú-nu izaqqapū* CUSAS 28, 75: 10 "(if) the equipment is broken or lost, they will pay an indemnity from their 'grain heap' (i.e. their commonly held property)". MPS (1, 3), JK/JW (2, 4), JW (5)

karû II "to be(come) short"

G 1. SB *lik-ru-uš napištašu* UF 16, 303 v 1 "his life shall dwindle" (s. Paulus 2014, 757, diff. Sommerfeld 1990, 31, who derives the verb from *qarāšu*).

2. NB *akkā'i annappil … ak-te-ra-ma* OIP 114, 63: 20 "how will I get paid? … I have become in need", s. Streck 1999, 293.

D 1. MB *danniš napištaka ku-ra-at* Emar 6/3, 266: 11 "your life is severely shortened"; *šumma napištaka mimma tu-kar-ra* ib. 15 "if you shorten your life in any way".
2. NA DN *ūmēšu arkūte* ⸢*li*⸣-*kar-ri* CTN 6, 5: 10 "may DN shorten his long days".

kāru "harbor; trading post"

OB lit. pl. *nadûšum ka-ru ina* GN CUSAS 10, 7: 7 "the harbors lie (ready) for him in GN".

****kāru B** (CAD K 239), s. ARM 26/1, 422. S. *kakkaru*.

kasāmu "to cut, chop; to weed"

OB *eqlam ak-su-um aškuk ešber u šer'am aškun* FM 6, 468 no. 67//68: 8 "I weeded the field, harrowed (it), broke up (the clods), and prepared the furrow".

kasāpu I "to break (off, apart)"

\+ **N** (the wheel(?) of the chariot) *i*[*t*!-*t*]*ak-sap* SAA 16, 25: 11 "broke".

kasāpu II "to make a funerary offering"; OB

G SB *kispa ta-kas-sip-ši* Lamaštu K 888: 27 (Farber 2014, 276) "you will make her a funerary offering".

\+ **Gtn** OB *kīma mītim kispam ak-ta-as-sí-ip-šum* AbB 13, 21: 9 "I kept making funerary offerings for him as if he were dead".

N OB lit. *kispum ul ik-ka-sà-ap* FM 3, 66 no. 4 i 15, s. 24, 31 "a funerary offering will not be presented".

JW (G), NR (Gtn), MPS (N)

kasāru, *kesēru* "to block, pave"

+ **D** OB *šaddaqdim ú-ka-sí-ir-ma lā libbilamma malī ú-ka-sí-ru [n]ārum itbal* ARM 28, 49 = ARM 33, 6: 17–18 "last year I did some paving, but unfortunately the river carried off everything I had paved".

kasāsu "to chew, to gnaw"

G 1. *a/u*: SB *[am]mīni eṭlam u wardatam* ⸢*ta-kàs-sa-si*⸣ KAL 9, 37 iv 38 "why do you gnaw (on) the young man and the young woman?" cf. // *ta-kas-si-i, ta-kas-sa/sà-si* in Muššu'u VIII 48 (Böck 2007, 274).
2. *u/u*: SB *ammīnim ti-ka-as-su-us-ma* AulaOr. (Suppl.) 23, 14: 4 "why do you chew up (my flesh)?"; s. also *ik-ta!-na-su-*⸢*us*?⸣ in BAM 1, 77: 25. CAD distinguishes two verbs based on vowel class, but this is not semantically justified.

D SB *ammīnim tuk-te-si-sí* ib. 21: 75 "why have you chewed up (his flesh)?"

+ **KaSāTu** "part of a table"; OA

GA-ZA-Dam ša ⸢*paššūri*⸣*m ša ammat u ūṭ bilam kablu annākam ibaššī* AKT 3, 66: 34 "bring the *k.* of the table measuring a cubit and a half. The (table's) leg(s) are here." The context suggests a mng. "tabletop" (Michel 2001b, 410).

JW/NJCK

kasilaqqu s. *kizalāqu*.

+ **kasîš** "bound" (?)

SB *sīqiš ka-siš* AfO 19, 51: 97 (prayer to Ištar) "tight(?), bound(?)" (in broken context, s. already AHw. 1049, 1567; von Soden 1975, 461), cf. *kasû* I?

kaslu "land drained by ditches"; + MB

1. MB (9 seah of barley) *ina mu-*[x *k*]*a-as-li ša ālim ša* PN MBLET 38 r. 2 "at the … of the *k.*-land of the town of PN".

2. LB [*k*]*a-sal* Or. 86, 53 no. 3: 2.

3. LB *adī ka-sa-la* CUSAS 28, 64: 4 "up to the land drained by ditches" (in description of land).

kaspu "silver"

NA unusual spelling: *ga-*⸢*as*!⸣*-bi gammur* StAT 3, 12: 10 "payment is complete" (s. Faist ib., 37). JK

+ **kaspu II** "chipped"; SB

Lex. *ka-a*[*z-b*]*a* = GAZ = *kàs*(GAZ)*-pu-um* CUSAS 12 p. 8: 27 (Ea).

kassibānû s. *kusīpu*

kassupu "broken"; + MA

MA 15 *nigallū ka-su-pu-tu* StAT 5, 75: 2 "15 sickles, broken".

kasû I "bound, fettered"

1. OA uncert.:
a) 402 *dulbātim ku-sú-a-tim* Prag 740: 10 "402 tied up *d.*" (s. *dulba/ātu*, a part or product of the plane tree).
b) *mulūḫāt*[*im*?] *ku*?*-sú-a-tim* Bab. 6, 188 no. 9: 4' "tied up *m.*"
c) Both *dulbātu* and *mulūḫātu* are of uncertain meaning. *kasû* (?) here either derives from an unknown noun *KuZūtu* in apposition, or from an adj. **KuZ'um* or **kuZi/uum* (cf. GOA § 7.2.3). Derivation from *kasû* offers a plausible etymology.

2. SB *utnennu anḫu ka-su-ú ša bēl lemutti ik-su-šú* ORA 7, 322: 80 "prayer of a weary, bound person, whom an adversary bound".

NJCK/JW (1), JW (1), MPS (2)

kasû II "a spice and dye plant"

1. OB 1 GUR *ka-si-i* FM 2, 25 no. 4: 7 "1 kor of *k.*" (in list of vegetables and spices).

2. LB Aram. pl. also in *ka-si-iá* dubsar 3, 170: 3.

3. For use in beer brewing s. Stol 1994, 175ff. His identification of the plant with *cuscuta* is uncertain, as, unlike *cuscuta, k.* is also used to achieve a red-purple color in wool. S. the disc. in Thavapalan 2020, 350–352 ("safflower"?) and Choukassizian Eypper 2019, who argues for "tamarind".

kasû III "to bind"

G SB *iramm(i) ka-sa-a-šú* Jiménez 2017, 48 "his bondage loosens".

D 1. OA "to arrest, to put in fetters": *šumma alākam ištē* PN *lā i-mu-ú kà-sí-a-šu-ma šēriāneššu* AKT 5, 4: 19 "if someone refuses to come with PN, put him in fetters and have him brought here"; sim. AKT 3, 87: 27; BIN 4, 25: 40; kt 88/k 970: 9, 17, 29, 32, 37 (s. Donbaz 2008, 211).

2. OA (if the intended husband does not come within two months and does not care for his (prospective) wife, they will give the girl to another husband) *a-ḫi-sà lā ú-kà-sà* TC 1, 67: 19 "he (the intended husband) will not 'bind' the man who marries her (*āḫissa*)" (// *a-ḫi*!*-sà ula ú-ša-Ga-ar* RA 76, 170: 20: from *nakārum* Š "to instigate enmity"?).

3. OA *adī* 5 *ūmē awātam ú-kà-sà šumma lā uk-ta-sí*!? *awīlam azakkarakkunūti* AKT 11A, 85: 22 and 23 "within 5 days he will 'bind' the matter. If he does not 'bind' it, I will mention the man('s name) to you" .

4. OA refs. in G mean "to bind by contract" rather than "to demand payment" (pace CAD K 252b s.v. *k.* 4). This mng. is however not attested for D (pace CAD K 253a *k.* 6). MPS (G), NJCK (D)

kāsu "goblet, cup; a capacity measure"

1. OA (the king) *kà-sú umallīma itbuk* (...) *umma šunuma šumma māmītkunu ninaddī damani kīma kà-sí-im lū tabik* Çeçen/Hecker 1995, 35 kt n/k 794: 34 and 41 "filled his cup and poured it out saying [...]. They said: 'if we neglect our oath, may our blood be poured out like (the blood from) this cup".

2. OA PN *kà-sá-am ša ilišunu išattī(ma)* AKT 7A, 294 tablet: 14 "(if) PN drinks the cup of their god" (i.e., apparently, if he swears an oath that he has told the truth).

3. OA *kà-sà-am* KÙ Prag 487: 24 "cup made of silver". S. also KTS 2, 31: 7; Prag 483: 14; 523: 17; and *pass.*

4. OA *ana kà-sí-im ramākka lā taddan* Fs. Matouš II, 116: 22 "do not give yourself (over) to the cup (i.e. to drink)!".

5. OB s. Guichard 2005, 2–13 and 211–213 for add. refs. NJCK (1–3), JW (4–5)

kasūsu "falcon"; + NA

ka-su-su SAA 7, 81: 3 (decoration on a dress pin made of gold).

kaṣādu "D to delay"

Dt OA *têrtušu lā uk-ta-ṣa-ad-ma* FAOS Bh. 2, 43: 37 "his report shall not be delayed".

kaṣāpu "to plan, think"

D 1. NB *ilū rabûtu ... [m]imma mala tu-kaṣ-ṣip qātka lušakšid* SAA 17, 90: 6 "may the great gods make your hand achieve whatever you planned".
2. NB *itti libbišu ú-kaṣ-ṣip* SAA 21, 21 r. 13 "he planned in his heart".

kaṣāru, *qaṣāru* "to tie, knot, gather, freeze"

G 1. "to gather": OB *enūtum* 17 *ka-aṣ-ra-at* FM 9, 220 no. 53: 5 "17 instruments have been collected".

2. "to freeze", said of ice:
a) OB *ina rîtim šurīpum ul ikkaṣir ina kalakkātimma šurīpum ka-ṣí-ir* FM 2, 140 no. 76: 17 "on the meadow the ice did not freeze, but in the (cold) stores the ice is frozen".
b) *[šu]rīpum* ⌜*ka-aṣ*⌝*-ru* FM 2, 145 no. 78: 9 "(because) the [ic]e is frozen".

3. "to arrange, organize": OB *awātam ša ṣuḫārī iqabbīki ku-uṣ-ri-ši* OBTR 39: 15 "the matter of which my servant told you – organize it" (s. the comm. in Langlois 2017, 14).

4. "to become angry" (s. *kiṣru* for the idiom *kiṣir libbi rašû*): OB *mimma bēlī ana annêtim ayyâšim lā i-qa-ṣa-ra-am* FM 2, 216 no.118 r. 23 "my lord must not become angry with me because of this!"

5. "to knot (textile)": MA *ana ka-ṣa-ri* EN *lišpura li-ik-ṣu-ru limḫiṣū* BATSH 4/1, 6: 13–14 "my lord shall write to me concerning the knotting; they shall knot and weave".

6. "to encase", mng. "to ratify": *ṭuppī tubbala ana kunukkī ša kiṣrāti tutār šumma adī* 1 ITU $U_4^{meš}$ *lā tattabal lā tuta''er lā i-ka-ṣu-ru-ni-ku* Chuera 22A/B: 26 "you will bring my tablet, (and) convert (it) into a sealed case-tablet. If you have not brought (and) converted (it) within a month, they will not encase (it) for you." Cf. Postgate 2013, 71.

N 1. OB *bītum šū lāma kuṣṣi li-qa-ṣí-ir* A.3936: 13' (cit. Charpin 1989–90, 99b) "this house shall be constructed before the cold season".
2. "to freeze", said of ice: OB *ik-ka-ṣí-ir*, s. *kaṣāru* G 2a. MPS/JW (G, N), JK (G)

kaṣāṣu, *gaṣāṣu* "to gnash (teeth), to grind; to rage; to trim, cut"

G 1. OB lit. *nimrī ga-ṣi!?-ṣú* Westenholz 1997, 100 r. 15 "my gnashing panther".
2. OB *aššum Amurrêti[m] ša* PN *irdê[m] kalûšinama ka-ṣa šībā* 1 *sinniš-tum ina bīrišina ul ibašš[ī]* FM 9, 218 no. 52 r. 10 "concerning the Amorite women that PN led here, they are all scuffed(?) (and) old. There i[s] not a single woman among them". N. Ziegler ib. p. 218, 220 derives *ka-ṣa* from *kaṣû* "to be cold", which cannot be excluded but seems less likely because one would rather expect a writing *ka-ṣa-a*.
3. SB *[gur₅-ru]-úš búr // [...] gaṣ*-GA-*ṣu* CTMMA 2, 15: 8, s. ib. p. 108 and TCS 3, 132 ad 434.
4. SB *šumma ubānu kaṣ-ṣa-at* SAA 4, 320: 7, r. 6 "if the finger is severed".
5. SB *šumma kubuš ḫašî ka-ṣiṣ* SAA 4, 292: 5 "if the cap of the lung is severed".

Gt OB lit. *ki-ṣa-aṣ šaḫurrūtim* Or. 87, 17 i 37 "the gnashing of the stupefied ones" (Streck/Wasserman 2018, 30: *kiṣṣā/aṣ* instead of *kiṣṣuṣ*).

D 1. OB 2 *ḫanî balṭūssunu ana pāṭi lirdûnimma ina pāṭi li-ka-ṣí-ṣú-šu-nu-ti* ARM 26/1, 582 no. 282: 21 "they shall take 2 Hanaeans alive to the border and mutilate them at the border".

2. SB [*lū g*]*u-uṣ-ṣú-ṣa ubānātīšu* KAL 2, 30 r. 6 "his fingers shall be mutilated".

+ **Š** OB *ša kīma rēʾûm ip*[*peš*]*u* [*k*]*issatam šu-*⸢*uk-ṣi*⸣*-iṣ* CUSAS 36, 71: 12 "have straw chopped up like a shepherd does".

kaṣâtu, *qaṣâtu* "early morning"

1. OB *mūšam adī ka-ṣa-tim šūpišma* ARM 18, 23: 10 "let (them) make (containers) during the night until morning".

2. OB *ša mūšam u qa-ṣa-tam ušallamū* ARM 18, 32: 11 "who will complete (the task by working) day and night" (s. Kupper 1996, 79–80 for further Mari refs.).

3. OB (animals) *niqûm ša ka-ṣa-tim* FM 12, 214: 12 "morning sacrifice".

4. NB *ka-ṣa-a-tum* SAA 17, 195: 4 in broken context.

5. Streck 2017, 599.

kaṣbittu s. *qāt ṣibitti*

+ **kāṣirtu** "female knotter, tailoress"; OB

1. PN *ṣuḫārki aššum kà-ṣí-ra-tim tašpurīm anūmma* 2 *kà-ṣí-ra-tim ana qāt* PN *apqidamma* OBTR 154: 11, 13 "you have sent PN, your servant, to me concerning female knotters; now I have entrusted 2 female knotters to PN".

2. 4 MUNUS *ka-ṣí-ra-tum* ARM 13, 1 xii 13; cf. ARM 26/1, 566 no. 265: 9 and perhaps FM 6, 43 ii 9 (Langlois 2017, 157).

kāṣiru "knotter, tailor"

1. SB *ka-*⸢*ṣir*⸣ *urpēti* KAL 3, 28: 4 "he who ties together clouds" (epithet of Adad), s. Frahm ib. p. 67.

2. In LB also tasked with laundry (s. Waerzeggers 2006a, no. 3 and p. 86).

+ **kaṣīʾ/yātu** "an aromatic, Cinnamomum cassia(?)"; SB, LB

1. LB in lists of aromatics:

a) ^{šim}*ka-ṣi-ia-*⸢*tú*⸣ AOAT 414/1, 73: 15 (after *qunnabu*).

b) 1/2 MA.NA *ka-ṣi-ia-t*[*u*4] Jursa 2009, 168 BM 61003: 2 "1/2 mina *k.*"

c) 1 MA.NA ⸢^{šim}⸣*ka-ṣi-ʾ-a-tum* ib. 167 BM 67001: 5 "1 mina *k.* (worth 1 shekel of silver)".

d) ^{šim}⸢*ka-ṣa-a-a-*[*tú*] ib. 151 BM 77429: 20.

e) *ka-ṣi-a-tu* ib. 161 BM 63707.

2. SB *ka-ṣi-*<<*ṣi*>>*-ḫa-tum* RAcc. 18: 6 Cf. AHw. 458, CAD K 266 s.v. *kaṣiṣiḫatu*.

3. Both Jursa 1997a and Zadok 1997 connect the word with Hebr. *qṣyʿh* "a powdered bark like cinnamon" (Zadok) and cf. Gr. *kassia*. Jursa 2009, 161f.: identification uncertain. Pasquali 2014 connects Eblaite *ga-zi-*(*a-*)*tum*/*ga-zi*, mentioned in connection with bread and flour.

****kaṣiṣiḫatu** s. *kaṣīʾātu*

kaṣru, + *qaṣaru* "bound, knotted, organized (of caravans, troops)"; + MA

1. OB of textile: ⸢GADA *qá-ṣa*⸣*-ra-*⸢*am*⸣ *ul ima*[*ḫḫarū*] ⸢*mīnum*⸣ *qá-ṣa-r*[*u-u*]*m ša balū* 2 ⸢*amātim*⸣ OBTR 138: 12, 14 "(my lady said:) 'They have not received the knotted textile.' What is a knotted textile without 2 servant-girls (to make it)?" (s. Langlois 2017, 138 for coll. and comm.).

2. MA PN GAL *kaṣ-ru-te* VS 19, 5: 23, 24 "PN, overseer of the organized (troops)", s. Freydank 1976, 113. Cf. VS 21, 4: 47.

kaṣṣāru "packing-supervisor"

1. OA 1/2 MA.NA *beʾūlāt kà-ṣa-ri-im* Prag 836: 14 "1/2 minas as *beʾūlātum*-capital for the packing-supervisor", cf. Prag 542: 8, 739: 9, 704: 16. Smaller amounts are mentioned in EL 170: 1, TC 3, 134: 18 (Matouš 1974, 169).

2. Early OB 2 *kà-ṣa-ré-en* ARM 19, 248: 2.

kaṣṣārūtu "function as packing-supervisor"; OA

ana kà-ṣa-ru-tim Prag 695: 2 (Matouš 1974, 169)

+ **kaṣṣu II** "a festival(?)"; MA

1. (wethers) *ana ka-aṣ-ṣi* Iraq 70, 159 no. 7: 3 "for *k.*" (among other ceremonial events).

2. (sheep) *ša ka-aṣ-ṣi ša naṣbete* MARV 2, 19 r. 19 "for the *k.* festival(?) and the *n.* festival(?)", s. Deller 1987.

3. (bread and sheep) [*ša*] *ka-aṣ-ṣi* Chuera 43: 2; (3 wethers) *ša ka-ṣi* ib. 4. S. disc. Jakob ib. p. 77.

kaṣû "cold"

OB lit. ⸢*lušqīka*⸣ [*m*]*ê ka-ṣú-ú-tim* AML 119: 80 "let me give you cold [wat]er to drink".

kaṣû II, *qaṣû* "steppe"

1. OB *ana ka-ṣí-im-ma īlī* ARM 14, 7 r. 6 "he went up to the steppe".

2. OB [*n*]*awâm ka*!-*ṣú-um malī* ARM 14, 121: 41 "the steppe is full of herds", s. Durand 1998, 384; [*naw*]*âm qa-ṣi-im* ... *likmi*[*s*]*ū* ib. 46 "let them assemble the [he]rds of the steppe".

3. OB *Ḫanû kalûšu ištū qa-ṣé-e-em ana šadîm ana rîtim ittalak* A.1187: 14, cf. ib. 18 (cit. Charpin 1989/1990, 99) "all the Hanaeans went from the steppe towards the hills for pasture".

4. On etym. s. Streck 2000, 101. The word is not attested in OA, but s. the difficult *kà-ZI-im* AKT 8, 149: 2 instead of expected *kà-ṣa-im*, and PN *ina Ga-Zi-im assī* AKT 2, 31: 16 "I called PN ...". MPS (1–2, 4), NJCK (4), JW (3)

kaṣû III "to be(come) cold"

G 1. OA *emārum ša upqim ina kà-ṣa-im iḫliq*(*ma*) Prag 804: 13 "(when) a donkey with an *upqu*-load perished from the cold".

2. OA in *šīmum kaṣī* "trade is cold", i.e. "has ceased, is at a stand-still", s. Veenhof 1972, 383f.; *kaṣāʾu* seems more straightforward than *kasāʾu* "to bind" as suggested by Veenhof, s. GOA p. 249 n. 6 and for the spelling *kà-ṣú* GOA § 3.2.1.1. Add. refs.: AKT 4, 39: 4; AKT 6C, 619: 10 and 654: 32; TPAK 1, 50: 48.

3. MA *tūr ūmū i-ka-ṣu-ú* BATSH 4/1, 6: 11 "the days will be cold again (and will not be suitable for washing)".

4. For FM 9, 218 no. 52 r. 10 s. *kaṣāṣu*. NJCK (1–2), JK (3), MPS (4)

kâšu "to flay, skin"; + MA

1. MA **a)** *mā ina mēlte mītū mā lā a-ku-ṣ*[*u*] BATSH 9, 37: 20 "(he spoke) thus: '(the donkeys) died in a flood' (and) thus: 'I did not skin (them)'".
b) *ina šipir mēlte mētū lā i*!-*ku-ṣú*!(text: SU) BATSH 9, 43: 4 "they (the donkeys) died in the wake of a flood, he did not skin (them)".
c) *ē*-class (also in Nuzi): *lā a-ke-e-ṣu* BATSH 9, 48: 11 "I did not skin (them)".

2. NB *lišānšu mittu ... ina patri ta-ku-*⸢*us-si*⸣ *u ina* x x *tankissi* OIP 114, 85: 15

"his tongue is dead … you flayed it with a dagger and cut it off with …".

JK (1), MPS (2)

kašādu "to reach, arrive; accomplish; conquer"

G 1. *ṭēmu ik-tal-da*!(KA) BATSH 4/1, 14: 5 "the decision reached me", s. the comm. p. 167; for *šd* > *ld* s. de Ridder 2018, 14.
2. LB ⸢*kul*⸣*-du* AOAT 414/1, 192: 12 "carry (it) out!" (at the end of the letter).

Gt 1. OB lit. [*li*]*-ik-ta-aš-da-ak-ki* VS 10, 214 viii 22 "[let] it reach you", s. Streck 2010, 569.
2. OB *šumma lā ki-iš-šu-*[*d*]*a-ti šuprīm-ma eqlam ana errēšim luddin* AbB 8, 71: 8 "(if you wish, work the field yourself.) If you cannot manage(?), write to me and I will give the field to a cultivator" (s. Streck 2003a, 68. The function of Gt is unclear).

Dtn 1. Matouš 1974, 169: OA *ḫa-ra-ka uk-ta-na-ša-ad* Prag 720: 8 "I constantly go on your trade journeys".
2. OB lit. *rū'am tu-uk-ta-na-aš-ša-di* CUSAS 10, 10: 25 "you constantly drive away a boyfriend".

Št OB *eqel pīḫātika šu-ta-ak-ši-id-ma* AbB 12, 5: 7 "have the field for which you are responsible finished!", cf. AbB 10, 191: 18; 12, 8: 14; 124: 9; 72: 27 (Streck 2003a, 122).

MPS (G, Gt, Dtn), JK (G), JW (Gt, Dtn)

kašāru, *kešēru* "to restore, replace, repair; to succeed, achieve; OA to compensate for(?)"

G 1. OA "to compensate for, to pay back(?)": (please make him pay the silver (...) and send it to me) *ḫu-bu-li*/*e ša a-ša-du-e*!*-tim aḫbulu lá-ak-šu-ur* AKT 2, 52: 16 "so that I can pay back/make up for my debt (or: the debts) which I incurred from the *šaddu'utu*-tax".
2. OB *u anāku annānūm ammīnim ke-èš-re-ku* RATL 18: 38 "and I, why should I succeed here?".
3. SB *šebirte ana ke-še*/*ši-ri* BAM 124 iii 57 // 125: 28 "in order to restore what was broken" (von Soden 1975, 461).

D 1. Early OB (men) *iš kà-šur saparrim* ARM 19, 64: 2 "for repairing carts"; also 114: 3; 324: 3.
2. OB (oil) *ana ku-úš-šu-ur eleppētim* (*labirātim*) FM 3, 218 no. 24: 3; FM 3, 229 no. 60: 15 "for repairing (old) ships".
3. OB *dūram ša išātum īkulu li-ka-ši-ru-ú* CUSAS 36, 11: 19 "they shall repair the wall that fire consumed"; cf. *dūrum lū ku-*[*š*]*u-ur* 7: 16 "the wall shall be in good repair"; ⸢*ku-še*⸣*-ra-a* 10: 24 "repair (the parts he set on fire)!"; cf. 12: 15.

Disc.: Pace CAD K 284–286, there is no need to assume three lemmata: *kašāru* A "to repair" and *kašāru* C "to replace", both *a*/*u*, are surely identical. Later *kašāru* B "to succeed, to achieve" (*i*/*i*), may well be another example of the shift from *a*/*u* to later *i*/*i* (s. Kouwenberg 2010, 77f.). Von Soden 1975, 461 proposed to interpret the instances given for *kašāru* B as elliptic use of the otherwise transitive verb.

kašāšu II "to feel dizzy(?) (a symptom of disease experienced after standing up)"

G 1. SB *itebbēma i-káš-šú-uš itebbē u ikammis* STT 91+: 85 = SA.GIG XXV 30 "he stands up and feels dizzy(?), he stands up and kneels down" s. Stol 1993b, 73.
2. The transl. "to feel dizzy" is suggested by the context. Von Soden proposed a basic mng. "to be(come)

heavy, bulky" (AHw. 462), based on the etym. from Arab. *k͟t͟t* "to be thick".

kašāṭu "to cut off"

1. OB lit. *lā ta-ka-aš-ši-ṭa-an-ni* YOS 11, 24 ii 9 "don't cut me off!"

2. OB [*n*]*īš ilī ša pī tuppi annī*[*m l*]*ā ni-ka-aš-ši-ṭú* [*lā n*]*imaššû* RATL L.-T. 3 iv 2 "the oath by the gods according to the wording of this tablet we shall not sever, we shall not forget". Cf. 1 v 9'''; 7 b, 4'.

kāšišu, + *kāsisu* "creditor, pledge-taker"

OB *ana ka-si-si-šu* AbB 10, 81: 8' "(a letter will go) to his creditor".

kašittu OB "recovered (stolen) goods"; SB "success, achievement"

OB *kīma ka-ši-it-tim šinīšu aštaprak-kum kaspam šūbilam* CUSAS 36, 145: 13 "like (chasing after) stolen goods I have already sent you two messages (saying) 'send me silver!'".

kaškaššu, + *kaškāšu* "overpowering"

Lex. *níĝ-ùl-la* = *ka-aš-ka-a-šum* CUSAS 12 p. 252: 165.

kašku "part of a field"; Nuzi

Negri Scafa 1982 (inalienable part of a parcel of land); Richter 2012, 193 with prev. lit.

kašmaḫḫu, *kašmāḫu* "first-class beer"; + OB

1. OB *kaš-ma-ḫa-am ukallam* AbB 9, 41: 23 "he is holding first-class beer for me".

2. NA *munaqqû* KAŠ.MAḪ *ša* P[N] KAL 3, 22: 5 "the libation vessel for first-class beer of P[N]".

kaššāptu "witch"

SB *kaš-šá-pat* SpTU 4, 149 ii 19, 24, 26 "she is a witch".

+ **kaššilu** "a profession connected to beer production"; OB; Sum. lw.

1. (PNN) *ka-ši-lu ša* KAŠ ÚS ARM 22, 57 A iii 12 "*k*.s for (making/handling) second quality beer"; *ša* KAŠ S[IG]$_5$ ib. 19 (coll. Durand 1987d) "for good quality beer".

2. [...] ^{lú}*ka-aš-ši-il*$_5$ ARM 23, 546 no. 580: 25.

3. 6 ^{lú}*ka-aš-ši-lu* ARM 23, 576 no. 609: 19.

4. PN *ka-aš-ši-il* OBTR 206 r. 13, cf. 207 iv 17.

5. ^{lú}KAŠ.ÍL *ša* GÌR-*šu marṣat* CUSAS 15, 158: 6 "the *k.* whose foot is wounded".

6. Durand 1987d. The logogr. KAŠ.ÍL suggests Sum. origin (cf. UET 3, 1401 r. 3).

kaššu "massive, strong"

SB *išāti ka-šiš-ti* SpTU 4, 129 vi 50 "mighty fire".

Kaššu I "an official"; OA

A general term designating officials in Anatolian towns and week eponyms in Kaneš (the latter only in the phrase *ḫamuštum ša kà-ší-im ša qāti* PN "the *ḫamuštum*-week of the official who took over from PN". Note also *ištū ḫamuštim ša Ga-«GA»-ší-im Kà-né-ší-im* PN *u* PN$_2$ *ilqe'u* kt c/k 782: 10–12 "from the *ḫamuštum*-week of the Kane-šite official (who) took over from PN and PN$_2$" (quot. in Dercksen 2011, 236). Lit.: Larsen 1976, 359f.; Kryszat 2004, 162f.; Veenhof 2008a, 226f. NJCK

Kaššu II s. *qaššu*

kašû II "to increase"

G Cf. D 1, below.

D 1. OB *agrum ša inūma ebūrim* ⌜*ú*⌝*-ka-aš-šu-ma ikkalu takšītum ana eṣēdim ina ḫalṣim* [*i-k*]*a*?*-aš-ši* … *ana* GN [*ana ku-úš*]*-ši-im ittalak* ARM 27, 26: 22 "the hired man who makes profit at the time of the harvest – profit increases(?) at harvest time in the district – he left for GN [to make pro]fit"; s. CAD T 88 *takšītu*.
2. OB *kasapka liqēma il–libbim ku-uš-ši* CUSAS 36, 36: 19 "take your silver and get your profit from it".

kâšu "to be late; to be merciful" AHw. *kâšu* III, CAD *kâšu* A and B

G SB [*u*]*zabbalma* : *i-kaš-ma* : *zubbulu* : *ka-a-ša* SpTU 1, 27: 10 "he protracts (the disease) : he delays : to protract : to delay" (commentary).

D NA [*atâ*?] *adu akanni tú-ú-ki-*[*iš*] SAA 1, 233: 13 "[why(?)] did you dela[y (it)] until now?"

Š MB *ul uš-ki-is-su-ma* CUSAS 17, 61: 19 "(DN) allowed him no pardon (but spilled his life-(blood) like water)".

kâšunu "you" (pl. obl. case)

1. NA also in letter: *ana ka-a-*⌜*šu*⌝*-nu* SAA 5, 34: 20.

2. LB *ana ka-šú-nu* dubsar 3, 75: 17 "for you".

kâta s. *kâti*

katammu "cover"; + NA

4 $^{giš?}$*ka-tam-a-ti* ⌜*te*⌝*ppaš* SAA 19, 156: 13 "you shall make 4 wooden(?) covers". S. *kadammu*.

katāmu "to cover"

G 1. OB with seed: *eqlam zēram ak-tu-um … aššum eqlim ša zēram ak-tu-mu* FM 7, 130 no. 36: 44–46 "I sowed the field (lit. covered it with seed) … regarding the field that I had sown". A mng. "to harrow", suggested by J.-M. Durand, ib. p. 132, is unlikely, s. *eqlam ša azrû* ib. 49 "the field that I had sown".
2. OB *ālī ina abnim ka-ta-mi-im izzīzamma* ARM 28, 44: 18 "my city stood up in order to cover (me) with stone(s)", s. FM 8 p. 107, and correct SAD 2, 64 *tamû* II G 1.
3. OB "to apply metal decorations to wood", s. Arkhipov 2012, 62f. with refs.

D 1. OB (oil) *ana ku-ut-tu-um ṣalmi* FM 3, 245 no. 95: 8 "for covering (= finishing?) a statue".
2. OB *panūki lā ku-*[*t*]*u-mu* AbB 7, 36: 5 "is your face not covered?" (perhaps indicating shame or grief, s. Kraus ib. n. b).
3. OB [*in*]*a bēlišunu* [*l*]*ā ú-ka-*⌜*ta*⌝*-mu-šu* RATL L.-T. 1 v 18" "I shall not hide him (= the runaway slave) from their master".

Ntn SB [*it-t*]*a-na-ak-tam* StBoT 36, 62 J2: 10' "is constantly covered", s. Wilhelm ib. 62: The logogr. spelling DUL.DUL-*tam* in TDP 40: 25, 70: 1 is likely also Ntn, pace AHw. 465 (D?) and CAD K 302 (Dt).

katanšarātu s. *kanasarru*

****katappu**, s. *katāpu*

katappû "bridle; double-edged"

SB *patri ka-tap-pe-e* Gilg. SB VIII 175 "double-edged dagger", s. SAD *patru* 5.

katāpu “a ceremonial weapon”

1. OB 1 ^{giš}*ka-ta-pu-um* KÙ.GI *muḫḫašu u išissu* KÙ.GI ARM 25, 608: 9 “1 *k*. made of gold, its top and its base made of gold”.

2. OB 1 ^{giš}*ka-ta-pu* ZABAR *īnātūšu* KÙ.BABBAR ARM 25, 608 ed. 1 “1 *k*. made of bronze, its eyes are of silver”.

3. OB *pādū ša ka-ta-pí* FM 7, 114 no. 30: 20 “handles for *k*. weapons”.

4. OB 1 *kà-tá-pum* KTT 53: 5, 15; 54: 10 (in lists of weapons and other objects).

5. OB Ebla PN *wakil* LÚ^{meš} *ka-ta-pí* Akkadica 126, 46: 3 “PN, overseer of the *k*.-bearers”, also in unpubl. OB Ebla text cit. RA 98, 123 n. 6. S. Kupper 2006.

6. MB s. Emar 6/3, 44, 45, 46.

7. For add. OB refs. and disc. s. Arkhipov 2012, 113f; s. also Watson 2014. Cf. CAD *katappu* b. None of the refs. for the weapon has double *p*, therefore *katāpu* instead of *katappu*.

katāru II “to wait(?)”

NA *ina libbi ni-ik-te-ti-*[*ir*] SAA 5, 249: 5 “we waited(?) there”.

katātu “to quiver, vibrate”; + OA

N(?) OA “to be annulled (of tablet)”: (silver will pass overland in the name of the Zuzu firm. When it arrives in the City) *tuppušu i-Ga-ta-at* CTMMA 1, 123 no. 86A: 14 “his tablet will be annulled(?)”, transl. M. T. Larsen.

NJCK/MPS

kâti, *kâta*, *kâtu* “you (fem./masc. sg. obl.)”

1. OB after prepositionally used *u*: *inūma ina* GN *anāku u abīya ka-ta nuštātû* AbB 14, 155: 12 “when I and you, my father, met in GN”. Cf. AbB 1, 21: 13; AbB 9, 108: 10; 76: 12; 129: 8; 125: 5; AbB 14, 85: 8 (Veenhof 2005, 209f.).

2. OB also for nom.: *šumma eqlum ka-a*[*-um*] *ka-ta ṣabat u šumma ya᾿um anāku aṣabbassu* ARM 26/2, 260 no. 404: 46 “if the field is yours, you take it! If it’s mine, I will take it” (a reading *at*!-*ta* is excluded by the photograph on https://archibab.fr/T7603).

katinnu “an implement; a weapon”

1. MB Emar (Pentiuc 2001, 145: *qaṭinnu*): *ga-di-nu* ZABAR Emar 6/3, 48: 2 *pass*., cf. *ka-ti-in-nu* Emar 6/3, 59: 4, 44: 10, 47:8, *ka-di-nu* URUDU RE 69: 11.

2. MB *ka-di-nu-*[*ma*?^{me}]^{š} PRU 6, 157: 11.

3. AHw. *kattinnu*. Huehnergard 1987, 398: “The writing with medial DI may reflect Hurrian intervocalic voicing.” Pentiuc 2001, 145 parses the word as *qaṭinnu*, but note that none of the refs. are spelled with *qa*$_1$. The interpretation as a weapon, perhaps “sickle-blade sword” has been suggested by Heltzer 1989 (cf. Hebr. *kīdōn*). For add. lit. s. Richter 2012, 197; Watson 2004.

+ **katkattu** “a box or chest”; MB

1. MB Qaṭna 4 *kat-kat-te*^{meš} *ša* ZÚ.GUL 3 *kat-kat-te*^{meš} *ša taskarinnim* QS 3, 12: 26f. “4 *k*. of ivory, 3 *k*. of boxwood”.

2. MB Alalaḫ (Niedorf 2008, 107 n. 403):

a) 6 *kat-kat-tù* ^{giš}TASKARIN AlT 441: 1 “6 *k*. of boxwood”.

b) ^{giš}*ka-at-ga-tu* AlT 421: 6, 8, 11; ^{giš}*ka-at-ga*!(TA)*-at-tù* ib. 3.

c) *ka-at-ka-at-te* AlT 438: 11.

d) *kat-kat-tum* AlT 417: 5, cf. 435: 21.

3. Inventories list the object among vessels or furniture, often made from wood. The ref. in AlT 417 was erroneously read *pa-pa-tum* in AHw. 824.

katrû s. *kad/trû*

kattû "guarantor"

1. Del. TIM 2 (= AbB 8) 101: 7 and TLB 4 (= AbB 3) 83: 20, both cit. CAD K 307 (Veenhof 2005, 210).

kâtu s. *kâti*

katû "to distrain, to take as security"; OA

G *amtam u wardam ša ak-tù-ú* kt 92/k 543: 31 (Bayram 2001, 3) "the female slave and male slave whom I took as security". S. also *ik-tù-ú-ma* Prag 537: 18; *kà-tí* AKT 6B, 337b: 20; *ni-ik-ta* AKT 7A, 276: 9; *ta-ak-ta* kt 92/k 293: 11; *ta-ak-tù-ú* ib. 14 and *ták-tá-a-ma* 328: 5 (s. Bayram 2000, 44–46).

Gtn *amtam ik-ta-na-tù-ú* kt 88/k 507b: 7 (Çeçen 1995, 53) "(why) does he keep taking the servant-girl as security?".

D *ku-tà-a-tí-a tù-kà-ta* AKT 6A, 86: 13 "you take things as security from me".

Disc.: Veenhof 2001, 154f. For *aq-tí-i* (kt j/k 97: 57), s. *qatû* II G. The meaning of *ik-ta-ma* (ATHE 35: 36 = OAA 1, 69) and *ak-tù-ú* (TC 2, 36: 39) is unclear.

NJCK

kâ/ātu, *gayyātu* "a type of barley"

1. SB ^{ú}*ka-a-t*[*u*] KAL 9, 52 l. e. 7 (list of medicinal ingredients).

2. CAD G s.v. *gajātu*. Cf. Hurr. *kade*, Hatt. *kait-*, Hebr. *gatāi* "barley bread" etc. It is disputed whether the word is originally Akk., Hurr., or other. S. Richter 2012, 197f. for lit. and disc.

3. S. also *qayyātu*.

+ **kawarḫu** "an animal"; OB

1. *ina panītim aššum ka-wa-ar-ḫi ašpurakkumma ka-wa-ar-ḫi šunūti ul tušābilam annītam bēlī išpuram mimma aššum ka-wa-ar-ḫi ina panītim bēlī ul išpuram* ... PN *illikamma* 4 *ka-wa-ar-ḫi ša maškī ḫa-ar-mu ilqē inanna anūmma* 3 *ka-wa-ar-ḫu*(sic) *ša maškī ḫa-ar-mu u* 2 *ka-wa-ar-ḫi ša* [*š*]*ārtim ana qāt* PN [...] ARM 27, 51: 5–13 "'earlier, I wrote you about *k.* but you did not send me those *k.*' This my lord wrote me. Earlier, my lord did not write me anything about *k.* ... PN came and took 4 *k.* enveloped in (their) skin. Now then I [entrusted] 3 *k.* enveloped in (their) skin and 2 *k.* with hair to PN".

2. M. Birot, ib. p. 112f., relates the word to the fish *kamāru* III. However, the words *kawarḫu* and *kamāru* are different, the det. *ku*$_6$ is missing, and skin and hair rather favor an animal with a hide.

kawāru "enclosure wall; edging"

1. OB *ammat u ūṭ uššū ana ka-wa-ar bītim mitḫāriš šuplam illikū* FM 8, 159 no. 45: 10 "the foundations for the enclosure wall of the temple uniformly went one and a half cubits deep".

2. OB as part of metalwork: 1 ^{gal}*ḫamrušḫu ka-wa-ar-šu ḫurāṣum* ARM 31, 258: 3 "1 *ḫamrušḫu*-cup, its rim edging of gold". S. Guichard 2015, 136–139.

3. AHw. 430 *kamar*(*r*)*u*, CAD K 111 *kamaru* A.

kawû, *kamû* "outer, outside"

OB DN *ša ka-we-tim* FM 12, 230 M.18084: 4 "DN of the outside" (in opposition to *libbi ālim* ib. 2 "inside the city")".

kayyamānu, fem. *kayyamāntu* "normal, regular, trustworthy"

1. OB [*in*]*a rēš erbîmma* [*in*]*a ka-ia-ma-an-ti-ia* [*k*]*amsāku* ARM 27, 29: 17 "I [was] kneeling(?) regularly in front of the locusts".

2. NA (may good news) *ka-a-a-ma-ni-u* ... *ana šarre* [*b*]*ēliya liqribāni* SAA 10, 251 r. 3 "constantly reach the king, my lord".

3. LB 1-*en mannu ka-ma-a-nu* AOAT 414/1, 221: 8 "somebody trustworthy" (cf. *mamma ka-a-a-ma-nu-u* CT 22, 141: 10).

kayyāniš "constantly"; + OA

OA *kà-a-a-ni-iš ana šēp bēlini nimta-naqqut* Günbattı 2014, 89 kt 01/k 217: 28 "we were constantly falling at the feet of our lord"; *kà-a-a-ni-iš ša ūmēni* ib. 51 "constantly through (lit. of) our days", i.e. "every day of our life"; s. also AKT 5, 13: 49. NJCK

kayyānu "constant, regular"

1. OB [*a*!]-*na ka-a-ia-an-tim udabbabū* FM 7, 105 no. 28: 37 "they shall talk constantly".

2. In commentaries "literal meaning" (Cavigneaux 1982, 237; George 1991, 154f. and Frahm 2011, 38 n. 137 for add. refs.).

+ **kayyanZu** (?) "a designation of property"; MB Emar

1. *eqlī ka-ia-an-ZA ša abīšu* (…) *ittadin* AulaOr. (Suppl.) 36: 13; cf. 83: 15 "he gave (PN) the fields (and?) *k.* of his father (instead of a debt of silver)".

2. *ka-ia-an-ZI-ia ša ālim u ṣēri* Iraq 54 1: 9 "my *k.* belong to the city and the open country", cf. Emar 6/3, 91: 18; 128: 3–7; ASJ 6 1: 7; RE 10:7; 13:9.

3. *mīnummê būšu*<*šu*> *bāšītušu u ka-ia-an-ZU-šú* Emar 117: 19 "all of his belongings, property and *k.*" (inheritance, cf. Emar 6/3, 5: 9, AulaOr. (Suppl.) 83: 10–12, 18).

4. *šumma mamma tuppa ša bītim šâšu qadū ka-ia-an-ZI-šu ušellâ* SMEA 30, 203 no. 6: 7 "if anyone produces a tablet concerning this house with its *k.*"; cf. ib. 205 no. 7: 24.

5. Pentiuc 2001, 93f. with prev. lit.; etym. unkn.

kazābu I "to be attractive", D "to fawn, flatter"

D 1. OB lit. *ku-uz-zi-ba-an-ni k*[*īma mī*]*rānim* ZA 75, 204: 106 "wag your tail at me l[ike a p]uppy!"
2. OB lit. *ul uk-ta-zi-ib* ZA 110, 43 iii 6 in broken context.

+ **kaZaššu** "a type of food"; MA; Hurr. lw.?

[n ^{dug}]*kallī* GIŠ.ŠE *ša ka-ZA-áš-še* MARV 3 16 = SAAB 18 p. 4 i 23 "[n] *kallu*-bowls with sticks of *k.*". S. Llop ib. p. 24.

kazāzu s. *gazāzu*

kazbu, OA *kuzbu* "charming, alluring; nice, friendly"

1. OA *atta ana awīli awātam ku-zu-ub-tám ištēt qarrib* kt b/k 95: 14 "you, put in a friendly word with the gentleman (or: gentlemen)", s. Balkan 1967, 410.

2. Ass. *kuzbu* corresponds to Bab. *kazbu* (GOA § 7.2.3); not from *kuzzubu*, pace CAD K 617a s.v. *kuzzubu* adj., as this would be **kazzubu* in Ass. NJCK

kazbittu s. *ṣibittu*

+ **kazuḫḫu** "a designation of shoes"; OB; Hurr. lw.?

1. 1 *mešēn ka-zu-uḫ-ḫi* ARM 30, 387 M.11311: 1 = ARM 25, 17 "1 (pair of?) *k.*-shoes".

2. 1 *mešēnu ka-zu-ḫu* ARM 23, 569: 2. S. Durand 2009, 167 for add. refs. and 165 for disc.

kazû s. *kizû*

kazzu s. *gazzu*

kē s. *kī*

kedru s. *kadāru*

kedrû s. *kad/trû*

+ **keltu**, *keldu* "health, well-being"; OB; Hurr. word

1. OB 1 *puḫādam ana ilī* ... *ana ke-el-ti-šu-nu tanaqqī* AlT 126: 23 "you sacrifice 1 lamb to the gods ... for their well-being"; cf. *puḫād ke-el-di-ia* ib. 37.

2. < Hurr. *keldi* (= Akk. *šulmu*). S. Schwemer 1995 for use in Hurr. and Hitt. sources; Richter 2012, 203f. with add. lit.

keltuḫlu, + *keltuḫul* "bowyer"; + OB; Hurr. word

OB [...] *ke-el-tu-ḫu-ul* Shemshara 2, 46: 23. S. Richter 2012, 206 for lit.

kepû "to bend, blunt"

D Del. ref. Hinke Kudurru i 13 (CAD K 313 ad 2): read *šur-bu-ú* instead of *kùp-pu-ú* (Borger 1975, 71b).

kerḫu "citadel, upper city, inner city; enclosure wall, enclosed area; a vessel"; + MA; + MB; Hurr. lw.

1. OB ⸢*Ištar bēlet ke*⸣-*er-ḫi-im* RATL 79: 6 "Ištar, lady of the inner city".

2. OB *nišīšunu ana ke-e*[*r*]-*ḫi-i*[*m*]^{ki} *ušērib* ARM 14, 66: 19 "I let their people enter the enclosed area". S. Durand 1997, 51: the area of the palace, distinct from the city.

3. MA *dūru ša ker*$_6$-*ḫe ša* GN Yamata/Shibata in Numoto 2009, 94: 2 "the wall of the inner/upper city of GN" (Mayer 2016, 226).

4. MB *adī balṭu ker-ḫa lizammī* Sumer 38, 124 iv 20 (Paulus 2014, 557 MNA 4 "for as long as he lives, he shall be deprived of (life in) the inner city".

5. A vessel:

a) OB 2 ^{gal}*ki-ir-ḫu* (of 1 1/3 mina and 2 shekel of silver, with an engraved AN-sign) ARM 31, 95: 1, s. Guichard 205, 214.

b) MB Qaṭna 1 *kir*$_{10}$-*ḫi* ZABAR QS 3, 17: 11 "1 bronze *k.*"

6. Richter 2012, 212 with lit.

kerku, *kirku* "roll (of papyrus, cloth)"; Aram. lw.

1. LB 1-*en kír-ku ša ina bīti maḫṣu* TBER 93–94: 16 (Joannès 1984, 72) "one roll of cloth which was woven in the house".

2. Kogan/Krebernik 2021, 440 (cf. Syr. *kerkā*); Abraham/Sokoloff 2011, 37 (loan from Aram. *krk*, not Akk. *karāku*).

kerru I, *karru*, *kāru* "male sheep"

Early OB 1 UDU 2 *ke-ru* ARM 19, 182: 2 "1 (female) sheep, 2 male sheep".

kesēru s. *kasāru*

ketrû s. *kad/trû*

kezretu, *kezertu*, *kazratu* "a type of cultic prostitute"

1. OB lit. *šumma* ⸢*ke*⸣-*ez-re-et liqabbir aštammaša elīya limqu*[*t*] CUSAS 10,

11: 14 "if she is a *k.* may she 'bury' (i.e. close down) her tavern (and) fall upon me". Note the parallelism with *qadištu* and *nadītu* ib. 12f. The verb is read *likappir* "may she clean" by Wasserman 2016, 236f. and AML p. 326f.

2. OB 44 *ᶠke-ez-r[e]-tum* FM 4, 216 no. 37: 3 (in list of musicians). Cf. N. Ziegler, ib. p. 87f.

3. OB lit. *ka-az-ra-a-tum-ma* UET 6/3, 889 (= Streck/Wassermann 2012: 199) ii 8.

4. Gallery 1980; Yoffee 1998.

kī, OA *kē* "like; how; as; if"

1. OA *kē*, s. GOA § 12.7.

2. MB lit. adverb (AHw. 469 *kī* B): *ki lūdirka ki lurāmki* ALL no. 11: 1 "how I want to embrace you! – How I want to love you!"

3. NB *kī adī* introducing a positive promissory oath: DN *u* DN_2 *kī mamm[a] bīt abīka īteṭ[ru] u ki-i a-di-i ina šībūtu u littūtu bīt abīka tulabbaru* SAA 17, 5: 7 "I swear by DN and DN_2 that nobody will take away the house of your father and that you indeed will make last the house of your father a long time in old age and in senility".

4. LB *kī ... kī* "either ... or" (s. CAD K 325 *kî* d): *ki-[i] kibtu u ki-⸢i⸣ saḫlê bēlu lušēbilaššu* AOAT 414/1, 103:8f. "may the lord send him either wheat or cress".

5. For *kī* + noun "in the way of" s. Mayer 2009, 431f., 439 with refs. S. also *kīkī*. NJCK (1), MPS (2–4), JW (5)

kīʾam "thus"

1. OA s. GOA § 13.5.4 s.v.

2. With *ša*: OB *ki-a-am ša uwaʾʾerukaʿ* FM 7, 38 no. 13: 8 "that is what I wrote you".

3. With pronominal suffix "to be suitable" (Mayer 2016, 226):

a) *ṣuḫārum ... ul ki-a-šu* AbB 14, 18: 25 "the servant is not suitable", cf. ib. 140: 33.

b) *awīltum ul ki-a-ša* AbB 2, 145: 19 "the woman is not suitable".

c) *awīlū annuttum ul ki-a-šu-nu* MHEO 1, 105 Di 985: 9 "these men are not suitable".

4. *kīʾamma* "just, simply": OB (a woman ... whose status as married wife is known to your ward) *ki-a-am-ma ittallak* CT 45, 86: 33 "is she simply to depart?" S. Veenhof 1976, 156f. with disc. and add. refs.

NJCK (1), MPS (2), JW (3–4)

kīʾāšu, *kâšu* II "to help"

SB *lú nir-da šu-bar-zi-aka-dè* : *awīlam ina šērtu ka-a-ša* SpTU 3, 67 ii 23 (*bīt rimki*) "to help a man in punishment" (Mayer 2016, 226).

kiʾāšum "to wrap up" (OA) s. *Kaʾāšu*

****kibarru** "boat made of inflated skins" (CAD K 329)

Read *ᵏᵘˢmaš!-ki!-ri* (Stol 1980–1983, 538).

kibbu I "an object made of metal or wood" s. *kippu* I

kibbu II, *gibbu* "burning; flame; a sacrifice"; + OB

1. OB lit. *ki-ib!-bu!* RA 86, 81: 5, s. *arāru* II.

2. Oil: **a)** OB *ana ki-ib-bi-im ša ilī* MARI 3, 38: 3 "for the *k.* sacrifice of the gods".

b) OB *ana gi-bi-im ša* DN ARM 7, 79: 4 "for the *g.* sacrifice of DN".

c) OB *ana ki-ib-bi-im [š]a elūnūm ālim u šaplān ālim* MARI 3, 39: 2 "for the *k*. sacrifice from above the city and below the city".

3. Animals: **a)** OB 1 *kalūmum gi-bu-um* ARM 21, 17: 9 "1 lamb, *g*. sacrifice". **b)** OB 1 *immerum gi-bu-um* ARM 21, 48: 11 "1 sheep, *g*. sacrifice".

4. Disc. with further refs.: Jacquet 2011, 38f. The var. *gibbu* shows an assimilation of *k* to *b*.

kibittu "full force, full strength"

ina ki-bi-it-te!(text: E) *ṣābim* ARM 10, 5: 8 "with troops in full force".

kibrītu "sulphur"; + OB; + MA

1. OB without case ending:
a) *ki-ib-re-e-et* UET 6/2, 193: 11 (= AML 148) among ingredients.
b) *ki-ib-ri-it* UET 6/3, 895: 24.
c) *ki-bi-ir-i-it* ARM 22/2, 323: 24.

2. MA *kib-ri-tu*$^{\mathrm{me[š]}}$ StAT 5, 1: 5.

3. The OB spellings illustrate a popular etymology < *kibir Ēt*/*Īt* ("bank of Ḫīt"), s. Stol 2009. Cf. Hurr. *kibridi*, Heth. *kibriti*- (Richter 2012, 209f. with lit.).

kibru, pl. *kibrātu* "border, rim, shore"

1. Lex. *kiš* = *ki-ib-ra-tum* Emar 6/4, 537: 712 (Sa), Sjöberg 1998, 276.

2. SB *līmurakka kib-ra* OBO 290, 88: 6 "may it spot for you a shore".

kibrû, *kubarû*, + *kibarû* "old man; grandfather"; + NA; Urarṭian word (?)

NA PN *mār* PN$_2$ *ana* PN$_3$ *ittidini ana* ^{lú}*ki-ba-ri-šú ra'āme* CTU B 02-04 "PN, son of PN$_2$, gave (it) to PN$_3$, to his grandfather for (his) affection" (s. Salvini 2014, 117 n22; Richter 2012, 209, cf. Hurr. *keweri* "elder").

kibsātu "deduction, compensation (for impurities)"; OA

1. *ki-ib-sà-tim* AKT 6B, 395: 7; *ki-ib-sá-tim* 6C, 671: 14; CUSAS 34, 35: 2.

2. VAT 9219: 4 (CAD K 339a s.v. 3) is published as VS 26, 47; in kt j/k 76: 4 (quoted ib.), read *ṣa-ḫu-ur* 'deducted' rather than *sà-ḫu-ur*. NJCK

kibsu I "step, path"

1. OB *alkā kuššidā ki-bi-is šēpīšunu* ⌜*liqê*⌝ FM 2, 68 no. 34: 13 "go, chase (them), track them (lit. take the step of their feet)!"

2. LB *ina kib-si anāku* dubsar 3, 160: 19 "I am on the way".

kibsu II "a garment"

1. LB (1 linen tunic) *ana kib-su nadī* Zawadzki 2013, 332 r. 4 "has been deposited for *k*."; cf. 359: 8.

2. LB (1 linen tunic – instead of a tunic for (covering) the throne) *ša ana ki-ba-su nadna ana* PN *mukabbî ana kussî nadin* Zawadzki 2013, 365: 4 "was given to PN, the mender, for (making) *k*. for the throne."

kibšu "a half-pack of a specific shape to be carried by a donkey"; OA

1. 4 ANŠE *ki-ib-šu-um* 1 *upqum* AKT 2, 34: 24 "4 donkeys with a *k*.-load and 1 with an *upqum*-load"; sim. TC 3, 192 pass.

2. ANŠE *ki-ib*!-*šu*!-*um ištēka lizzīz* BIN 4, 56: 25 "let the *k*.-donkey stay with you".

3. 20 *muttātum ša ki-ib-ší-im* 8 *muttātum ša upqim* TC 1, 16: 4 "20 half-packs of the *k*.-type and 8 half-packs of the *upqum*-type"; sim. CCT 5, 29a: 4.

4. *k.* is typically used in apposition and contrasts with *upqu.* S. Veenhof 1972, 2–4; Dercksen 2004a, 279–282. NJCK

kīdam "outward, outside"

1. OB *ki-dam-ma īpulūninni[m]a u attalkam* ARM 26/1, 309 no. 145: 6 "'Out!', they replied to me, and I left".

2. OB PN *ki-da ki-da-ma issī* ARM 26/2, 523 no. 530: 34 "PN yelled '"Out! Out!'".

kīdānu, + *gīdānu* "outside"; + NA

1. Early OB [x] *maršidātum* [x [n]]^{na_4}*ki-da-nu* ARM 19, 460: 15 "[x] foundation stones; [x] outer stones".

2. BÀD *ša gi-da-a-⌜ni ga⌝mmur sē⌜re⌝* SAA 15, 94 r. 6 "the outer city-wall is finished and plastered".

kidinnû II "a fabric or textile"

1. LB 10 MA.NA ^{síg}*ki-din-nu* (...) *kūmu šīpāti* CT 55, 834: 1 (Zawadzki 2013, 487 no. 582) "10 minas of *k.* (for a *ṣibtu* of DN's bed) instead of wool".

2. Zawadzki 2006, 26. Kleber 2011, 88f. suggests to read *kiṭinnû*; likely "cotton". S. further Quillien 2019 on prices and properties.

kidintu, *kitintu* "a linen(?) garment"; LB

1. 1-*et* ^{síg}*kid-ni-tum ḫišiḫtum* AOAT 222, 38 (CT 49, 165): 8 "1 valuable woolen *k.*".

2. Zadok 1982, 174f. for disc. and etym. Cf. *kidinnû.*

kīdu "outside"

OB 60 ESIR *ki-da-ti-ša aprus* Finkel 2014: 18 "I apportioned 60 (measures of) bitumen regarding her (the ship's) outside".

kidudû "rites"

1. OB *aššum ki-du-di[m] abī iš[puram] abī īdē kīma šamnum marṣu inanna* PN *šamnam ipšušanni* ARM 28, 147 r. 7 "my father had written to me concerning the rites. My father knows that the oil was difficult to get. (But) now PN has anointed me with oil".

2. Diff. J.-R. Kupper ib. p. 209: Related to *kâdu* II "to take into custody" and *kādu* "watch"? JW/FJMS

kigallu, + *gigallu* "socle, pedestal"

1. OB 2 *ki-ga-al-lu* ZABAR FM 3, 96 no. 7 iii 31 "2 bronze pedestals".

2. OB ^{giš}*gi-ga-al-li ša nūbal* DN ARM 23, 183 no. 198: 3 "(glue for) the base of the palanquin of DN". S. Arkhipov 2012, 168f. with add. refs.

3. SB *iṭṭapil* KI.GAL.LA Šūpê-amēli 80 "the pedestal was treated with disrespect".

4. SB AfO Bh. 32: *ki-gal-lum* WBC vi 24. *ki-ga-lum* ib. viii 55. *ki-[gal-lum]* ib. v 20.

5. NA *ki-gal-lu ša* DN SAA 13, 47 r. 9 "pedestal of DN".

kigamlu s. *gigamlu*

kikallû s. *kagallu*

kikamunu, *kukumnu* "triple"; Hurr. word

S. Richter 2012, 201f. with lit.

kīkī adv. "how?"

1. SB (who will say later on:) *ki-ki-i* PN ... *dīkti annīti [iddūk]* BagM 21, 345 no. 2 ii 30 "how did PN win this battle?", cf. *ki-i-ki-i* no. 4: 44, no. 9 iv 9.

2. CAD *kīkî* , AHw. *kikī.*

+ **kik(k)iʾānu**? "a foodstuff"; OA

1. 15 ŠE *ana ki-ki-a-né ašqul* kt 88/k 71: 44 "I paid 15 grains (of silver?) for *k*." (s. Albayrak 2002, 2).

2. *ša* AN.NA 10 GÍN *u* 1/3 MA.NA *lū šeʾam lū ki-ki-a-né ina* GN *lišʾumū* kt 93/k 151: 13 "may they buy barley and/or *k*. in GN for 10 or 20 shekels of tin" (unpubl., court. C. Michel).

3. Cf. *kikkirânu*? NJCK (1–2), FJMS (3)

+ **kik(k)innu** "a metal object; tripod?"; MB Qaṭna; Hurr. word

1 *ki-ki-in-nu* URUDU QS 3, 12: 5, s. Richter 2005, 41f. (< Hurr. *kig*= "three").

kikittu "a snake(?)"

CAD K 351 "mng. unkn.", hapax. Von Soden 1975, 461 prefers to read *gán-gíd-da* = *muš-ki ki-it-ti* in CT 19, 31 iii 7 (= Antagal F 157, s. MSL 17, 216), s. AHw. 684 s.v. *muškû*.

kikiṭṭû, + *kikiṭṭu*, + *kikkiṭṭu/û* "ritual"; + OB

1. OB lit. *amrātima ki-ki-ṭa ša ilim* ZA 110, 41 57 "you are versed in the god's rite".

2. OB lit. *ki-ik-ki-iṭ-ṭum* CUSAS 32, p. 133 8 ii 10 (= AML 21); *ki-ik-ki-ṭá-ša* ib. p. 144, 42: 24; YOS 11, 4: 20 (= AML 102).

3. Del. BMS 30 r. 29, read: *ki*-⸢*mil*!⸣-*tu* (Mayer 2016, 227) or *qí*-⸢*iš*?-*tu*⸣ (Lenzi, http://shuilas.org/P395021.html).

4. SB KÌD.KÌD.DA-*e tāmarāti latkūti* Iraq 72, 110 iii 17 "reliable rituals and readings", cf. ib. 21 (Mayer 2016, 227). On the logogr. s. Maul 2009, 78–80.

MPS (1–2), JW (3–4), FJMS (3)

kikkirânu, *kikkirênu* "pine or juniper seeds"

1. OB *ki-ki-re-nu u ballukkum* FM 2, 25 no. 4: 14 "(5 liters) of *k*. and *b*. aromatics" (in list of vegetables and spices).

2. LB $^{\check{s}im}$ŠE.LI Jursa 2009, 151 BM 77429: 11 (in list of aromatics for a censer).

3. Richter 2012, 214.

kikkiru s. *kakkaru*

kikkišu "reed fence, reed wall"

1. OB lit. *igār igā*[*r k*]*i-ki-iš ki-ki-iš* Finkel 2014: 1 "wall, wall! Reed wall, reed wall!"

2. OB É.DÙ.A *ki-ki-šu-um* VAS 22, 1: 1 "house plot, (surrounded by) a reed-fence".

3. OB *mannum ša ina* ^{gi}*ki-ki-ši-ia qanâm i-ša-la-*[*ṭú*?] ARM 26/2, 269 no. 405 r. 12 "who will be there to cut the reed in my reed fence?"

kikunû s. *gigun*(*n*)*û*

kilallān "both, two, pair"

In RA 28 (quot. CAD K 354 lex. section) read *ki-la-ta-an* (Borger 1985, 352).

+ **kilaʾūtu**, *kilʾūtu*, *kilûtu* "an offering or a festival"; OB

1. *inūma šarrum ki-la-ú-tam*!(PI) *ušbu* ARM 22, 276 i 40 "when the king was present at the *k*.", cf. *inūma ki-*[*la*]-*ú-tam ušbu* ARM 30, 337 M.11928: 4; sim. ARM 30, 435 M.6699: 14.

2. (barley) *ana šutērsî ša ki-la-ú-tim* FM 12, 117 M.15087: 7 "for the preparation of the *k*.".

3. *inūma ki-il-ú-tim* ARM 30, 303 M.12187: 21; *inūma ki-lu-ú-ti* FM 12,

220 M.12789: 5 *kil'ūtim/kilûtim* "at the occasion of the *k*."

4. (beer bread, barley and malt) *ana qerīt* DN *u ki-la-ú*!*-tim ša* DN2 ARM 7, 263 i 7 "for the banquet of DN and the *k*. of DN2".

5. The refs. s.v. *qilāsātu* (AHw. 921; CAD Q 251) belong here. S. von Soden 1985, 27; Charpin 1989–90, 104; Jacquet 2011, 60f. with further refs. and disc. Derivation from *qalû* "to burn" (Charpin, followed by Jacquet), although semantically attractive, is uncertain. The third consonant /'/ rather points to *kalû* "to hold back". However, the noun pattern leaves doubt about any Sem. origin. The suggestion of Fleming (1993) to connect the word with *kalû* "lamentation priest" is not convincing.

+ **kiliḫu?** "a designation of cloth"; MA

(garments) *ša birme ša ki-li-ḫi ša* PN MAH 16086 (Assur 2, 95ff.) A ii 5, 14; B ii 7, 15 "of multi-colored cloth of *k*. of PN".

+ **kilkillatu** "reed, straw (of metal)(?)"; OB

1 *ki-il-ki-il-la-tum* KÙ.GI BagM 21, 167 no. 115: 3 "1 golden *k*.", also ib. 9, 11. Cf. *kilkillu*.

kilkillu, *kikkillu* "a reed structure"

Also a room made with or from reed to contain the oath-symbol of Šamaš (Reiter 1989 and 1991).

+ **k/qillirītu** "a piece of jewellery"; OB

[1] *ki-il-li-ri-tum* KÙ.GI ARM 25, 656 = ARM 32, 336 M.11206 r. 8. Arkhipov 2012, 81.

killu s. *ikkillu*

+ **k/qilṣ/z/satum** "decorative(?) part of a weapon"; OB

(2 *kakku*-weapons) *qadūm Ki-il-Za-tim u siggurrī* ARM 32, 349 M.7298: 6 "with *k*. and *s*." Arkhipov 2012, 114.

kiltu s. *kaltu* and *keltu*

kilzappu s. *gerṣeppu*

kīma "like, instead of; when, as; that"

1. Early OB *anāku kī-ma* PN *ku'āšimma taklāku* AS 22, 12: 5 "I rely on you in place of PN".

2. OB with numerals:
a) *ki-ma* 1-*šu* 20-KAM *ašpurakkumma* AbB 9, 28: 6 "as I have written to you once, (I have written to you) 20 times".
b) "about, circa(?)": OB *aššum bītiya ša ki-ma šalāšīšu tuppī ušābilakkumma* AbB 6, 196: 11 "as for my house, concerning which I have sent my letters to you about three times".
c) For the mng. "amounting to" cf. Finet 1956, 113 § 46e.

3. *kīma inanna* "right now": *ina ki-im-na-an-na* AbB 13, 180: 18.

4. For OA s. GOA §§14.4.13, 26.3.16–19.

kimaḫḫu "grave"

1. OB (textile(s) for) [*k*]*i-ma-ḫi-im ša* PNf FM 4, 196 no. 25: 7 "the grave of PNf".

2. Lundström 2000; Felli 2012, 83–86.

+ **kimartu** "ramp"; MB

1. *pūtu* 1.KÁM.MA *ki-ma-ar-tum* AulaOr. (Suppl.) 55: 6 "the first front side: a ramp".

2. Cf. *kamaru* (CAD K 111). Pentiuc 2001, 103.

kimdu "a (felted?) fabric"

1. OB *ḫayyû ša ki-im-di* T. 407: iv 14 (ARM 30, 43) "*ḫayyû*-textiles of *kimdu*-type".

2. S. *kamādu*.

kimku s. *kinku*

kimru I "heap(ing); an offering(?)"

NA 1 *immeru ana kim-ri* SAA 12, 71: 6, 9 "1 sheep for the *k.* offering(?)".

+ **kimsu**, *kinsu* "bringing in (of harvest)"; MB

ina ki-in-si ebūri UET 7, 20 r. 5 "when the harvest is brought in" (van Soldt 1978, 499).

kimṣu *kinṣu*, *kiṣṣu* "knee, shin, calf"

1. [...*i*]*ttatbakā ki-im-ṣa-a-*⸢*ia*⸣ KAL 9, 18: 15 "my legs are paralyzed".

2. For the measurement (= *eṣemtu*, 3/4 of a cubit) s. Powell 1987–1990, 473.

kimtu "family"

1. OB *k*[*i-i*]*m* ⸢*sa*⸣*-al-la-at* Finkel 2014: 35 "kith and kin" (abs. state, cf. *ṣeḫer rabī*).

2. SB (a woman who gives birth to a baby) *lā urabbû šeršuma lā urappašu kim-is-su* ... *lā ippallasu kim-is-su* SpTU 5, 248: 46f. "(but) does not raise his (her husband's) baby and does not enlarge his family ... so that he does not see his family".

+ **kīna/ākam** "truly"; OA

1. OA *ina* GN *tēzibannīma ina qāti mūtim ki-na-kam ūṣī* kt h/k 73: 5 "you have left me behind in GN, and I have truly escaped from the hand of death" (s. Sever 1995, 14 and Michel 2006, 170).

2. Alternatively – because of the suffix *-ākam* – an adverb of place, cf. Mari OB *kinnikêm* (Kouwenberg 2012, 65 n. 121). NJCK/JW

kinattu, *kinātu*, + *kannātu* "staff, employee", NB "colleague, peer"; + OA

1. OA *ki-na-tám ištēn ṭurdam* kt n/k 1065: 13 "send me one employee" (s. Çeçen/Gökçek 2016, 249).

2. OB defining a measure: (beer) *ina sūt ki-na-te-e* Or. 63, 317 no. 4: 4 "according to the menials' measure", used throughout the Tell Leilan beer archive (van de Mieroop ib. 310f.), Chagar Bazar (Lacambre 2008), and Tell Rimah (OBTR 17, 18). S. also Chambon 2011, 138–140.

3. SB *ana kan-n*[*a*]-⸢*a*⸣*-tú gabbi šapir* Iraq 67, 268: 21 "(this inscription was copied and) sent to all the colleagues", s. George/Frame ib. 270.

4. Ur III *é gi-na-tum*, *gi-na-ab-tum* is considered Akk. by Heimpel 2009, 164f., but a Sum. etymology is more likely. S. the proposals by Steinkeller 1989, 80f. (< **lú gi-na íb-túm-e-a* "the one who bears the guarantee"), and Sallaberger 2011, 357 (a Diri compound for *é šutum*. Cf. [*šu*]*-tu-um* = *é gi-na-ab-du*$_7$ = *šu-tu-um-mu* Diri v 298).

NJCK (1), JW (2–4), NR (4)

kindabašše, + *kiddapašše*; NA *kindabassi* "a garment"; MA; + NA; + OB; Hurr. word?

1. OB 15 *ki-in-*<*da*>*-ba-ša* 1 GÍN.TA CUSAS 15, 68: 1 "15 *k.* (for) 1 shekel each".

2. MA x *ki-da-pa-še* Iraq 35 pl. XIII no. 1: 1.

3. NA **a)** *šazbussu ša* ^{túg}*kín-da-ba-se* SAA 7, 166: 2 "a consignment of *k.*".

b) ^{túg}*ki-in-da-*[*ba-se*] SAA 7, 176 r. 5.

4. Cf. Ugar. *k*(*n*)*dwṯ* (Richter 2012, 529 with prev lit.); Gaspa 2018, 285. S. AHw. 358 *ḫurdabašše*.

kindu s. *kandu*

kingu s. *kinku*

kiništu, *kinaštu*, *kinaltu*, *kinartu* "priesthood, religious staff"

Logogr. LÚ.UKKIN CT 49, 122: 4; 140: 9; 147: 4; 160: 3; 168: 1, 6; 170: 5; 182: 4; 190: 3 (von Soden 1975, 461).

kinku I, *kingu*, + *kimku* "sealing, sealed tag, sealed bag"

1. OB 304 *ki-in-kum* NÌ-1-GÍN.TA BagM 24, 155 no. 202 vii 1 "304 sealed tags at one shekel each (1229 at 1/2 shekel each, 1202 at 1/3 shekel each)"; s. also BagM 21, 160 no. 109: 1, 110: 1; TLT 57 r. 4; ARM 24, 213: 3.

2. OB *tadbibtam ana ūmī arkātim ana tuppi ki-im-ki-ma-an iškunū* ARM 26/1, 169 no. 37: 15 "they would have placed endless complaints on the sealed tablet".

3. NB *ki-in-gu* OIP 114, 81: 33.

4. AHw. *kingu*, *kinkum* II; CAD *kinku* A.

kinnāru "lyre"

1. Lex. ZA.AN.MÙŠ = MIN (*za-na-ru*) = *ki-in-na-ru* Emar 6/4, 545: 392.

2. 2 *ki-in-na-ra-tim* ARM 23, 180: 12; s. also ARM 21, 298: 17, 20; ARM 23, 213: 29, 32; ARM 25, 547 r. 9.

3. Cf. Ebla *gi-na-*LUM MEE 4, 572. S. Huehnergard 1987, 138; Pentiuc 2001, 98; MUŠ *gi-na-rí-im* MEE 4, 116 iv 1 "lyre snake" (s. Sjöberg 1996, 17). According to CAD K 387, a "Wsem." lw. However, the word seems to be the inherited Sem. word replaced by the Sum. lw. *balangu* in Mesopotamia.

+ **kinnāruḫuli** "lyre player or maker(?)"; Hurr. lw.

^{lú}*ki-in-na-ru-ḫu-li* AlT 172: 7 (s. Dietrich/Loretz 1964, 192). S. Richter 2012, 207 for disc. and lit.

+ **kinnikâ** "quickly"

Lex. *ki-in-*⸢*ni-ka*⸣*-a* = MIN (*zamar*) AOAT 50, 364: 80 (malku), s. ib. p. 232 and cf. *kinnikêm*.

+ **kinnikê(m)** "there"; OB

1. *išpur* PN *ana* GN *anūmma dūkāšu u ki-ni-ke-em lā idūkūšu* ARM 26/2, 67 no. 310: 15 "PN wrote to GN: 'kill him here!' but they did not kill him there".

2. (PN will reach his goal) *ki-in-ni-ke-em ara*ʾʾ*ub u ina lîtim azzâz* ARM 26/2, 40 no. 211: 14 "I will rage there and be present in victory".

3. *ki-in-ni-ke-e-em ḫarrānātūšunu ana takšītim ... uṣṣû ina ūmīšu ḫarrānātim akallā* ARM 26/2, 526 no. 532: 10 "their caravans will go out (to make) profit over there – at that time, I will detain the caravans".

4. *alānū ša in māt* GN *ša ki-in-ni-ke-e dannū* GN$_2$ GN$_3$ *u* GN$_4$ *ša ki-in-ni-ke-e dannū ullîš alānū kalûšunu passū* OBO SA 6 p. 73f. (A.315 +): 17, 19 "the cities of the land of GN, those which are there, are they strong? GN$_2$, GN$_3$, and GN$_4$, those which are there, are they strong? In addition, all the cities are in poor condition".

5. *muškēnū ša ki-i*[*in-n*]*i-k*[*e-e*]*m* ⸢*puḫ-ḫurū*⸣ ... *ittalkū* ARM 33, 394f. no. 185: 22 "the *muškēnū* who were assembled there left".

6. *ki-in-ni-ke-em lā uḫtallaq* ARM 28, 50 r. 12 "I shall not go to ruin over there".

7. The interpretation as deictic adverb is largely based on the opposition with *anūmma* in ARM 26/2, 310 and comparison with later *akannaka* "here" (MB – LB, Durand 1988, 440 n. d). Hrůša 2010, 232 favors the mng. "quickly, immediately" based on the entry *kinnikâ* = *zamar* in malku (s. *kinnikâ*). Etym. *kī* + (*a*)*nnī* + *kī'am*?

+ **kinnimmu?** "morning meal"; < Sum. *kin nim*.

SB AfO Bh. 32 (reading uncert., s. *naptanu*): KIN.NIM WBA v 18; ⌜KIN.NIM⌝ WBC iib 21*, Da Riva 2012, 67.

kinsikku, + *kissiku* "end of the workday"; Sum. lw.

1. OB *ina ki-ìs-si-ki-im* FM 3 p. 68: 5; FM 1 p. 82: 30 "in the late afternoon".

2. Streck 2017, 599.

kinsu s. *kimsu*.

+ **kinṣu II** "gathering"; LB

1. In *mala kinṣiya* etc. "as much as I etc. can":

a) *mala kin-ṣi-ni uṭṭatu ninanšâmma* dubsar 3, 179: 15 "we will bring as much barley as we can (lit. according to our gathering)".

b) (I pray) *mala kin-ṣi-ía* dubsar 3 (= TCL 9, 80), 106: 26.

c) (I will be tireless) *mala kin-ṣi-ia* BIN 1,66: 10.

2. Pace AHw. 478 *kimṣu* 1 and CAD K 374 *kimṣu* 1b1'a', not from *kim/nṣu* I "knee", but from *kinṣu* II; cf. *kamās/ṣu* "to gather".

kīnu, OA *kēnu* "true, honest, legitimate"

1. For the legal formulae with *šalmu* and *kēnu*, expressing joint liability, s. Veenhof 2001, 148–152. Note the unique variant *ina qaqqad kēnišunu u balṭišunu rakis* ICK 2, 43: 19–21.

2. OA *ke-na-ma* "really", especially in *šumma ke-na-ma* "if really": *šumma ke-na-ma awīlum ina murṣīšu kabit* AKT 9A, 41: 27 "if the man is really seriously ill"; also AKT 6B, 310: 24. NJCK

+ **kīnu II** "true value"; OB

1. 1/3 MA.NA *ḫullum u šewerum nībum* 18 GÍN KÙ.GI *ki-nu-um* FM 1, 140 A.486+: 43 "the nominal value of the ring and the coil is 1/3 mina, the true value is 18 shekels of gold".

2. 10 GÍN *nīb šewerišunu u* 1 GÍN *nīb kanīktum* 8 GÍN *šewerum ki-nu-um* 2/3 GÍN *kanīktum ki-nu-um* 3 GÍN *kanīktum nībum* 2 1/2 GÍN *ki-nu-um* ib. 65f. "10 shekel is the nominal value of their coil and 1 shekel is the nominal value of(!) the sealed medal. 8 shekel is the true value of the coil, 2/3 shekel is the true value of the sealed medal. A sealed medal of 3 shekel nominal value (and) 2 1/2 shekel true value".

kinūnu; Ass. *kanūnu*, + *kenūnu* "kiln, hearth, fireplace, brazier; a festival, a month"

1. OA lit. *ká-nu-nam paḫḫuram tusappiḫ* AML 150: 5 "she scattered the assembled hearth", s. OB lit. *ki-nu-na-am pu-⌜ḫu!⌝-ra-am usappiḫ* AML 157: 10; *ke-e-nu-nam puḫḫuram usa*[*ppiḫ*] AML 152: 4; 154: 6; *ištū ke-e-nu-ú-na-am usappiḫuma* AML 154: 12 "after she had scattered the hearth" (i.e. dispersed those gathered around it).

2. OA (the two brothers who have divided the inheritance) *ukultam i-kà-nu-nim* *išberū* kt 87/k 253: 16 "have broken food (bread?) in/over the hearth", s. Hecker 1997, 169f., apparently a symbolic act).

3. OA (for the life of his family and himself PN dedicated) *kà-nu-na-am mušanwer* [...] RIMA 1, 10: 12 "a brazier that illuminates [...]".

4. OA In expressions referring to the extinguishing of the hearth as a symbol for the extinction of a family:

a) *bēt abīka ana kà-nu-nim bali'im ištaknū* AKT 6D, 765: 14 "they have made your father's house into an extinguished fireplace".

b) PN *ša kà-nu-ni-im bali'im* AKT 11A, 47: 6 "PN of the extinguished fireplace" (i.e. who died without offspring?).

c) (unfortunately, the mother of your *amtu*-wife has died ...) *mā'ē ina kà-nu-nim lū tatbuk* kt 93/k 916: 10 "she (the *amtu*-wife) must pour out water over the hearth" (quot. in Michel 2008a, 186 with n. 26).

5. OB lit. *ina pūt ki-nu-ni-im ina išertim šinā atḫâ wašbāma* AML 156: 10 "in front of the hearth, in the chapel, two companions are sitting".

6. For the festival in OB, s. Jacquet 2011, 43 with disc. and refs.

7. MN, in Nuzi also *ša arḫi kè-nu-né-t*[*i*] *ša* ⌜*āl ilāni*⌝ JEN 554 (ZA 77, 129): 6, Wilhelm ib. 132 with add. refs.

8. *kanūnu* is the Ass. form of *kinūnu*, and some instances of *ganūnu* listed in CAD G s.v. *ganūnu* A 2 should be assigned to this noun as Assyrianisms (pace J. G. Westenholz 2000). It is to be distinguished from OB *ganīnu* "storage room or building" in spite of its logogram GÁ.NUN(.NA). For OA *k/g/qanīnu* (kt 91/k 502: 3) s. *ganīnu*.

NJCK (2–4, 8), MPS (1, 5–6), JW (7)

kīnūtu "loyalty"

SB *abulla ke-e-nu-ti apt*[*e*] SAA 3, 19: 4 "I opened the gate of loyalty".

kipa'u s. *kab/pa'u*

kiplu "twisting, twine (also as decoration)"; + OA; + OB

1. OA *anneqē ki-ip-lá-am ša amuttim* AKT 11A, 167: 33 "rings (with) a *k.* of meteoric iron".

2. 2 *annuqū ša amuttim ki-ip-lu* KÙ.GI kt a/k 1072: 2 "two rings of meteoric iron (with) *k.* (of) gold" (with a weight of 16 shekels), s. Çeçen 1997, 220 n. 11.

3. OB 65 *ki-ip-lum* KÙ.BABBAR BagM 24, 140 no. 198 r. iv 2 "65 silver *k.*"

NJCK (1–2), JW (3)

kippatu, *kibbatu* "loop, circle"

1. OB *elep teppušu e-*[*ṣ*]*i-ir-ši-ma e-ṣi-ir-ti ki-*[*i*]*p-pa-tim* Finkel 2014: 6f. "the boat that you will make, draw it with a circular plan!"

2. OB 2 *ki-ib-ba-at* KUŠ.EDIN *ša qabli šarrim* ARM 24, 122+ (= ARM 32 p. 264f.): 7 "(gold for) two hoops for the purse on the king's belt". S. Arkhipov 2012, 169 with add. refs.

3. OB as ring handles: (1 silver *mašqaltu*-cup with) 1 *sugūnu* 2 *ki-ip-pa-tum* ARM 31, 159: 5 "1 handle and 2 rings".

4. NA [x *in*]*a* 1 *ammatim* : *kip-pu-tú ša āli* SAA 5, 15 r. 7 "the perimeter of the town is [n] cubits".

5. NA 2 *ki-pa-te ša nīrī* StAT 3, 8:7 "2 rings for yokes".

MPS (1, 4), JW (2–3), JK (5)

kippu I "loop, trap; coil (of intestines); ring"

1. "ring" (made from metal):

a) OB 1 SAG *ki-pí* (made from silver) TLT 57: 5. S. Guichard 2005, 286.

b) OB among commodities collected as tax: (oxen, sheep, gold cups, gold rings) *ki-ip-pu* (silver cups, silver rings …) Fs. Charpin 265f. (M.12631): 1. S. Chambon/Guichard ib. 247f.

c) We assume the refs. cit. CAD *kibbu* A denoting an object made from wood or metal to be rings, coils, or otherwise curved items. Cf. *kippatu*, *kapāpu*.

2. SB *kip-pu tarṣu* SpTU 5, 247 v 7 "taut snare".

3. NA 25 GAG AN.BAR *ša ki-pa-ni* SAA 16, 40: 3 "25 iron nails for loops".

+ **kippu II** "a water bird"

1. Lex. *kib*[mu][šen]//[*ki*]-*ib* = *ki-pu* Emar 6/4, 555: 58.

2. OB KI.IB {x}[mušen] Edubba'a 7, 100: 14 (in list of birds, section of water birds which starts in l. 11 of the text). S. Black/Al-Rawi 1987, 125 for Sum. *ki-ib* as a water bird.

3. OB *šumm*[*a m*]*ê ki-ip-pi tušabšal* YOS 11, 26 iii 38 (MC 6 p. 88) "when you want to prepare *k*.-soup" (recipe).

kīpu "a garment"; + SB

1. SB 1-*en ki-i-*[*pi*] SpTU 4, 128: 69; 1-*en* [túg]*ki-i-pi ša iṣi* ib. 95 "1 *k.* for wood(?)".

2. NB 1 [gada]*ki-i-pi* dubsar 7, 38: 26. S. Zawadzki 2006, 190.

kipunannu "a small household item"; + MB Emar

1. OA Prag 429: 28 (// OIP 27, 55: 34); JEOL 33, 134 No. 17: 19; AKT 6B, 335: 15; kt 88/k 418: 11 (s. Bayram 2016, 21). In 2 *mi'at ki-KU-na-né* Prag 429: 24 (// OIP 27, 55: 28 *ki-Bu-*) and 51, KU may be an error for *BU*, or *kikunannu* is a by-form of *kipunannu*.

2. *ina libbišu* 1 *ki-pu-na-nu* GUŠKIN Emar 6/3, 43: 9 "in its centre one golden *k.*" NJCK (1), JW (2)

kiqillatu "dung hill, refuse dump"; Aram. lw.

1. *ki-qí*!-*il-te* SAA 6, 200: 5 (context broken).

2. The ref. TCL 9, 58: 34, now SAA 6, 32 r. 3, cit. CAD Q, 252 s.v. *qilûtu* belongs here (Deller in id./Mayer/Oelsner 1989, 262).

3. AHw. 483 "Zwangsverkauf", CAD K 401 "mng. uncert." Cherry 2017, 166–169 argues for a lw. from Aram. *qyqlh*, *qyqlt'* "garbage heap, dunghill". Cf. Aram. *qlqlt'* in Tell Fekheriye: 22. Parpola 1976, 195; Greenfield/Shaffer 1983, 124f.

kirādu "a container"

1. OB *šu-úš-ši-im sugūnim naktamim u guḫaṣṣim ša ki-ra-di-im ṣeḫrim* ARM 31, 238: 8 "(metal for) *š.*, *s.*-ornament, cover, and wire-decoration of a small *k.*"

2. For and add. refs. s. Guichard 2005, 213f.

kirānu s. *karānu*

kirbānu, *kurbannu*, *kurbānu*, + *kurbi'ā-nu*? "lump, clod"

1. Lex. *lag* = *ku-ur-*⸢*ba*⸣*-nu* Emar 6/4, 537: 149.

2. OB 10 MA.NA *ku-ur-bi-a-nu-um* Shemshara 1, 67: 25 "10 minas of (metal) lumps".

3. OB in divinatory use:

a) *u ki-ir-b[a]-na-am ša* GN *ublūnim muttatam aššum têrētim šūpušim maḫrī-ya aklā* ARM 23, 317 no. 153: 23 "they brought a clod of earth from GN. I kept half with me for making oracles (and sent the other half to my lord); cf. ib. ll. 29, 32.

b) *anūmma ki-ir-ba-an* GN GN_2 *u* GN_3 *ana ṣēr bēliya uštābilam elī ki-ir-ba-ni šunūti bēlī têrtam līpuš* ARM 23, 366 no. 184: 5, 11 "I have sent my lord clods from GN, GN_2, and GN_3 (so that) my lord may perform an oracle on these clods".

c) OB [*umma nīnuma*] *balūm ki-i*[*r-ba*]-*nim ke-e*[*m tēpuš*] ... *umma šuma* ... *b*[*al*]*ūm ki-ir-ba-nim têrē*[*tim*] *nušeppeš* ARM 26/1, 269 no. 103 r. 2–5 "[we said:] 'you (performed an oracle) without a clod of earth?' ... (and) he replied: '...we (always) perform oracles without a clod of earth'". S. also ARM 26/2, 119 no. 346: 17.

d) *aššum kaspim ša galamaḫḫu ša ki-ir-ba-na ana qātim taškunu* AbB 9, 166: 7 "concerning the silver of the chief lamentation priest, in (whose?) hand you put a clod" (mng. uncert.).

4. OB *warkī ebūrim ki-ir-ba-num ana* PN *linnadin* ARM 26/1, 42 A.2342 r. 5 "the clod shall be given to PN after the harvest".

5. NB *kur-ban-nu šīḫu*! *ma'da kī lā pašrā ul ṭābu ana erēši* OIP 114, 92: 12 "the clods of the estate are many. If they are not broken up, it will not be good for ploughing".

kirḫu s. *kerḫu*

+ **kirikaru** "a bird"

1. Lex. *kar-kar-e*[mušen] = *ki-*[*ri-ka-ru*] UET 7, 139: 13 (Ḫḫ 18, 61).

2. OB *ki-ri-ka-ru-um*[mušen] Edubba'a 7, 100: 67 (in list of birds). Perhaps variant of *karkarru* and/or *kurkurru* C, s. Al-Rawi/Dalley 2000, 107 and Veldhuis 2004, 261f.

kiriktu, + *kariktu* "blocking of the water supply in a canal, weir"; + OB

OB (bring bricks to the palace) *ka-ar-ka-at ēkallim ḫu-Bu-ur* ARM 26/2, 380 no. 455 r. 16 = ARM 33, 490 no. 235 "and block off(?) the weirs of the palace". The text mentions strong rainfall previously, which fits this interpretation.

kirīku s. *karīku*

kirimmu "a part and position of the arm(s); a garment"

1. OB [túg]*ki-ri-im-ma-ka šurriṭma kubbitanni* SEb 2, 51: 4 "tear up your *k*.-cloth and honor me!"

2. *k.* usually refers to the cradling and nursing of infants. The textile is therefore likely a type of wrap or shawl. Despite CAD's objections (K p. 406), it may originally denote a bodypart (cf. AHw.'s "Armbeuge" following B. Landsberger), as indicated by Sem. cognates (Kogan/Militarev 2002, 315).

kirippu "(oil) jar"; Ur III, Mari

1. Ur III *ki-ri-ip ar-gi₅-núm* CUSAS 3, 511: 65; 972: 17, 88; 975: 18, 89 (s. also CUSAS 4 p. 22) "(oil) jar of *a*.". W. Sallaberger CUSAS 6, 359: *ki-ri-ĝá* with unknown mng.

2. OB 1 [[dug]*ki*]-*ri-pu šaman šurmēnim* 1 [dug]*ki-ri-pu šaman asim* 1 [dug]*ki-ri-pu šaman za-ba-lim* FM 11, 8: 4–6 "[1] *k*. of cypress oil, 1 *k*. of myrtle oil, 1 *k*. of juniper oil". NR (1), MPS (2)

kirissu "an accessory, a decorative pin or clasp"; + MB Qaṭna

1. OB lit. *ki-ri-is-sà-am siBtam uḫḫa tibba našī zikru* Or. 87, 19 ii 7 "the man carries a pin, a *siBtum*, an *uḫḫu*, a harp".

2. MB Qaṭna *ki-ri-iz-zí-na* QS 3, 12: 39 "6 pins (edged with gold)". The word is hurrianized, as indicated by a gloss marker and ending *-na* (s. the comm. ib. p. 87).

3. SB [...] *šiddu u ki-ri-is-si* THeth. 23 p. 96: 149 "curtain and pin".

kirītu, + *karītu* "a rope"

LB 2 *ka-re-e-tum* RSM 66: 18 "2 ropes" (among similar implements; s. Streck 1995a, 27 n. 79).

kirizzu s. *kirissu*

+ **kirkirdanu?** "mng. uncert."; MB Emar

kakkam ša šarrim kir-kir-da-na liššû Emar 6/3, 18: 19 "the weapon of the king, the *k.*, they shall carry". For disc. and lit. s. Richter 2012, 214. Suggestions include "in perpetuity(?)" (Fleming 1992, 164 n. 284); emendation to *kir-kir-ra*!*-nu*, denoting a type or quality of bronze (Durand 1989a); a glosse of *kakkam* deriving from Hurr. *karkarni* "weapon" (Adamthwaite 2001, 105).

kirku s. *kerku*

kirlammu, + *kirlimmu* "a container"; + OB

1. 1 ^{dug}*kír-li-ma-am* 1 *mākaltam* ARM 27, 152: 14 "1 *k.*-container, 1 dish".

2. 3 *mākalātim* 3 ^{dug}*kír-li-mi* ib. r. 7 "3 dishes, 3 *k.*-containers".

kirratu I "an ornament"

1. MB part of a chair: 1 KUŠ DUḪ.ŠI.A *ana* 1 *kir-rat* ^{giš}GU.ZA BagF 21, 335: 1 "1 rawhide for 1 *k.* of a chair", s. Sassmannshausen ib. 395.

2. CAD *girratu*; AHw. *kirru*, *kirratu*; CDA *kirratu*.

+ **kirratu II** "a large vessel"; NA

1. (100 *kakkabānu* birds) *issi*! *ki-ru-*⌜*te*!⌝ SAA 7, 148 iii 12 "from the *k.* vessel".

2. 50 ditto *ki-ru-tú* SAA 7, 149 ii 11 "50 ditto (fish): (from the) *k.* vessel".

3. UZU *kìr-ru-tú* SAA 7, 164: 5 "meat: (from the) *k.*".

4. [*k*]*i-ru-tú*? SAA 7, 151: 17 in broken context).

5. Back-formation from the fem. pl. of *kirru* I "a big jar". SAA 7 translates "meal".

kirru I "a big jar"

1. Lex. A = *ki-ir-rum*, var. *gi-ir-ru* Emar 6/4, 537: 23 (Sa), cf. KÍR.A Emar 6/4, 88 (Ḫḫ X A 26), s. Sjöberg 1998, 242f.

2. OA 4 *luḫusinātim u* 2 *ki-re-en* PN Prag 629: 2 (Matouš 1974, 170). Cf. OB *qerru* (AHw. 918a).

3. OB 5 *sikkāt ki-ir-ri-im* FM 3, 96 no. 7 iii 33 "5 pegs for a *k.*" (followed by knives and vessels); [*s*]*ikkāt ki-ir-ri* ib. 42 "pegs for a *k.*".

4. OB *eqlam ša epettû šuprīmma ki-ra-am lušpuk* AbB 2 157: 14 "write to me (the name of) the field that I have to 'open' so that I may pour out the *k.*" (Stol 1995b, 201).

5. Sallaberger 1996, 102; Guichard 2005, 214–217.

kirru II "(region of the) clavicles"

1. OB as part of a *kakku*-weapon, s. ARM 32 p. 111 + n. 353 (M.12099: 9–10, unedited).

2. AHw. *kerru* III.

kirṣitu s. *erṣetu*

kirû "garden"

1. Lex. *kiri*6 = *kí-ru* Emar 6/4, 537: 465 (Sa), Sjöberg 1998, 266.

2. OA *ana* (...) *ki-ri-im damqim ša mera Aššur šumšu ēnēka lā tanašši'u*(*ma*) Günbattı 2004, 252 kt 00/k 6: 65 "you shall not raise your eyes to (i.e. desire) (...) the good garden of any Assyrian".

3. OA 4 *eql*[*ātim*] *u ki-ri-a-am ša ṭiḫi eqlātēšuma* "4 fields and a garden adjacent to his fields" kt o/k 52: 6, s. Albayrak 2001, 308; sim. kt a/k 583b: 18 (quoted Dercksen 1996, 202).

4. OA *kunuk* PN *rabī ki-ri-a-tim* kt 87/k 253: 1 "seal of PN, chief of the gardens", s. Hecker 1997, 169.

5. OB *ana* gišKIRI6 *ēkallim ša* GN *ašūḫī āmurma* FM 8, 44 no. 5: 4 "I saw pines for the garden of the palace in GN".

6. OB *ana* gišKIRI6 *nillikma šaššūgī nīmur* FM 8, 55 no. 11: 9 "we went to the garden and saw *š.*-trees".

JW (1), NJCK (2–4), MPS (5–6)

kīru "oven, kiln"

Fem. pl. *ki-ra-ti-ia*, used for bitumen, in OB Finkel 2014: 21, s. *iṭṭû*. *uštarkib* ⌜*ki*⌝*-ra-ti-*[*ia*] "I loaded my kilns" ib. 25. [*k*]*i-ra-ti-*⌜*ia*?⌝ ib. 32.

kisalluḫḫu "courtyard sweeper"; + SB

1. OB 13 f*ki-sa-lu-ḫa-tum* FM 4, 215 no. 36: 3. Cf. N. Ziegler ib. p. 89f.

2. SB lúKISAL.LUḪ-*ḫa* YOS 1, 45 ii 23; Borger 1975, 72a; Schaudig 2001, 375 (no. 2.7).

+ **kisamu** "an aromatic (and alcoholic?) drink(?)"

OB *ki-sa-mi-im* ARM 21, 106: 13, s. *ballukku*.

kisānu s. *kīsu* II 9d

kisibirrītu s. *kisibirru*

kis(s)ibirru, *kus*(*s*)*ibirru*, + *ki*/*usa*/*imaru* "coriander", pl. fem. *kisibirrā*/*ētum*

1. A spice: **a)** OB *ki-sí-bi-ra-tum* FM 2, 25 no. 4: 8 "(10 liters of) coriander" (in list of vegetables and spices).
b) OB *ki-is-sí-bi-ri-tam* OBTR 140: 17.

2. A metal ornament:
a) For OB s. Arkhipov 2012, 47f.
b) SB na4GU.ZA-*bir-tú* KÙ.GI AOAT 46, 295 no. 9 iv 21 "(1) coriander seed made from gold" (s. ib. p. 314).

3. Var. *ki*/*usa*/*imaru* (?): MA *ku-si-ma-ri* MARV 43: 4 (Stol apud Postgate 1980, 67*. Cf., perhaps, OAkk *šutuḫḫā-tim ūlū ki-sa-ma-ri* FAOS 19 Di 7 (OAIC 52): 7 "*š.* or *k.*".).

4. Instead of *ki-is-si-bi-ir-ri* VS 16, 102: 24 (AHw. 486 *kisibirrītu*, CAD K 421 *kisibirru*), read with AbB 6, 102 *ki-is-si-bi-ir-re-tim* (fem. pl.).

kisikkû, + *kisikku* "(jar for) funerary offering"; + OB

(3 liters of cypress oil) *ina* 1 dug*ki-si-ik-ki* FM 1, 76 A.2761: 6 "in one *k.* jar".

kisimmu "a type of cheese"

S. Stol 1993c, 106f.

kisirru "a tool"; NB

1 giš*ki-is-si-ru ša libitti* dubsar 7, 39: 31 "1 *k.* for bricks". Alternatively *ki-is-kir*!*-ru* "board" (s. the disc. Tarasewicz ib. p. 184).

kisittu, pl. *kisnātu*? "trunk, branch"; + OA;

1. OA 1 *emmeram Zu-Ba-am* 20 NINDA *u eriqqam ša ki-is-na-tim ina šattim inaddinūnim* KTK 94: 8 "they will give me one *ZuBum*-sheep, 20 loaves and a wagonload of branches per year". Veenhof 1970, 368b.

2. 3 *ereqqātim ša ki-is-na-tim* kt f/k 81: 10 "three wagonloads of branches" (unpubl. court. K. R. Veenhof).

3. MA also "expense account" (Jakob 2009, 23): (bread, beer, and barley) *ana ki-si-te laput* Tell Chuera 54: 22 "are registered in the expense account". S. Jakob ib. p. 85.

4. SB *nakru rubû* (var. *māt rubê*) *ina ki-si-it-ti-šú* … Šumma izbu 14: 75 (De Zorzi 2014, 710) "the enemy – the prince (var.: the country of the prince) ... from his lineage".

NJCK (1–2), JW (1–3), MPS/FJMS (4)

****kisītu A** (CAD K 423)

The ref. KAH 2, 84: 35 belongs to *kisittu* (Borger 1975, 72a) or *kišittu* (RIMA 2, 149 with n. 35).

kiskirru, *kiškirru*, + *kis/škarru* "board", NB "a type of temple contribution"; + MA

1. Lex. *dúr* = *ki-iš-kàr-rù* = *dapārum* Emar 545, 267, cf. 268. Pentiuc 2001, 187.

2. Early OB 29 ^{giš}*ki-is-kàr-ra-tum* ARM 19, 460: 10.

3. OB lit. [*n*]*alban uqnîm ke-eš-ki-ir-ri*! *eb-bi-i* AML 88: 2 "brick mold of lapis lazuli, board of pure (gold)"; cf. ⸢*ki-iš*⸣-*ki-ir e-eb-b*[*i-im*] AML 92: 2; ⸢*ki*⸣-*is-ki*-[*ir*]-⸢*ru*!?⸣ *ša ḫurāṣim* AML 95: 19 "board of gold".

4. OB $^{\text{giš.ḫi.a}}$*ki-is-ka-ar-ri* OBTR 287: 4.

5. MA 67 *ki-iš*-⸢*ki*!?⸣-*ru-tu ša ḫurāṣe* Chuera 63: 1 "67 golden platelets". Note the pl. *kiškirrūtu* instead of *kiškirrētu*.

6. NB (dates) *ina mašīḫi ša sattuk ina ki-is-ki*-⸢*ri*⸣ *ša ina maššartu ša* MN Zawadzki 2013, 629: 3 "in the measure of the regular offering from the *k*.-payment as the *maššartu* of MN (were given to PN)."

kisnātu s. *kisittu*

kissatu "fodder, food, chopped straw"

1. Early OB *amtum ki-sa-tum* IB 1779: 12 (Isin 4, p. 130) "slave girl responsible for fodder(?)".

2. OB for humans: (beer and barley) *ana ki-sà-tim ša ṣuḫārē* AbB 12, 133: 20 "for the food of the servants". Cf. ARM 26/2, 77 no. 324 n. f.

3. OB (one ox, killed) *ki-is-sa-at barbarim* CUSAS 9, 341: 2 "wolf fodder".

4. NA ^{še}*ki-su-tú ekkulū* SAA 19, 47 r. 5 "they eat fodder".

kīsu II, *kīšu* + pl. *kīsātu*, + pl. *kīsānū* "bag, moneybag"; + OA

1. OA *kīma ki-Zi-i ina ēkallim išriqūni* Günbattı 2014, 101f. kt 01/k 219: 4 "after they had stolen my pouch in the palace".

2. OA *inūmi ki-sà-am tušebbalanni šāptam šuknam šāptum ina ālim waqrat* BIN 6, 7: 16 "when you send me a/the pouch, provide wool for me, wool is expensive in the City" (sim. BIN 4, 9: 18).

3. OA 1 ^{túg}*išram ki-sà-am tadmīqtaka* PN *naš'akkum* ICK 1, 88: 16 "PN is bringing you one belt-with-pouch (as) your *tadmīqtu*-loan".

4. OA in *k. nadā'um*, a symbolic act in connection with the transfer of a house (Veenhof 2010, 108f.):
a) *ki-ša-am* PN (…) *bēt* PN_2 *tamkārišu iddīma* PN_3 (…) *bētē iš'amma ki-ša-am nadā'am ēmurū* kt 87/k 324: 24 and 31

"PN laid down the pouch in the house of PN2, his agent; (when) PN3 bought the house, they saw the laying down of the pouch", s. Hecker 2004b, 283 n. 11.

b) (let nobody harm my paternal house) PN *u atta ki-ša-am idʾā ki-ša-am taddiʾā* TC 2, 39: 29 "PN and you must lay down the pouch. Have you (already) laid down the pouch?". Cf. AHw 490 s.v. *kīšam*.

5. As a qualification of gold (shape or quality?):

a) 1 GÍN KÙ.GI *ki-ša-am ša iṣṣēr* PN PN2 *īšūʾu* KTK 99: 1 "1 shekel of *k.*-gold, which PN2 owes to PN"; sim. AKT 7A, 211: 9

b) *ki-ša-am ša ma-tim* kt c/k 440: 15 "(gold which is) *k.* of the land" (court. J. G. Dercksen).

6. *ša ki-ší-a* as a qualification of iron: (they placed a great vow (stating): how much pure iron, (iron) *ša Ḫa-ar-ša* and (iron)) *ša ki-ší-a altaqqeʾu* kt n/k 67: 11 "of *k.* I have received" (sim. ib. 6, 16, 29; n/k 66: 1, s. Donbaz 2001, 84f.; CCT 5, 2a: 37). The reading and interpretation of (iron) *ki-ší-a* (or *ki-diri*?) are uncertain. Since *Ḫa-ar-ša* seems to be a geographic name (Donbaz 2001, 87), *ki-ší-a* may be one as well.

7. For OA *ki-i-šu-ma* (TC 2, 26 r.17), s. *Kaʾāšu*. For the alternation of *kīsu* and *kīšu*, s. GOA § 3.2.5.1.

8. NA 10 MA.NA URUDU *ki-si ša* PN StAT 2, 148: 1 "10 minas of pocket copper belonging to PN", cf. 149: 1.

9. (Vessel with) leather wrapping for vessel (differently Guichard 2005, 217–219 who proposes to interpret *kisu* as an animal, hence a zoomorphic vessel):

a) OB 1 [gal]*ki-su* ARM 31, 80: 4 "1 cup (with) wrapping".

b) OB 1 *ki-su ša sugūnī* ARM 31, 80: 20 "1 (cup with) wrapping, with handles".

c) OB 1 [gal]*mašqaltum ki-su ša sugūnī* ARM 31, 153: 17, 154: 7 "1 *m.*-cup (with) wrapping, with handles".

d) MA 30 ⸢x x x⸣[meš] *ša ki-sa-a-ni* AoF 17, 70: 5 "30 (vessels?) with wrappings, cf. ADD 1023: 6 (cit. CAD K 420 s.v. *kisānu*).

10. OB var. *kīšu*:

a) 1 [kuš]*ki-šum ša uqnî šadî* VS 22, 84: 14 (AoF 10, 52f.) "1 *k.*-bag with lapis lazuli from the mountains".

b) 1 *ki-ša-am ša kaspim* ARM 10, 58: 15 "1 *k.*-bag of silver"; cf. 59: 13; s. also FM 6, 62: 21; M.9344 (ARM 32 p. 469): 3'; UET 5, 60: 5; YOS 13, 158: 1.

11. OB pl. *kīsātu*: *ina ki-sa-ti-ni i nīkul* ARM 26/2, 76 no. 314: 25 "we shall pay for provisions from our (own) purses" (s. Arkhipov 2018, 169).

NJCK (1–6), JK (7), JW (8, 10–11), MPS (9)

kīsu III, *kišû* "bond, fetter"

SB *ina ki-šu-ú lamû* ORA 7, 318: 29 "they have surrounded with a fetter".

kiṣallu "tarsal calcaneus"

On the mng. s. Cohen 2018, 135.

+ **kiṣiptu** "calculation"; NA

ki-ṣip-ta-šú šalimti aštur AfO 25, 52: 5 "I wrote down its complete calculation", s. Reiner/Pingree ib. 53 (< *keṣēpu*). S. also *kiZiBtu*.

kiṣirtu "thickening, constriction"; OB "rental payment"; M/NA "envelope"

A *k.*-envelope (MA) contains a duplicate or summary of the text inside, whereas the term *maknaktu* refers to an envelope only containing author and addressee; both are sealed (de Ridder 2020, 32–35). JK

kiṣru "knot"

1. OB lex. [*k*]*a-kéš šu-si ĝìr-*[*ĝu*10] = *ki-*⸢*ṣi*⸣*-ir ubān šēpiy*[*a*] CUSAS 12 p. 157 xi 11 (Ugumu) "the joint of my toe".

2. OB lit. *ibtuq nakram kī ki-ṣí-ir abīḫim* FM 14 i 24 "he cut off the enemy like the knot of a cord".

3. *kiṣir libbi* "anger": OB *ana annêtim mimma ki-ṣí-ir libbi bēlni lā iraššênêšim* FM 2, 210 no. 117: 41 "my lord must not at all become angry with us because of this!"

4. As an ornament: OB (cups) *ša ki-ṣí-ir* ARM 21, 222 = ARM 31, 9: 7, 8 "with knot-decoration", s. Guichard 2005, 137.

5. MB "a harvest tax": *ki-iṣ-rù* BagF 21, 45: 1, s. Sassmannshausen ib. p. 230.

kiṣṣatu s. *gizzatu*

kiṣṣu "shrine, chapel"

1. OB lit. *mamman ul iṭeḫḫī ana* ⸢*ki-iṣ-ṣi*⸣*-ia* Westenholz 1997, 100 r. 10 (text B) "no one will approach my sanctuary".

2. SB pl. *ki-iṣ-ṣa-na* Jiménez 2017, 302: 6.

3. NB *ilū rabûtu iggagūma ul irrubū ana ki-iṣ-ṣi-šú-nu* SAA 18, 124 r. 6 "the great gods will be become angry and not enter their chapels".

kīša, *kīšam*(*m*)*a* "certainly, allegedly, supposedly"; + OA

1. OA lit. *ki-ša bīrum lamnum ki-ša šittum abiktum* AML 150: 2f. "certainly, bad vision; certainly, robbed sleep".

2. OA (are you my servants or the servants of the man of Ḫarsamna) *ki-ša-ma kakkam naš'ātunūma urkēa tattanallakā* 01/k 217: 42 (Günbattı 2014, 89) "allegedly carrying a weapon and following me around?" (also c/k 266: 25 quoted in GOA § 13.5.6 s.v. *ki-ša-ma*).

3. OB *ki-ša-ma ūmakkal šisâmma panīka lūmur* CUSAS 36, 221: 11 "do by all means summon me for just a single day so I may see your face!"

4. *ki-ša-ma* (< *kī* + *ša* + *-ma*?) ironically states a false assumption ascribed to the addressee: "you apparently think that … (but in fact …)". Cohen 2006, 561f.; Wasserman 2012, 138–153.

MPS (1), NJCK (2), JW (3)

kišādum "neck, bank"

1. OB *ki-ša-ad-ka kaqqaram uštakšid-m*[*a*] AbB 7, 187: 6 "she made your neck reach the ground" (idiom indicating humiliation?).

2. OB string of beads, s. Arkhipov 2012, 81–84 with add. refs.; of vessels, s. Guichard 2005, 130.

kišdu "acquisition, attainment"; + NA

1. OB (5 women) *ki-ši-id qātim ša šarrim* FM 2, 120 no. 72: 89 "personal (lit. of the hand) acquisition of the king".

2. NA [*k*]*i-šid littū*[*ti*] SAA 2, 6: 416 "attainment of old age"; s. the disc. Watanabe 1987, 191.

kišeršu "prison"

OA *i-ki-šé-er-ší-im ana mū'ātim nad'āku* AoF 35, 24 kt 86/k 48: 7 "I am thrown into prison to die".

kišertu "bondage, captivity"

OB *inūma* <*ina*> *ki-še-er-tim wašbātama* KTT 372: 5 "when you were sitting in prison".

kišittu "achievement, acquisition, conquest"

1. OA also "costs, liabilities" (Veenhof 1972, 416f.):

a) 1/2 TÚG *ḫuluqqāʾē ki-iš-da-tum ša* PN ICK 1, 53: 13 "the loss of half a textile is PN's liability".

b) *ana gamrēšunu nisḫātēšunu a-ki-iš-dá-té-šu-nu izzazzū* TC 3, 247A: 21 "for their expenses and taxes they are liable in proportion to their liabilities"; sim. kt 88/k 97B: 8 and 35 (s. Çeçen 1995, 56).

2. OB *ki-iš₇-da-at bītišunu* FM 2, 34 no.10: 11 "assets of their house".

NJCK (1), MPS (2)

kiškanû "a tree"; + OB

1. OB 1 *qaštu ša* GIŠ.KÍN 1 GIŠ.KÍN MU.DU ARM 23, 205 no. 232: 1–2 "delivery of 1 bow made of *k.* and one (log of?) *k.*". S. also Arkhipov 2012, 121 sub *qaštu*.

2. OB [giš]*ki-iš-ka-nu* ARM 24, 277: 50.

3. NB GIŠ.KÍN *muḫramma* OIP 114, 10: 12 "get *k.*-wood for me" (probably used for the bows mentioned in l. 14), s. also GIŠ.KÍN ib. l. 16, 22.

4. NB GIŠ.KÍN *magarra* OIP 114, 63: 4 "*k.*-wood for wheel(s)".

kiškattû, *kitkittû* "(industrial) kiln, forge; craftsman; engineer (as part of the royal army)"

1. OB (silver) *ina ki-iš-ka-te-ia* ARM 23, 532 no. 561 "in my forge" (memorandum).

2. NA [L]Ú *kit-kit-ta-a-te ša šarrim sammuḫ* SAA 12, 83: 19 "he is has joined in with the craftsmen of the king".

3. NA [lú]*kit-ki-te-e* ⌜*ša*⌝ *ē*[*kalli*?] SAA 19, 167 r. 1 "craftsmen of the p[alace(?)]".

****kiškīru** "an object" (AHw. 491)

The ref. RA 36, 147 belongs to *kiskirru* (s. already CAD K 424).

kišpu "sorcery"

Lex. *uḫ* = *ki-iš-pu* Emar 6/4, 537: 75 (Sjöberg 1998, 247).

kiššā/ēnu "a legume, vetch"

1. OA *ki-ší-ni* (…) *zarʾam* kt g/k 18: 14 "*k.*, winnowed" (cit. Balkan 1974, 38 n. 34).

2. OB *ki-ša-nu* (as fodder for oxen) CUSAS 34, 59 i 8, 9, 12, ii 6.

3. Stol 1985, 130–132; Postgate 1987, 94; Zeeb 2001, 190–192.

kiššatu I "all, totality"

1. Lex. *sag* = *ki-iš-ša-tu* Emar 6/4, 537: 323 (Sa) "head = totality", Sjöberg 1998, 261.

2. Lex. *a* = *ki-iš-ša-tum* Emar 6/4, 537: 26 "water = totality".

****kiššatu II/B** s. *kiššātu*

kiššātu "debt-slavery, indemnity, theft"; + OAkk

1. Lex. **a)** *udu-zíz-àm* = *immer kiš-šá-ti* "sheep of theft", after *immer šur-qí* "stolen sheep" MSL 8/1, 15: 87.

b) *kiš-šá-tum* = *sartum* AfO 21 pl. r. 2 "*k.* = falsehood" (s. 4 below).

2. OAkk "indemnity": *šībūt kiš-ša-tim* MVNS 3, 102 "witnesses of indemnity", s. Gelb 1984, 164.

3. SB "theft": *úš-tag nam-lilib*(IGI-IGI) *nam-zíz-ta dib-ba* // *laptān dāmi ša ina šurqi* (*u*) *kiš-šá-ti ṣabta*/*i* Borger 1973 i 29 "stained in blood, who was captured for theft or robbery".

4. Borger 1973, 175 on the mng. "theft". The refs. listed s.v. *kiššatu* (AHw. 492

"Emmer", CAD K 459) belong here. In general s. Kraus 1984b, 266–277; Wilcke 1991; Westbrook 1996.

kiššūtu "power"; + OB

1. OB lit. *il ki-iš-šu-tim gašru* RA 86, 81: 6 "strong god of power".

2. OB *šarrūt ki-iš-šu*[*-tim*] ARM 28, 172: 6 "powerful kingship".

+ **Kištu** "an agricultural product"; OA

1. *Ki-iš-tám u šaḫerēn kunukkīma ištē* PN *šēbilīm* BIN 6, 20: 30 "send me *K.* and a pair of *šaḫeru*-footwear under seals with PN".

2. *alānē er-bi-i ti'āmte u ki-iš-tám šēbilam* OIP 27, 6: 6 "send me acorns, shrimp and *K.*".

3. 2 *naruq ki-iš-tám iṣṣēr* PN *u* PNf *aššitišu* PNf_2 *tīšū* kt o/k 106: 3 "PN and his wife PNf owe 2 'sacks' of *K.* to PNf_2" (also ib. 10, s. Albayrak 1998, 10).

4. *g*/*k*/*qištu* is a rarely mentioned agricultural product, measured by capacity (*naruqqu* "sack" = ± 120 liters and *karpatu* "jar" = ± 30 liters), and doubtless to be separated from *qīštu* "forest" and *qīštu* "present". Dercksen 2001, 44 with n. 24. NJCK

kīšu s. *kīsu* I

kišubbû, + *kišuppû* "uncultivated land"

OB lit. *ki-šup-pa-šu* CUSAS 10, 1: 21.

kišukku "prison; grate"

1. SB *uššiṭū ki-šuk-*[*ki*] ORA 7, 322: 67 "they made harsh [my] prison".

2. NB 2 *ki-šuk-ku*^{meš} dubsar 7, 39: 10 "2 grates (of bronze)".

kitinnû s. *kidinnû*

kitintu s. *kidintu*

kitītu "a fabric"; OB; + MB

1. OB 1 ^{túg}*ki-ti-tum* ARM 21, 219: 22 (priced at 5 shekel); cf. 318: 2; 349: 11, 2.

2. OB *kišādum ki-ti-tum ḫašmānim* ARM 21, 282 ii 4 "red-purplish scarves of *k.*"; *paršīgum ki-ti-*[*tum*] ib. vii 14 "headdresses of *k.*"

3. OB 3 MA.NA *ki-ti-tum šà* SIKI 2/3 MA.NA 5 GÍN BIN 10, 79: 1, 3 "3 minas of *k.* containing 2/3 minas and 5 shekels of wool".

4. MB ^{túg}⌈*ki*⌉*-ti-tum* MBLET 56 r. 5.

5. Durand 2009, 159f. Based on etym., a linen fabric (s. *kitû*), but lex. refs. and the south-Bab. text BIN 10, 79 suggest that it may be (partially) made from wool (s. also Michel/Veenhof 2010, 216f.). S. also *kidinnû*, *kidintu*.

kittu II "part of a bowl"; + OB

OB lit. *šaknū ki-it-tu*!? *aparikku u purussu ina libbiki* AML 27: 9 "a *k.*, an *a.* and a plug are placed in your (the fermentation's vat) inside".

kitmu "cover"

OB *aššum nubāl ḫurāṣim ki-it-mi nussuḫim* ARM 13, 18: 6, cf. 8 "concerning the stripping of the plating of the palanquin". Cf. ARM 13, 21: 3, 6 (Arkhipov 2012, 64).

+ **kitmultu** "mutual grudge"

šarrū kit-mu-ul-tú ippušū SpTU 2, 35: 20 "the kings will hold grudges against each other" (Streck 2003a, 21).

kīttu "truth"

1. Lex. *zi* = *ki-it-tum* Emar 6/4, 537: 170 (Sa), otherwise *níg-zi* (Sjöberg 1998, 255).

2. NB plene spelling *kit-tu-ú*:

a) In question: ⌜*kit-tu*⌝*-ú ša* ... *kī pī annî idabbubū* OIP 114, 110: 12 "is it true that they speak like this?".

b) Elsewhere: *kit-tu-ú* ... *bēlī lumassīma* ib. 38: 42 "my lord should find out the truth".

3. NB adverbial acc.:

a) *kit-tu annâ ḫīṭū'a* OIP 114, 1: 32 "truly, this is my fault".

b) *ša'al kit-ta kī pî annî ana* PN *iqtabi* ib. 33: 9 "ask if he truly spoke to PN".

c) ⌜*kit*⌝*-ta* ib. 35: 25 in unclear context.

kitturru "salamander(?), toad(?)"; SB

1. *šumma kit-*⌜*tur*⌝*-ru ina bīt amēli innamir* K. 3726+ iii 46 (*šumma ālu* 38.65') "If a salamander(?) is seen in a man's house." FJMS

kit(t)ur(r)u "a chair; throne"; + OA

1. OA *u ki-tù-ra-am* PN [...] *lublam* AKT 5, 11: 34 "PN shall bring the *k*.".

2. NA 2 ^{giš}*ki-tú-ri-a-te* ZA 74, 78: 24 "2 *k*."; ^{giš}*ki-tú-u-ru* ⌜*dan*⌝*nu* ib. 28 "(1) strong *k*." S. Deller/Finkel ib. S. 87f.

3. NA in PN: KI.DUR-I BATSH 6/2, 95 l.e. 1 "the throne is praised".

JW (1–2), JK (3)

kitû, OA/MA *kitā'u*, pl. *kitā'ātu* "flax, linen"

1. OA *ki-ta-am ša Tuttul* Kt 93/k 196: 8 "1 linen fabric from Tuttul" (s. Michel/Veenhof 2010, 216–218).

2. OB *šūt* GADA UET 7, 73 ii 87 (Westenholz 1997, 148ff., Sg. letter) "flaxworkers (lit. those of flax)".

3. MA *aššum ki-ta-e ša* GN BATSH 4/1, 3: 5 "concerning the flax (that grows in) GN (...locusts have not eaten it)".

4. NA 1 ^{túg}KID *peṣû* StAT 3, 1: 32 "1 white linen-garment". Although the logogram KID is used (= akk. *kītu* "a mat"), the context and determinative *túg* suggest the reading *kitû*.

kizalāqu, *kasilaqqu* "sealed tablet(?)"

NB *ka-si-laq*!*-qu ša* PN PN$_2$ *u tupšarra-šunu ina* GN [...] *išṭurūma* SAA 17, 39: 5 "the sealed tablet(?) which PN, PN$_2$ and their scribe wrote in GN". Cf. already AHw. 1569.

+ **kizibtu I** "lie"; EA; NWSem. lw.

ki-zi-ib-tu ina panīka awâtu iqbû ana kâta ZA 86, 100: 5 "were the words I was saying to you lies in your opinion?". S. Huehnergard ib. p. 105 and cf. AHw. 467 *kazābu* II, *kazbūtu*.

+ **kiZiBtu II** "a garment"; NA

[x T]ÚG *ki-ZIP-te ša puškāyi* CTN 2, 1: 5 (uncert.). Cf. *kuzippu* "cloak"?

kizû, *kazû*, + *kezû* "animal trainer, groom"

1. OB *ka-zi-i* UET 7, 73 v 181 (between *šā'ilī* "dream-interpreters" and *ṭābiḫī* "butchers"; Sg. letter, Westenholz 1997, 148ff.). The by-form *kazû* is otherwise only attested in Ugar. and Nuzi.

2. OB lit. *Šagadirika ki-zu-*[*ka*] (// *kuš*$_7$) ASJ 19, 262: 6 "Š. is your groom" (preceded by *kartappu* l. 5).

3. MB KUŠ$_7$ DN WZJ, p. 574: 10f. (Sassmannshausen 2001, 55).

4. NB PN *ke-e-zu-*⌜*ú*⌝ OIP 114, 15: 1.

+ **kizûtu** "office for herd management"; OAkk; OB

1. OAkk È.A *ki-zu-tim* Banca d'Italia 1, 229 r. 3; 2, I-60: 4, r. 1 "delivered by the office for herd management". S. Such-Gutiérrez 2018, 134.

2. OB *awīlu šū mādiš ki-*[*z*]*u-tam u asût*[*am i*?*-le*?]*-e* ARM 26/1, 570 no. 270: 8 "this man is very [adep]t at(?) herdsmanship and medicine".

kû, fem. + *kūtu* "belonging to you, your"

1. Lex. *ku-ú* // ⸢*ku-ú-tu*⸣ = *attū*⸢*ka*⸣ // *att*[*ūki*?] AOAT 50, 366: 100 (malku) "your = belonging to you".

2. Sg. fem.: MA *sinništa ku-a-tu* Chuera 15: 6 "the woman belonging to you".

3. Pl. masc.: **a)** MA *ku-a-ú-te ṣābē* Chuera 4: 14 "your troops".
b) MA *immerē* ... *ku-a-ú-te* Chuera 10: 19 "your sheep".

4. MA in broken context: *yā'u lā ku-a-ú* [...] *ù ku-a-ú ku-a-ú*(-)*um*[*-ma*?...] BATSH 4/1, 29: 7f. De Ridder 2018, 262–264. MPS (1–3), JK (4)

ku'āti, + *ku'ātum* "you (gen./dative/acc. sg. masc.)"

Lex. *ku-a-tum* = *ana kâšunu* AOAT 50, 366: 101 (malku) "to you".

kubādu s. *kubātu*

kubā'ātu (BIN 4, 70: 11) s. *kuppû* II 6.

kubarinnu, + pl. *kubarinnātu* "a vessel"; + MA

1. 5 ANŠE Š[E *ku-ba*]*-ri-nu ša* ⸢*pî ṣaḫri*⸣ ... *ku-ba-ri-nu šanā'ītu* ...*ku-ba-ri-nu šalāšītu* 2 *ku-ba-ri-na-tu ša annaki* CUSAS 34, 44: 1–4, 8 "5 donkey-loads of b[arley (?)] (in) a ⸢*k.*⸣ with a small opening; (3 donkey-loads and 2 seahs in) a *k.* of second size; (2 donkey-loads and 2 seahs in) a *k.* of third size; 2 *k.* (made) of lead".

2. Sallaberger 1996, 55, 113: < *kubāru* "thick" + diminutive *-innu.*

+ **kubāšu** "a kind of bread"; OA

1. 1 *me-at* NINDA *ša mazītim ku-ba-ša-am* CUSAS 34, 36: 13 "100 loaves *ša mazītim* (and) a *k.*".

2. 1 *me-at ù ku-ba-šu-um* kt 93/k 513: 12 "100 (loaves) and a *k.*" (also ib. 14 and 28, quoted in Michel 2016, 229 n. 44).

3. Perhaps related to NB *kubbušu*, a kind of cake or bread (CAD K 483 s.v.) and MB *kubāsu*, mng. unknown but part of a list of cereals and vetches (CAD K 482a s.v.). S. Michel 2016, 229. NJCK

kubātu, *kubādu* "honors", in Emar: "a ceremony"; + MB Emar

1. *ēntu kakkī ilānī ana ku-ba-ti tanaššī kīmē ku-ba-da ugammarū* [...] Emar 6/3, 369: 31 "the high priestess carries the weapon of the gods for the *k.*; when they finish the *k.* [...]".

2. *ana pani bābi ša qabli ku-ba-da ana gabbi ilānī eppešū* Emar 6/3, 373: 36 "before the gate of battle they perform a *k.* for all the gods".

3. LÚ^{meš} *ku-ba-di* Emar 6/3, 366: 8 "honorable men (?)" (after list of bronze amounts and individuals).

4. On the ceremony ("sacrificial homage") s. Fleming 1992, 162–169; 2000, 95f.

+ **kubbillu**, *kunbillu* "a bucket for coal or embers(?)"; MB Qaṭna

1. 1 *ku-bi-il-lu* URUDU : *ta-ru-uš-ḫé* URUDU QS 3, 13: 14 "1 copper *k.* (gloss:) copper coal hod(?)".

2. 1 *ku-un-bi-il-lu* ZABAR QS 3, 12: 7 "1 bronze *k*." (listed after *zābil išāti* "fire carrier").

3. The Hurr. gloss *tarušḫe* is a device designation ending on *=ušḫe* derived from *tari-* "fire". This suggests a type of bucket for coal, embers or ashes (s. Richter 2005, 33f.). Richter in id./Lange 2012 considers a connection to *kabbilu* in MB Emar (s. *qabbilu*).

kubbulu "lame, crippled"

NA logogr. ^{lú}GÌR.AD$_4$ SAA 17, 79: 11, s. *karāmu*.

kubburu "very thick; an additional payment"; + MB Emar

1. MB *ku-ub-bu-ru ša bīti na-di-*⌜*nu*⌝ CunMon. 13, 4: 13 "the *k*. of the house has been paid", s. J. G. Westenholz 1993.

2. MB *ku-bu-ru bīti nadnū* Emar 6/3, 111: 22 "the *k*. of the house have been paid". S. also Scurlock 1993 with add. Emar refs.

kub(b)uttu "honoring gift"

1. MB Ugar. [*k*]*u-bu-ut-ta-tum*^{meš} RSO 14, 239 RS 88.2158: 35.

2. S. Huehnergard 1987, 135: *kubuddati* in PRU III is perhaps an Ugar. form.

kubbutu s. *kupputu*

kubdu s. *kubtu*

kubsu, pl.? *kubsātu* "laundering(?)"; Ugar. lw.

S. AHw. 498 s.v. *k/qub/psu*, read A^{meš} *ku-ub-sà-ti-ša* (Huehnergard 1987, 136, cf. ^{lú}*ka*$_4$*-bi-s*[*ú*] PRU 6, 136: 8 "launderer" in a list of Ugar. words for professions).

kubšu "headdress, cap"

1. OB (wool for) *ku-ub-šu* TH.87.47 (cit. ARM 30 p. 51). S. Durand 2009, 51–53 for logogr. refs. (SAG.ŠU) and disc.

2. MB 10 $^{\text{túg.me}}$*ku-ub-šu* PRU 6, 158: 13. S. Huehnergard 1987, 139f.: Perhaps *kupšu* in light of NWSem. cognates. S. also Pentiuc 2001, 108f.

kubtu, *kubdu* "lump of metal"

OB (lead) *ana ku-ub-di ša šaparrim* ARM 32, 229 M.18468: 11 "for sinkers on hunting nets". Arkhipov 2012, 18.

kūbu II "a building"

Lex. *é-nìgin = bīt ku-ú-bi* CUSAS 12 p. 40: 44 (Kagal).

kubūsu "a qualification of baskets and doors, handle(?)"

OB 4 ^{giš}PISAN *ku-bu-si* ARM 24, 277: 55 (c. ARM 30 p. 180 and 183).

kubuttû, *kubuddû* "abundance; a weight; bequest"; + OB, + MB Emar

1. OB "a weight": *qadū ku-bu-ut-t*[*u*] *ša* 10 GÍN ARM 25, 174*: 6 "with an additional 10 shekel"; *ku-bu-ud-de-e* ARM 25, 384 r. 11.

2. MB Emar "bequest": *ku-bu-da-e annûti ana* PNf *aššatiya add*[*inš*]*i* RE 8: 17 "I herewith give these bequests to my wife PNf"; cf. CunMon. 13, 14: 13; AulaOr. (Suppl.) 1, 71: 17; *ku-bu-da*^{meš} ib. 22: 2. S. Pentiuc 2001, 107f.

3. Durand/Joannès 1990.

kūdanu "mule"

1. MA ^{anše}*ku-du-nu* BATSH 18, 35: 5, 25; 36: 4, 48.

2. NA 20! *uttarāte* 10 *ša sīsê* 10 *ša* ^{anše}*ku-di-ni* SAA 5, 215: 8 "20 *u*.-type chariots, 10 with horses, 10 with mules”. JK (1), MPS (2)

kuddimmu “a spice plant, cress(?)”; + MA

1. MA *ku-di-mu* AoF 1, 78: 5, 11, 17, 31 (among other foodstuffs).

2. MA ^ú^*ku-di-mi* StAT 5, 90: 7 (among ingredients for a salve).

3. For “cress” s. Stol 1983–1984, 29f. (= Bab. *saḫlû*?).

kudurru II “a basket, wooden container”

1. MB 1-*en ku-dú-ra* (of bread) Emar 6/3, 387: 15, 13.

2. MB ^giš^*ku-du-ru* (for fruit) Emar 6/3, 369: 88 (as a wooden container also in Nuzi).

****kuddunu** “to seek sanctuary”

For the ref. cit. AHw. 1569 s. SpTU 2, 22 iv 3, but read with Schuster-Brandis 2008, 255 iv 34: DINGIR.MEŠ-*ú-ka da-an* DINGIR-*ú-a* DINGIR-*ka iḫeppe* “your gods are strong (but) my gods break your god(s)”. FJMS

+ **kuduḫe-** “departure(?)”; Hurr. word in MB Qaṭna

adī ÉRIN^meš^ *ḫu-ra-te* : *ku-du-ḫa-še-ni-eš* QS 3, 2: 17 “until the *ḫurādu*-troops (that are) ready for departure(?) (arrive)”, s. the comm. ib. p. 50.

kuduktu “a wool measure”; Nuzi; Hurr. word

= 1 1/2 minas, s. Wilhelm 1988; Richter 2012, 233.

kuduppânu “a sweet variety of pomegranate”

Lex. *ku-dup/du-pa-nu* = *matqu*, *dašpu* AOAT 50, 363:55f. (malku) “*k.* pomegranate = sweet, syrupy”.

+ **Kuʾītu**? “a decoration or type of vessel”; OB

1. 1 ^gal^*pašlu KU*?(*ma*?)-*i-tum* ⸢KÙ.BABBAR⸣ ARM 24, 83 = ARM 31, 78: 3 “1 silver *pašlu*-cup (of) *K*.-style(?)”.

2. S. SAD 1, 75 s.v. *pašlu* 2. S. *qû* II or *kuyātu* (a plant-shaped decoration in Qaṭna, s. Guichard 2005, 257)?

kukittu “inappropriate behaviour”

SB *uštād*[*ir eṭlūti ša* GN *in*]*a ku-kit-ti* Gilg. SB I 84 (s. 67) “he inappropriately vexed [the young men of GN]”.

kukkallu s. *kakkullu*

kukku I “cake”

1. Lex. *laldabû* = *ku-uk-ku* AOAT 50, 385: 110A (malku) “*l.* cake = *k.* cake”.

2. *kuk libbim* “cake of the belly, stomach”: OB lit. *rēš ku-uk libbim* AML 53: 17 “top of the *k.* of the belly”, s. Geller/Wiggerman 2008, 156.

3. OB (oil) *ana ku-uk-ki* KTT 178: 3 (s. also 72: 1) “for cakes” (for the meal of the king).

4. Logogr. and syllabic spelling: SB GÚG *ku-uk-ka* SpTU 4, 156: 6.

kukkub(b)u, pl. *kukkubātu* “a vessel”; + OA; + OB

1. Lex. *ku-ku-bá-t*[*um*?] Ugar. 5, 130 iii 9 (sg.?)

2. OA 3 MA.NA 10 GÍN *ana ku-ku-ba-tim šalāš ašqul* AKT 4, 20: 3 “I paid 3 minas and 10 shekels (of copper?) for three *k.*”; also AKT 8, 346: 7 and 13. Veenhof 2010, 105 with add. instances; id. 2017a, 462.

3. OB [1] *ku-ku-ub* 5 SÌLA ARM 31, 23: 9, s. also Sallaberger 1996, 51.

4. OB (wool, bread, and oil) *ina ku-ku-bi-im ublūnim* AbB 10, 55: 8 "they brought me in a *k.*".

5. MB Ug. 2 *ku-ku-ba-tu* PRU 6, 158: 2; 3. S. Huehnergard 1987, 136 (alphabetically attested, perhaps a loan from Akk. in Ugar.).

6. MB Qaṭna: 60 ^giš^GU.ZA ^giš^TASKARIN : *ku*!-*uk-ku-be-na-še* QS 3, 16: 1 "60 boxwood chairs (gloss:) (of) *k.*(-type)". This Hurr. form is also attested in Alalaḫ, s. CAD K 499 s.v. *kukkubu* ad f. It is unclear whether it belongs to this lemma.

JW (1, 3–6), NJCK (2)

kukkudru "stomach"

Of a human: OB lit. *ippuḫanni ku-ku-id*?-*ri* AML 30: 37 "my stomach set me on fire".

kukkullu s. *kakkullu*

kukkušu, + *kakkušu* "a low quality flour"; + OA

1. Lex. *ḫalāṣu* = *ku-*[*u*]*k-ku-šu* AOAT 50, 376: 228 (malku) "*ḫ.* flour = *k.* flour".

2. Early OB *ku-ku-šu* ARM 19, 329: 1.

3. OA (silver) *miḫrātim ša kà-ku-uš almattim* AKT 6B, 473: 10 "the equivalent of the *k.* of/for the widow".

MPS (1), JW (2), NJCK (3)

kukru "an aromatic plant"

SB *ḫibištu* : GÚR.GÚR [*ša ḫup*]*pê iqtabûni* ^šim^GÚG.GÚG : *ḫi*[*bi*]*štu* : ^šim^GÚR.GÚR SpTU 1, 49: 31f. "*ḫ.* is called *k.* plant [of] *ḫ.*, ^šim^GÚG.GÚG is *ḫ.* (and) is *k.* plant" (commentary). Stol 1979, 16ff.; Jursa 2009, 162.

kukullu s. *kukkallu*

kulbābu "ant"; + OB

OB *ina qaqqarim īlû ištū ab*[*u*]*ssim ša šu*[*dduri*] *ana bīt gal*[*lā*]*bim ša bāb šudd*[*uri*] *ī*[*lû*? *ištū*] *bīt gallābim ana bā*[*b*] *bīt* DN *ašar šinīšu īlû* [*an*]*a*? PN *l*[*ū*] *iqbûnimma ana šulum bēliya uzakkīma têrētum šalmā inanna ku-ul-ba-bi* [*š*]*unūti u kirbānam* [*ša*] *abussim ša šudduri* [*akn*]*ukamma ana ṣēr bēliya* [*ušābil*]*a*[*m*] ARM 26/1, 498 no. 242 r. 9 "they came up from the ground. They [came up(?)] from the storeroom of *š.* to the barber's house at the *š.* gate. They came up [from] the barber's house to the gate of DN's temple in two places. They verily told(?) PN and he made a purification for the well-being of my lord, and the extispicies were sound. Now I [se]aled those ants and a clod of soil [from] the storeroom of *š.* and [sent] it to my lord".

kulīlu II "an accessory, jewellery"

In Mari, always made from silver and offered to goddesses (s. Arkhipov 2012, 84 with add. refs. and disc.). Cf. Ebla *gú-li-lum* "bracelet(?)" (Pasquali 2005, 137–139).

+ **k/qullānu** "a tool"

1. *kúl-la-ni* ARM 21, 258: 26; *ku-ul-la-ni* 267: 2 (Charpin 1989–90, 105).

2. 1 *ku-ul-la-nim ša šipir ṣalam šarrim* ARM 22, 203+ vi 2 (Durand 1990d, 173) "a *k.* for fashioning a statue of the king".

kullaru "a disease"; + SB

kul-la-ri šumšu SpTU 4, 152: 7f. (description of disease:) "*k.* is its name"; *kul-la-ar ašî šumšu* ib. 9 "*k.* with(?) *ašû* disease is its name".

+ **kul(l)išu** "a district"; Early OB; foreign word

1. *šar* 9 *ku-li-ší* Shaffer/Wasserman 2003, i 14 "king of the 9 *k.*"

2. [...] *ku-li-šu-um ikkirma* ib. v 1 "the *k.* rebelled".

3. *Amurram ina kúl-li-⌜ší⌝-šu iṭrussu* Ahmed 2012, 257 Haladiny 84 "he turned the Amorite away from his *k.*"

4. The word is only attested in royal inscriptions from Simurrum, where it clearly denotes a geographical unit. Its origin remains unknown (s. Shaffer/ Wasserman 2003, 13f.).

+ **kullitannu** "a vessel"; OA; Anatol. lw.

1. 22 1/2 ŠE KÙ.BABBAR *aššikkātim u ku-li-ta-nim* Prag 624: 9 "22 1/2 grains of silver for flasks and a *k.*".

2. 6 *ku-li-ta-nu* AKT 6B, 335: 17.

3. 10 *ku-li-ta-nu* AKT 6B, 516: 9.

4. Cf. Luwian *kullit-* "a vessel (for oil and honey)", s. Dercksen 2007, 33f.

NJCK

kullizu "ox driver; leading ox"

MB 1 *alpu kul-li-zu šī[bu]* MBLET 5 r. 7 "1 aged leading ox".

kullu "to hold"

D 1. OB *ēkallam li-ki-[i]l* FM 7, 102 no. 27: 13 "may she administrate the palace".
2. MA with *ana* "to stop at":
a) *ana* GN, GN2 *u* GN3 *uk-ta-i-lu-ni* BATSH 4/1, 6: 20 "they stopped in GN, GN2 and GN3".
b) *ana* GN *lā* ⌜*ú*⌝-*ka-i-lu-ni ana* GN2 ⌜*uk*⌝-*ta-i-lu-ú-ni*⌝ ib. 25f. "they did not stop in GN, (but) they did stop in GN2".
Dt Streck 2003a, 112:
1. OA *ša ittīya uk-ta-i-lu-ni-ni ša''il* TPAK 1, 50 30 "ask those who have been held with me!". Cf. 110: 6; 156a: 7; 194: 18.
2. OB *šumma kaprum šu uk-ta-al* ARM 26/1, 323 no. 156: 30 "if this village can be held".

S. also *kutallu.* MPS/JK/JW

kulluBu s. *galābu*

kullumu "to show; to assign"

1. Lex. *pàd* = *ú-kál-li-mu* Emar 6/4, 537: 695 (Sa), Sjöberg 1998, 276.

2. OB *bīt rēd[îm] li-ka-al-li-im* AbB 13, 85: 29 "he shall assign (him) the soldier's house".

+ **kulluṣu** "shrivelled(?)"; OA

ŠE-*um kà-lu-ṣú-um* AKT 10, 16: 12 "shrivelled(?) barley"; sim. AKT 10, 24A: 3 // 24B: 7. NJCK

kulukku s. *kalakku*

kulūlu "crown, crenellation, ledge"

SB *šumma ṣēru ištū ku-⌜lu⌝-li ša nērebi ušqallilamma* KAL 1, 12: 28 "If a snake is hanging from the sill (above) the entrance".

kulupinnu, *kilupinnu* "hatchet-like tool with which straw was chopped"; OA; Anatol. lw.

1. OA 10 *ku-lu-pì-ni tibnam* Prag 549: 10 "10 *k.* for straw". S. also VS 26, 196: 2.

2. In CAD K 528b correct the ref. Kültepe 211 to Ka 382.

3. Dercksen 2007, 34.

kūm, *kû*, + *kūmma* "instead (of)"

1. NA var. *kūma*: *ku-ma* 1/2 [MA.NA KÙ.BABBAR] StAT 1, 36: 2 "instead of 1/2 [mina of silver]".

2. In locative case with pronominal suffix: NA *mār* PN *ina kussî ina ku-mu-uš-šú tus*[*sēšib*] SAA 1, 8 r. 11 "instead of him, you had the son of PN s[it] on the throne".

3. LB var. *kû* < *kūw* < *kūm*: *ana ku-*⸢*ú*⸣ AOAT 414/1, 129: 12; Nbn 916: 16; TCL 13, 200: 6. JK (1), MPS (2, 3)

kumānu "a surface and linear measure"

1. MB *ku-ú-ma-ni* [GÍ]D.⸢DA-*šu*⸣ Ekalte 74: 2 "(a vineyard…) (1) *k.* is its length".

2. Watson 2011: Cf. Mycenaean *kama* "a plot of land", Greek *kamán*? Powell 1987–1990, 476f., 485; Chambon 2008, 142f. (= *šiddu* in Emar, 1/4 *iku*).

kumāru "border(?), edge (referring to terrain, framed jewelry); a part of the constellation Cygnus"

1. LB 2 *šá-an-šú šá ku*!*-ma-ri* ArOr 33, 21: 3 "two framed sun-disc ornaments" (von Soden 1975, 461), cf. [*šá*]*-an-šu*^meš^ *ša ku-mar-ra-a-tú* CT 55, 309: 3.

2. *ku-*⸢*ma*⸣*-ru* KÙ.GI *ša tamlê* PTS 2950: 14 "golden framed ornament with inlaid work" (Beaulieu 2003, 383).

kumru, + MB Emar *kamru* "priest"

1. OA (silver) *ištē ku-um-ri-im* AKT 8, 325: 9 "due by the priest". S. also AKT 4, 48: 34 (of Adad); AKT 5, 53: 34 (of Ea-šarrum); AKT 6A, 129: 31 and 36 (of Šamaš); and pass.

2. MB Emar:

a) LÚ^meš^ GAL ^lú.meš^*kà-ma-ri* Emar 6/3, 446: 38 "the nobles and priests"; ^lú.meš^*kà-ma-ru* ib. 17.

b) [D]N *ka-ma-*[*ri*] Emar 6/3, 378: 48 "DN of the priests".

c) D[N *bē*]*l ku-ma-ri* Emar 6/3, 373: 134, cf. 468: 3 "DN, lord of the priests".

d) *ku-ma-ri* Emar 6/3, 274: 17.

e) Some refs. may also be interpreted as *gammaru* ("whole populace") or derivatives of *kamāru* IV "to heap up" (s. Pentiuc 2001, 95f. for disc. and lit.). The forms are NWSem. pls. Cf. Ugar. *kmr*, syllabically spelled *kù-um-ru* PRU 3, 69–70: 21–24 (Huehnergard 1987, 95). NJCK (1), JW (2)

+ **kumruttu** "(attributes of) priesthood"; OA

*ku-um-ru-tám tuka*ʾʾ*al* kt c/k 18: 12 (s. Dercksen 2015b, 38f.) "she (your *amtum*-wife) holds the attributes of priesthood" (the addressee is a priest of Ištar). NJCK

kumû "a waterfowl, crane(?)"; + OB

1. OB ⸢*ku*!*-mu*!⸣*-um*! Edubba'a 7, 100: 23 (in list of birds). Black/Al-Rawi 1987, 124 read ⸢x⸣*-mu-um*, Al-Rawi/ Dalley 2000, 106 offer as an alternative reading *iz-zi-du*.

2. SB *ku-ma-a*^mušen^ *umašširma* OBO 290, 88: 14 "I released a crane".

+ **kumurtu** in *bēt kumurti* "temple, chapel(?)"; OA

1. *be-et ku-mu-ur-tim ša* DN *aṣṣēr bētiʾa imqutma be-tí-a iddī*(*ma*) Kuzuoğlu 2016, 36 kt 88/k 487: 9 "the chapel(?) of DN has fallen on my house and has wrecked (lit. thrown down) my house".

2. Presumably an abstract noun derived from *kumru* "priest" (less likely a derived feminine "priestess"). NJCK

kumzillu s. *kunšillu*

+ **kunāmu** "mng. unkn."; OB

OB lit. ⸢*ṭābiš*⸣ *iššakkan ku-na-mu-um mūša adī šērim* Or. 87, 20 ii 23 "a *k.* is pleasantly placed from night until morning" (s. Streck/Wasserman 2018, 32).

kunāšu "emmer"

OB (2 seah 3 liters) *ku-na-ši…ublakki* AbB 7, 10: 5' "I brought you (2 seah 3 liters of) emmer".

kunda/iraššu s. *kandarasānu*

kuninnu "a vessel (clad with bitumen)"; + OB, + MB Emar

1. OB ^giš^*ku-ni-in?-nu* ARM 31, 472 no. 172 r. 10.

2. OB 1 ^gal^*gu-ni-nu* KÙ.BABBAR ARM 31, 477 no. 177 r. 18.

3. MB 2 *ku-ni-nu* (of silver) Emar 6/3, 43: 13, 14.

4. S. Sallaberger 1996, 88; Guichard 2005, 193.

kunnu "established, just"; + OB

OB lit. PN *ku-nu-um* FM 14 ii 30 (s. also 29) "PN, the just one".

kunnû "honored, beloved"; + OB

OB lit. *mārum ku-un-nu-ú-um* (// *zi-dè áĝ*) CUSAS 10, 14: 31 "beloved son".

+ **kunnunu** "to fill"; SB

1. ⸢*ku*⸣*-un-*⸢*nu*⸣*-nu kunūnūšu* Gilg. MB Ur 56 "his storerooms are filled".

2. Denominated from *kunūnu*, var. of *ganūnu*. George 2003, 305 suggests a reading *ku-un-nu* {*nu*} "is well off", which is semantically unsatisfying and presupposes a mistake.

kunnūtu "tending"

For AHw. 1569 s. NB SAA 17, 130: 5.

kunšillu, + *kuršillu* "(thorn used as) teasel; textile worker using a teasel"; + MB Emar

1. Lex. ^kuš^BAR.SÍG = *ku-ur-ši-il-lu* Emar 6/4, 548: 186. Previously known attestations use the determinatives TÚG or UZU.

2. (pieces of meat) *ana ku-um-zi-il-li u sekrim* FM 12, 220 M.18014: 2 "for the carder and the *s.* priestess".

3. On the profession s. Sassmannshausen 2001, 88.

kunukku "seal"

1. OB *ina ku-nu-ki-ia ù ku-nu-uk mārī kārim* FM 2, 285 no. 130: 18 "with my seal and the seal of the merchants", s. *kanāku*.

2. On cylinder-shaped beads in Mari s. Arkhipov 2012, 48, 84–86.

3. S. also *qanû*.

kunūnu s. *ganūnu*

kunūšim, + *kunūšin* "you (dative pl. masc.)"

Lex. *ana ku-nu-ši-in* = *ana kâšunu* AOAT 50, 366: 103 (malku) "to you".

+ **k/gunurû** "yesterday"; SB; Sum. lw.

1. Lex. *ūmu gu/ku-nu-ru-u/ú* = *timālu/i* AOAT 50, 370: 162 (malku) "yesterday's day = yesterday".

2. < Sum. *u*4*-ku-nu-ri-a*, s. Hrůša ib. p. 87.

kupatinnu, *kuptatinnu* "pill, pellet"

OB lit. *ša qātīya ku-up-ta-ti-in ṭīdim* AML 29: 11 "clay pellet in my hands".

kupīru "bitumen(?)"

S. SAA 11, 16 for the interpretation as var. of *kupru*.

kuppu "cistern, water source, reservoir" s. also *quppatu*

Disc. Bagg 2000, 152f. (a reservoir rather than a spring).

kuppû I "eel(?); a bird"; + OB

1. OB lit. *ku-pí-i* CUSAS 10, 7: 5, cf. *pāštu* 1.

2. OB GÚ.BÍ^{mušen} Edubba'a 7, 100: 43 (in list of birds).

3. NA ⸢*kīma ku*⸣*-up-*⸢*pe*⸣*-e šurbuṣā* RINAP 3/2, 46: 76 "(all my soldiers) had to camp like eels" (in description of flooded campgrounds, von Soden 1975, 462). Grayson/Novotny in RINAP 3/2, following Luckenbill, read *quppê* "(as though they were in) cages", but note that the inscription uses *qu*$_1$ throughout.

kuppû II "snow, ice"; + OA

1. OA masc. sg.: *kīma ku-pá-um mādūni* AKT 6B, 329: 19 "since there is much snow".

2. OA fem. sg.: *kīma ku-pá-ú-um mādatni* AKT 7A, 284: 16 "since there is much snow".

3. OA *ku-pá-um ippaṭṭarma ana* 10 *ūmē uṣṣī'am* CCT 3, 48b: 5 "once the snow starts melting, I will leave within ten days".

4. OA *kē i-ku-pá-im allak* AKT 5, 18: 49 "how can I travel in the snow?" (also ib. 50)

5. OA *innapṭar ku-pá-e-em išaqqal* AKT 10, 2a: 11 "he (the debtor) will pay at (the time of) the melting of the snow" (sim. ib. 2b: 16).

6. OA fem. pl.: *nēnu i-ku-pá-a-tim nirtanappud* BIN 4, 70: 11 "we have been wandering about in the snow".

7. NA *ku-pu-u šērida* SAA 5, 142: 6 "bring down ice!"

8. NA *lā zī[nu] lā ku-up-p[u] i-zi-nu-nu-[ni]* SAA 5, 26: 10 "it 'rained' neither rain nor snow".

9. NA *ku-pu-u* KASKAL^{meš} *uṣṣabbit* SAA 5, 146: 7 "snow has blocked the roads".

10. NA *ku-*⸢*pu*⸣*-[u] qarḫāte annāka ida''inūni* SAA 15, 41: 9 "(my lord knows, that) snow and ice are strong here".

11. NA *ana šadê ša ku-pe-*⸢*e*⸣ SAA 19, 26: 12 "to the snowy mountains".

NJCK (1–6), MPS (7–8, 11), JW (9–10)

kupputtu "one-seah vessel"; + MB

MB [^{d}]^{ug}*ku-*⸢*up*⸣*-pu-ut-tu šizbi* MBLET 50: 7 "[x] *k.* of milk".

kupputu "block(-shaped)"; + OA

1. OA *allānū mišlum kà-pu-tù-tum* CCT 2, 36a: 13 "oak resin(?), half solid (half powder)". S. *tasīku*.

2. OA *sāmtum mišlum kà-pu-tum mišlum araktum* AKT 6C, 649: 9 "carnelian, half block-shaped, half oblong".

3. OA uncert.: *ina tamalakkim kà-pu-tim ṣaḫrim šaknū* AKT 5, 66: 24 "(tablets) are placed in a small square(?) container". JW/NJCK

kupputu "to collect" s. *kapātu*.

kupru "dry bitumen, pitch"

1. OB *ku-up-ra-am ana qaqqadišu* ⸢*iš-ša*⸣*-ap-*⸢*pa*⸣*-ku* Haradum 2, 23: 15 "they will pour(!) bitumen over his head", cf. TCL 1, 238: 32.

2. OB Mari *bīt k.* (an office): (silver) *ina bīt ku-up-ri-im maḫir* ARM 23, 524 no. 553: 9 "is received in the house of bitumen", cf. ARM 23, 530 no. 558: 10; ARM 21 p. 189 n.7.

3. a) Together with *iṭṭû* used for waterproofing a ship in OB lit. Finkel 2014: 21, s. *iṭṭû*.
b) ESIR.UD.DU⸣ *kīdû* "dry bitumen for the outside" ib. 32.

4. 12 *eleppētim annêtim ku-up-ra-am u iṭṭâm iṣ-ṣé-nu-nim* FM 2, 45 no. 14 r. 5 "they loaded for me 12 ships with dry bitumen and liquid bitumen"; cf. also ib. 7, r. 9, r. 11, r. 15, r. 18, r. 21.

5. Stol 2011–2013b. S. *kupīru*.

kupru "shepherd's hut" s. *gupru*

kupsu "bran, sesame residue"; + OB

1. *aššum šīri*? *u ku-up-*⸢*si*⸣ KTT 376: 6 "because of the flesh(?) and the bran".

2. SB 7 *ṣalam ku-up-si* Lamaštu, Assur memo 29 (Farber 2014, 279) "7 figurines made from bran".

kuptatinnu s. *kupatinnu*

kupû, + *kupa'u*, + *kipa'u*, *kapa'u*, *kaba'u* "canebrake"; + MB Emar

1. Lex. (malku) **a)** *ka-pa/ba-'-(ú/u)* // *ku-pa-*⸢'⸣-[x] = MIN (*appāru*) AOAT 50, 336: 76 "canebrake = swamp".
b) *ka-pa-'-ú/u* // ⸢*ku*⸣*-p*[*a- ...*] = MIN (*apu*) ib. 79.

2. MB Emar (second narrow side) *ki-pa-ú* AulaOr. (Suppl.) 1, 7: 7 (description of field); s. Hrůša 2010, 215.

3. *kupû* (AHw. 509, CAD K 555f.) and *kab/pa'u* (AHw. 417, CAD K 18) are variants of the same word. *b* only occurs in NA sources of malku and attests to the typical *b/p*-change of NA.

kurangu, + *kuri'angu*, + *kuri'āgu* "a cereal"; + MA; + LB

1. MA ŠE *ku-ri-an-gu* Salvini 1998, 187: 5. Cf., perhaps, the Nuzi PN *Ku-ra-an-ge* (NPN 230).

2. NA *še'u gabbu* ŠE.LIL^{meš} ⸢*ittaṣadū*?⸣ SAA 19, 20: 8 "all the barley and *k*. have been harvested(?)".

3. LB *ku-ur-ia-a-gu* AOAT 254, 112 no. 13: 2 (part of a delivery for the temple, besides sesame).

4. The MA attestation disproves the older suggestion that *k*. is a loan from Persian *guri/anj* "rice" (10th cent.), although it may be a *Kulturwort* of Indo-Aryan origin. S. also Stol 2007b.

kurāru "carbuncle, a skin disease"; + OB

1. OB *ša ku-ra-ra-am marṣu* RA 90, 4: 16 "he who was afflicted with carbuncles".

2. For *kurāru* (II) "knob" s. *karru*.

kurā'u s. *kurû* II

kurartu, *k/gura/ištu* "a disease; a plant"

S. Fincke 2011, 181–184: A skin condition often affecting the head.

kurdinnu "an aromatic plant"; + NA

2 GÍN ^{šim}*kur-di-*⸢*nu*?⸣ SAA 7, 146: 7 "2 shekels of *k*.".

kurdiššu "pile of straw"

NA ^{še}*kur-diš* SAA 15, 326: 3 in broken context.

kurgarrû "a performer, transvestite(?)"

LB ^{lú}KUR.GAR.RA^{meš} *lā tumaššara adī* 2 ^{lú}KUR.GAR.RA^{meš} *ušaršadūma ana panī šarri išapparūni nubatti lā ibêt* dubsar 3, 21: 10 "don't release the *k*. Until they establish(?) 2 *k*. and send them to the king, he(?) shall not stay overnight!"

+ **kurḫu** "workshop"; NA; Hurr. lw. (?)

1. ^{é}*ku-ur-ḫu šū ētapaš* CTN 3, 2: 3 "this workshop – I have constructed (it)".

2. ⌜é⌝*kur*-⌜*ḫu*⌝ *adī* ⌜*gušūrī*⌝[*šu*] [*tarbā*]*ṣi mūṣû* StAT 3, 14: 4 "a workshop with its roof beams, a courtyard and exit". S. also StAT 3, 3: 7.

3. 3-*su ša* ⌜é*kur*⌝-*ḫi* WVDOG 132, 49: 4 "his third of a workshop".

4. *mešlu tarbāṣi ša* é*kur-ḫi* StAT 2, 263: 8 "half of the courtyard of the workshop".

5. é*kur-ḫu*!(RU) *tarbāṣušu* Sadberk 30: 8 "the workshop and its courtyard".

6. *tarbāṣu* é*kur-ḫu ina libbi* Assur 28: 8 "a courtyard: a workshop in its center".

7. Radner 1997, 274f.

kuriāgu s. *kurangu*

kuriangu s. *kurangu*

+ **kurībtu**? "a type of land"; NA; Aram. lw.(?)

1. (1 homer of) *ku-ri-bat*! *ina muḫḫi na*[*ḫalli*] SAA 6, 137: 4 "*k.*-land on the wa[di]".

2. Cherry 2017, 172–174 suggests a lw. from Aram. *krb*(ʾ) "ploughed or tilled field".

kurību "cherub"; + NB

ku-ri-bu ul tādur SAA 19, 4 r. 14 "you did not fear the cherub".

kurinnu, pl. *kurrinātu* "a neck ornament; a divine symbol"; + NA

1. NA 2 *ku-ri-nat* ⌜KÙ⌝.[BABBAR] *issaknū* SAA 7, 58 iii 19' "they set aside 2 sil[ver] *k.*"

2. NA *ku-ri-nat* 3 GÍN SAA 7, 73: 4 "a(?) necklace (weighing) 3 shekel".

3. Postgate 1994a, 244.

kurištu "vulva" s. *gurištu*; for the disease s. *kurartu*.

kurkānû, *kurkânu* "a medical plant"

1. LB *kur-ka-nu* Jursa 2009, BM 34005 and ib. p. 162.

2. S. Kinnier Wilson 2005 (perhaps a type of maidenhair fern); Thavapalan 2020, 183 (turmeric?).

kurkizannu, *kurkuzannu*, + *kukkuzannu* "piglet"; + OA

1. 1/3 GÍN *šiʾim ku-ku-za-nim* AKT 6C, 719: 9 "1/3 shekel, the price of a piglet" (in a list of expenses).

2. Often as PN in OA, e.g. *Ku-ku-za-nu-um* ATHE 14: 24; *Ku-ku-za-num* Prag 580: 21.

3. OB lit. *ku-ur-ku-za-an* (// *zé-eḫ tur-re-e*) *lū tātakal ribiṣ* CUSAS 10, 14: 6 "piglet, indeed you have fed, sit down!"

4. *kīma ku-ur-ku-za-nim tulê libbika tēniq* ib. 21 "like a piglet you sucked at the teats of your (own) belly".

5. Borrowed into Hurr. as *kuzinkari*, s. Haas 1993, 265, Richter 2012, 231.

NJCK (1–2), MPS (3–4), JW (5)

kurkû "goose"

1. OB KUR.GI4!mušen Edubba'a 7, 100: 2 (list of birds).

2. NA 2 KUR.GImušen!meš CTN 6, 99: 3.

3. NA 1 KUR.GImušen CTN 6, 101: 1.

4. NA 1 KUR.GImušen *māt A-ra-me-i* CTN 6, 112: 16 "1 goose from the land of the Arameans".

5. LB *bīt kur-ki-i ṣullilma* dubsar 3, 171: 17 "roof the goose house!"

kurkurrānu "pot bellied sheep"

See Steinkeller 1995, 56 (< *kurkurru*).

FJMS

kurkurru, *kukurru* (a vessel); + Ur III

Ur III n ^{dug}*ku-kur-rú* CUSAS 3, 1267: 1.

NR

\+ **kurmadillu** "a bird"; OB, MB

1. OB (barley as fodder for) 4 *kur-ma-di-lu* (that stay in the courtyard of the palace, mentioned between ducks and a gazelle) KTT 154: 3. Cf. *tarmazilu* CAD T 238?

2. MB *kur-ma-di-il-lum*^{mušen} BagF 21, 361: 19 (list of fattened birds).

3. MB 1 *kur-ma-di*!*-lum*^{mušen} BagF 21, 125: 9.

\+ **kurmišu** "a foodstuff, perhaps a cereal or spice"; MA

kur-mi-šu AoF 1, 78: 4, 10, 16, 30 (listed after cereals and before *kuddim-mu* and sesame).

kurmittu "an insect"; + OB, SB

OB ?*-kúr-ki* = *kur-mi-it-tum* UET 7, 93 r. 13, between *šāʾilullu* (an insect?) und *ilulāya*). Cf. Sjöberg 1996, 230. Cf. *kurṣiptu*.

kurnû s. *qurnû*

\+ **kurrapû** "(official) legal document"; LB; Greek lw.

LB *enna agâ iturruʾ ina epēšu kur-ra-pe-e ana* PN OECT 9, 42: 5; 28 "the prebend, which had returned thereafter by means of making a *graphē* to PN", s. McEwan 1984, 240f. Lw. from Greek < γραφή/*graphē*.

NR

\+ **kurru III** "flour-based depilatory paste"

1. Lex. **a)** *šinṭu, gerdu // šipat kur-ri* AOAT 50, 417: 193–4 (malku) "plucked wool, scraped off wool // wool of *k.*"

b) [*zì-d*]*a-ti // zì-da kur-*[*ri*] CT 19, 39 = KDP 28 I 39.

2. OB (hides) *ša ina ku-ur-ri-im nadû* OIM A.3556 (cit. Deller 1985, 328) "that have been placed into *k.*"

3. OB *šī ibūma maškam ina ku-ur-ri-im ušēlī* ARM 26/1, 87 no. 6: 18 "she (the bitch) herself came and lifted (a piece of) skin from the *k.* (in order to eat it)" (Mayer 2016, 227; diff. Groneberg 1993, Heimpel 1996c, Scurlock 1997, who attribute the passage to *kurru* II "a body part", perhaps "groin").

4. SB *ana ummi danni nasāḫ*(*i*) *kur-ra ša aškāpi labira* (...) SÚD BAM 147: 13–15 "to remove a high fever, grind up old *k.* (with var. medicinal plants)"; cf. BAM 315 I 33; AMT 63, 2: 6.

5. SB *kur-ru ša aškāpi* Lamaštu II 28 (Farber 2014, 99) var. *kur-ra, ku-ur-ra* "*k.* of the leather workers"; Lamaštu III 67 (ib. 135), among ritual ingredients.

6. NA in a penal clause, s. CAD Q s.v. *qerdu*; CAD S 20 s.v. *sadru*; AHw. 1002 s.v. *sadru* 7. S. also StAT 2, 243: 7.

7. NA in *ša kurrišu* (?) (a profession): *ša kur-ri-šu* ADD 953: 3 and CAD S 20 (*sadrišu*), s. also Kinnier Wilson 1972, 86.

8. LB (flour) *ana kur-ru ša aškāpī* AnOr 8, 20: 11–12 "for the *k.* of the leather workers", sim. AUWE 5, 1: 2.

9. n *ši-ḫa-ṭu ša ina bīt karê ana ku-ur-ru* Nbn. 345 "n sheep skins from storage for *k.*"

10. (cow hides) *ittī* 4 SÌLA *qēm buqli* 4 SÌLA *qēm bitqa ana kur-ru idī* TCL 6, 44: 23–24 "put (them) together with 4 liters of malt flour and 4 liters of *bitqa*-flour into the *k.*"

11. Deller 1985.

kurrû "short" (pl. of *kurû*); + NA

1. OB field name: *dimātum ku-ur-re-tum* YOS 12, 380: 2 "short towers".

2. NA 68 ^{túg}GÚ.È *kùr-ri* StAT 3, 1: 33 "68 short *naḫlaptu*-garments".

+ **kurrukummu** "curcuma"; SB, < Aram. *kūrkemā*

2 *gír-e kur-ru-ku-um-mu* SpTU 2, 50: 5 "2/24 shekel curcuma". Cf. *kurkānu*.

kursālu, *kuršalû*, *kuršilû* "a basket"; OB AHw. *kursālu*, CAD *kuršallu*.

1. OB ^{gal}*ku-ur-sa-lum ša ša-wi-nim bābušu išissu* KÙ.BABBAR ARM 25, 501 = ARM 31, 34 r. 16 "1 *k*.-cup of *š*.-wood(?), its opening and its base of silver".

2. 1 ^{giš}*ku-<ur>-sa-lu ša-wi-lu šaptāšu* KÙ.BABBAR GAR.RA *sugūnšu* KÙ.BABBAR ARM 31, 37: 36 "1 *k*. of *š*.-wood(?) its rim (lit.: lips) silver plated, its handle of silver". S. also ARM 31, 166: 3; 177: 1; 237: 1; 172: 8''.

3. Of bronze:

a) 1 *kur-ša-lu-ú* ARM 31, 37: 51.

b) 2 *ku-ur-ši-lu-ú* ARM 31, 223: 2.

4. S. Guichard 2005, 219f. However, ARM 31, 37 throws some doubt on the identity of *kursālu* (Guichard: *kursalû*) with *kurša/ilû*, as it contains one of each. Note also that the former is not made from solid metal in the known refs., but plated or equipped with metal components. Cf. *kunšillu*, *kuršillu* "thorn, teasel" instead?

Kursānu "a container for oil"; OA

1. OA *šinā ku-ur-sà-né* Ì.GIŠ CCT 6, 8b: 7 "2 *k*.-containers with oil".

2. OA 3 *ku-ur-sá-num re-eš*$_{15}$*-tum* 2 *ku-ur-*⸢*sá*⸣*-num marrurum* CCT 1, 42b: 5 and 6 "3 *k*.-containers with first-quality (oil and) two *k*.-containers with bitter (oil)".

3. *g/k/qursānu* (or *-annu*) is to be kept separate from *kursinnu* II, from which it differs in both form and meaning. It may be the OA counterpart of (^{kuš})*gusānu*, a leather bag (OB, MA). *Pace* Durand 2009, 176 they may be independent borrowings from the same source. S. Veenhof 2012, 191–193. NJCK

kursimtu, *kurṣimtu*, *kursittu*, *kurṣindu*, + *kuršiddu*, + *kurṣinnu*, + *kussimtu* "scale, plate; a snake"; + NA

1. OB lit. *aṣbat ku-ur-ši-da-am ṣerri lā šiptim šinnāšu mirmerrum lišānšu herīnum* AML 106: 3 "I seized the viper, a snake impervious to spell(s), whose twin fangs are a (lightning) flash, whose tongue is sharp grass"; *kur-ṣi-nu-*⸢*um*⸣ AML 109: 25.

2. NA designation of a door: 15 *ku-si-mat* SAA 1, 203: 8 "15 (doors) with (metal) plates" (in list of doors).

kursinnu I "ankle, lower leg"; + OA

1. OA lit. *muḫḫam ša kur*^{ur}*-sí-na-tim adī šabā'im ekkulūni* OA Sarg. 27 "they eat the upper part of the lower legs until being satisfied".

2. OA *qaqqadātum ištaplāma* [*k*]*ur-sí-na-tum e-ta-l*[*i-a*...] "heads have gone down, ankles have gone up" Prag 735: 26, s. *qaqqadu* for an OB parallel.

3. OA *kur-sí-na-tim* TPAK 1, 209: 12 (in a list of meat dishes); perhaps also *ku-ur-<sí>-na-am* kt j/k 97: 37 (s. Günbattı 1997, 109), s. *gurnu*.

4. OB *ištū anāku muḫḫam amazzaqu šū ku-ur-si-na-tim linakkis* A.111: 29 (Durand 2006, 27) "as soon as I have sucked the marrow out, he shall cut off the hock." MPS (1), NJCK (2–3), JW (4)

kursinnu II "a private fund (OA); a container (NA)"

1. OA: **a)** *lū naruqqum lū kur-sí-nu-um lū ba'abtum malā* PN *ēzibu* (…) *ša* PN$_2$ ICK 2, 157: 18' "be it a joint-stock fund, a *k.*-fund, or outstanding debts, whatever PN left behind (…) belongs to PN$_2$" (also ib. 24').

b) *ina kur*^{ur}*-sí-na-tim ša bēt abīka e*-15 MA.NA URUDU *ša* PN *mimma ulā nilqā* St. Meriggi p. 119: 4 "from the *k.*-funds of your father's firm we have not taken anything except (the?) 15 minas of copper of PN" (corresponding to *ina naruq* PN "from PN's joint-stock fund" in KTH 9: 4).

c) *ina ku-ur-sí-nim ša* PN AKT 8, 175: 7 "from the *k.*-fund of PN (1 1/3 minas of silver have been deposited for them)".

d) *gameršu* PN *ša ṣuḫārtim ina ku-ur-sí-na-tim ilaqqē(ma)* AKT 3, 36: 9 "PN will receive his expenses(?) for(?) the girl/servant from the *k.*-funds" (sim. RA 60, 134 Thierry: 18 and 23).

e) A *k.* is a fund owned by a particular person or firm, from which silver or copper can be taken to meet certain obligations, often in the context of a testimentary disposition. It is parallel to *naruqqu* "joint-stock fund", lit. "sack", and may likewise originally denote a container (s. 2, below). According to Schwemer (2005–6, 222) it is likely to be borrowed from Hittite and thus to be kept separate from *kursānu.* S. Veenhof 2012, 191–93.

2. NA 2 *kur-si-na-te ša kutalli* StAT 3, 8: 9 "two *k.* for the neck (of a pack animal)". NJCK (1), JK (2)

kurṣindu s. *kursimtu*

kurṣiptu, + NA *gurṣiptu* "an insect"; + OB, SB, NA

1. OB lex. ⸢*giriš*$^{!}$⸣*-du* = *kur-ṣí-ip-tum* UET 7, 93 r. 4. Cf. Sjöberg 1996, 229.

2. MA/B in PNN:

a) ^{I}*Kur-si-ip-te/tu* MARV 6, 58: 3.

b) ^{mí}*Kur-si-ip-te/tu* ZABR 7, 358 no. 6: 1.

c) ^{mí}*Kur-ṣip-te* Franke/Wilhelm 1985, 22: 1.

3. SB *lú-kar-ra-bi giriš-gin*$_7$ *dím-ma-a saĝ-bi m[u-un-šú]* : *munnaribšu kīma kur-ṣip-ti šumm[utti (bup?)pan]īšu* ⸢*saḫip*⸣ Iraq 57, 210 (Lugale 98) "the one who fled it (i.e., the enemy land), his face is overwhelmed like a swatted *k.*" (transl. after Mayer 2016, 228. Diff. George, ib. 220: "covered his face like a butterfly at rest"). For the swatting of *k.* (Sum. *giriš*) cf. Ninurta's Exploits (l. 98 and 441).

4. NA *giṣṣiṣīka ayyābīka [akī gu]r-ṣip-ti lā alqutu* SAA 9, 3 iii 24 "did I not collect your haters and foes [like] ⸢*k.*⸣?"

5. NA logogr. MUŠEN.TUR in GN: ^{uru}MUŠEN.TUR-[*na-š*]*i* Subartu 14, 10: 9, cf. ⸢^{uru}⸣*kur-<ṣip>-te*⸢^{mušen}⸣*-na-ši* no. 14: 6.

6. Mayer 2003, 378 n. 18 suggests "horsefly" rather than "butterfly" based on lexical and med. texts associating them with oxen and possibly blood-sucking. The plant *k. eqli* can then be understood as "stinging nettle". The interpretation as "butterfly" was based on the entry (KA) GIRIŠ = *sāsu* "moth" in Ḫḫ XIV 296–7 (Landsberger 1934, 134), which is otherwise written UR.ME or ZIZ$_{(4)}$. As the known refs. do not contain any identifying characteristics of butterflies, the mng. of *k.* remains uncertain. For etym. cf. Militarev/Kogan 2005, 164: Jud. *kərāza*, *karzəbā*, *karzubbā*, Hebr. *karsäpät*, all species of locusts; Gez. *k^{w}arāzi* "ant"; Tgr. *karse* (a stinging insect).

kurṣû "fetters"

1. OB lit. [*k*]*ur-ṣe-e-šu-nu* Haul 2009, 330: 7 "their fetters" (context broken).

2. *abbuttašu ugdallab* ^{giš}*ku-ur-ṣú-šu iḫḫeppī maškanšu ippaṭṭarma* ARM 26/1, 282 no. 15 r. 6 "(a slave, …) his slave-hairstyle will be shorn off, his shackles will be broken, his fetter will be loosened", cf. ib. 11, r. 2.

kuršillu s. *kunšillu*

kuršilû s. *kursālu*

+ **kuršittu**? "an insect(?)"; OB

OB *aš-dím* = *kur-*⸢*ši*$^{?}$⸣*-tum* UET 7, 93 r. 5, between *kurṣiptu* (s. above) and *pērurūtu* "mouse".

+ **Kuršu** "a piece of furniture?"; OA

5 *ku-ur-šu ša ašar utupte ibaššīʾū ikkunukkēʾāma libbišīʾū* AKT 3, 77: 28 "let the 5 *k.*that are among the furniture remain (there) under my seals". Possible equivalents are *guršu* "peg" (lex., s. CAD G 141b s.v. *guršu* B) and *kursû*, a household furnishing (OB, s. CAD K 567b s.v.). NJCK

kurû I "short"

1. OA PN *ku-ri-um* AKT 6C, 722: 9 "PN, the short one".

2. Referring to honeybees(?): OB lit. *arkum ē tuṣṣâmma* ⸢*ku*⸣*-ru-ú-um ē tattallak* AML 78: 10 "oh long one, do not go out! Oh short one, do not depart!" S. also *kurrû*. NJCK (1), MPS (2)

+ **kurû II** "hireling"; MB; WSem. lw.

(PNN) *ku-ra-ú dimti bītima ina kaspim* Ekalte 34: 4 "hirelings of the hamlet and house (paid) by means of silver". Cf. Hebr. *kry*, Arab. *krʾ* "to hire out, lease".

kūru I "depression"

SB *minâ ēpuš ku-ú-r*[*u*] AulaOr. (Suppl.) 23, 44: 2 "why have I become depressed(?)".

kurukku "a kind of duck or goose"; + OB

OB *ku-*⸢*ru-kum*⸣^{mušen} Edubba'a 7, 100: 3 (in list of birds after *kurkû* "goose").

kurullu, *kurillu* "grain heap; heaps of corpses"

1. OB *têrētim ana ku-ru-ul-*[*li-im*] *qabārim ušēpiš* (…) *šalamtašu iqbir* ARM 26/1, 564 no. 263: 12 "I had extispicies for the burial of the corpse heap performed. (…) (each) buried their corpse.

2. OB 6 *ku-ru-ul-la-tim ša tarmīktim ša karānim* FM 11, 187: 13 "6 bundles of vine-prunings".

3. CAD *kurullu* C "calamity, catastrophe" (Mari only) is probably not a separate word. Heimpel (2003, 279 n. 312) suggests "some kind of makeshift morgue".

kurummatu "food allocation, ration" s. *kurummu*

+ **kurummu** "food allocation, ration"

ŠUKU *ku-ru-um-ma-am ul īšū* AbB 12, 67: 24 "I do not have any rations". Cf. *ku-ru-um* BWL 72: 31 cit. CAD K 579 s.v. *kurummu* and emended to *ku-ru-um-*<*mat*> in AHw. 513a, sub 1d.

kurun(n)u "a type of beer or wine"

1. OB 20 MA.NA GI.DU$_{10}$.GA *ana* ^{kaš}*ku-ru-nim* ARM 23, 291 no. 364: 2 "20 minas of 'sweet cane' for *k.*".

2. SB *ana nibīt šumiya izakkar kalīšunu* KURUN.NAM // KURUN.[NAM?] Jiménez 2017, 252: 39 "they all name fine beer (*kurunnu*) after my name".

kuruppu "a basket; a reed structure; shop"

1. OB lit. *ku-ru-*⸢*pu-ú-ki*⸣ *mašḫū* AML 27: 7 "your (the fermentation vat's) baskets (with malt) are measured".

2. On mng. "shop" (as a reed structure) in LB s. Baker 2010a; Jursa 2009, 167.

kurussu, + *karis*(*s*)*u* "strap of leather"; + NA

1. Lex. [^{kuš}LÁ.LÁ = *ku-ru-us*]*-su* = *ka-ri-su* Emar 6/4, 584: 3. Pentiuc 2001, 94.

2. 1 ^{kuš}*kur-si-u* SAA 7, 134: 5.

kuruštû "fattener"

1. OB UDU$^{ḫi.a}$ *ku-ru-uš-te-e* FM 1, 25 M.15077: 14 "sheep of the fattener".

2. OB (fat-tailed sheep) *ša ku-ru-uš-te-em* ARM 24, 45: 19.

kusarikku, *kušarikku* "bison"

1. Lex. IDIM = *ku-ša-ri-ku* Emar 6/4, 537: 688 (Sa), Sjöberg 1998, 276.

2. OB lit. *ku-sa-ri-*[*k*]*u-u*[*m*] *iggeltê* AML 124 r. 5 "the bison has been roused".

3. OB lit. *šinā zaqrān nawrān ku-sa-ri-ka-an* CUSAS 18, 2 r. 13 "two tall radiant bison".

4. OB ⸢ALAN *ku-sa-ri-ik-ku* FLP 2312 "bison figurine". Ellis 1989.

kusīpu I, pl. *kusīpātu* "bread (morsel)"; OB "split wood"; + OB, + NB

1. OB 2 *gušūrū rabûtum* 100 ^{giš}*ku-sí-pá-tum ana ṣullul bīt littētim* ARM 23, 446 no. 522: 2 "2 wooden beams and 100 split wooden boards (as rafters) for covering the 'house of stools'".

2. NB *ku-sip-pe-ti nad*[*â*] OIP 114, 109: 20 "bread crumbs are thr[own](?)".

kusīpu II, *kusibānu* "a plant"

Lex. *ṣerri ku-si-ba-ni* Emar 6/4, 551: 5 (Ḫ̮ḫ̮) "snake of the *k.* plant", s. AHw. *k.* 2 and CAD *kassibānû*.

kusītu "an outer garment, a coat"; + MA

1. OA logogr. ^{túg}BAR.DUL$_5$ CTMMA 1, 121 no. 85A: 12 and kt n/k 1697: 63 (s. Çeçen/Erol 2018, 58).

2. MA ^{túg}BAR.DUL$^{(meš)}$ Assur 2/4,)5ff. MAH 16086 A ii 4, 11, 13; B ii 14, 19.

3. LB 20 *ku-sa-a-tum ina šaddānū kinṣāma* dubsar 3, 135: 16 "gather 20 *k.* garments in boxes!"

4. LB (blue-purple wool) *ana adilānu ša* ^{túg}*ku-si-tum šarrat Sipparim* Zawadzki 2013, 624: 5 "for the *a.*-tassel for the robe of the Queen of Sippar".

5. Logogr. BAR.DIB in NA ^{túg}BAR.DIB *ša* DN CTN 6, 56: 7 "coat of DN". Cf. Borger 2010b, 275.

6. Zawadzki 2006, 117–118; On OA s. Michel/Veenhof 2010, 234. On the *eleppu ša k.* ("*k.*-ship") in N/LB s. Kleber 2008, 297–301. NJCK (1), JW (2–6)

****kussalili** s. *kuzallu.*

+ **kussimtu I** "branch"; OB

100 *gušūrī šuruptam qanî* ^{giš}*ku-us-sí-im-tam u sikkātim* ARM 28, 152: 8 "100 logs, firewood, reeds, branches and pegs".

kussimtu II “scale, plate” s. *kursimtu*

kussu, + *kūsu*? “a gold ornament”; + NB?

Uncert.: NB *ku-ú-su* BM 84129: 8 (cit. Roth 1989–1990, 25). S. also *k*/*qūšu* and *kuštu*.

kussû, + *kissû* (MB Emar) “chair, throne”

1. OA (when our brothers arrived) *lū ana bikītišunu lū a-ku-sí-im ša ummišunu ṭabbu'im* AKT 8, 184: 10 “for bewailing them and for removing our mother’s chair”; also ib. 15 and 185: 14.

2. OB lit. *qūlam attadī elī ku-sí-a-tim* AML 29: 14 “I have cast silence on the chairs”.

3. OB *nāš* GU.ZA UET 7, 73 i 29 (Westenholz 1997, 148ff.) “chair-bearer”.

4. Fem. pl.: **a)** OB lit. *ku-us*$_4$*-si*$_{20}$*-a-at g*[*i*]*zîm* OECT 11, 1: 9 “thrones of *gizi* cane”.

b) ^{giš}GU.ZA-*a-at ḫurāṣi* YOS 11, 23: 18 “thrones of gold”.

c) *wašbūt ku-sà-at uqnîm ellim* RA 38, 87 r. 5 “seated on thrones of pure lapis lazuli”.

d) NA *ku-si-a-te* ZA 74, 78: 21.

5. Masc. sg.: OB ^{giš}GU.ZA-*um še-bi-ru-um* BagM 2, 58 iii 11 “a broken chair” (Mayer 2016, 228).

6. NA *ku-si-iu-u* StAT 2, 233 r. 5.

7. LB ⸢4 ^{giš}GU.ZA⸣^{meš} *ša ḫilēpu* AOAT 414/1, 183: 4 “4 chairs of willow wood”.

8. MB Emar var. *kissû* (Pentiuc 2001, 102–3):

a) ^{giš}NÁ *ki-is-sà-a* Emar 6/3, 370: 79 “one bed, one chair”.

b) *enūma mārū* GN ^{ezen}*ki-is-sà ana* DN *ippašū* Emar 6/3, 385: 2 “when the people of GN perform the throne-festival for DN”; cf. ib.: 1, 27; 370: 113.

NJCK (1), MPS (2–4, 7), JK (6), JW (5, 8)

kusullu s. *k*/*guzullu*

kuṣṣu, *kūṣu* “cold, winter”

1. Lex. *se-*⸢*e*⸣ = LUL = *ku-uṣ-ṣú-um* CUSAS 12 p. 13: 248 (Ea).

2. OA *ku-ṣú-um* AKT 8, 253: 19 “it is winter!”

3. OA *ana ku-ṣí-im nimū'at* AKT 8, 262: 20 “we will be dead by winter!”; sim. kt n/k 715: 22 (Günbattı 2016, 278).

4. OA unusual spelling: *ana ku-ú-ṣí-im* KTS 2, 40: 26.

5. OA pl.: **a)** *annākam kīma ku-ṣú dannūnīma* AKT 8, 189: 36 “since the cold is severe here”.

b) *ku-ṣú sanqū* AKT 11A, 18: 16 “winter has arrived”.

6. OA a disease: (winter has arrived) *assurre emārum ištēn u šinā ku-ṣa-am ē iršī'ū*(*ma*) AKT 11A, 18: 18 “under no circumstances shall one or two donkeys catch cold” (cf. CAD K 596a s.v. *kuṣṣu* 3 “chill, ague” said of humans).

7. OB ⸢*ku*⸣*-uṣ-ṣa-am-ma* [*b*]*ēlī ammīnim lā iqbêm* FM 3, 263 no. 129: 13 “why did my lord not tell me in winter?”

8. OB *ku-úṣ-ṣum u* ⸢*uklum*⸣ *ikallanni* AbB 8, 100: 9 “cold and darkness are detaining me”.

NJCK (2–6), MPS (1, 7), JW (8)

kuṣṣudu “to delay”; OA

1. *nāruqqaka* […] x *tu-uk-ta-ṣí-id*! Prag 762: 10 “you held back […] your capital” (Matouš 1974, 170).

2. AHw. s.v. *kaṣādu* (G not attested)

kuṣṣuru “well tied”; + OB

OB lit. *ipṭur maksîšu ku-uṣ-ṣú-ru-ú-tim* AML 14: 13 “he loosened its well tied shackles”.

kušarikku s. *kusarikku*

kušartu “repair, patch”

MB (*alluḫaru*) *ana ku-šar-ti* (for a wagon) BagF 21, 385: 3. S. Sassmannshausen 2001, 60.

****kušāteanu** s. *kušātu*

****kušātu** (CAD K 598)

In HSS 13, 323 read *ana* ZÍD.DA! *ṭe*$_4$-*a-ni* (Deller in id./Mayer/Oelsner 1989, 266).

kušīru “success”

1. OB lit. [*išk*]*unki* DN *ana ku-*⸢*ši*⸣-*ri* AML 27: 5 “DN [ma]de you successful”.

2. OB (when outlaws are among us) *mīnum ku-ši-ir-ni* RATL 175: 5 “how shall we succeed?”; *mimma ku-ši-ir-šu-nu* [*lā ib*]*aššī* ib. 7 “let there be no chance of their success!”.

3. OB *kīma* 20 *līmi ṣābim an*[*a*] *ayyâšim gu-ši-ru* Shemshara 1, 68: 18 “(the tin will give) me success like 20,000 soldiers”.

kušru III “damage to be repaired”; OB

rukūbu ... *ku-uš-ra-am īšū ku-šu-ur-ša linakkirma eleppum lā imât* AbB 3, 35: 24f. “the barge has some damage – the damage shall be removed so the boat won’t ‘die’” (cit. CAD s.v. *kušru* C without transl.). S. Frankena 1978, 120–122 (< *kešēru*).

kuššatu “a garment”; OA; + OB

1. OB 1 ^{túg}*ku-úš-ša-tum* ARM 23, 297 no. 375: 11 and pass.

2. OB 6 ^{túg}*ku-ša-at gi-zu* … *ana lubbuš* ^{lú}GAL.KU$_5$ ARM 22, 164 = FM 2, 197: 1 “6 shorn *k*.-garment for dressing the section chief”.

3. Durand 2009, 54f. with add. refs. and disc.

kuštu, + *kussu*? “a rush”; + NA?

(an estate adjoining) *ku-su*! SAA 6, 275 r. 9. *kuštu* < *kultu* > *kussu*?

kušû “an aquatic animal”

1. Lex. *ku-šú*! = KÚŠU = *ku-šu-ú* CUSAS 12 p. 21: 29 (Syllabary A).

2. Disc. Loktionov 2014 (“crocodile”?).

MPS (1), FJMS (2)

+ **k/qūšu** “a precious stone”

1. OB 12 *Ku-šu* ARM 7, 247 r. 4 (coll. MARI 2, 95), among other precious stones (von Soden 1985, 278). Sim. ARM 21, 247: 31; ARM 25, 635 (= ARM 32, 475 M.12299): 6.

2. Arkhipov 2012, 49: Perhaps to be connected with the ornament *kussu*.

kušurrāʾu “compensation, indemnity”

OAkk only in the phrase *šībūt kušurrāʾim*, s. Gelb 1984, 264 for add. refs. and 274–276 for disc.

kutallu “back of the head, rear part”

1. OB *bēlī* DN *ku-ta-al-la-ka likīl* CUSAS 36, 221: 17 “may my lord DN stand guard behind you!” Cf. CAD K 516 s.v. *kullu* 5 a; also AbB 10, 203: 7.

2. NB *alpu attuʾa ku-tal nīrišu u alap ritta ittašizzū* OIP 114, 91: 8 “my ox, the (one at the) rear part of his yoke, and the plough ox have been standing”.

kutallūtu "reserve-duty"; + NB

kī ku-tal-lu!*-ta šu-ú tukāl* OIP 114, 2: 35 "if you keep him(!) for reserve-duty".

kutānu, *qutānu* "a woollen textile"; + OAkk

1. OAkk ^{túg}*ku*$_8$*-tá-nu* CUSAS 13, 146: 3.

2. On OA s. Michel/Veenhof 2010, 212, 234.

3. Rare in OB Mari: 1 *ku-ta-na-am* A.2881 (Fs. Dercksen, 122: 13); ARM 13, 101: 29 (s. Durand 2009, 55).

+ **Kutaru (?)** "mng. unkn"; OB

(4 men loaded barley on donkeys and went away.) *ina ku-ta-ri-im ībirū gerram īzibūma arrī iḫmirūma* ARM 33, 210: 9 "they crossed in *k*. They left the road and hurried through water ditches". S. the comm ib. p. 443.

kutinnu "a textile"; OA

Not a variant of *kutānu*: 1 ^{túg}*kutānum ša* PN 1 *ku-tí-num ša* PN$_2$ PIHANS 96, 3: 9. S. Michel/Veenhof 2010, 235.

kutlānu "the one of the embankment (bird name)"

OB *ku-ut-la-nu-um*^{mušen} Edubba'a 7, 100: 38 (in list of birds).

kutlu, pl. *kutlātu* "rampart, embankment"

1. OB 2 *nēšū ina ku-ut-li-im ša abullim ... irbiṣūma* ARM 26/1, 273 no. 106: 9 "2 lions crouched at the rampart of the city gate".

2. OB 90 A.ŠÀ [A.GÀ]R *ku-ut-la-tim*^{ki} ARM 27, 33: 6 "90 (dikes of) field-area, [territor]y of the embankments".

3. OB *ana ku-ut-la-tim*^{ki} *ikšudūnim ana* GN *re-bi-tim ul īrubūnim* ARM 27, 116: 4 "they arrived at the ramparts but did not enter central GN".

4. ⸢A.⸣GÀR ŠE *ina ku-ut-*⸢*la-tim*^{ki}⸣ ARM 27, 109 r. 1 "(n) territory of grain at the embankments".

5. J.-M. Durand, ARM 26/1, 273 n. a ad no. 106: "haie". J.-M. Birot, ARM 27 p. 91 n. a ad no. 33: "barrière, clôture, barrage en roseau". Heimpel 2003, 217 n. 132: "a feature of the outside of the wall close to the city gate". The refs. rather favor a rampart or embankment than a (reed-)fence.

kūtu, *kuttu* "a container"; + OAkk

1. OAkk ^{kuš}*ku*$_8$*-tum* SCTRAH 31: 4, 249: 2. (Such-Gutiérrez 2018, 146: "Deckenleder").

2. OB (68 jars of wine) [*š*]*a* 6 ^{dug}*ku-ut-ta-*[*tim*] ... (58 jars of old wine) [*š*]*a* ⸢6⸣ ^{dug}*ku-ut-ta-tim* FM 11, 71: 2–5 "for 6 *k*. containers".

3. OB 1 ⸢^{dug}⸣*ku-ut-tim* (in broken context) ib. 40: 12.

4. Cf. G. Chambon ib. p. 24; Guichard 2005, 219 with add. refs.

kutuktu s. *kuduktu*

kutultu "rampart, embankment"; + OB

Lex. *si-il da-ĝu*$_{10}$ = *ku-tu-ul-ti qinnatiya* CUSAS 12 p. 157 x 9 (Ugumu) "bottom crack". M. Civil ib. with commentary p. 158 suggests "stopping of my anus".

kutummu "covering, veil"

1. OB ⸢n⸣ [^{tú}]^{g}*ku-tu-mu* ARM 24, 210 iii 27 (coll. ARM 30, 497).

2. OB ^{túg}*ku-tu-um-mi elī mārtim niddī* ARM 26/1, 106 no. 10: 15 "we placed the veil over the girl".

3. Durand 2009, 55f.

kutūtu "security"; OA

1. *bēt ubrišu ṣabtāma ku-tù-a-sú ša* 1 1/2 MA.NA KÙ.BABBAR *ana maḫri-kunu lublūnim*(*ma*) AKT 5, 74*B: 23 "seize his quarters so that they can bring here distrained property of his to a value of 1 1/2 minas of silver".

2. *ku-tù-a-té-a uššeram* kt 92/k 543: 60 (s. Bayram 2001, 4) "release my distrained property to me"; s. also AKT 6A, 86: 13 (s *katû* D, above); CCT 3, 11: 12. NJCK

ku'u s. *qû* II

kuyātu s. *Ku'ītu.*

kuzallu, + *kuzzallu* "shepherd"

Nuzi ⸢PN LÚ⸣ *ku-u*[*z-z*]*a-al-li* AdŠ 3, 110: 10 (misread in CAD K 587b and AHw. 515a s.v. *kussalili*).

kuzbu s. *kazbu*

+ **kūzu** "pitcher"; LB; Aram. lw.

ku-ú-zu BM 84129: 8. Cf. Aram. *kwz*, Mand. *kwz'* (Zadok 2020a with coll.).

kuzu'ātu s. *kasû* I

k/guzullu, *kutullu*, + *kusullu* "bundle of reeds or wood"; + OB

1. OB of wood: 1 ^giš^*ku-su-lu-um* JCS 26, 136 (IM 52599): 2, 8, among wooden items.

2. LB 4 *ṣābu ūmu* 4 *me* 20 KI.MIN (= *gu-zu-ul-lu*) *ana muḫḫi atūnu ultu muḫḫi* (...) *adi atūnu ša* 1-*en amēlu* 15 *gu-zu-ul-lu inašši* CT 55, 426: 14 "4 men will carry 420 bundles of reed to the oven, from the (…) to the oven every man will carry 15 bundles (each time)"; *gu-zu-ul-lu* ib. 7, 15, s. van Driel 1992, 175.

Q

\+ **qa'ālu** "to gather"; OB, SB

G OB *qāt nišīkunu ṣabt[ānim] qí-i'-la-nim-ma ana libbi māti[m] atlakānim* MARI 5, 179: 16 "take your people by the hand, gather together and depart towards the inner country", s. Durand ib. 180. Cf. hebr. *qhl* (Charpin 1989–90, 94).

D SB Perhaps in *tillātīšu ú-qa-i-la ana* GN *ušēribu* King Chron. 2 37 r. 9 (= AOAT 326 no. 24) "he gathered his auxiliary troops and led them to GN" (cit. CAD Q, 75 s.v. *qâlu* B). Mayer in Deller/Mayer/Oelsner 1989, 267.

qabaltī'u, *qabassī'u* "middle"

NA [n] KÙŠ *rūṭu ša ṣalam qa-ba-si-e* CTN 3, 95 B 24 "[n] + 1/2 cubits is the central statue", cf. *annî ša* É [NU?] ⸢*qa*⸣-*ba-si-e* ib. B 20 with comm. p. 162 (Deller in id./Mayer/Oelsner 1989, 255).

qabaltu, *qabassu* "middle"

1. OA lit. *qá-ba-al-tí qaqqadātīšunu* OA Sarg. 61 "the middle of their heads", cf. *galābu.*

2. NA *issu libbi siparrē ipta[ṭar(šu)] [is]su qab-si ēkallim ussēṣ[ī]* CTN 3, 8: 5 "(his pledge) has freed (him) from fetters (and) he has brought him out from the center of the palace" (Deller/Mayer/Oelsner 1989, 256).

qabālu s. *qubbulu*

qabāru s. *qebēru*

qabassī'u s. *qabaltī'u*

\+ **qabbāru** "undertaker, a person associated with funerary rites"; MB Emar

1. PN [lú]*qa-ba-ru* Emar 6/3, 124: 25.

2. *ana dārīti šangûma u rabi ša* DN *u ana* [lú]*qáb-ba-ri šūtma* Sigrist 1993, 6: 27 "he is the *šangû*-priest and superintendent of (the temple of) DN and the undertaker forever".

3. *mamman šanûma ištū bīt* DN *u ištū* [lú]*qáb-ba-rù-<ti> lā unakkaršu* ib. 30 "nobody else shall remove him from the temple of DN or from the office of undertaker".

4. Pentiuc 2001, 143. Cf. *qēbiru.*

****qabbātu** (CAD Q, 2; AHw. 886b)

For ARM 10, 80 (= ARM 26/1, 424 no. 197) s. *qammatu.*

\+ **qābilu** "receptacle"; MB Emar

1. 1 *qà-bi-l[u]* ZABAR CunMon. 13, 14: 5 "1 bronze *q*.".

2. among other bronze objects:
a) 2 *ruqqu* ZABAR 4 *qà-bi-lu* ZABAR Emar 6/3, 33: 7, cf. 297: 4 "2 *ruqqu*-vessels of bronze, 4 *q*. of bronze"; s. also CunMon. 13, 21: 6.
b) *qà-bi-lum* AulaOr. (Suppl.) 1, 22: 8. (weighing 60 sekel).
c) *qà-be-lu* RE 8: 9 (weighing 70 sekel).

3. Pentiuc 2001, 146f.: NWSem. *qbl* "to receive", "receptacle". J. G. Westenholz 2000, 40: connection to *kablu* "stand". Richter in id./Lange 2012: possible connection to *kubbillu*, a container for coal or embers. Cf. *qablītu.*

qabbiru s. also *qabbāru* and *qēbiru*

qabla “in the middle”

OB *i*!-*na*! *qa*!-*ab-la* ARM 8, 43: 8 (coll. MARI 1, 110). Cf. *qablē*.

****qablānu** (CAD Q 3) s. *qablē* 1.

qablay s. *qablē*

qablē, *qablay* “in the midst”; OAkk, OA

1. OAkk **a)** *in qàb-lá-ì ti-ba-a*[*r*] *šadū’im* RIME 2, 127: 10 “in the midst of mount Tibar” (coll. Sommerfeld 2013, 250). Note that the spelling with *ì* points to a form *qabla’i* rather than *qablay*(*i*), as *i* is used for /*yi*/ in OAkk. **b)** *qáb-li* GN *bīssu ibnī’ū* RIME 2, 114: 51–53 (after photo) “(in) the middle of GN they built his temple”. The spelling with *li* represents *qable*/*ē*. Cf. the spelling *in qàb-lí* GN for *in qabli* (RIME 2, 52: 13 and pass.). Hasselbach 2005, 169; Kogan 2011, 41. Sommerfeld 2021, 587 n. 218 interprets *qable* as constr. state with epenthetic vowel.

2. OA (GOA p. 454):
a) *i-qá-áb-le ḫarrānim* CCT 1, 10a: 5 “in the middle of a journey”.
b) *ištū qá-áb-le*! *šadu’im* CCT 6, 40b: 1–2 “from the middle of the mountain”.

qablītu “middle; container; scales”

1. OB lit. *ina* ⸢*qá-ab-li*⸣*-tu šamā’ī* [...] *lizzīzma* AnSt. 33, 148: 37 “let her stand in the midst of the heavens” (Mayer in Deller/Mayer/Oelsner 1989, 267).

2. OB *ištū* GN *mūšam qa-ab-li-tam ittābitūnim* ARM 26/2, 500 no. 524: 6 “they escaped from GN in the middle of the night”; cf. ib. 10 (Charpin 1989–90, 92).

3. OB *nīq barārtim* ⸢*ina qa*⸣*-ab-li-tim* KTT 345: 5, “sacrifice of the evening watch, at midnight” s. SAD 1, 12 *barārītu* 1.

4. Container:
a) OA *qá-áb-li-tám ša taskarinnim* AKT 4, 35b: 25 “a boxwoood container”; 2 *qá-áb-li-a-tum* … *aḫḫuzātum* kt m/k 69B: 24 “two containers with inlays”, s. Hecker 2004b, 286; sim. AKT 8, 186: 4.
b) In the expression *qablītam erru’um* “to empty, to clear out the container”, an act accompanying the sale of a house or a slave, probably referring to the transfer of records of ownership and attendant obligations (Postgate 2003, 131). New refs.: *murrī qá-áb-li-tim* Prag 502: 24 “the one who empties the *q*.”; kt 88/k 310: 15, s. Bayram 2016, 19.
c) OB ^{giš}*q*[*a-a*]*b-li-tum* UD.KA.BAR GAR.RA T. 344: 30 “*q*. plated in bronze”; ^{giš}*qa-ab-li-tum* ARM 24, 212: 6; 213: 6 (both cit. Charpin 1989–90, 92).

5. Scales: OB lit. *dám-gar-ra lú e-ri-na-ĝu*$_{10}$ *a-na ma-dù-an-na* // *tamkāram nāšī qa-ab-li-ti-ia mīnam ēpuš* A. 2789: 4 (Guichard 2015, 357f., 367f.) “what did I do to the merchant who holds my scales?” (Charpin 1989–90, 93).

6. LB refs. for ^{túg}MURUB$_4$-*tum* are likely defective spellings of ^{túg}MURUB$_4$ ÍB.LÁ (Oelsner in Deller/Mayer/Oelsner 1989, 276).

JW (4c, 1–2, 5–6), MPS (3), NJCK (4a–b)

qablu I “middle, center”

1. Lex. *i* = *íb* = *qa-ab-lum* Emar 6/4, 537: 432 (Sa), Sjöberg 1998, 265.

2. NB TÚG *ša* MURUB$_4$ CT 56, 382: 8 (Oelsner in Deller/Mayer/Oelsner 1989, 277).

3. S. also *qabla*, *qablē*, *qablû*.

qablu II “battle”; + OA

OA only in the DN *Bēl qablim* “Lord of battle”: *Bēl qá-áb-li-im* kt n/k 32: 10, s.

Günbattı 2014, 129; kt 92/k 1048: 6, s. Çayır 2006, 7; sim. ib. 1045: 18f. with <*ša*>, s. Çayır 2006, 12. NJCK

qablu III "grove, forest"

1. NA (trees) *ina* ^{giš}MURUB$_4$-*šú*-⸢*nu*⸣-*ma* SAA 5, 34 r. 32 "are in their groves".

2. NA ^{giš}*qab-lu* SAA 13, 144: 9.

3. Deller in id./Mayer/Oelsner 1989, 256: Probably the NA word for "forest", perhaps to be connected to *ḫablu*. – CAD Q 16 *qablu* C. AHw. 1555 *gablu* "Hügel".

qablû "mid, middle, median"

1. OB *dūram qa-ab-le-e* FM 2, 12 no. 1: 14 "the middle wall".

2. Del. ref. AOB I 98: 7, read *qa-ab-*⸢*li ú-te*⸣*-ṣi* (now RIMA 1, 154 no. 18: 7). – S. also *qabla*, *qablē*, *qablu* I.

qabru, + *qubru*? "grave"

1. OAkk uncert.: ^{túg}BAR.DUL$_5$ 10-*tim ana qú-ub-ri* Banca d'Italia 2, I-61: 3 = CUSAS 27, 236: 4 "10 garments for burial", cf. ib. r. 4.

2. SB *mūtu* ... *našûšu ana qab-rim* Jiménez 2017, 252: 44 "death … has borne him towards the grave".

3. SB *innannū qab-ri pāliḫš*[*a tu*]*rru* Fs Kraus, 196 iii 28 "to bring back her worshipper from the grave" (Mayer in Deller/Mayer/Oelsner 1989, 268; Mayer 2017, 28).

4. *mītu ša ina qab-ri nī*[*l*]*u* LKA 83: 2 "the dead one who lies in the grave" (Mayer 2017, 28).

****qabsu** (*AHw*. 886), the refs. belong to *qabaltu* (CAD Q and von Soden 1985, 275).

qabû I "speech, statement"

1. OB *qá-ba-ka* PN *imaḫḫar* AbB 10, 207: 10 "(if you are truly my brother) PN will accept your statement"; *qá-ba-ni ul ilqē* AbB 10, 171: 45 "he did not receive our words" (Charpin 1989–90, 93).

2. OB *pīqat mimma bēlī qa-ba-šu ana* DN *iddin* ARM 26/1, 223 no. 84: 14 "did my lord perhaps somehow give his word to DN?" (Charpin 1989–90, 93).

qabû II "to speak"

G 1. OB *mīnam lu-uq-bi* ARM 4, 34: 15 "what (more) shall I say?" (Charpin 1989–90, 93).

2. NA *i-qab-bu-u-ni* SAA 6, 101: 18 (whoever comes forward and institutes a lawsuit or litigation against PN or his sons) "saying:", cf. SAA 6, 106: 3; 102 r. 3, all from the archive of Aplaya (Deller in id./Mayer/Oelsner 1989, 256 on CAD Q, 33 mng. 3 a 2').

3. NA [*ina*] *muḫḫi ša qa-ba-šú-nu-u-ni* SAA 1, 260: 15 "concerning what they are told (they refuse to listen)" (Deller in id./Mayer/Oelsner 1989, 256 on CAD Q, 37 mng. 4e).

qabuttu "(animal) stall"; + MA

MA (barley) [*ina*] ⸢*bīt*⸣ *karme* [*ša*?] *qa-bu-te tabik* BATSH 9, 84: 11 "is heaped up in the storage of the stable". JK/JW

qabūtu "a container, a flask or pitcher"

1. NA 1 ^{dug}*qa-but* CTN 6, 55: 1 (alongside meat, probably as an offering).

2. NA 386 *kuzippē ša* GN *ina qa-bu-te* 50 (…) ⸢SUM⸣ *ina qa*-ZAG *lā karrū* StAT 3, 1: 36f. "(in total) 386 garments from GN (are) in the *q*.-container: 50 (garments) have been handed out and are not placed in the *q*.-container". Considering the large number of garments, *q.* may be containers for tokens rather than the commodities themselves, as proposed in AHw. 890 and Deller in id./ Mayer/Oelsner 1989, 256. The latter suggests applying this interpretation to several NA passages cited in CAD Q s. v. *qabuttu* "corral, fold". Radner *apud* StAT 3 p. 37 proposes to read *ina qabûte* "as ordered".

3. For the mng. "flask, pitcher" s. Leichty 2000.

+ **qabûtu** "word"; OB

qà-bu-sú ša PN [*ē*]*teppeš* FM 2, 266 no. 128: 28 "I used to do what PN said".

qadādu "to bow down"

G 1. OB [*ana awāt*] *bēliya iq-du-du* ARM 26/2, 205 no. 386 r. 3 "they bowed down [at the command?] of my lord" (Charpin 1989–90, 93 with add. refs.).
2. SB *kišāssu iq-ta-da-du* SpTU 2, 2: 72 "he bent his neck".

Gtn SB *kīma urbatu nīltu ki-šad-su iq-ta-da-du* // *ki-šè ḫé-en-gá-gá* SpTU II 2: 72 "like trailing rush they repeatedly bent his neck" (von Soden 1985, 276).

D OB lit. PA.SAG.LAGAB-*e* [*g*]*ú ba-gúr* // *nissatum u*[*q-da*]*-di-da-a*[*n-ni*] Charpin 1992, A.1258+ r. 4 (= LAPO 16 no. 22) "despair made me hang my head".

qadāšu "to be(come) pure"

D 1. OA *ammala dīn kārim panîm urram* PN *ú-qá-du-šu-ma allītiš itam-mā*(*ma*) Prag 681: 26 "in accordance with the earlier verdict of the *kārum* they will 'purify' PN tomorrow and he will swear the day after tomorrow".
2. OA (on the day that PN left) *gāmer awātim nu-qá-di-ìš* Prag 711: 5 "we have 'purified' the arbitrators of the case".
3. SB *kī ša* DN *īpušu ú-*⸢*qad*⸣*-diš ṭiṭṭa akriṣ* K.2387+ r. 3 // K.5022+ r. 9 "like DN did, I purified, I pinched off clay" (Mayer in Deller/Mayer/Oelsner 1989, 268).
4. "to treat as sacred" (Pentiuc 2001, 142f.; Mayer 2017, 28):
a) MB Emar *ina ūmi qa-ad-du-ši ša kissi ša* DN Emar 6/3, 385: 28 "on the sanctification day of the throne festival of DN".
b) MB Emar *ilānī* GN *gabba ištu akali šikari ú-qa-da-šu* Emar 6/3, 369: 6 "they sanctify all gods of GN with bread and beer". S. Fleming 1992, 158–162 with add. Emar refs.
c) SB *eṭ*[*emmī*] *kimt*[*iš*]*u salāti*[*šu*] *tu-qad-dáš* LKA 84: 3 "you sanctify the ghosts of his family, his clan".
5. In BAM 234: 23 (cit. CAD Q 46b) read *ú-qa-diš*.

Dt SB *ina ūmi mitgurti liq-te-diš* SpTU 3, 80 i 40 "on an auspicious day he shall purify himself" (Streck 2003a, 113).

JW/NJCK (D), MPS (Dt)

qadilû, *kadilû*, + *qudullû* "a cloak"

Lex. [^{túg}*gada*] ⸢*an-ta dul*⸣ // *taktīmu* // ⸢*qa-dul*⸣*-lu-u* KAL 8, 110 r. vi 25 (murgud) "linen cloak = *taktīmu*-cloak = *q.*-cloak".

qadištu, *qašdatu*, *qaššatu* "a type of priestess"

1. OA (PN has married PNf, sister of PN$_2$) *qaqqassa pati šawītam ina šaḫāti-ša ulā ušeššab qá-di-iš-tám ina* GN *u* GN$_2$ *ula eḫḫaz* AKT 1, 77 tablet 7 "he has uncovered her head, he shall not let a *šawītu* sit next to her (and) he shall not marry a *qadištum* in GN or GN$_2$" (// envelope 9).

2. OB lit. *šumma qá-aš-da-*⌜*at*⌝ CUSAS 10, 11: 12 "if she is a *qadištu*-priestess" (parallel to *nadītu* and *kezretu*).

3. *qa-aš-ša-tum* ARM 23, 211 no 236: 21 *pass*.

4. Charpin 1989–90, 99b: The interpretation of *qaššatu* as a Mari-var. suggested in CAD Q 147 is supported by the co-occurrence of *qaššatu* and the cstr./abs. state *qa-aš-da-at*. For the metathesis *š*/*d* cf. *ḫuddušu* < *ḫašādu* (ARM 23 p. 298). NJCK (1), MPS (2), JW (3, 4)

qadū "together with; because, since"

1. Early OB *aššumi wardim šu'āti qá-dum maškiya allakakkum* AS 22, 12: 38 "on account of this slave I come to you with my skin".

2. OB [*q*]*a-du*! *murṣiya etbīma* FM 1, 95: 14 "I rose in spite of being sick (lit. 'together with my sickness')".

3. OB with suff.: *qá-du-uš-šu* AbB 12, 9 r. 5. The refs. for suffixed forms in VS 2, 74: 16 and Idrimi 76 are to be deleted (s. Mayer 2017, 29).

4. OB "because, since" (Charpin 1989–90, 94):
a) *qa-du-ú kaspam ana ēkallim lā išqulu* A.2535: 4' "because he has not paid the silver to the palace".
b) *qa-du mamman lā īpulušunūti* A.1017: 65 "since nobody replied to them".
c) *qa-du-ma anāku ana šitappurim a-ta-aš-šu-*<*šu*> ARM 28, 152 no. 105: 15 "because I was in distress about sending (letters) repeatedly".
d) FM 7, 6 no. 1: 14, s. *karāru*.

5. Edzard 1978. S. also *adī*.

qadû I "owl"

1. SB *iṣṣūru qa-du-ú ša ištass*[*û*] *ina šitassîšu minâ ilqē* Westenholz 1997, 46: 53 "the bird, owl, which kept crying, for all its crying, what did it achieve?"

2. SB *kīma qa-di-i ina ḫarbī nadûti lirbiṣ* Sumer 38, 124 iv 18 (= AOAT 51, MNA 4) "like an owl he shall lurk in the barren wasteland" (Mayer in Deller/Mayer/Oelsner 1989, 268).

qadû II "to hoot"

OB *kīma qadî*[*m*] *mūšam u urriš* [*q*]*a-du-um-ma a-qa-ad-du* M.9050 (cit. ARM 26/1, 201 n. 9) "like an owl, I will really hoot day and night" (Charpin 1989–90, 94). Other known instances show *i*-vocalisation.

qadû III "a type of bread"; MB

1. MB Emar: n ^{ninda}*qa-d*[*u*] Emar 6/3, 442: 4; 1 ^{ninda}*qa-du-ú* Emar 6/3, 460: 18.

2. CAD *qadû* B. Cf. *qadūtu*.

qadullû s. *qadilû*

+ **qadūmu** "an adze"; OB

1. *pāš qa-du-mi* ARM 25, 589: 4, r. 1 "adze of *q*.(-type)" s. MARI 3, 279 (Mayer in Deller/Mayer/Oelsner 1989, 268).

2. ^{giš}*qa-du-mu* M.12179 iii 5 (of *musukkannu* wood, cit. Arkhipov 2012, 142).

qadūtu, *qaduttu* "mud, sediment; dregs; a type of bread for offerings"

1. SB *qa-du-ut-tum ul āmur qa-du-ut*[*-tum* …] VS 24, 107: 5 "I did not see the mud [I did not …] the mud" (Mayer 2017, 29).

2. A type of bread:
a) MA [n ^{ninda}*q*]*a-du-a-tu* (of 1 liter each) KAL 9, 64: 4.
b) NA ^{ninda}*qa-du-*⌜*tú*⌝ SAA 7, 205: 2; RA 69, 183: 11, 38 (Deller in id./Mayer/Oelsner 1989, 257).

3. In Gilg. MB Ur 16 read *qa-*⌜*qa*⌝*-ru*? instead of *qa-*⌜*du*⌝*-t*[*um*] (AHw. 892 *qadūtu* 7; CAD Q 53 *q.* 2), s. George 2003, 302. – Llop 2011, 257f.

qaḫālu s. *qa'ālu*

qajātu s. *qayyātu*

qakkabu s. *kakkabu*

qalālu I "to be(come) small, weak"

G 1. OB 2000 *ṣābum qa-al* ARM 6, 7: 12 "2000 troops are too few" (Mayer 2017, 29).
2. OB PN ... *iq-li-il* FM 9, 123 no. 22 r. 9 "PN has become discredited".
3. SB *qātāšu u šēpāšu i-qal-li-lu* SpTU II, 34: 4 "his hands and feet will weaken" (Mayer in Deller/Mayer/Oelsner 1989, 268).
4. SB *lemnum u ayyābum birkāšu i-qal-li-la* BagM 2, 59 iv 31 "the knees of the evil and the enemy will become light" (i.e. their movements will become swift; s. Mayer 2017, 29).

D OB *šattam berkīya qú-li-il* IPLA 38: 15 "lighten my knees this year!". Also in OA, s. *birku*.
****Nt** (AHw.) s. Streck 2003a, 130.

qalālu II (AHw. 893) s. *naqallulu*

qalāpu "to peel, strip off"

OB (loan of silver) *ana gišimmarī qá-la-pí-im* VS 29, 48: 5 "for stripping off palm (fronds)" (Stol 2004a, 124).

qâliš "silently"; + OB

OB lit. *urrī qá-li-iš ul attillam* Iraq 81, 243: 14 "(throughout) the days, I cannot rest in silence".

qalītu "parched grain"

NA ^{še}*qa-la-te* CTN 3, 3: 9 (Deller in id./Mayer/Oelsner 1989, 257).

qālītu "pan for roasting grain; female roaster"

NA 1 *qa-li-te* URUDU Iraq 31, 152: 6 "1 roasting pan of copper".

qallalu "tiny"

For the spelling QÀL-*su*/*si* cf. the PNN ^{I}QÀL-*lu-su* ADD Appendix no. 1 xii 2, ^{I}QÀL-*lu-si* StAT 1, 4: 2, read *Qallussu*/*i* "tiny one" (Deller in id./Mayer/Oelsner 1989, 257).

+ **qallatu II** "roasted"

Lex. *sa* = *qàl*/[*q*]*a-al-la-tu* VAT 9719 iv 24 // AfO 16, Tf. XI 48 (Izi, cit. CAD Q 61 s.v. *qallatu* B "mng. unkn." and AHw. 894 s.v. *qallu*(*m*) I, 1b). Sumerian *sa* means "to roast". FJMS

****qallatu B** (CAD Q 61) s. *qalû* I

qallu, NB pl. *qallalūtu* "small, light; slave"

1. OB DUMU^{meš} *lāsimī qa-a*[*l-l*]*u-tim* ARM 26/2, 183 no. 373: 19 "members of the light couriers" (Charpin 1989–90, 94).

2. MB *azamrâti qal-la-tim* VS 24, 122: 6 "light lances" (Mayer in Deller/Mayer/Oelsner 1989, 269).

3. MB *qīpi qál-le-e lâti u alpīšu* RA 66, 169: 71 "overseer of the slaves and his cattle" (reading with Sassmannshausen 2001, 121 n. 2090).

4. NB *qal*!*-la šū miqti ina muḫḫišu* OIP 114, 12: 16 "that slave is affected by the *miqtu*-disease".

5. NB pl. *qallalūtu*(?), s. Cole 1996, 162 ad. l. 29: ^{lú}*qal-la-lu-*(*ú-*)*tu*/*ti* OIP 114,

74: 29; 79: 4, 18; 82: 7; 83: 26. Perhaps Akkadographic spelling [lú]*QAL-LA-lu-(ú-)tu/ti*.

qallupu "peeled"; NA

lurintu qa-lu-up-tú StPohl SM 10/2, T 35: 19 "peeled pomegranate" (von Soden 1985, 277).

qalpu "stripped, peeled"

1. In MB refs. to clothing read *qá-tan-tum* instead of *qá-líp-tum*, based on the spelling SIG-*tum* in OIC 22, 140 no. 17: 3' (Sommerfeld 1990, 30f.).

2. NA 1 [túg]GÚ.LÁ *qa-lip-tú* StAT 1, 39: 8. S. also Sommerfeld in Deller/Mayer/Sommerfeld 1987, 213.

qalqālu?, *qalqallu*? "a type of flour; a beer-bread product"; + NA

1. MB 1/2 SÌLA BÁPPIR … *ša* 3 *qal-qal-lum* BagF 21, 256: 2 "1/2 *qû* of beer-bread for 3 *q*."; sim. 257: 1; 258: 3. S. Sassmannshausen 2001, 347.

2. NA *adī simdi* ZÍD.KA.GAL.GAL SAA 12, 69: 12, 21; 70 r. 13 "(flour provisions) together with *simdu*-flour and *q*.

3. NA NINDA.ZÍD.GAL.GAL.LA NINDA.LÚGUD.DA NINDA.GÍD.DA Gaspa 2009–2010 p. 118 A.187: 45' "*q*.-bread, short bread, long bread", s. Gaspa ib. 119.

4. It is uncertain whether the flour (always logogr.) is identical with the syllabically attested commodity *q*. The editors of SAA 12 and SAAo prefer a reading *kakkallu*, taking KA as a phonetic complement (ZÍD.[ka]GAL.GAL). CAD takes it to be a writing of *samīdu* (CAD S 115b s.v. *samīdu* B). For LB s. Jursa 2010, 706. – Cf. *qulqultu*.

+ **qāltu** "attention, consideration?"; OB

1. *elī bēl qa-al-ti-im* PN *ana qa-al-ti-ia izzīzam* ARM 27, 116: 51f. "PN commanded my attention(?) more than (any other) man who needs attention(?)".

2. Noun pattern *PaRāSt* from *qâlu* "to be silent; to heed, pay attention"? M. Birot, ib. p. 203f. translates "silence" (var. of *qūltu*).

qalû II "to burn, to roast"

G 1. OB *ḫamūsam* ... *iqqurū u* [udu]A-LUM[ḫi.a] *išātam iq-lu-ú* FM 8, 118 no. 34: 51 "they destroyed the memorial stone and roasted the *alum*-sheep in fire".

2. OB *šumma ina kīnātimma ḫumūssu iqqurū u* [udu]A.LUM-*šu iq-lu-ú* FM 8, 123 no. 36: 21 "if they really destroyed his memorial stone and roasted his *alum*-sheep".

3. *a-ja/ji-li iq-lu-ú* FM 8, 125 no. 37: 6" "they burnt my *alum*-sheep".

N 1. OB *šumma ḫamūsum innaqqar u* [udu]A-LUM[ḫi.a] *išātam i-qa-[lu-ú]* FM 8, 118 no. 34: 55 "if a memorial stone is destroyed and *alum*-sheep are roas[ted] in fire".

2. OB lit. *iq-qa-al-lu-ma* FM 3, 68 no. 4 ii 3 "they will be burnt".

3. SB *kīma saḫlê li-iq-qa-lu* SpTU 3, 100: 20 "he shall be roasted like cress (seeds)" (Mayer in Deller/Mayer/Oelsner 1989, 269).

Disc.: Mayer 2017, 30.

qâlu "to pay attention, to heed, to be silent"; + OA

G 1. OA *ana awâtim ša šiprēni qú-⸢ul⸣(-ma)* Günbattı 2014, 90, kt 01/k 217: 66 "heed the words of our envoys!".

2. OB *ana milkiya qú-ul-[ma]* Finkel 2014: 2 "heed my advice!"

3. OB *inanna sinništum ana ramāni-šama i-qa-al* ARM 26/1, 200 no. 57: 13 "now the woman can (only) pay attention to herself" (Charpin 1989–90, 95 with add. refs.).
4. SB ^{d}*utu di-níg-gi-na-zu giš ḫé-em-ma-ra-ni-in-lá* // ^{d}*Šamaš ana dīn kīttika li-qu-ul-ka* VS 24, 59 i 5f. (= *mīs pî* IV, Walker/Dick 2001, 161 l. 12b) "May Šamaš heed your true decision".
5. SB *ana šipṭi u purussê i-qal-ši* D[N] BM 75974: 9 (cit. Mayer 2017, 30, now Bennett 2021, 202f. l. 57') "DN heeds her for judgement and decision"
6. SB *šumma qutrīnum ina sarāqika i-qu-ul-ma wark*[*ānūm ni*]*piḫšu ištappū* UCP 9/5, 373: 3 (Finkel, AfO 29/30, 50 no. 2) "if the incense settles after you shake it up and smokes more strongly afterwards" (Mayer in Deller/Mayer/Oelsner 1989, 269).
7. In SBH p. 152 no. 34: 9f. (quot. CAD Q 72, lex. section) read *ta-qa-al-lu* instead of *-la* (Borger 1985, 352).
8. The PN cit. CAD Q 75a as *Sîn-ana-*ḪI.GAR^{ki}*-li-qú-ul* is to be read …*-li-ip-p*[*a-li-is*] (AbB 9, 32; JCS 14, 129 n. 13).
9. II/ā: **a)** MA *bēlī wardīšu li-qa-a-al* BATSH 4/1, 12: 31 "may my lord take care of his servants!".
b) MA *igārātīma u tarbāṣa ša* TÚG *li-qa-al* BATSH 4/1, 6: 10 "may he take care of the walls and enclosure of the textile (storage?)".
c) Nuzi *atta ammīni qa-la-ta* HSS 14, 12: 9 "you, why are you doing nothing?" (Deller in id./Mayer/Oelsner 1989, 266).
d) De Ridder 2018, 389 n. 7.

+ **D** Charpin 1989–90, 95:
1. OB *adī ṭēmšu uqattû* [...] *ú-qí-il* ARM 26/2, 365 no. 449: 9 "until he (= PN_1) had finished his report, he (= PN_2) paid [close?] attention".
2. OB *ākil karṣiya u qābī lā damqātiya maḫar abīya* [*l*]*i-qí-lu-ma igirrê dum-miq* A.730: 23 (cit. ARM 26/1 p. 385 n. 43) "may they silence those who slander and denigrate me in front of my father, and you improve my reputation!"

Š Charpin 1989–90, 95:
1. *mannum lā idâm bēlī úš-qí-il-ma* ARM 26/1, 169 no. 36: 20 "who, unreasonably, brought (it) to my lord's attention" (transl. after Heimpel 2003, 195).
2. *ana ṭēmim ša ašpurakkum šarram šu-qí-il*$_5$ ARM 26/2, 215 no. 388: 29 "bring the message that I wrote you to the attention of the king!"

Disc.: The alleged Gt (von Soden 1981a, 150 and Sommerfeld 1990a, 31) is not confirmed: The PN *Iliš-ku-tu-ul* is likely a contraction of **Iliška-uṭul* "look at your god" (Stol 1991, 196 and Streck 2003a, 78).

MPS (G), NJCK (G), JW (G, D, Š)

qâlu B s. *qa'ālu*

+ **qalullā'u** "discredit, disgrace"; OA

awīlū ša (...) *qá-lu-lá-ni ētanappušū*[*ni*] Prag 714: 9 "the men who keep discrediting us". Var. of *qulālu*. NJCK

qamāmu "to dress hair in a certain way"; + OB

OB lit. *qa-am-ma-*[*a*]*t* Haul 2009, 330: 7' (// [*g*]*ullubat*), in unclear and broken context. Cf. *qammatu*.

qamlu s. *gamlu* 1.

+ **qammatu** "a prophetess"; OB

1. 1 ^{munus}*qa-ma-tum ša* DN ARM 26/1, 424 no. 197: 6 "1 *q*. of DN"; ARM 26/1, 426 no. 199: 42.

2. *šārtam u sissik*[*tam ša* munus*qa*]*-am-ma-*[*tim*] ARM 26/1, 431 no. 203: 11 "the (strand/lock of) hair and the seam of the *q*."

3. A descriptive term derived from the *qamāmu*-style of hair dressing (sim. *kezertu, kuzīru*). Charpin 1989–90, 92.

qamû "to burn"

Š SB *šaptān mulammināti Girra ú-ša-aq-ma* ORA 7, 318: 10 "he makes Girra burn the defaming lips".

****qâmu** (CAD Q 79)

Read *li-*⌜*qi*⌝*-bi*!*-u* (SAA 1, 82 r. 9, Deller in id./Mayer/Oelsner 1989, 258).

qanānu "to make a nest"

1. SB *šumma ina šupal mayyālti amēli ṣerru iq-nun-ma rabiṣ* ZA 71, 114: 20 "if a snake has made (its) nest beneath a man's bed and lies in wait" (Sommerfeld 1990, 31), cf. *qinna iq-nun-ma* KAL 1, 9 v 9.

2. SB *šumma summatu ina bīt amēli qá-na-at-ma* SpTU 2, 32 r. 12 "if a dove is nesting in a man's house".

3. SB (if a fox) *ina imitti amēli iq-nun-ma* NÁ*-iṣ* SpTU 2, 33: 12 "makes a lair to the right of a man and lies in wait".

4. *i*-class: SB *šumma sinūntu ... iq-ta-ni-in* ib. 17 "if a swallow has built a nest".

\+ **q/kanaqurtu** "a plant producing an aromatic oil"; OB

1. 44 DUG$^{\text{ḫi.a}}$ Ì *qa-na-qú-ur-tum* 30 DUG$^{\text{ḫi.a}}$ LÀL FM 7, 114 no. 30: 4 "44 jars with *q*. oil, 30 jars with syrup".

2. 2 DUG LÀL 2 DUG [*k*]*a-na-qú-ur-tim* ARM 21, 100: 1 "2 jars with syrup, 2 jars with *k*.".

3. 2 DUG Ì *ka-na-qú-*[*ur-tim*] 3 DUG LÀL FM 11, 144: 2 "2 jars with *k*. oil, 3 jars with syrup".

4. 20 DUG Ì *ša ka-na-qú-ur-ti* ŠÀ.BA 19 DUG Ì *ana* [*na*]*kkamti šarrim šūrubū* 1 DUG Ì PN FM 11, 62: 16 "20 jars with *k*. oil, among them 19 jars of oil have been brought into the storeroom of the king, 1 jar of oil is for PN".

5. The original form seems to be *qana-qurtu* rather than *kanakurtu*, suggested by J.-M. Durand, ARM 21, 120 n. 1. The form *kanaqurtu* is conditioned by a dissimilation similar to *kaqqadu* < *qaqqadu* and *kaqqaru* < *qaqqaru*.

qandalu, *kamdalu* "a household item"; + MB

1. OB *qa-an-da-lu* ARM 7, 102 r. 1 (coll. MARI 2, 79; prev. read *k*[*a*]*-a*[*n*]*-d*[*a*]*-l*[*u*] in CAD K s.v. *kandalu*).

2. MB ⌜*ša qan-da-le-e*⌝ BagF 21, 85: 2.

3. The NB refs. cited in AHw. 897 s.v. *qandalû* and CAD K 148 s.v. *kandalu* belong to *gidlu* (Stol 1983, 299 and s. *gidlu*).

qannu, *qarnu* "border, environs, outside; fringe, hem"; + Nuzi

1. Var. *qarnu*:

a) *bēlī qātīšu ina qa-ra-an ṣubātīya ušakkil* WZKM 86, 480: 8 "my lord wiped his hands on the hem of my clothes" (Mayer 2017, 30).

b) *bēlī* PN *qa-ra-an ṣubātišu elīya ittadī* ARM 26/1, 530 no. 251: 17 "my lord PN cast his hem over me" (Charpin 1989–90, 95 with add. refs.).

2. As preposition also in MA: [*ina*] *bīt karmi ša qa-an-ni ša utūni pappi*[*ri*] VS 21, 23 r. 12 "in that part of the granary which is close to the beer-bread oven"

(Deller in id./Mayer/Oelsner 1989, 258).

3. Nuzi *ana ālānī qa-an-na-ti* HSS 14, 132: 2; 124: 15 "(barley) for the border towns" (Deller in id./Mayer/Oelsner 1989, 266).

4. SB *qa-an-ni ana ēkalli allaku* BagM 13, 145: 4 "right before I go to the palace" (Deller in id./Mayer/Oelsner 1989, 258).

5. SB *ultū ūmu ša qa-ni-šú tētiqušu* TCL 6, 49 r. 12 (RA 18, 166) "from the day you crossed her (bed's) edge", cf. UET 7, 8 r. 1–3 (Mayer 2017, 30).

qanû I "reed, tube, arrow"

1. Lex. *gi-umbin* // *qa-nu-ú ṣupur* SpTU 2, 51 iv 13 and cf. 23–30 (reeds of var. lengths, s. Mayer in Deller/Mayer/Oelsner 1989, 269).

2. Lex. *zánaru* = *za-na-ru* = *qà-an tá-bi-tum* / *qà-an tá-bi-ti-iš* Emar 6/4, 545: 391 (an instrument, reading after Y. Cohen 2010, 825f. Cf. Pentiuc 2001, 92 (KA-[*a*]*n*-DA-BI-*tum*).

3. OB [*enūtu*]*m ša qa-ni-im* FM 9, 220 no. 53: 13 "[instrumen]ts made of reed".

4. SB *aššum* GI *nākis abbunnati* JNES 33, 332: 12–13 "concerning the reed that cuts the umbilical cord" (i.e. a broken reed with a sharp edge, Mayer in Deller/Mayer/Oelsner 1989, 270).

5. NA in *ša muḫḫi qanâte* (CAD Q 91): [lú]*ša muḫḫi qa-*<*na-*>*a-te* SAA 6, 35: 9, or perhaps *qa'âte* (Deller in id./Mayer/Oelsner 1989, 258).

qanû II "to keep; to buy, acquire"

G 1. OB *ammīnim adī inanna alpī u immerī lā ta-aq-né-e-ma* A.1884: 24 (cit. Charpin 1989–90, 95f.) "why have you not kept the oxen and sheep until now?"

2. OB *li-iq-ni-šu* AbB 13, 24: 12 "let him keep it" (in broken context). Cf. AbB 2, 177: 19.

D 1. OB *ana pūḫāt wattarī ú-qa-an-nu-ú* ARM 4, 86: 34 (coll. Durand apud Charpin 1989–90, 96) "they (want to) acquire substitutes for the auxiliaries".

2. MB: On *li-ga-an-ni-ma* in MDP 10 pl. 12 v 3 and MDP 6, 43 iii 8, both cit. CAD Q 91 ("mng unkn.") s. Paulus 2014, 396, 401 (MŠ 3 v 2) and 466, 469 (MAI I 6 iii 8'), who derives this word from *genû*.

N NA MÍ *táq-qí-nu-nu* StAT 2, 41: 2 "(until) the woman was purchased".

JK (N), JW (G, D), FJMS (D)

\+ **qanuḫḫe** "reed cutter, arrow maker"; OB Alal.

[lú.]meš*qa-nu-ḫe-en* AlT 277: 3 (AOAT 282, 513 no. 7). Akk. *qanû* + Hurr. *-ḫḫe* (Zeeb ib. 437; Richter 2012, 185).

qapādu s. *ḫapādu*

qapīru "a container"; Aram. lw.

On etym. s. Cherry 2016, 203f.; Abraham/Sokoloff 2011, 46. < Aram. *qpyr* "a measure of capacity".

qappatu, *qabbatu* "a basket (made of palm leaves or iron)"

1. Lex. *gi-gur-im-ma* = *qap-pa-tum*; *gi-gur-*[di-il]*dil* = MIN SpTU 2, 51 i 23–24 (Ḫḫ IX, Mayer in Deller/Mayer/Oelsner 1989, 270).

2. Lex. [*pap-š*]*e-*[*er*] = [*pa*]*p-nir* = *qa-pa-tum* ASJ 18, 232 r ii 14 (Nippur emesal vocabulary).

3. LB (5 minas of silver for) [an].bar*qab-ba-a-ti* dubsar 3, 74: 14.

qâpu I "to buckle, to sag, to become dilapidated"

1. SB *ana tanūqātīša dūr šadî i-qup-pi-ši* AfO 50, 22: 17 "at her roar the walls of the mountains buckle for her" (Mayer 2017, 31).

2. OB lit. *šadûm i-qù-pa-am-ma* CUSAS 10, 5: 6 "the mountain buckled upon me".

qâpu II s. *qīʾāpu*

qaqânu "*qaqû*-like bird"

SB *qa-qa-⌜a⌝-nu issu libbi aṣūdātīkunu lēšu lēkul* SAA 2, 15 vi 23 "may the *q*. eat the dough from your bowls" (Mayer 2017, 31).

qaqdâ s. *kakdâ*

\+ **qaqqadāniš** "importantly"; SB

<qa>-qa-da-niš idâl SpTU 3, 61: 17 "he will roam about importantly".

qaqqadānu, + *qaqqadannu* "with large head"

1. OB *Qa-aq-qa-da-an* ARM 16, 170; M.7405 (Charpin 1989–90, 96).

2. MB *Qa-qa-da-an-ni* MRWH 12: 9' (Sommerfeld 1990, 31).

3. LB *Qaq-qa-da-ni-tu* OECT 10, 152: 17 (family name, Oelsner in Deller/Mayer/Oelsner 1989, 278).

****qaqqadānû** (CAD Q 100)

The refs. belong to *qaqqadānu* (Deller in id./Mayer/Oelsner 1989, 258).

qaqqadu "head"

1. OA *ša q*. "head-dress": (if she prostitutes herself) 1 *ṣubātam tūdittaša u ša qá-qí-dí-ša eṭṭerši(ma)* kt 94/k 487: 11 "he will take away from her 1 garment, her toggle-pin and her head-dress" (s. Veenhof 2018a, 43); sim. AKT 8, 215: 23.

2. OA "the best" (sg. and pl.): 11 *ṣubātē damqūtim watrūtim qá-qá-ad* TÚG$^{hi.a}$ kt m/k 135B: 11 "11 textiles of extra high quality, the topmost quality of the textiles"; sim. kt 87/k 146: 8 (pl.) (both court. K. Hecker).

3. OA "original amount, principal": *qá-qá-ad kaspīʾa šēbilam* AKT 8, 256: 10 "(I do not need the interest of the silver), send me the original amount of my silver"; sim. AKT 6, 136: 16.

4. OB *eperam ina qa-qa-di-šu lippuṣma* ARM 26/1, 537 no. 257: 22 "let him pound dirt on his head" (in damaged context, possibly referring to a punishment). Cf. *eperam ina qa-qa-di-šu inappaṣu* A. 2071: 14 (cit. Charpin 1989–90, 96).

5. OB *anāku qa-qa-di ana imittim ūlūma ana šumēlim ul ušasḫir* ARM 28, 48: 8 "I did not turn my head right or left", i.e. "I have served no other".

6. OB *kursinātum itēlīʾāma qá-qá-datum uštaplā*$^{sic?}$ A.4285+: 42 "ankles have been lifted up and heads put down" (Charpin 1989–90, 96).

7. OB *qa-qa-da-at mātim* ARM 26/1, 536 no. 256: 15 "notables of the country" (Charpin 1989–90, 97 with add. refs.).

8. OB *šulmum šinā qa-qa-du-šu nīram inaṭṭal* ARM 26/1, 328 no. 161: 5 "the cleft – it was two-headed – was looking at the yoke" (ref. to extispicy, transl. after Heimpel 2003, 238).

9. *q. kullu* "to abide by"; + *ana* "to resign oneself to, to lean towards" (Charpin 1989–90, 97, s. CAD Q, 112 "to be in readiness for"):

a) *ana isiktim ša bēlī īsiku qa-aq-qa-ad-ni i nukīl* A.288: 42 "so that we shall comply with the assignment given by my lord".

b) *aššum kī'am ana awātim qa-qa-di ukālšu* ARM 26/2, 285 no. 411: 56 "I therefore heed him in this matter".

c) *ana salīmim qa-qa-su ukīl* ARM 26/2, 280 no. 410: 7 "he was leaning towards peace". S. Charpin 1989–90, 97b with add. refs.

10. *q. kabtu*: **a)** *ina qa-qa-di-im ka-ab-di-im* ⌜*ana* G⌝N *bēlī iṭeḫḫī* ARM 33, 346 no. 154: 59 (= FM 2, 116) "my lord shall approach GN with honor"; sim. ARM 33, 229 no. 92 r. 15 (= ARM 26/1 no. 148).

b) For *q. kubbutu* "to honor" (CAD Q 112, 3' a') s. also ARM 26/2, 365 no. 449: 28, 34.

11. For cephalomorph vessels s. Guichard 2005, 63, 154f., 264–287 with refs.

12. Del. the refs. TIM 2, 16 cit. CAD Q 106 ad 1b5', read after copy *ga-am-lam imtaḫaṣ* (Sommerfeld 1990, 31).

13. On spellings indicating regressive dissimilation (*kaqqadu*) s. Edzard 1983, 134f. Note the spelling variations *qá-qá-as-sú* Haradum II, 23: 7, but *ka-ka-di-šu* ib. 15 (s. *gālābu* D and *kuprum*), cf. *ka-ka-da-ša* CUSAS 18, 4: 36.

NJCK (1–3), JW (4–13)

+ **qaqqadūtu** "leadership"; NB

[*q*]*aq-qad-us-su* SAA 21, 5: 5, in broken context.

qaqqaršu(m) "on the ground"

OB lit. *ka-qa-ar-šu tušūmida šēpīya* RB 59 = Fs. Reiner 192: 32 "you set my feet on the ground".

qaqqaru "earth, ground"

1. OA figuratively in *qaqqar ši'āmātim* "area of purchases": *annākam i-qá-qá-ar ši'āmātim wašbāku u šīmum ma'ad* AKT 5, 19: 2 "here I am staying in an area where purchases can be made and there is a lot of trade"; sim. TPAK 1, 144: 5 and 145: 11.

2. OB *qa-qa-ar napištini niše''ī* RA 81, 144 A.649: 26 "will we search for land to live on?" (reading after Charpin 1989–90, 97).

3. OB *ana qa-qa-ar ḫadānim ana* GN *akšud* ARM 26/1, 176 no. 40: 22 "I have reached GN, the locality of the appointment" (transl. Heimpel 2003, 198). For add. Mari refs. s. Charpin 1989–90, 97f.

4. SB *eršī qaq-qa-ru* K. 9252: 10 (*šigû* prayer) "my bed is the ground" (Mayer in Deller/Mayer/Oelsner 1989, 271).

5. SB *ina qaq-qar tamḫāzi* K.6331: 5 "on the battle ground", [*ina qaq*]*-qar tuqmati* ib. 22 (Mayer in Deller/Mayer/Oelsner 1989, 271).

6. SB *ina qaq-qar pu*[*šqi qāta ṣabāt*]*u* Fs Kraus, 196: 26 "to [take by the hand] on a difficult stretch" (Mayer in Deller/Mayer/Oelsner 1989, 271).

7. NA (stone slabs) *ša šarru ina muḫḫi izzazzuni qaq-qu-ru inaššiquni* George, Iraq 48, 144–5 r. 4 "on which the king stands and kisses the ground" (Deller in id./Mayer/Oelsner 1989, 259).

8. NA (wine) *ša qaq-qi-ri* CTN 1, 3 ii 5; *ša qaq-qa-ri* 6: 49b; [*ša muḫ*]*ḫi qaq-qi-ri* 4: 6; 14: 21 (Deller in id./Mayer/Oelsner 1989, 259).

9. LB *qaq-qar mala qaq-qar* TBER pl. 72 AO 20175: 48 "(PN will exchange with PN_2 and PN_3) land for land" (Oelsner in Deller/Mayer/Oelsner 1989, 279).

10. For BATSH 4/1, 2 s. *tarāṣu* I G 1.

NJCK (1), JW (2–10)

+ **qaqqû II** "fin?"; SB

Lex. *pa ku*₆ = *qa-aq-qu-ú* CUSAS 12 p. 49 iv 4 (Izi) "wing of a fish = fin" (followed by *qulēpti nūni* "fish scale").

qaqqullu s. *qāqullu*

qaqû "a bird"; + OB

1. OB *qa-qú-um*^{mušen} Edubba'a 7, 100: 53 (in list of birds).

2. *qa-qù-ú*^{mušen} A.1394: 15 (Charpin 1989–90, 98).

3. OB *ḫiṭītu ina eqlim ina lā maṣṣar* MUŠEN *qá-qé-e*^{meš} *ra-bu-um ibbaššû* AbB 6, 179: 11 "major losses are occurring in the fields caused by lack of protection (against) the *q*.-birds"; (during the night, the wild cows,) *kala ūmim qá-qú-ú*$^{mušen.ḫi.a}$ *eqlam ana š*[*am*]*ê uštālī'a* ib. 17 "(during) the whole day, the *q*.-birds are carrying the field skyward".

4. OB (barley as fodder for) ⌜5⌝ *qa-qú-ú*[^{mušen}] KTT 164: 6.

5. SB *tamšīl* [*p*]*aspas* // U₅.SI[M]$^{mu[še]n}$ *qa-qu-u* // *qa-qu-ut-/tú* SpTU 3, 99: 21, cf. 20 (Mayer in Deller/Mayer/Oelsner 1989, 271). S. *qaquttu*.

6. Cf. Aram. *qāqā*, Hebr. *qīq* ("pelican"). S. also *qaqânu*, *qiqû*.

qaqullu s. *qāqullu*

qāqullu, *qaqqallu* "a plant; a bird"

1. The refs. cit. CAD Q 125 s.v. *qaqullu* "a type of field" belong here. The preceding sign read KU in CAD is in fact DU₆: *Tīl-qāqullu* is a place name (Oelsner in Deller/Mayer/Oelsner 1989, 279).

2. S. extensively de Ridder/Zomer 2019 (an alkaline plant, perhaps *Suaeda fruticosa* or *Suaeda vera*, "shrubby seablite"). For the container s. *kakkullu*.

+ **qaquttu** "a bird"

qa-qu-ut-/tú SpTU 3, 99: 21, s. *qaqû* 5.

qarābu "battle, fight", Aram. lw.

Cf. Syr. *qrābā* (Kogan/Krebernik 2021, 441; Abraham/Sokoloff 2011, 46).

****qarādu A** "mng. uncert." (CAD Q 126)

1. For EA 69: 30, EA 87:25 and ABL 633+ (now SAA 16. 63) s. *qarādu* II.

2. For BWL 252 s. *qarādu* I.

3. The final ref. cit. in CAD (ABL 101, now SAA 10, 350) is too damaged for interpretation (*ug-da*-[...]).

qarādu I "to pluck (hair, wool)"

SB *ila*! *i-taš*!*-mar maḫḫūti ṣīḫiš qit-rad-ma* BWL 252 iii 17 "praise god (and) pluck (the beards / hair of?) the ecstatics while laughing!" (reading after von Soden 1985, 276).

qarādu II "to be(come) warlike, heroic", D "to encourage"

+ **Gt** SB *aššu taq-tar-du-ma šadê tanāru* Anzu III 120 "because you have proven yourself to be heroic and defeated the mountains" (Mayer 2017, 31).

D 1. MB *qú-ru-ud-mi ana šarri bēlika* EA 69: 30, 87: 25 "encourage the king, your lord". Diff. Moran 1992, 160 who translates "urge with loud cries" based on an assumed verb **qarādu* III (s. also Civil 1984a, 294f. with ref. to *lú gù-mur-ak* = *qar-du-um* MSL 12, 157 A: 342 which has been included in CAD G 50 s.v. *gardu*).

2. SB *ṭēm šarrī mu-qar-ri-di-šu* ... *uparrir* BagM 34, 144 ix 1 "I have thwarted the plan of the kings who encouraged him" (Mayer 2017, 31).

3. NA *sangû uq-ṭa-ri-da-áš-šú* SAA 16, 63: 26 "the priest has encouraged him".

S. CAD s.v. *qurrudu.*

qaraḫu "to freeze"

S. *qarḫu.*

qarānu "to pile up"

OB lit. *bāštī a-qá-ra-an* AML 130: 5 "I will pile up my dignity".

qarāru "a garment" s. *qarrāru*

qarāru, *garāru* "to turn over; to writhe, grovel; to be(come) frightened; to flow, to overflow"

G 1. Lex. *ga-ra-ra* = *palāḫu* SpTU 2, 39: 3 "to writhe = to fear".
2. OB lit. [*in*]*a ur-ši-ma-aq-ru-ur ina mayyālim* CUSAS 10, 8: 21 "[in] the bedchamber I tossed and turned on the bed".
3. NA *lā illakūni ig-du-ru* SAA 1, 179: 10 "they do not come. They have become scared".
4. NA [*š*]*īrīšu ittaṣa*[*r*] [*m*]*ā ig-du-ru-u*[*r*] [*m*]*ā bārû ētarbūni* [*u*]*ssani'a* [*i*]*g-du-ru-ur* [x x *l*]*ā ig-ru-ur* [... *m*]*ā ūmu itta*[*lak š*]*īrūšu* .[..] SAA 10, 304 r. 4–9 "he watched its (the sheep's) flesh (and) became frightened. The exorcists entered (and) a second time he became frightened. [But then(?)] he did not become frightened (and) the day came and its flesh [became good(?)]".

Gtn NA *asseme mā ig-da-na-ru-*[*ru m*]*ā atâ ta-ag-da-*⌜*na-ra*⌝-[*ra*] SAA 5, 95: 7f. "I heard that they are constantly scared. Why are you constantly scared?"

Š NA *libbī ú-sa-ag-ri-r*[*i*] SAA 16, 15: 22 "frightened my heart".

N 1. MB *ana šēpī bēliya 2-šú 7-šú aq-qá-ra-ar* Emar 6/3, 266: 5 "twice 7 times I grovel at my lord's feet".
2. SB [*šumma ṣēru* ...] ... *ana muḫḫišu iq-qa-*⌜*ri*?*-ru*?⌝ KAL 1, 9 iv 25 "when a snake … wriggles down on him".

Ntn 1. SB *ašar imēru it-taq-ra-ar-*[*ru*] MSL 9, 109: 6a "where a donkey kept rolling around" (// *iq-qá-ri-ru*).
2. SB [*šumma ṣēr*]*ū ina sūqim it-ta-naq-ra-ar-ru* KAL 1, 9 vi 19 "when snakes are constantly writhing in the street".
3. NA *ina muḫḫi šēpē ittagal it-AT-na-aq-ra-ra* SAA 16, 20 r. 5 "(the patient) looked at his feet and kept bending over".

Disc.: CAD *garāru* A "to turn or roll over" and B "to shy away, become scared" belong together (MSL 10, 23 n. 1). S. also *qirīru.*

qarāšu "to cut off, break off"

1. LB ⌜ŠE⌝.NUMUN *atar ša ina birišu<nu> irri*[*š*]*ū amīlu akī alpišu iq-qàr-áš* CUSAS 28, 75: 16 "more field(s) that they cultivate jointly – each (of them) will take his cut(?) (of the harvest) according to (his share in) the ox(en)". The interpretation of this passage is uncertain (s. the comm. ib. p. 219).

2. AHw. 903a *qarāšu* = *garāšu* II "to drive off" (*UG-ta-ar-ša-an-ni* in ARM 2, 28: 9, 19) may belong here (s. Streck 2000a, 88–9).

qarbātu (CAD Q 128) s. *qerbetu*

qardam(m)u "villain, wicked person" Mayer 2017, 31, SB:

1. *ul ulteṣṣu qar-da-mu* Or. 61, 25: 29a "the wicked one will not get away"; *kāsû qar-da-mu* ib. 33b "who binds the wicked one".

2. *rāsib qar-da-mu* BM 34179: 4 "(DN,) who smites the wicked one".

3. *kāšid qar-da-mu* (// *lú-gil-gil*) CTMMA 2, 18: 9 "(DN,) who overcomes the wicked one".

qardu "heroic"

1. Lex. *sag* = *qar-*⌈*du*⌉ Emar 6/4, 537: 336 (Sa), Sjöberg 1998, 262.

2. *manzāz maḫrika lū qar-du* TIM 9, 55: 17 "your attendants shall be valiant!" (dupl. of JRAS 1920, 568: 14, cit. CAD Q 131a ad c as [*nāš*] *azmarīka lū qar-du,* after Mayer in Deller/Mayer/ Oelsner 1989, 271).

qarḫu "ice, frost"; Aram. lw.

For etym. s. Cherry 2016, 206f. (Aram. *qrḥ*, itself a loan from Hebr.?).

qāribu "a bird"

1. NA PN: [I]*Qa-ri-bu* SAA 6, 147 r. 3.

2. The word might correspond to Bab. *āribu* "crow" (Deller in id./Mayer/Oelsner 1989, 260).

****qarittu** (CAD Q 132)

The form *qar-da-a-ti* belongs to *qardu* (Borger 1985, 352; Mayer 2017, 31).

qarnānu "with (large) horns"

OB as PN: *Qa-ar-na-an* M.13349, M.11856 (cit. Charpin 1989–90, 98).

qarnu, *qannu* "horn"

1. OA as a container: *qar-nam ša rīmim* (...) *šamnam ṭābam mallīʾ*[*am*] Çayır 2016, 97 kt 97/k 185: 7 "fill for me the horn of an aurochs with sweet oil".

2. OB *qa-ar-*[*n*]*a-at rīm*[*ī*] *ītenerrišanni* ... *lū* 20 *lū* 30 *qa-ar-n*[*a-a*]*t rī*[*mī*] ... *šūbilam* ARM 28, 43: 6 "he constantly asks me for the horns of aurochsen ... Send me 20 or 30 horns of aurochsen!"

3. OB (bronze) *ša* ⌈*qar-na-at ṣalam ilim*⌉ FM 3, 100 no. 7 vi 13 "for the horns of the divine statue".

4. OB of chariots:

a) OB *qar-na-at narkabtim ša ašnugallim* FM 3, 101 no. 7 vii 28 "horns of a chariot (made) of alabaster".

b) *qar-na-at ašnugallim ša* 1 *narkabtim rēštîm* ib. 33 "horns of alabaster for 1 first-class chariot".

c) 2 ^{giš}GIGIR GAL *qar-na-šu-nu* ^{na_4}GIŠ.NU$_{11}$.GAL ARM 21, 253: 6 "2 big wagons, their horns (made) from alabaster"; cf. 254: 2, 22; 311: 2; 312: 2 (Mayer in Deller/Mayer/Oelsner 1989, 271) and ARM 23, 57 no. 68: 4; 452 no. 531: 4; 440 no. 516: 2; ARM 22, 204 r. iii 27; ARM 26/2, 176 no. 370: 50'.

d) OB (bronze) **a)** *ana* 4 *qar-na-tim ša rukūbi* FM 3, 118 no. 10 iii 8 "for 4 horns of a *r.*-chariot".

e) *qar-na-tim ša rukūbi* ARM 22, 207 r. 7 "(for) the horns of the *r.*-chariot" (Charpin 1989–90, 98).

5. OB as part of a (temple) building:

a) *inūma* PNf *qar-ni ina bīt* DNf *ušbu* ARM 23, 194 no. 218: 4 "when PNf dwelled in the 'horns' of the temple of DNf" (Mayer in Deller/Mayer/Oelsner 1989, 271).

b) *qa-ra-an dūrim elī aḫim ša nā*[*rim*] M.5130+: 18 (cit. Charpin 1989–90, 99) "the horn of the wall overlooking the river bank".

6. LB *qa-an-nu ša ṣabīti* dubsar 3, 72: 6, 10 "gazelle's horn".

7. S. Guichard 2005, 149; Arkhipov 2012, 151 (on *q.* as part of weapons and vehicles in Mari). S. also *qarranu.*

NJCK (1), MPS (2–4, 6), JW (4–5, 7)

qarnû "horned"

S. also *qarranû.*

qarpāsu, + *karpassu* "a fine textile; cotton?"; + LB

1. LB 20 *ka-⸢ar-pa⸣-as-su* RA 83, 69: 11; 1-*en ka-ar-pa-⸢as-sà⸣* ib. 23, s. Beaulieu ib. 71.

2. CAD Q opted to delete this lemma and read *qar-aru*(PA) in the two known NA refs. This sign value is rare, however, and the new LB refs. suggests that the word was borrowed into Akk. after all.

qarrādu "hero, warrior"; + OA

1. OB lex.: [*ši-li-i*]*g*? = ⸢KAxŠID⸣? = *qá-ra-du-u*[*m*]? Klein/Sefati 2019, 90 i 43, cf. *qú*!?-*ra*?-*du*?-*u*[*m*] ib. 46.

2. OA lit. 7 *li-me-e qá-ra-du-a ša irātim ūmišamma maḫrīʾa ekkulūni* OA Sarg. 21 "7 thousand are my warriors, who eat breast pieces in my presence each day"; sim. ib. 30.

3. OA lit. *libbum qá-ra-ad* kt 91/k 502: 18 "the heart/belly is a hero" (s. Kouwenberg 2018/19; perhaps from *qardu*). FJMS (1), NJCK (2–3)

qarrādūtu "heroism, valor, bravery"

1. OB LI.LI.ÌZ ZABAR *ša rigimšu ṭābu ana simat qar-ra-du-ti-šu šūluku ušēlī* RIMA 1, 58 no. 6: 12 "(PN) has devoted a bronze kettledrum with good sound, befitting his valor" (Mayer in Deller/Mayer/Oelsner 1989, 271).

2. SB *qar-ra-du-ta a i-ban*!*-na-a*ʾ *libbūkku* SpTU 1, 1 iii 6 "you shall not fancy heroism in your heart!" (Mayer in Deller/Mayer/Oelsner 1989, 271).

+ **qarranu** "horn, pincer (of a scorpion)"

1. OB lit. *sâdum qà-ra-na-k*[*a*] YOS 11, 87: 3 "your two horns – smiting".

2. SB *ez-zi-*<*iš*> *qar-ra-nu-ka a-na na-*[…] AMD 1 p. 236 no. 13: 2 "angrily your horns are…", s. Finkel ib. 237.

3. Cf. *qarnu*, *qarnû*, *qarranû*.

+ **qarranû** "horned"

1. SB *qar-ra-nu-u* BL 185: 1 (Borger 1985, 352).

2. Cf. *qarnû*, *qarranu*.

qarrāru, *qarāru*? "a garment"

1. NA ^{túg}*qar-ra-ru* SAA 16, 53: 10 (Deller in id./Mayer/Oelsner 1989, 258).

2. K 880b, quot. AHw. s.v. *qarrāru* and CAD s.v. *qarāru*, is now SAA 16, 53.

3. S. Gaspa 2018, 328f. S. also *birmu* 4.

+ **qaršu** "cut-off? (as a designation of clothing)"; OB

uṭublu qar-šum ARM 22, 166: 1; var. *gàr-šu-tum* T. 341: 5; *qa-ar-šum* M.5681 i 8 (Durand 2009, 108–9 with add. refs. and disc.). The word almost exclusively qualifies *uṭublu*. It could refer to shaping ("cut-off"), texture, or pattern of a fabric. Cf. OA *GarZu*?

+ **qasābu** "to listen", D "to pay close attention to"; OB; Amor. lw.

D (I am being held here) *u awāt* DUMU *yamīna ú-qa-ás-si-ib* A.1958: 14 (cit. Charpin 1989–90, 99a) "and I am paying close attention to word (about) the Yaminites". Cf. Hebr. *qšb*.

+ **qasāmu** "to divide (the period of divination)"; OB; Amor. lw.

têrētim ana šulum ḫalṣim u ālim GN *ša* ITI 1-KAM *ušēpišma lupputā aq-sa-am-ma ša* U$_4$ 15-KAM *ušēpišma šalmā*

FM 2, 71: 8 "I had omens taken concerning the well-being of the district and the city of GN for a month. They are unfavorable. I divided (the period of divination) and had (the omens) taken for a period of 15 days. They are favorable." S. Sasson 1994, who connects the word to NWSem. *qsm* "to divide, apportion, to practice divination" (s. Gesenius 1987–2010, 1177; DNWSI 1018; Wehr 1985, 1024f.).

qaṣāru s. *kaṣāru*

+ **qaṣīru** "harvesting"; EA; NWSem. word.

u lāmi nileʾʾu ZÚ.SI.GA *ba-qa-ni* : *qà-ṣí-ra* EA 244: 14 "and we are therefore unable to do the sheep-plucking : harvesting". Moran 1992, 298 n. 1.

qaṣû s. *kaṣû* II

qašādu "to purify"; + OB

D OB *šumman ṣuḫāram šâti ana qú-úš-šu-di-im tapqidānim* ARM 10, 27: 28 "if you had entrusted those boys to me for purification" (Charpin 1989–90, 106).

****qašdatu** s. *qadištu*

qāširānu s. *qāširu*

+ **qāširu?** "mng. unkn.; part of a property"; NA

NA (a field adjoining) *qa-ši-ra-ni ša bīt* P[N] StAT 2, 60: 4. JK

****qaššatu** s. *qadištu*

qaššu "part of the temple of Aššur"

1. OA (they will pay back the silver) *inūmi rubāʾum ana bēt* DN *ana qá-ší-im errubu* kt j/k 9: 12 (s. Çeçen 1998a, 121) "when the king enters the *q.* in the temple of DN"; sim. kt n/k 306: 5 (s. Bayram/Çeçen 1995, 8 n. 26), both cit. Dercksen 2001, 45 n. 35.

2. OA (PN built ...) *siḫerti i-Za-ri ša bēt* DN *u mušlālam qá-ša-am watmānam ša* DN RIMA 1, 26: 16 "the entire(?) *iZārum* of the temple of DN, and a *mušlālum*, *q.*, (and?) the cella of DN", alternatively "a sacred *mušlālum*".

3. Whether the OA official (s. *Kaššu*) belongs to the same root (QDŠ) as proposed in AHw. is doubtful, as he does not appear in connection with the temple. S. CAD *kaššu* A and B.

NJCK (1, 2), JW (1, 3)

qaštu "bow"

1. OB 10 gišBAN *ša lišānūšina* 10 GÍNàm ZABAR FM 3, 95 no. 7 iii 17 "10 bows whose 'tongues' are of 10 shekel bronze each".

2. SB *ilat qá-áš-ti ūṣu u išpati* AfO 50, 21: 13 "goddess of bow, arrow, and quiver" (Mayer in Deller/Mayer/Oelsner 1989, 272).

3. SB gišPAN *Elamti* SAA 3, 19: 10 "Elamite bow".

4. NA *bīt qašti* "quiver": É gišBAN CTN 3, 96: 24.

5. LB ⌜gišPAN *ša daprāni*⌝ AOAT 414/1, 194: 8 "a bow of juniper wood".

6. Archer: LB 10 *ṣābu ana iltēn* lúBAN *ša* PN Jursa 1999, 169 BM 42384 r. 3 "10 men for one archer of PN", s. Jursa ib. p. 101.

7. Bow-fief: LB (10 men) *ana* gišBAN *i*[*na pan* P]N Jursa 1999, 233 BM 43300+: 15 "are [at the disposal of P]N, for the bow-fief", s. Jursa ib. p. 101.

8. S. Mayer 2009, 425f. on expressions for "to draw a bow" (*matna ana qašti kunnu*; *qašta mullû*), "drawn bow" (*qaštu malītu*), and "relaxed bow" (*qaštu ramītu*).

9. S. Arkhipov 2012, 121 for add. Mari refs.

qâšu s. *qī'āšu*

qāt ṣibitti, *qaṣṣa/ibitti*, + *kaṣbitti* "stolen property"

NB (3 thiefs) *ša ka-aṣ-bit-ti-šú-nu ina* IGI [lú]SUKKAL CT 55, 163: 5 "whose loot is with the vizier", cf. 9, 10.

qatālu "to kill, slaughter"; NWSem. lw.

OB *inūma ḫâra iq-tu-lu* ARM 25, 761: 10 "when the donkey foal was killed" (Mayer in Deller/Mayer/Oelsner 1989, 272). S. Charpin 1989–90, 100a for add. refs.

qātamma "the same, similarly"

1. OB *qātam qātamma*: *ammīnim qa-tam*(-)*ka-tam-ma tabrītum ana ṣēriya lā illakam* ARM 26/2, 334 no. 433: 15 "why did the (news of their) appearance not come to me in the same way?"

2. For add. Mari refs. s. Charpin 1989–90, 100a.

qatāpu "to pluck"

G 1. *aššum karānim ša* GN *ka-ṭá-pi-im* Miscellanea Eblaitica 2 p. 44 n. 54 A.2415 "concerning picking the grapes of GN" (Charpin 1989–90, 100a).
2. OB *karānum lā iq-qa-at-ta-ap* … *ūm karanim qa-ta-pi-im iktašdam* ... *karā-nam li-iq-tu*(sic)*-pu* FM 11, 188: 8 "the vine must not be plucked … the day of vine plucking has come … may they pluck the vine".
3. MB *ana* PN 6 MU.KAM *qa-ta-pa akāla iddinaššu* RE 90: 7 "he gave him (a vineyard) for 6 years to pick and eat", i.e. as usufruct. S. also Ekalte 94: 7.

N s. G 2 above.

qatāru I "incense"; + NB

Fem. pl. *qa-tar-ra-a-*⸢*ti*⸣ OIP 114, 35: 22.

qatāru II "to smoke, fumigate", D also "to make somber, dejected"

G Lex. *bi-i* = NE = *qa-ta-rum ša īnē* CUSAS 12 p. 9: 37 (Ea) "to become gloomy, of the eyes".

D 1. OB lit. *qú-tu-ru panūšu* AML 30: 35 "his face is made somber".
2. Del. ref. ABL 570 (CAD Q 167b as Dtn), read *kīma uq-ta-t*[*e*!*-ru*] SAA 10 323 r. 5 "as soon as they have fumigated".

qāti "in accordance with" s. *qātu*

qatinnu "a profession; verger?"

1. MB Emar: PN *ka-di-in-nu* Emar 6/3, 44: 11.

2. NA *rab q.*: [PN GAL]-[lú]*qa-ti-ni ša turtānī* StAT 1, 23: 6 "PN, the *rab-q*. of the *turtānu*-officials". S. also Radner ib. 114–116.

3. Postgate N. et al. 2019, 141f.: "the precise role of the *qatinnu* in Assyria is unknown … he has a function associated with the temple, while not … being a 'priest' with ritual duties".

JW (1), JK (2), MPS (3)

qatnu "thin"

1. OA (silver) *ana e-ṣé qá-at-nu-tim* AKT 6A, 274: 15 "for thin (pieces of) wood".

2. MB lit. *pappam qà-ta-tam* ALL no. 11 r. 8 "thin curl".

3. NA 1 TÚG *qat*!*-a*!*-tú*! *adirtu* GADA SAA 7, 62 iv 8 "1 thin, dark linen garment"; 1 TÚG *qat*!*-a-tú adirtu* ib. ii 15.

4. LB GARIM *qat-nu ina ḫuṣṣēni ša* PN TBER pl. 31 AO 8599: 25, a "Flurname"? (Oelsner in Deller/Mayer/Oelsner 1989, 280). If *q.* is attribute to *tamertu*, fem. would be expected.

S. also *qalpu*.

NJCK (1), MPS (2–3), JW (4)

qattanu "very thin, fine"

1. OB (trees) *qa-ta-nu-tum* ARM 23, 547 no. 581: 5 and *pass*. (von Soden 1985, 276).

2. LB *uṭṭatu qa-at-ta-tum* CT 57, 68 i 5 "thin (stalks of) grain" (von Soden 1985, 276).

qattāpu s. *katāpu*

qattatu s. *qattanu*

qatû I, fem. *qatītu* "finished, completed"

SB *nāri ḫé-gál-lim lā qa-ti-ti* SpTU 2, 5: 5 "endless river of plenty" (von Soden 1985, 276).

qatû II "to come to an end", OA also "to chop"(?); + OA

G 1. OA lit. *ša Amurrê kīma appīšunu šamāṭim išaršunu aq-tí-i* OA Sarg. 57 "the *penis*(*es*?) of the Amorites I chopped as if cutting their noses". Cf. Sem. QṬʿ "to cut off, break off" (Stol apud Hecker 2001, 59; Alster/Oshima 2007, 15; Kouwenberg 2015, 169), s. also *qāṭû* "woodcutter" and *qettāʾu* "cane cutter" (Aram. lw. in LB). Alternatively, *išaršunu* may derive from *išrum* "a scarf or belt" (s. Kouwenberg 2015, 168f.)

2. OA *warḫam u* 2 *ūmē i-qá-tí-ma kaspam išaqqal* kt j/k 60: 6–7 quot. in Veenhof 1995/96, 15 "(he will pay (back) the silver when a month and two days have ended".

D 1. OB lit. *ú-qá-at-tu-ú zikra* AnSt 33, 146: 10 "they ceased speaking" (Mayer in Deller/Mayer/Oelsner 1989, 272).

2. MB *ina ḫušaḫ ramānišu kimtašu li-qat-ti* Sumer 38, 125 v 3 (= Paulus 2014, 557 MNA 4) "he shall ruin his family through his own hunger" (Mayer in Deller/Mayer/Oelsner 1989, 272).

Št 1. OB lit. *i nu-⌜uš-ta⌝-aq-ti nēpištu*! *râmimma* CUSAS 10, 12: 7 "let us complete the deed(!) of love-making".

2. OB lit. [*āta*]*kkul libbika šu-ta-aq-ti-a-am ina ṣēriya* ZA 75, 204: 120 "let the constant consummation of your desire come to completion in me!"

3. *eqlam lu-uš-ta-aq-ti* ARM 26/1, 259 no. 94: 11 "I shall have the field finished".

NJCK (G), MPS (G, Št), JW (D)

qātu "hand", pl. *qātātu* "guarantee"

1. OB *qa-ta-tim uddanninūšum* [*šū*]*ma* 1/3 MA.NA *kaspam ša qa-ti-šu ugdammer* FM 9, 71: 36 "they increased(?) the guarantee for him, and [he] spent 1/3 mina of silver himself out of his own pocket".

2. *qá-at-ka-ma bāʾiʾat* ARM 28, 1 r. 15, s. SAD 1, 24 *bâʾu* I e, f.

3. "Conditions" (of weather):

a) [*išt*]*ū ūmū iṭṭebûma qa-tum ištaḫnu* MARI 6, 339: 82 "[aft]er the weather has become good and the conditions have become warm (again)".

b) *lāma kuṣṣim appiš qa-*[*t*]*um šaḫnat* ARM 28, 104: 27 "before the winter, when conditions are (still) warm".

c) J.-R. Kupper, ARM 28 p. 153, transl. "les circonstances sont propices", but the two refs. show that *šaḫānu* is not used metaphorically but has to be taken literally as "warm", said of weather.

4. "list" (s. CAD Q 197 mng. 14): OB *qá-ti tamkārī awīlum* PN *išmēma umma šuma tamkārī ša pī qá-ti annītim am-*

mīni lā tugammeramma ittīya lā innamrū AbB 13, 130: 8, 12 "the gentleman PN has seen the list of merchants and said the following: 'why have you not assembled the merchants according to this list, and (why) did they not meet with me?'" (s. the comm. ib. p. 117).

5. *q. leqû* "to advocate for, intercede on s.o.'s behalf": OB *ana annītim ḫiṭītim ša ublam qá-ta-ti-ia ittī* DN *liqî'a* AbB 13, 164: 6 "for this sin which I commited, intercede for me with DN"; *inūma qá-ta-t[i-i]a telteqî* ib. 8 "as soon as you have interceded for me" (letter to a goddess).

6. With loc. "by one's own hand": Nuzi *emūqa lā elqēmi qà-tu4-šu-ma-mi iddinumi* IM 70801: 10 "'I have not taken (the donkeys) by force – he gave (them to me) himself'" (cit. Deller in id./Mayer/Oelsner 1989, 266).

7. OB *qāti* in prepositional use mng. "in accordance with":
a) URUDU.ŠÁR.A *damqam qá-ti kārim ... idnaššumma* AbB 11, 153: 17 "give him good copper alloy in accordance with the market".
b) 2 *wardī* 2 *amātī qá-tim ālim šāmam šūbilam* N 1182: 21 "buy me 2 male and 2 female slaves according to (the price set by) the city and send them to me" (cit. AbB 11 p. 99 n. 153b, photo https://cdli.ucla.edu/P276333).

8. For add. Mari refs. s. Charpin 1989–90, 101–3.

qatûtu "finishing, result"

MB *qá-tu-tum ša ibaš[š]û* [...] JCS 37, 137, no. 5: 3 "the result that occurred" (Richter 1992).

qaṭṭā'a s. *gaddā'u*

qaṭû "to approach, to wander about"; + NA?; Aram. lw.

1. NA [*umm*]*i šarre bēliya iq-ṭi-ú* SAA 13, 188 r. 6 "[who(?) ...] approached(?) [the moth]er of the king, my lord".

2. NB *bēlī lumaššir li-qeṭ-ṭu* OIP 114, 80: 26 "may the lord release (the silver) and may he (the slave) (freely) wander about". Pace Cole 1996, 171, prefix *li-* speaks for G rather than D. The spelling with *ṭu* favors a lw. from Aram. (pace Abraham/Sokoloff 2011, 46f.). The text has another Aram. lw. in l. 22, s. *qubbulu*.

+ **qa'u** "mng. unkn."; NA

[*i*]*na muḫḫi qa-'i iḫturup karṣīya ikkal* SAA 19, 91 r. 22 "he slandered me earlier because of ...". M. Luukko ib. p. 96: = *qi''u*, "because of envy". But *qi'u* "envious, jealous person" CAD Q 285 is with AHw. 1584 rather *qin'u*.

qa'u s. also *qû*

qawali s. *qawili*

qawili, + *kabilli* "designation of a vessel", Hurr. word

OB Alal. *ka-bi-il-le-na* AlT 127: 3, s. Richter 2012, 187f.

qawu s. *qû*.

qayyalu "taciturn; pious; attentive, eager"

LB PN: [f]*Qa-a-a-al-*[*tu4*?] OECT 10, 215: 14 (Oelsner in Deller/Mayer/Oelsner 1989, 277).

qayyātu "tiger nut; a mixture of roasted barley and tiger nut"

1. OB *kīma qa-a-ia-tum ana zērim lā illaku* RATL L.T. 3 v 29' "like *q.* does not sprout (the seed of PN shall not rise)".

2. OB 4 SÌLA *qa-ia-tum* KTT 89: 7, 10 "4 l of *q*." (as travel provisions on a ship).

3. MB Emar [z]i.da*qa-i-ti* Emar 6/3, 460: 32 "*q*.-flour" (Pentiuc 2001, 144f.).

4. LB *ša qa-a-a-at*meš OECT 9, 60: 11 (among foodstuffs).

5. LB *qēme qa-a-a-tum* dubsar 3, 156: 40; *qa-a-*[(*a*)-*tum*] ib. 26.

6. S. extensively Dornauer 2018, 95–139. S. also AHw. 1179 s.v. *šaqqājūtu* (von Soden 1985, 276 "enthülste Gerste") and CAD K s.v. *ka'ātu*.

qebēru, *qabāru* "to bury"

G 1. OA *ana pani qubūrim ša ašar abūni qá-áb-ru-ni* AKT 6A, 273: 35' "in front of the grave where our father is buried".
2. (you never send me even a single shekel of silver) *inūmi ina bubūtim amūtu ina kaspim ta-qá-bé-ra-ni* kt a/k 478b: 13 "are you going to bury me with silver (only) after I have died from hunger?", quot. in Veenhof 1998, 127 n. 22.

+ Š 1. OB *mala šu-uq-bu-ru ušālšu* FM 8, 110 no. 32: 10 "I repeatedly asked him about (the silver) that he had had buried".
2. OB *têrētim ana kurull*[*im*] *qa-ba-ri-im ušēpiš* ARM 26/1, 564 no. 263: 13 "I had omens taken for the burying of the (corpse) heap" (Charpin 1989–90, 103a).

N 1. OA (as long as she lives she will stay in PN's house) *ina bētim ša* PN-*ma ta-qá*!(ŠA)-*be-er* Sadberk no. 28: 8 "(and) she will be buried in PN's house as well" (s. Veenhof 2017b).

NJCK (G, N), JW (Š), MPS (Š)

+ **qēbiru** "undertaker"; OB, SB

1. OB lit. *libbi erṣetim qé-*⌜*bi*⌝*-ir-ti-šu iṣṣa*<*ba*>*at* CUSAS 32, 7o vi 12 // *qé-*⌜*bi*⌝*-i*[*r-ti-šu*] CUSAS 32, 8i iii 5 "it seized the heart of the earth, its undertaker".

2. SB *mūtānū ina māti ibbaššû nišū qé-bi-ra* [*ul iraššû*] AfO 26, 54 r. 11 "there will be pestilence in the country, the people [will have no] undertaker" (Richter 1992).

qēmītu "female (flour) grinder"

1. LB (dates, rations for) *qé-me-tum ša* GN *ša qāt* PN *rab amīlāti ša* PN2 *sepīri ša qé-me-tum* Jursa 1999, 152 BM 42353: 1, 3 "the female grinders of GN, under the responsibility of PN, the supervisor of the female slave girls, for the scribe of the female grinders".

2. LB *sepīri ša qé*!*-me-e-*⌜*tum*⌝ Abraham 2004, 71: 5.

3. In AHw. 479 s.v. *kimtu* 2c.

qēmu "flour"

1. OA *naruq qé-ma-am ša ta-ba-lá-tim* VS 26, 124: 7 "a 'sack' of flour for making(?) *tabalātum*"; s. also AKT 9A, 18: 32.

2. OB PN *ša qé-mi* ARM 7, 127: 4 (s. MARI 2, 80) "PN, in charge of flour" (Charpin 1989–90, 103a).

3. Pl.: OB *qé-me-šu-nu ī*[*šû*] FM 3, 278 no. 133: 12 "th[ey] have their flour".

NJCK (1), JW (2), MPS (3)

qēmû (CAD Q 209) s. *qēmītu*.

****qerbâ** (CAD Q 210 "inside")

The passage ARM 12, 121: 25 is perhaps to be understood as a quote or saying: "for five days (it's being said) 'stay near (*qé-er-ba-a*) the well, the fire is coming!'" (Durand 1997, 383–5 no. 660 following Charpin 1989–90, 103a). Spelling, syntax, and context render a hapax *qerbâ*/*ā* with an unexplained adverbial suffix unlikely.

qerbetu "environs, meadowland"

1. OB lit. *ballat qé-er-bé-tum ina dāmīšunu* FM 14 iii 6 "the environs are soaked with their blood".

2. SB *ukannīka qer-bet kīma ummika* SpTU 2, 21: 19 "(the steppe begot you as if it were your father), the meadow nourished you as if it were your mother"; *muttallik qer-bé-e-tú* ib. 20 "who roams the meadows" (Mayer in Deller/Mayer/Oelsner 1989, 272).

3. For the refs. AHw. *qerbetu* 2e = CAD *qarbātu*, Parpola in SAA 1 p. 224 and SAA 5 p. 233 suggests the mng. "personally(?)".

qerbiš "nearby, promptly"

1. OB [...] *birīt* PN *u awil* GN [*šakn*]*ā ulāšuma qé-er-bi-iš-ma panam iršê* ARM 26/2, 180 no. 372: 22 "[the terms?] between PN and the man from GN are established. If not, they will soon be finalized" (Charpin 1989–90, 103; Heimpel 2003, 325f., Mayer 2017, 32).

2. *atta tīdē kīma qé-*⸢*er*⸣*-bi-iš bīt āl* GN *bītum maṭû* RATL 173: 12 "you know that nearby, the house in the town of GN – the house is wretched".

qerbu "inside"

1. OAkk *in qir-bí-su* CUSAS 27, 245 r. 3 "(the fuller inspected the wool:) from among it (2 1/3 minas are assigned for making donkey reins).

2. Del. the ref. BE 15, 184: 12 cit. CAD Q 226, mng. 4, read *I-na-É-kur-taš-man-ni* (Sommerfeld 1990, 31).

qerbû "inner, middle"; + OA

1. OA *ina*/*ana mātim qé-er-bi-tim* AKT 3, 45: 11 and 12; *ana mātim qé-er-bi-tim* kt v/k 89: 7, s. Günbattı 1995, 109 and Dercksen 2001, 58 n. 105.

2. OA unclear: *ṣí-li-a-*<*nu*>? *qé-er-bi*$_4$*-ú-tum* AKT 9A, 167: 10 "the middle containers"? NJCK

****qerdu** s. *gerdu*

qerēbu "to come near"

G 1. OA stative *qurub* (GOA § 7.2.3, s. also *qurbu* adj. in CAD Q 215a s.v. *qerbu* adj. 2):

a) *kasapka qú-ru-ub mimma libbaka lā iparrid* Prag 483: 25 "your silver is close, do not worry at all!".

b) *ḫarrānī qú-ur-ba-at* AKT 6A, 129: 53 "my business trip is imminent".

c) *lū awâtum qú-u*[*r*]*-ba lū awâtum dannā* AKT 4, 66: 6 "whether the matters are urgent or whether the matters are serious".

Gt OB lit. *šun*[*ātu*]*m qì-it-ru-ba* Gilg. OB Nippur 2 "dreams are quite near".

Š NB *emūq ša šarru ú-šaq-rib* SAA 17, 67 r. 9 "the force that the king led".

NJCK (G), MPS (Gt, Š)

qerītu "banquet, invitation"

1. OB lit. *uštēṣī'am*! ⸢*qé*⸣*-ri-i-tam* AML 27: 11 "I made an invitation go out" (referring to the scent coming from the fermentation vat?).

2. OB (flour) *ana qé-ri-it kinātēšu* Tell ed-Dēr 153: 25 "for the banquet of his colleagues" (Richter 1992).

3. For the *q.* festival or sacrifice s. Jacquet 2011, 59f. with disc. and refs.

qermu "a garment, cloak?"

1. NA *qer-me* GE$_6$ *za-ki-u* StAT 3, 1: 12 "(one) pure black *q.*"; *qer-me* GÙN ib. 23 "(seven) multi-colored *q.*".

2. Pl. *qerāmū*: 1-*en* ^{túg}*qé-er-mu šá-tú-e* 1-*en ša kitê* ... 2 ^{túg}*qé-ra-a-mu* SpTU 4, 128: 22 ... 91 "1 woven *q.* garment, 1 made of linen ... (together) 2 *q.* garments".

3. LB 1-*en* ⌜^{túg}⌝*qé-er-mu* AOAT 222, 42: 13 "1 *q.*-garment"

qersu "part of the wooden frame of a canopy"; + OB

1. OB lit. *ūm gimkim qe-er-su-ú iššak-kanū* 1 *imērum iddâk ilū u enūt*[*um*] *ina libbi* ⌜*qé*!-*er*!⌝-*si*! *uṣṣû ilum ana bītišu šarrum ana* ⌜*ēkallišu*⌝ *illak* FM 3, 68 no. 4 ii 8–12, s. Fleming 2000a, 490f. "on the day of the *g.* ritual the canopy frames will be installed. 1 donkey will be killed. The gods and the utensils leave the canopy frames. (Each) god will go to his temple, the king will go to his palace". CAD Q 270 *qirsû* "mng. unkn.". Pace Charpin 1989–90, 105, not *kirṣû* "lump of clay".

2. OB *šuddun ḫu-u*[*r-pa-tim* ...] *qadūm* ^{giš}*qé-er-si-ša* ARM 27, 124 r. 5 "to let deliver the ca[nopy ...] together with its wooden frame".

3. a) OB 1 *ḫurpatum rabītum* 16 *awīlū* 10 ^{giš}*qé-er-su* 20 *awīlū* 5 *muzzazzū* 5 *awīlū* 14 *murudû* 2 *awīlū* ŠU.NIGIN 43 *awīlū ša ḫurpatim rabītim* FM 3, 65 M.6873 "1 big canopy, 16 men; 10 tent frames, 20 men; 5 posts, 5 men; 14 lattices, 2 men. Together: 43 men for the big canopy".
b) 10 ^{giš}*qé-er-su* 3 *murudû* 2 *awīlū našû* FM 3, 66 (unpublished) "10 wooden frames, 3 lattices. 2 men carry (them)".

4. AHw. 1584 *q.* 2; AHw. 918 "ein hölzerner Verschlag"; CAD 269 *qirsu* A "a sacred area", B "a wooden object", and *qirsû* are the same word; s. May 2010. The word was hith. only attested in NA, prompting a connection to Aram. *ʿarīs*, cf. Arab. *ʿarīšah* (Deller in id./Mayer/Oelsner 1989, 263).

qeršu I "strip (of meat, dough, leather, fabric)"

AHw. 918 s.v. *qeršu*, CAD Q 270 *qiršu* A and B.

qeršu II "a payment"; OB
CAD Q 217 s.v. *qiršu* C. Possibly identical with *qeršu* I.

1. OB (silver for PNN) *aššum qé-er-ša-am lā imḫurū* BagM 21, 187 no. 132: 9 "because they did not receive the *q.*".

2. *ana* GN *nikšudma* [*u*] *qí-ir-ša-am ana rēdî* [*n*]*iddin* M.8196 (cit. Charpin 1989–90, 105) "we arrived in GN and gave the soldiers *q.*".

3. *qí-ir-ša-am u*[*l īšū*] ARM 33, 3: 24 "they have no *q.*"

qerû "to invite, to summon"

G SB (resin) *qé-ri* (var. *qé-*⌜*e-ri*⌝) *ilī rabûtim* YOS 11, 23: 5 // RA 38, 87: 7 "that summons the great gods" (Mayer in Deller/Mayer/Oelsner 1989, 273).

+ D 1. SB ^{lú}ḪAL *tu-qar-ra-ma* Or. 57, 147 r. 10 "(then) you call the diviner" (Mayer in Deller/Mayer/Oelsner 1989, 273).
2. LB *ana qur-ru-ú naptanu* YOS 17, 351: 4 "(vessels) for an invitation to a meal" (Or. 57 p. 163). Cf. AHw. 930a s.v. *qurrû* "zusammengerufen (?)".

qīʾāpu "to believe; to entrust"

D MB Bogh. *attunu lā tù-qa-a*[*p*(-*pa*)] KUB 3, 47: 7 "you shall not believe" (von Soden 1985, 276).

+ **Št 1.** OB *ittī tamkārim ina* GN *annākam šu-ta-qí-ip-ma* FM 1 p. 128: 30 "acquire the tin on credit from a merchant in GN"; *uš-ta-qa-ap-pa-am-ma* ib. 33 "I will acquire (the tin) on credit" (Charpin 1989–90, 96; Mayer 2017, 32).
2. S. Streck 2003a, 125 (Št is caus. to pass. N).

qīʾāšu "to bestow"

G 1. SB *qa-a-a-i-šat balāṭi* Sumer 38, 126: 8 (= Paulus 2014, 558 MNA 4) "(DNf) who bestows life" (reading after Sommerfeld 1990, 31).
2. Del. the PN Marduk-*ta-qi-šu* (BE 14, 32: 7 cit. CAD Q 161a ad 2c2'), read [x x] ᵈMarduk TA ⌜ITI⌝?.DU₆?.KÙ (Sommerfeld 1990, 31).

D SB *kurunnu napšat nišī ú-qa-a-šú kala dadmē* Jiménez 2017, 248: 14 "I bestow upon all inhabitants fine beer, the life of land".

qību "command, declaration"

LB PN: *Ina-qí-bi*-DN SpTU 1, 128: 1, 12 (Oelsner in Deller/Mayer/Oelsner 1989, 280).

qiddatu "downstream, downward direction"

On *qiddat ūmi* "afternoon" s. Streck 2017, 603.

+ **qiddūtum** "bulge"; OB

bīt PN *ša ina panītimma qí-du-*[*tam illik*]*u* ARM 26/1, 499 no. 243: 6 "the house of PN which ⌜developed a bulge⌝ some time ago" (Charpin 1989–90, 104; transl. Heimpel 2003, 269).

+ **qidmē** "in front of"; OAkk.

1. Ebla lex. IGI.ME = *gi-ti-ma-a* MEE 4 p. 357, 128, s. Steinkeller 1984; Krebernik 1984, 165f.

2. IGI^{me} DN *izzâz* FAOS 7, Rim C 9: 15 "(his statue) stands before DN"; sim. Frag 3 I 2; MAM 3 p. 319 no. 12: 6;

3. PN *wāšib* IGI^{me}-*śù* FAOS 7, MŠ 8: 6 "PN, his courtier".

4. ITI *Baḫir* IGI^{me} PBS 9, 119: 4; AS 17, 20: 6 "the first/earlier month Bahir".

Cf. AHw. s.v. *qadmu*, *qudmu*, CAD s.v. *qudmu*.

****qilāsātu** s. *Kilaʾūtu*

Read *KI-la-ú-tim* in all refs. (MARI 2, 96; Charpin 1989–90, 104a; von Soden 1985, 277).

qilpu "skin, peel; bark for tanning?"; + Ur III

1. Ur III 1 *kuš udu qí-il-pu-um* CUSAS 3, 892: 1 "1 bark-tanned sheep-skin". S. Sallaberger 2011, 358.

2. OB *ḫazannu qí-il-pu-um* FM 2, 25 no. 4: 4 "(15 liters of) *ḫazannu*-onion skins" (in list of vegetables and spices).

NR (1), MPS (2)

qiltu "a lye plant"; + MA

MA ᵘ*qi-il-ta* SI^{meš} StAT 5, 11: 2 "*q.* (with) 'horns'"; *qi-il-*⌜*tu*⌝ *qarnānû* 41: 8 "*q.*, sprouted".

qilûtu s. also *kiqillatu*

qimmatu "tuft (of hair), plume; crown of a tree"

1. a) OB lit. *šakān qí-im-ma-tim mēlul pērēte* Streck/Wasserman 2018, 17 i 38 "setting of hair, whirling of locks (is yours, Ištar)".

b) *surru qí-*⸢*ma*⸣*-ti šārta* ib. i 47 "letting the locks dance, the hair".

2. MA 6 *qi-im-ma-tu ša tabarre* [SUMUN] MARV 4, 138: 16 and pass. "6 tufts of old red wool" (for wrapping or decorating royal weapons), s. Dercksen 2005b, 123–125.

3. SB *qim-mat* // SUḪUR Jiménez 2017, 248: 4 (cf. also *qim-mat* ib. 254: 52), cf. *wasāmu*.

4. Instead of *qí-im-ma-*[*ti-ia*] (CAD Q 253 *qimmatu* 1a), read in Gilg. MB Megiddo r. 1 *di-im-ma-*[*tu*?], s. George 2003, 346.

qinītu I "acquisition, property (acquired through royal grants)"

1. NA *ammar qí-ni-su-u-ni issēšu* BagM 24, 220: 20 "as much property (acquired through royal grants) as is with him (belongs to DNN)".

2. S. Deller 1991.

qinītu II "rival, concubine"

qí-ni-tú/tum Lambert 1975, 102/4 ii 2', 21'; iii 19. S. Edzard 1987, 59f.

qinnatu "anus"

1. Dual: Lex. *ku-du-ĝu*$_{10}$ = *qí-in-na-ta-a-a* CUSAS 12 p. 150: 25 (Ugumu) "my buttocks".

2. Of sheep: OB lit. *qí-in*!*-na-tum* Fs. Geller 132 i 14 (list of sheep body parts).

qinnazu "whip; a work unit"

1. OB PN *ša* PN$_2$ … *ana* ^{kuš}ÙSAN *iṣbatu wuššer* AbB 13, 46: 25 "release PN, whom PN$_2$ has seized for a *q.*-unit".

2. S. *kapālu*.

qinnu, + *qīnu* "nest; family; guild"

1. SB *qinnu šapiltu* SAA 3, 30: 3 "lowly family".

2. NA "guild": *qí-in-nu gabbu ša ṣarrā-pī* AfO 32 p. 43: 27 "the entire guild of goldsmiths" (Deller in id./Mayer/Oelsner 1989, 263).

3. Var. *qīnu*: NA PN *ša qi-i-ni* PN$_2$ SAA 5, 93: 7 "PN of the family of PN$_2$".

4. NA writing ^{lú}*qin* StAT 2, 81: 15.

5. Fem. pl. NB 2 ⸢*ù*⸣ [3?] ^{lú}*qin-na-a-ti ana pan aḫīya illakā* OIP 114, 1: 24 "2 or [3?] families will come to my brother".

S. also *qanānu*.

MPS (1, 3), JW (2, 5), JK (4)

qīnu, *qin'u* "jealousy, envy"; + OA

1. OA *i-qi-in-im aššumi tappā'išu naš<p>ertam uštēbilam* AKT 5, 18: 12 "(do not think:) Out of jealousy he sent me a letter about his partner".

2. OA *ūmam ina qí-in-e-em ša ebāruttī'a lā al-té-e* AKT 11A, 95: 38 "nowadays, I can no longer manage as a result of the envy of my colleagues".

3. SB *ina* U$_4$ 8 DN [x (x)] *ša qí-na-i uṣṣī* Emar 6/3, 446: 107 "on the 8th day – DN […] of envy goes out" (s. Pentiuc 2001, 149). Alternatively *ša ki-na-i* "of Canaan" (Fleming 2000, 169f.).

4. SB *riddu qí-nu elī aḫḫīya ittabikma ša ilānī umašširūma* RINAP 4, Esarh. 1 i 23 "persecution (and) envy fell upon my brothers and they forsook (the will) of the gods" (s. Frahm 2009).

5. The OA refs. render a loan from Aram. as proposed by von Soden 1977, 193 doubtful (Cherry 2016, 285). For a possible Sum. equivalent *nimin* s. Civil 1990 (with Frahm 2009, 37–39).

6. Cf. SB *qenû* "to be jealous" (CAD Q 209f.) and NA *qi'(')u* < *qin'u* (CAD Q 285a s.v. *qi'u*). JW (1, 3–6), NJCK (2)

qīptu "belief; office; loan, credit"

1. NA *qip-tú ša ēkalle lū karānu lū kaspu* WVDOG 94, 17: 1 "loan of the palace, be it wine, be it silver", also ib. 10 (Deller in id./Mayer/Oelsner 1989, 263, s. also 267).

2. LB (silver) *ana* KIB-*tum ša lā baṭ?-lu? u? ana tamṭītum ša* ⌜*immer*⌝ *ginê* Iraq 43, 133 AB 244: 6 "for a loan without interruption (?) for partial payment of regular-offering sheep", alternatively *kibtu* "wheat" (Oelsner in Deller/Mayer/Oelsner 1989, 281).

qīpu "trustworthy (person)"

1. OB PN *u* 2 *qí-pa-ni* PN CUSAS 36, 78: 20 "PN and 2 trustees of PN"

2. LB DUMU [lú]*qí-i-pi* OECT 10, 399: 29 (Oelsner in Deller/Mayer/Oelsner 1989, 281).

qīpūtu "trust"

1. OB *kīmā tupšar* MAR.TU *qí-pu-ti yâttum ul leqêt* ARM 27, 151: 10 "how does the scribe of the Amorites not trust me (lit. has taken my trust)?"

2. [*q*]*i-pu-ti ul teleqqê* ib. 11 "you do not trust me".

+ **qiqû** "an animal?"; NA

[... *a'īlu*] *ša bīt kūdini* [...] *a'īlu ša bīt qi-qi-i* SAA 15, 332: 5 "either a 'mule-house man' or a '*q*.-house man' (shall come to me)" in broken context. Von Soden (1985, 277) suggests a connection to *qaqû* "a bird".

qirīru "wick"

1. SB ⌜*qi*⌝*-ri-ru u nūru* KAL 9, 53 r. 4 "wick and light" (*tākultu* ritual).

2. In 3R 66 x 32 cit. CAD Q 268 (= SAA 20, 40 r. iv 32') read *qí-ri-ru* (Deller in id./Mayer/Oelsner 1989, 263).

3. S. *qarāru* "to writhe", "to coil, twist".

qirmu s. *qermu*

qirnātu s. *qurnātu*

+ **qirratu**, *qerretu* "leftovers, scrap"; OAkk; OB

1. Oakk *qir-ra-at* KÙ.GI OSP 2, 19: 1; 22: 12 (s. ib. p. 43) "leftover gold".

2. OB (8 1/3 minas of silver for plating lances: 8 minas and 9 shekel are the finished work) 5 GÍN! *ribbatum* 6 GÍN! ⌜*qé-er-re*⌝*-tum* ARM 25, 194 = ARM 32 p. 329 A.4540: 9 "5 shekel are the (unused) remainder, 6 shekel are scrap".

3. OB *qé-er-re-tum* (of gold) BagM 21, 138 no. 89: 10.

4. S. Arkhipov 2012, 63f. with disc. and add. refs. The word may derive from *qarāru* in the meaning "to overflow", also said of molten metal. This would then refer to spillage occurring during the casting process.

qirsu s. *qersu*

****qirsû** (CAD Q 270) s. *qersu*

qīrtu s. *qīru*

qīru, + *qīrtu* "hot bitumen"

1. OB PN *qí-ir-ti meḫret dimtim iškun-ma u išātam ina libbi qí-ir-ti ippuḫma dimtum imqut* ARM 26/2, 83 no. 318: 9–13 "PN placed bitumen in front of a tower and then lit a fire in the middle of the bitumen and the tower collapsed" (Charpin 1989–90, 105).

2. NA *ina pūti ūmāte ša atta qi-ru ta-ṣu-u-ni* CTN 3, 46: 6 "in return for the work days on which you … bitumen" (Deller in id./Mayer/Oelsner 1989, 263 emends *ta-ṣu-<lu>-u-ni* in view of *li-ṣu-lu* in the following sentence. The mng. of either reading remains unclear.)

3. S. Stol 2011–2013b; 2012, 57.

qiššû "a melon, a cucumber"

S. Stol 1987a.

qīštiš "to the forest"; + OB

OB lit. *niqterib qí-iš-ti-iš* Gilg. OB Nippur 1 "we have come close to the forest".

qīštu I, *qīltu* "gift"

1. OA (silver) *inūmi* PN (…) *aššassu ēḫuzu ana aššitišu qí-iš-tám addin* "when PN married his wife, I gave silver as a wedding gift to his wife" kt 88/k 340: 13, s. Bayram/Kuzuoğlu 2015, 33–35 with add. refs.

2. For add. Mari refs. s. Charpin 1989–90, 105.

3. LB *qí-il-ta-a* dubsar 3, 160: 21.

4. The two OA instances cit. CAD Q 277a s.v. *qīštu* 2a belong to *g/k/qištu*, an agricultural product, s. *Kištu*.

NJCK (1, 4), MPS (2–3)

qīštu II "forest"

OB *qí-[š]a-a-tim ša* GN FM 2, 162 no. 87: 6 "forests of GN", s. *gušūru*.

qīšu I "granted, oblate"

1. OB (grain) *ana qí-iš* PN ARM 23, 410 no. 465: 3 "as a gift for PN" (Charpin 1989–90, 105).

2. LB PN lú?*qí-ši-šú ša* PN_2 dubsar 3, 67: 28 "PN, oblate of PN_2".

qīšu II, *qēšu* "forest, thicket"

With *ē*: SB *ina qé-e-š[i]* Jiménez 2017, 166 Ia 2.

qitmu "chrome alum, black alum"

1. OB lit. *qit!-ma šaptāšu kalûm panūšu* AML 51: 7 "black paste are its lips, yellow-ochre paste is its face", s. *qí-it-ma šaptāš[u]* ib. 50: 19.

2. OB *innuḫaram qí-it-ma-[am] u šammam pālišam ina panīšunu liššûnim* ARM 26/1, 298 no. 134: 8 "they must supply white alum, black alum, and drill-emery as soon as possible"; s. also no. 297: 7, 12 (Charpin 1989–90, 105).

3. *q.* is probably chrome alum (black alum) which is used in leather tanning. While itself purplish-black in color, it is not a dye (pace CAD and AHw), although it can be used as a mordant.

4. The mng. "black discoloration" (CAD Q 282) is doubtful, the ref. ARM 13, 18 cit. ib. likely belongs to *kitmu*.

qītu "end"

OB [*adī*] *qí-it* ITI 1-*kam* ARM 26/2, 83 no. 320: 7 "until the end of the first month".

qû I "thread, string"

1. OB lit. *i-qí-im tušēšibanni* ALL no. 1 ii 10 "you have made me sit (tied) in a string".

2. OB lit. (holding spindles) *ina uṣṣi līli iddû qú-a-ti* Or. 87, 20 ii 18 "they throw threads into the spread of the evening" (Streck/Wasserman 2018, 20).

3. SB *išpartu unūt qé-e-šú ušarsad kalāma* Jiménez 2017, 250: 18 "the female weaver fastens all her weaving (lit. thread) tools".

4. LB in list of pieces of meat: ⸢uzu⸣[*q*]*u*-⸢*ú ša immeri*⸣ Jursa 1999, 181 BM

42425+: 3 "a sheep's sinew(?)". S. Jursa ib. p. 67.

qû II, + *qa'u*, + *qawu*, + *qu'u*? "a measurement, litre; a measuring vessel"

1. OA 7 *qú-a-tim kirānam* kt a/k 1060: 20 "7 *q*.-measures of wine" (quot. Dercksen 1996, 232).

2. OB a measurement: GIŠ *ša* n *ammatu u* n *qa-a* ARM 23, 547 no. 581: 3 and pass. "trees, n cubits (in length) and n *q*. (thick)" (von Soden 1985, 277); A.1863 (Charpin 1989–90, 105).

3. OB "a vessel":

a) 1 *qa-wu-um* ARM 31, 344 no. 7: 12.
b) 1 ^{gal}*qa-ú* KÙ.BABBAR AWTL 115: 16. S. Guichard 2005, 287–8.

4. MB Emar

a) ^{dug}*qú-'u-u* Emar 6/3, 369: 4; 2 *qú-'u-ú* ib. 93 "2 *q*. (of second-quality beer)"; 6/3, 306: 11.
b) [x x] ^{dug}*qú-a-ta* Emar 6/3, 306: 12.
c) Alternatively a NWSem. lw. *ku'u*, cf. Ugar. *kw* "a recipient, a measure" and Off. Aram. *k'* "a certain measure of capacity" (Pentiuc 2001, 105).

5. SB *qu-ú Šamši* Jiménez 2017, 34 "cup of Šamaš", s. *ḫī'āqu* Š.

6. NA [*l*]*aḫannī ša ḫurāṣe ša* [n] SÌLA!-*a-a* SAA 13, 134: 18 "golden bottles holding [n] litres each".

NJCK (1), JW (2–4), MPS (5–6)

qû III "copper"

1. OB lit. *qé-e dibbāšu* CUSAS 10, 1: 28 "its twin panels were copper".

2. S. Mayer in Deller/Mayer/Oelsner 1989, 274.

qubbâtu, + *qubbūtu* "mourning, wailing?"

1. NA *qu-bu-tu ina qabli ālešu* AfO 21, 44 pl. 8 (VAT 9968): 16 "there was wailing in the town" (s. Bloch 2013, diff. Deller in id./Mayer/Oelsner 1989, 265).

2. S. AHw. *qu*(*b*)*batu*, CAD Q s.v. *qubbātu* "mng, unkn." The ref. ABL 988 is now SAA 5, 156. For disc. s. Bloch 2013 (< *qubbû* "lamentation"). Diff. Cherry 2016, 209f., who discusses a connection to Aram. *qbb* "to suffer fever, to shiver feverishly".

+ **qub(b)û?**, pl. *qub*(*b*)*i'ānu* "a vessel?"; MB Emar

1. 3 *qú-bi-ia-nu* KÙ.GI Emar 6/3, 282: 8, cf. 3 "3 golden *q*.".

2. 1 *kutmu* ḪÉ LA BI *ina libbišu* 3 *qú-bi-ia-nu* KÙ.GI CunMon. 13, 25: 17 "1 cover of …, in its centre 3 golden *q*."

3. 2 *qú-bi-ia-nu* KÙ.GI *ša paššūrim* AulaOr. (Suppl.) 1, 97: 2 "2 golden *q*. for the table" (listed among vessels).

4. Pentiuc 2001, 107 rejects a connection to *quppu* II based on the spelling indicating a III/weak root. Assuming *-ānu* to be a pl. ending, we propose a connection to NWSem. *qb'* "cup, goblet" (s. DNWSI 983; DUL 681 s.v. *qb't*). Cf. *qupāḫu* and *qabūtu*.

qubbulu "to accept"; + NB; Aram. lw.

1. NB *sarrūti lu-qab-bil-ma luddâkka* OIP 114, 60: 28 "I will take the criminals and give (them) to you".

2. NB *adû amīlu šū akanna ina qāt* PN *apṭurušu anāku ú-qa-ba-al-šú* OIP 114, 80: 22 "now I will take the man whom I ransomed here from PN".

3. On etym. s. Kogan/Krebernik 2021, 441 (cf. Syr. *qabbel*; Aram. *qbl*, DNWSI 979).

****qubburu** (CAD Q, 292) s. *qebēru* D (von Soden 1985, 277; Richter 1992, 21).

qubirtu s. also *qubrūtu*

\+ **qubrūtu** "an underground structure?"; MB

1. *qú-ub-ru-tum ša* PN Ekalte 63: 3 "*q.* of PN".

2. (a vineyard and) *qú-ub-ru-tu ša* ^{giš}KIRI$_6$.GEŠTIN Ekalte 94: 2 "the *q.* of the vineyard"

3. Mayer 2001 translates "Begräbnisstätte", but the association with a vineyard suggests that this is a commercially or agriculturally used structure. Perhaps underground storage?

qubūru, + *qubāru* "grave, tomb; funerary gift"; + OAkk; + OA

1. Early OB PN *ana abu abīka ana abīka qú-bu-ra-am ušābil* AS 22, 15 r. 3 "PN sent a funerary gift for your grandfather (and) your father". S. also 11: 27.

2. Early OB *ana ṣūbāti qú-bu-ri-im ana leqûtim iš[pu]ršu* AS 22, 12: 21 "he sent him for the collection (?) of burial garments".

3. OA *ana tarbītim ukultim u qú-bu-ri-im ša mer'u'āt* PNf AKT 5, 40: 2 "for the costs of upbringing, the food and the tomb of the daughters of PNf"; also AKT 6A, 251: 6; AKT 8, 297: 11; TPAK 1, 212: 2; kt m/k 69: 44 (s. Hecker 2004b, 287).

4. Fem. pl. in SB *qu-bu-ra-te-šú-nu* SAA 3, 22: 10. Also *qa-bu-rat* ib. 34: 11, pace CAD Q 293 and von Soden 1991, 194, who correct *rat* to *re*.

5. SB *qu-ba-ru-šú ḫursānu* SpTU 5, 257: 17 "his grave is a mountain".

JW (1–2), NJCK (3), MPS (4, 5)

qudāsu "a ring"

Perhaps the normal Assyrian word for "earring" (s. Postgate 1994a, 224). S. Sjöberg 2003, 252f. for lex. refs. (Ebla).

quddu I "an axe, adze"

1. OB lit. *ana nūnim māḫirim qú!-du rakbūšu* CUSAS 10, 7: 6 "adzes are riding for the fish going upstream" (in parallel with *pāštu*, reading after Wasserman 2011).

2. The ref. ABL 1079: 9 cit. AHw. 926 belongs to *(q)udīni* (Deller in id./Mayer/Oelsner 1989, 264).

S. also *qundu*.

\+ **quddumu I** "advance payment"; MA

5 *qu-ud-du-mi-šu maḫir* Podany 2002, 6: 10 "5 (kor of barley) he receives as his advance".

\+ **quddumu II** "to be black as *qitmu*?"; SB

D (if the nails of her fingers/toes) *qud-du-ma* SpTU 4, 149 ii 31 "are black as *qit/dmu*(?)" (preceded by *pūṣa tukkupā* "are spotted with white dot(s))"; iv 39 (followed by *du''umā* "are dark" and *ṣalmā* "are black"). Denominated from *qitmu*, var. *qidmu* "a black dye"?

qudīni s. CAD/AHw. s.v. *udīni*

qu'ītu s. *Ku'ītu*

qulālu "discredit"; + OB

šumma ... ina puḫur ṣābim qú-la-li-šu lā aškun ARM 27, 151: 40 "I surely did not discredit him among the assembled troops" (Mayer 2017, 32).

Cf. OA *qalullā'u*.

qulēptu "scale, scaly skin; husk, bark"

1. Lex. *pa ku*$_6$ = *qu-lep-ti nūni* CUSAS 12 p. 49 iv 5 (Izi) "fish scale". S. also *qaqqû* II.

2. OB 1 GAL *ša qú-le-ep-ti* KU$_6$ KÙ.BABBAR ARM 31, 479f. no. 177

r. 15 "1 *kāsu*-cup with silver fish scales", s. ib. p. 150, 213.

3. SB *šumma izbu kīma purādi u ṣerri qú-lep-tú saḫip* SpTU 2, 38: 21 "if an anomaly is covered with scaly skin like a carp or a snake" (Mayer in Deller/Mayer/Oelsner 1989, 274).

4. LB ^{kuš}*qu-lép-du* Iraq 45, 189: 21, 44 (Oelsner in Deller/Mayer/Oelsner 1989, 282).

+ **qullānu** "an implement made of bronze"; OB

1. (bronze) *ana qúl-la-ni ša šipir ṣalam šarrim* ARM 32, 283 vi 2 (s. FM 3, 120 no. 12: 2) "for *q*. for the work on the king's statue".

2. (2 mina 2 shekel bronze) *ana* 2 *qúl-la-ni* ib. 38.

3. (1 mina of bronze) *ana* 1 *qú-ul-la-nim ša šipir šamšatim* ib. 284 vi 18 "for 1 *q*. for the work on a disk".

4. (1/2 mina 3 shekels bronze) *ana qú-ul-la-ni* ARM 21, 267: 2.

5. (bronze for) 12 *namê u* 4 *qúl-la-ni* ARM 21, 258: 26 "for 12 *n*. and 4 *q*.".

6. S. Arkhipov 2012, 135.

+ **qullītu II** "a vessel"; LB

1. 1 *qu-ul-*⸢*li*⸣*-ti* UD.KA.BAR Iraq 59, 115 no. 28: 4 "1 *q*. of bronze"

2. 1*-et qu-ul-li-tum* UD.KA.BAR BM 82607: 8 (cit. Roth 1989–1990, 27), dupl. BM 101980 (NABU 2005/51).

3. Likely backformation from the fem. pl. of *qullû*, *qulliʾu* "a bowl".

qulliʾu s. *qullû*

qullu, *qūlu* "ring"

1. OB 1 MA.NA *kaspum šīm qú-ul-li-im* VS 22, 86: 15 "1 mina of silver, the price for the *q*." (von Soden 1985, 277).

2. NB *qu-ú-*⸢*li*⸣ *kipidma* OIP 114, 35: 27 "take care of the rings!"

3. S. Postgate 1994a, 240–242.

qullû "a bowl"; + OB

OB lit. *iḫpī qú-li-a-am ša libbišu* UET 6/2, 399: 10 (ZA 75, 181) "it broke the *q*.-bowl of his heart" (Mayer 2017, 33).

qullulu "despised"

S. Deller in id./Mayer/Oelsner 1989, 264.

qullulu "to blind" s. *gullulu* II

qullupu s. *qallupu*

qulmû, *ulmu* "an axe"

1. OB 1 *qú-ul-mu-um ša kaspim* ARM 26/2, 387 no. 463 r. 9 "1 silver *q*." S. Arkhipov 2012, 122.

2. SB *qúl-ma-a ina qāt imittišu tušamšāšu* 1904-10-9, 18 r. 14 = AMD 8/2, 313ff., 8.42: 43'' "you make (the figurine) carry a *q*. in its right hand" (Mayer in Deller/Mayer/Oelsner 1989, 274).

3. SB *ina qul-mé-e qaqqassu tamaḫḫaṣ* K.2387+ r. 26 // K.5022+ r. 30 "you hit it (= the substitute image) on the head with a *q*." (Mayer in Deller/Mayer/Oelsner 1989, 274).

****qulpu B** (CAD Q 301)

In Ḫḫ XXIV 144 read *zir-pu* (Mayer in Deller/Mayer/Oelsner 1989, 274).

qulqullu "a wrapping used to package textiles or a textile itself"; OA

1. PN *qú-ul-qú-li liššīʾa* Prag 539: 29 "PN shall bring the wrapping". S. also Prag 718: 23; AKT 2, 35: 8, 13; AKT 4, 36: 20; AKT 6B, 313: 33; TPAK 1, 153: 9.

2. In "Matouš 24a": 19 quoted in CAD Q 301-2 s.v. *qulqullu* 1a end, read *qú-ul-qú-le-kà* "your *q*.s". NJCK

+ **qulqultu** "a kind of flour"; MB Emar

Lex. [NINDA.ZÍD?].IŠ *qúl-qúl-tum* Emar 6/4, 560: 103 (Ḫḫ XXXIII). Pentiuc 2001, 151 considers this word a local variant of Akk. *qalqālu* (a type of flour).

qūltu "dead of night; silence"

1. OB lit. *qù-la-tu šaknāku* CUSAS 10, 15: 43 "silence has been your lot".

2. OB (ration) *ša qú-ul-tim ša nabrî* OECT 13, 263 r. 4 "for the night-time during the *nabrû*-festival".

Cf. *qāltu*.

qumaḫḫu s. *gumāḫu*

qumāru "upper arms and shoulder section?"

MB 1 *ḫullān qú-ma-ri liqtum* AoF 24, 97: 12 "1 shoulder wrap (?) of choice quality". S. van Soldt ib. 102.

+ **qumbutu** "a building"; NA; Aram. lw.?

1. É *qu-um-bu-tú* ⌜x⌝ […] SAA 14, 63: 1.

2. […S]UHUR É *qu-um-ba-t*[*e* …] CTDS 7: 5 (cit. Cherry 2016, 2010) "adjoining the *q*.".

3. S. Cherry 2016, 210–212: Cf. Palm., JBA, Syr. *qwbh, qwbt*ʾ "pavilion, vault"? Note also the place name ^{URU}*qu-um-ba-te* SAA 14, 44: 4, 6.

qunātā "woad (*isatis tinctoria*)"; LB; Aram. lw.

LB ⌜*ina šīpāt qu-na-a-ta talammu* Fs. Lambert 170, 16: 2 (s. also 10) "you wrap (it) in woad-dyed wool". Cf. *uqnâtu*.

qundu "a plant; an implement"

The NA ref. ADD 978 (*qu-un-di erê*) might belong to *quddu* I (Deller in id./ Mayer/Oelsner 1989, 265).

qunnabu, *qunnubu* "an aromatic; cannabis, hemp?"

1. SB [^{šim}*q*]*u-nu-bu zappašu* SAA 3, 38 38 r. 11 "[h]emp is his bristle".

2. NA ŠIM *Išḫara qu-nu-bu* ZA 73 p. 252 no. 12: 2, 4 "the salve of Išḫara is hemp" (Deller in id./Mayer/Oelsner 1989, 265).

3. LB ^{šim}*qu-un-na-bu u kaṣīyātu* AOAT 414/1, 73: 14 "hemp and cassia(?)". Cf. Jursa 2009, 164 with further refs.

qunnunu "curled, coiled"

1. OA as PN: (*a-*)*Qà-nu-tim* CCT 1, 37a: 16; TCL 21, 202: 11 "the curly-haired one". Both refs. were erroneously cit. AHw. 438 s.v. *kannūtu* and CAD K 157 s.v. *kannûtu* (s. Sturm 1995 with add. refs.).

2. NA as PN: ^{f}*Qa-nu-*⌜*un*⌝*-tum* CTN 1 pl. 11 (ND 6212): 19 (Deller in id./ Mayer/Oelsner 1989, 265).

+ **qūnu** "creator"; MB Emar; NWSem. lw.

1. *Dagan qu-ni* Emar 6/3, 381: 15 "Dagan the creator" cf. 379. 5, 382: 16.

2. *Dagan bēl qu-ú-ni* Emar 6/3, 373: 88 "Dagan, lord of creation".

3. Cf. Hebr. QNH "to create". S. Feliu 2003, 239f. Diff. Pentiuc 2001, 150f. (QW/YN "to compose/sing a song of lamentation").

+ **qupāḫu** "a container"; MB Emar
In inventories of containers:

1. *qú-pa-ḫu* CunMon. 13, 27: 6.

2. *qu-pa-ḫu* Emar 6/3, 186: 9, cf. 283: 19 (of bronze).

3. J. G. Westenholz 2000, 69: Cf. Hurr. *ku-wa-ḫe* "helmet"? (s. Richter 2012, 225 with lit.); Pentiuc 2001, 150 compares NA *qabḫu* "a vessel" and NW-Sem. *qbʿ* "cup, goblet", for which s. also *qub*(*b*)*û*,

quppatu "box, basket"; + MB Emar

In description of a divine statue: (On his head 1 golden *laḫu*) *qú-pa-at-šú* KÙ.BABBAR GAR CunMon. 13, 25: 7 "his *q*. overlaid with silver".

quppu II, pl. *quppātu* "box, cage; guffa"

1. OB lit. *quppī addī eṭlam*⸢*ma*⸣ *u sukannīna luṣbat*! AOAT 267, 192 i 16–18 "I threw my cage on the young man, and may I catch the dove".

2. NB [*lū*] *qu-pu lū kalakki* SAA 18, 106: 7 "[either] a guffa or a kelek".

3. LB [^{lú}*šá m*]*uḫḫi qu-up-pu* Zawadzki 2013, 444 r. 4 "supervisor of the box".

4. LB (silver) *ana šu-li-ia* 5 *qu-up-pi-e ša* GN Zawadzki 2013, 609: 12 "for *transporting* five *q*.-boxes from GN".

5. Fem. pl., referring to a type of granary (MA):

a) (barley) *ša* PN [*ša*] *ištū bīt qu-pát-te ša qabal tarbaṣi ša* PN_2 PN_3 *iššuranni* Chuera 81: 4 "belonging to PN, which PN_3 took from the *q*.-building in the courtyard of PN_2".

b) (the entire harvest) *ina bīt karme* ⸢*ina*⸣ *adri ēkallim ina qu-pát-te tabik* MARV 3, 4: 10 "is stored in a *q*. in the granary of the threshing floor of the palace".

c) (barley) *ana bīt qu-pát-t*[*e*] ⸢*ta*⸣*bik* Chuera 62: 3 "is stored in the *q*.-building".

d) (barley) *ina bīt qu-up-<pa->te ša pī adri ēkalli ša* GN *tabkuni* AOAT 247, 131: 19 "barley from the granary, which was heaped up at the gate of the threshing floor of the palace of GN".

e) Delete *qup-pat* KAJ 199: 3 (AHw. 928 *q*. 2b; CAD Q 308 *q*. A 1c), s. Freydank 1997, 132.

f) S. Jakob 2003, 325–327 (a storage unit for grain).

S. also *quppatu*.

qūqānu "an insect; an eye disease"

On *q*. of the eye s. Fincke 2000, 196f.

qurdu "warriorhood, heroism"

1. OB lex. ⸢KAxBAD?⸣ = *qù-ur-du-um* Klein/Sefati 2019, 91 ii 32.

2. SB *in-di na*[*m-e*]*n-na-zu* // *qur-di* [*bēl*]*ūtika* Ešḫ n5: 38 (Maul 1988, 100), cf. sum. *in*/*en*/*an-ti*, *in-te* (Borger 1985, 353).

3. SB *ušappâ qur-rad*!(MAR)*-su* KAR 104: 4 "I praise his heroism" (Mayer 2017, 33). FJMS (1), JW (2–3)

qurnātu, + *qirnātu*? "a foodstuff?"

1. OB (oil) *ana qí-ir-na-tim* FM 2, 193 no. 97: 4, unclear.

2. J.-M. Durand apud Charpin 1980/90, 106 ad *qurnātu*: "(déesses) à corne". Since the Akk. word is rather *qarnu* and there is no DINGIR determinative, and since the structure of neither ARM 19, 365 nor FM 2, 193 no. 97 requires a god (name) this hypothesis is rather improbable. Perhaps it is a PN?

qurnu s. *qurnātu*, *qurnû* II

\+ **qurnû II** "a vessel"; OB

1. (2 5/6 minas and 8 shekel of silver) *ana* 1 *qúr-ni-i-im* ARM 31, 15: 7. S. Guichard 2005, 288.

2. Cf. the PN *qú-ur-ni-*{x}*ia* Edubba 1, 6: 17 and s. Sanmartín 2019, 352 ("with (small) horns"?).

q/gurpis(s)u, *q/gursip(p)u* "helmet"

1. OB $^{\text{na}_4}$*gabî ana šipir qúr-pí-si* SAG ARM 22, 308: 2 "alum for making helmets of prime quality"; 1 *qúr-pí-su* SAG ARM 24, 204: 1; 23, 233: 1; 24, 324 iv 19 cf. iii 21; *qúr-pí-su* ZABAR ARM 24, 277: 46 (Mayer in Deller/Mayer/Oelsner 1989, 275).

2. OB *mārū ummênī ša* ... *qur-pí-si* FM 3, 169 no. 15 r. 9 "artisans for … helmets".

3. OB ^{gi}*qúr-si-pu* in ARM 7, 255: 2 is a misreading for ^{gi}GUR.ZI!.DA!; s. Durand 2009, 87.

4. OB 1 *qúr-pí-su* SAG *ša kappī* AWTL 80: 1 "1 first-quality helmet with plumes".

5. MB 3 *gur-pí-sú*^{meš} PRU 6, 132 r. 5 (s. Huehnergard 1987, 117).

6. S. Kendall 1981. S. also Richter 2012, 228.

qurqurratu "sculptress"

S. *qurqurru.*

qurqurru "a craftsman, sculptor, carver"

The mngs. "metal worker" and "coppersmith", based on the logogr. URUDU.NAGAR, should be abandoned. On the mng. "sculptor" or the like, s. for instance Westenholz 1987, 360; Lambert 1991.

qurrubtu, *qurubtu* I "a group of officials"

AHw. *qurrubu*, CAD *qurubtu.*

S. Postgate 2007, 20 (small contingents within the *kiṣir šarrūti*).

qurrudu I "bald" s. *gurrudu*

+ **qurrudu II** "brave, heroic"; OB

1. 19 *ṣābī q*[*ù*]-⸢*ru*⸣-*du-tim* ... *aṭarradakkum* CUSAS 36, 210: 32 "I will send you 19 brave troops".

2. For *qurrudu* "to make into a hero" (CAD Q 320) s. *qarādu.*

quršu s. *g/quršu*

+ **qurubtu II** "delivery"; LB

1. *qu-ru-ub-tum ina bīt* PN BM 54555: 6 (AOAT 254, 115) "delivery for the house of PN".

2. *qu-ru-ub-t*[*um*] *ina* GN CT 49, 123//122//182: 7 (Jursa 2006, 191) "delivery for GN".

q/gurunnu "heap"

1. SB masc. pl.: *kīma gu*!-*ru*-⸢*un*⸣-*né-e ana karšišunu kamsū* Iraq 67, 274: 14 "(scribal learning) is stored like heaps (of goods) in their minds", s. George/Frame ib., 276.

2. NB *adi imat kī eperti agâ ina* [*g*]*u-ru-un-nu šaknat* OIP 114, 103: 20 "how long will it be before those bricks are placed in a heap?"

+ **quššu?** "a festival"

1. OB *inūma qú-úš-ši-im* MN FM 3, 251 no. 103: 7 "on the occasion of the *q.* festival in MN".

2. (animals) *ina qú-ši-im* ARM 21, 48: 19 "during the *q.*".

3. Durand 1995, 184; Jacquet 2011, 34. < *qdš* "to be pure".

quššudu s. *qašādu.*

qūšu s. *k/qūšu*

****qutāntu**

Read ^{kuš}*qu-lép-du*, now Iraq 45, 189: 21, 44 (Oelsner in Deller/Mayer/Oelsner 1989, 282).

qutānu "something thin"

NA (n estate) *qu*!-*ta*!-*nu*! SAA 6, 275 r. 6 "a narrow strip".

S. also *quttunu*.

qutāru "fumigant"; + NB

KÙ.GI *ša uznī* OIP 114, 70: 11, 21 "fumigant for the ears".

\+ **qutīptu** "a textile"; MB Emar

1 ^{túg}*qu-ti-ip-tum* J. G. Westenholz 2000, 21: 14. S. Durand 2009, 87 (from *qatāpu* "to pluck", also said of textiles).

qutrīnu "incense"

The mng. "censer" (CAD Q 324) does not apply to the known refs. (Mayer in Deller/Mayer/Oelsner 1989, 275).

qutru "smoke"

1. OB (3 sheep and 1 leg of lamb) *ša qu-ut-ri-im* FM 12, 227 M.6667 r. 6 "for smoking".

2. Lex. *be* = NE = *qú-ut-ru* Emar 6/4, 537: 305 (Sa), Sjöberg 1998, 261.

quttunu "very thin"

OB "thin piece of wood": 5 MA.NA *imḫur-ašar* 2 MA.NA *qú-tu-nu* ARM 23, 677 no. 619: 2 "5 minas of *i.*-wood and 2 minas of thin logs" (Charpin 1989–90, 106).

qutû "Gutian"; + MB; + MA

1. OB 1 *kāsu qú-tu-ú* KÙ.BABBAR ARM 31, 34 r. 14 "1 silver Gutian cup" (s. Guichard 2005, 288).

2. OB *ana qú-ti-im* [*n*]*a-ri* Shemshara 2, 136: 48 "for a Gutian, a singer". S. also TLT 92, 6; 100 r. 16; 102: 4.

3. MB 1 ^{túg}GÚ.È *gu-di-tum* MBLET 55: 5 "1 Gutian cloak", also 61 r. 3.

4. MA 1 *ṣubātu qu-ti-ú* Iraq 35, pl. XIII no. 1: 7 "Gutian garment".

qu'u s. *qû* II